NATIONS OF THE MODERN WORLD

ARGENTINA   H. S. Ferns
*Professor of Political Science,
University of Birmingham*

AUSTRALIA   O. H. K. Spate
*Director, Research School of Pacific Studies,
Australian National University, Canberra*

AUSTRIA   Karl R. Stadler
*Professor of Modern and Contemporary History,
University of Linz*

BELGIUM   Vernon Mallinson
*Professor of Comparative Education,
University of Reading*

BURMA   F. S. V. Donnison
*Formerly Chief Secretary to the Government of Burma
Historian, Cabinet Office, Historical Section 1949–66*

CYPRUS   H. D. Purcell
*Professor of English
University of Libya, Benghazi*

DENMARK   W. Glyn Jones
Reader in Danish, University College London

MODERN EGYPT   Tom Little
*Managing Director and General Manager of
Regional News Services (Middle East), Ltd, London*

ENGLAND
A Portrait   John Bowle
*Professor of Political Theory, Collège d'Europe
Bruges*

FINLAND   W. R. Mead
Professor of Geography, University College London

EAST
GERMANY   David Childs
Lecturer in Politics, University of Nottingham

WEST GERMANY	Michael Balfour *Reader in European History, University of East Anglia*
MODERN GREECE	John Campbell *Fellow of St Antony's College, Oxford* Philip Sherrard *Lecturer in the History of the Orthodox Church, King's College, London*
MODERN INDIA	Sir Percival Griffiths *President India, Pakistan and Burma Association*
MODERN IRAN	Peter Avery *Lecturer in Persian and Fellow of King's College, Cambridge*
ITALY	Muriel Grindrod *Formerly Editor of* International Affairs *and* The World Today *Assistant Editor* The Annual Register
KENYA	A. Marshall MacPhee *Formerly Managing Editor with the* East African Standard *Group*
LIBYA	John Wright *Formerly of the* Sunday Ghibli, *Tripoli*
MALAYSIA	J. M. Gullick *Formerly of the Malayan Civil Service*
MOROCCO	Mark I. Cohen *Director of Taxation, American Express* Lorna Hahn *Professor of African Studies, American University*
NEW ZEALAND	James W. Rowe *Director of New Zealand Institute of Economic Research* Margaret A. Rowe *Tutor in English at Victoria University, Wellington*

NIGERIA	Sir Rex Niven *Administrative Service of Nigeria, 1921–54 Member, President and Speaker of Northern House of Assembly, 1947–59*
PAKISTAN	Ian Stephens *Formerly Editor of* The Statesman *Calcutta and Delhi, 1942–51 Fellow, King's College, Cambridge, 1952–58*
PERU	Sir Robert Marett *H.M. Ambassador in Lima, 1963–67*
POLAND	Václav L. Beneš *Professor of History and Geography, Indiana University* Norman J. G. Pounds *Professor of Political Science, Indiana University*
SOUTH AFRICA	John Cope *Formerly Editor-in-Chief of* The Forum *and South Africa Correspondent of* The Guardian
THE SOVIET UNION	Elisabeth Koutaissoff *Professor of Russian, Victoria University, Wellington*
SPAIN	George Hills *Formerly Correspondent and Spanish Programme Organiser, British Broadcasting Corporation*
SUDAN REPUBLIC	K. D. D. Henderson *Formerly of the Sudan Political Service and Governor of Darfur Province, 1949–53*
TURKEY	Geoffrey Lewis *Senior Lecturer in Islamic Studies, Oxford*
YUGOSLAVIA	Muriel Heppell and F. B. Singleton

NATIONS OF THE MODERN WORLD

THE SOVIET UNION

THE SOVIET UNION

By
ELISABETH KOUTAISSOFF

PRAEGER PUBLISHERS
New York · Washington

BOOKS THAT MATTER

Published in the United States of America in 1971
by Praeger Publishers, Inc., 111 Fourth Avenue,
New York, N.Y. 10003

© 1971 in London, England, by Elisabeth Koutaissoff

All rights reserved

No part of this publication may be reproduced, stored
in a retrieval system or transmitted in any form or by
any means, electronic, mechanical, photocopying, recording
or otherwise, without the prior permission of the Copyright
owner.

Library of Congress Catalog Card Number: 79-133088

Printed in Great Britain

Preface

My gratitude goes to those who have helped me in the task of writing this book : David Foreman, M.A., for his contribution to the chapter on Literature and Art; to Dr Violet Conolly, O.B.E., who gave so generously of her time and knowledge to check various points and read the typescript; to my former colleagues of the Russian and East European Centre, University of Birmingham, whose stimulating range of interests broadened my understanding of modern developments in the USSR; to Joanna Pohl, who patiently deciphered my writing and was always willing to retype additions, alterations, and other tiresome changes; to the editor of the *New Zealand Slavonic Journal* for allowing me to use parts of an article published in 1969, entitled 'Recent Demographic Trends in the USSR and their Possible Implications'; to David Fanning for bravely tackling the time-consuming task of compiling the index; and above all, to my publishers, for I kept them waiting and to their patience I owe the completing of this book.

Wellington E.K.
October 1970

To the memory of the late
Alexander Baykov
Professor of Soviet Economics
University of Birmingham
a pioneer of Soviet Studies
in the English-speaking world

Contents

	Preface	9
	List of Illustrations	13
	Maps	14
	Abbreviations	15
	Acknowledgements	16
	Introduction	17
1	The Twenty-third Congress of the CPSU	23
2	The Communist Party of the Soviet Union	31
3	Economic Planning	67
4	Industry	88
5	Agriculture	107
6	Demographic Trends	129
7	Education	141
8	Literature and the Arts	178
9	Science	206
10	Daily Life	221
11	Conclusion	230
	Appendix A Chronology of Events	241
	Appendix B Population Figures	246
	Appendix C List of Personalities mentioned in the Text	250
	Bibliography	276
	Index	280

List of Illustrations

[*All are inserted between pages 144 and 145*]

1. Malozemel'skaya Tundra, north of the Arctic Circle
2. Reindeer-racing at a collective farm in the Olekminsky region, Yakut ASSR
3. Landscape in the Daghestan ASSR, North Caucasus
4. A branch of the canal dissecting the steppe in the Uzbek SSR
5. Leningrad. View of the Winter Palace from Strelka, Vasilievsky Island
6. The Kazan Cathedral, Leningrad
7. The fifteenth-century Registan Square in Samarkand
8. The Bratsk hydropower-station on the Angara river
9. A section of the Bokhara-Urals gas pipeline
10. The Kremlin, seen from the Moscow river embankment
11. The Moscow television tower
12. Derricks of the Neftyanye Kamni oilfield over the Caspian Sea
13. Norilsk, a 'black blizzard'
14. Lenin Avenue, Norilsk
15. The factory district of devastated Stalingrad
16. Leningrad under siege, 1942
17. Russian ballet—*Cinderella*, the ball scene
18. Photograph of the earth from about 70,000 kilometres, taken by Zond-7 automatic station
19. Stalin with delegates to the Tenth Young Communist League Congress in 1936
20. Moscow, May 1960. Nikita Khrushchev addresses the USSR Communist Work Team Conference
21. Leonid Brezhnev speaking at the unveiling of the Lenin Memorial at Ulyanovsk
22. Alexei Kosygin meets representatives of Scottish sports organisations
23. May Day celebrations in Moscow, 1966
24. The monument to the first sputnik in Moscow
25. A TU-144 supersonic passenger plane

Maps

1	The Coalfields of the Soviet Union	70
2	The Oilfields of the Soviet Union	85
3	General Industrial Regions of the Soviet Union	91
	The Soviet Union, Physical and Political	*facing page* 240

Russian Abbreviations

Cheka	Vserossiiskaya chrezvychainaya komissiya po bor'be s kontrrevolutsiei i sabotazhem (All-Russian Extraordinary Commission for the Struggle against Counter-revolution and Sabotage).
DOSAAF	Dobrovol'noe obshchestvo sodeistviya armii, aviatsii i flotu (Voluntary Society for Assisting the Army, Aviation, and Fleet).
GOELRO	Gosudarstvennaya komissiya po elektrifikatsii Rossii (State Commission for the Electrification of Russia).
GPU	Gosudarstvennoe politicheskoe upravlenie (State Political Administration).
GTO	Gotov k trudu i oborone (Ready for Toil and Defence).
KGB	Komitet gosudarstvennoi bezopasnosti (State Security Committee).
LAPP	Leningradskaya assosiatsiya proletarskikh pisatelei (Leningrad Association of Proletarian Writers).
LEF	Levy front v isskustve (Left Front in Art).
MAPP	Moskovskaya assosiatsiya proletarskikh pisatelei (Moscow Association of Proletarian Writers).
NKVD	Narodny kommissariat vnutrennikh del (People's Commissariat of Internal Affairs).
RAPP	Rossiiskaya assosiatsiya proletarskikh pisatelei (Russian Association of Proletarian Writers).
RSDRP	Rossiiskaya sotsial-demokraticheskaya rabochaya partiya (Russian Social Democratic Workers Party).
UKP	Uchebno-konsul'tatsionnyi punkt (Study-Consultation Office).
VAK	Vysshaya attestatsionnaya komissiya (Supreme Attestation Commission).
VAPP	Vserossiiskaya assosiatsiya proletarskikh pisatelei (All-Russian Association of Proletarian Writers).
VKP(b)	Vsesoyuznaya kommunisticheskaya partiya (bol'shevikov) (All-Union Communist Party, Bolshevik).
VUZ	Vysshee uchebnoe zavedenie (Establishment of Higher Education).

Acknowledgements

THE PHOTOGRAPHS in this book are by courtesy of the Novosti Press Agency, London.

Acknowledgement is also due to the following for quotations:

Calder and Boyars Ltd. and October House Inc.: Evgeny Evtushenko, 'The Heirs of Stalin', from *The Poetry of Yevgeny Yevtushenko*, selected, edited, and translated by George Reavey; © 1965 by George Reavey.

Oxford University Press and Basic Books Inc., Publishers: Andrei Voznesensky, 'To B. Akhmadulina', from *Antiworlds and the Fifth Ace*, edited by Patricia Blake and Max Hayward, translated by Stanley Kunitz; © 1966, 1967 by Basic Books Inc., New York.

Oxford University Press and Basic Books Inc., Publishers: Andrei Voznesensky, excerpt from 'Oza', section II, from *Antiworlds and the Fifth Ace*, edited by Patricia Blake and Max Hayward, translated by Max Hayward; © 1966, 1967 by Basic Books Inc., New York.

Note Throughout this book the term 'billion' is used in the American sense of one thousand million.

Introduction

IN 1967 THE SOVIET UNION celebrated the fiftieth anniversary of the October Revolution and the leadership of the Communist Party of the Soviet Union looked back in pride to its achievements. Half a century earlier Lenin and his small dynamic Bolshevik Party had spearheaded an armed rebellion against the short-lived Provisional Government which had been set up when Nicholas II, the last Tsar, had been forced to abdicate in March 1917. The Bolshevik uprising was to be the first step to end the Old World Order and establish throughout Europe the Dictatorship of the Proletariat. Although the proletariat in western Europe failed to respond, the Bolsheviks, after seizing power in St Petersburg (now Leningrad) and Moscow, established control over the whole country. In bitter fighting during a civil war which lasted for three years (1918–20) they defeated all their opponents – Tsarist officers, peasant anarchists, and various socialist parties half-heartedly supported by Britain, France, and Japan. They also subdued the nationalist movements which were tearing asunder the multinational empire after the Tsar's abdication. To assuage national aspirations, the vast country spreading from the Baltic to the Pacific was transformed into a Union of Soviet Socialist Republics, each with its own language and culture, national in form, yet socialist in content. The constitution of the USSR, adopted in January 1924, granted each of the major or Union republics its own government and the right to secession, but the monolithic unity of the Communist Party precluded the latter contingency. Smaller national groups were given the status of autonomous Soviet Socialist Republics or that of national districts; they, too, could use their vernacular in schools, in court proceedings, and official documents; the study and publication of their folklore and literary production received encouragement and often financial support.

In 1928, under Stalin's leadership, economic planning on a national scale was introduced. The aim of the first Five-Year Plan (1928–32) was to achieve rapid industrialisation and transform a largely agricultural country into a modern industrial state. The cost of industrialisation fell heavily on the shoulders of the peasants, who were dragooned into merging their individual holdings into large collective farms on the grounds that large-scale agriculture is more profitable than peasant farming, and in the hope of breaking down peasant individualism and their resistance to selling agricultural produce at low state-fixed prices. Rapid industrialisation found its justification when Hitler's armies invaded Russia in June 1941. The country's armament industry proved an adequate match for the German war-machine and, after four years of the most devastating war in the history of mankind, the German invaders were driven back to Berlin.[1]

Within that momentous half-century (1917–67) a backward country had become one of the industrial giants of the twentieth century and its scientists had inaugurated the exploration of outer space. The cost of progress had been tremendous in human errors, lives, and suffering, but the price of suffering is not an item that can be entered into a balance sheet.

When Lenin and his Party, numbering hardly more than 200,000 members in a country with a population of well over 150 million inhabitants, seized power in 1917, they were not even sure to retain it for any length of time. So much so that Lenin expressed his confidence in the future of Soviet power when by mid-January 1918 it had already outlasted the Paris Commune of 1870 by five days.[2] Fifty years later the Communist Party of the Soviet Union (CPSU) numbered 12 million members and was not merely in complete control of Russia, but had ceased to be the sole *ruling* Communist Party in the world. One-third of the human race now lived under communism and the capitalist countries, though unexpectedly resilient and still dangerously powerful, were losing their colonial empires and were being slowly squeezed out from what had become 'the third world'.

Yet, despite her spectacular achievements, the Soviet Union was beset by grave problems. The most obvious and dangerous were the dissensions within the ranks of the communist camp. In Yugoslavia, since 1948, when Tito had broken relations with Stalin and withstood the economic pressures directed against his country, the League of Yugoslav Communists had been pursuing an independent line and carrying out ambiguous policies described in Moscow as

[1] Britain and the USA sent arms to the USSR by sea around the North Cape to Murmansk and Archangel, and along the single-track railway through Persia. The courage of the sailors who manned the arctic convoys under constant threat of German submarine and bomber attack in icy weather conditions is a chronicle of gallantry, but in military terms this help constituted only a small fraction of the armaments expended by the USSR in World War II.
[2] Report to the Third Congress of Soviets, 11 (24) January 1918. *Works*, 4th edition, Vol. 26, p. 413.

INTRODUCTION 19

rightist deviationism. More ominous was the growing chasm between China, astir with a recklessly revolutionary fervour, and the USSR, increasingly reluctant to shoulder the astronomical costs of China's industrialisation. Less obvious, yet no less worrying, were the unforeseen developments at home. Lenin's forecasts that every cook should become competent to partake in state affairs had not been realised. Instead, a rigid and numerous bureaucracy had consolidated its powers, keeping cooks and other unauthorised persons well away from any decision-making councils. Indeed, things had gone so far that it was necessary to speak of 'democratisation' at least at the lower echelons of power, i.e. the local Soviets. These are elected by universal suffrage from among candidates nominated by local committees of the Communist Party or the League of Young Communists (*Komsomol*), local trade unions, scientific institutions, or collective farms. In 1967, among the 2 million of these part-time representatives of the people, well over half were not members of the Communist Party.

Contrary to Engels' prognostications, the state had not withered away; instead, its functions had expanded far beyond the sphere of politics. The resolution of the Twenty-third Congress of the CPSU, held in March 1966, recorded that

> the Congress emphasises the importance of further strengthening the Soviet state and developing socialist democracy in every way.... It is especially important that the role of the Soviets of People's Deputies be enhanced so that they may make full use of their powers in carrying out the task of economic and cultural construction ... and show more initiative in solving planning, financial, and land questions and in guiding enterprises of local industry and everyday social and cultural services to the population.

Even the most critical Western sovietologists had to concede that the Soviet cultural revolution had succeeded. Illiteracy was a thing of the past. The smallest paleoasiatic nationalities, still making a living from reindeer-breeding, trapping fur animals, and fishing in the icy waters of the Arctic Ocean, now had their *written* languages, and boarding-schools where children got an eight-year education. Every major republic had its Academy of Sciences. The state was allocating nearly 20 per cent of its Budget expenditure to science, culture, and education. Yet half a century of communist education and of psychological conditioning through mass communication media had failed to produce the superior type of humanity, the *Homo sovieticus*, who alone could make a living reality of communism. Instead, the man in the street, whether in Moscow or Vladivostok, was manifesting the same consumer mentality as did his counterparts in Paris or New York. For him, peaceful competition with the West meant a rising standard of living, the craving for which had been exacerbated by years of shortages, self-sacrifice, and 'jam tomorrow'. He was longing for better housing, buying only the better goods and allowing warehouses to get cluttered up with shoddy, unsold, and unsaleable household articles. The young failed to appreciate the magnitude of the progress made and brushed aside comparisons with what things were like in 1917 as irrelevant to their own days. They took for granted what their elders admired as wonders. Sample sociological surveys, inaugurated in the 1960s, revealed a dangerously distressing contempt for manual work among urban teenagers and a determination to leave the countryside among rural youths. Other surveys showed that in some schools up to 60 or 70 per cent of pupils in their final year were better informed on scientific and technical matters than the teaching staff, a factor that contributed to their youthful arrogance.

Boomeranging expectations of a better life were being thwarted by shortages of higher-protein foods and fresh fruit (always a problem in northerly countries) because agriculture was still unprofitable, inefficient, and incapable of meeting the demands of an urban population no longer content to live on black bread and cabbage soup.

In vain Nikita Khrushchev, First Secretary of the CPSU from 1953 to 1964, had appealed in lengthy and impassioned speeches for an increase in agricultural production, and devised coercive measures to divert collective farmers from giving too much time to their half-acre family plots. The peasantry persisted in their passive resistance, grand schemes of cultivating dry steppes and even semi-deserts or sowing maize under any latitude hardly raised the volume of food production, while the flight from the land of the better educated, able-bodied younger generation was threatening rural depopulation. Even in industry, returns on investment were becoming alarmingly low. Apparently the command economy was no longer capable of coping with the growing variety and complexity of production.

In October 1964 the Central Committee of the CPSU forced Khrushchev to resign. The reasons for his removal are still not clear; it may have been a manoeuvre to placate Mao Tse-Tung, whose personal hostility towards Khrushchev was poisoning the relations between the two countries; or it may have been Khrushchev's failure to promote agricultural production by his ill-advised reforms; it was also rumoured in the West that he fell out with the military for trying to cut down on defence expenditure in his overconfidence that the partial nuclear test-ban treaty with the USA and Britain was an adequate guarantee against any Washington-backed attack by the resurgent *Wehrmacht* now at the disposal of the 'Bonn revanchists'. Yet another factor may have been his ignorance of modern methods of management which, since the advent of the computer and the introduction of mathematical methods into economic planning, revealed the hollowness of his ambitious slogans of 'catching up and overtaking America' in production per head of population. At any rate, it was after his retirement that at the March and September (1965) Plenums of the Central Committee of the CPSU his agricultural policies were revised and the new economic reforms began to be cautiously introduced.

The latter had been under discussion among mathematical economists since the early 1960s, but were not publicised so long as the Party leadership persisted in decreeing unrealistic goals based on unreliable and often falsified statistical data supplied by obsequious bureaucrats. However, decrees and administrative adjustments failed to produce the abundance of material goods envisaged and the rates of growth of the Soviet economy which had been so remarkable for so long were slowly grinding to a halt. The reforms introduced since January 1966 (described further) and a scientifically devised new Five-Year Plan were essential for the Soviet Union to take her place among the affluent societies of the modern world. The drafting of this eighth Plan (for 1966-70) had been preceded by lengthy discussions on the extent to which 'economic levers' could be used within a centrally planned economy. It was the first plan to have been elaborated by mathematical economists using a vast flow of electronically computerised information. Perhaps an account of the USSR today should start with a description of the rather unspectacular Twenty-third Congress of the Communist Party held in March 1966 to discuss various aspects of policy and adopt the draft of the eighth Five-Year Plan.

The half-hearted reforms discussed at the Congress and the measures taken in the following years all reflect the slow and painful adaptation of men burdened by a recent tragic past to our present-day technological era and its numerous and unforeseen social consequences; an adaptation not made easier by the vastness of the geographical area, quite well endowed with mineral wealth but climatically not favoured by nature and inhabited by peoples of different ethnic origin who have not yet overcome differences and tensions, some of which go centuries back, while others are being created by present-day conditions.

Chapter 1

The Twenty-third Congress of the CPSU

FOR THE SECOND TIME in Soviet history the meetings of a Party Congress were held in the huge hall of glass and steel of the Palace of Congresses, completed in time for the previous (Twenty-second) Congress in 1961. Contrasting with the adjacent ancient churches of the Kremlin, this ultra-modern building rises like an architectural symbol of the country's entry into the world of tomorrow.

The Twenty-third Congress was not marked by any sensational events such as the secret speech made ten years previously at the Twentieth Congress by N. S. Khrushchev, in which he denounced Stalin's crimes. That speech, though never published in the Soviet Union, marked the high-water mark of de-Stalinisation, which had been discreetly started after the death of the great dictator in 1953. Although temporarily halted by the Hungarian uprising in 1956, de-Stalinisation has continued its slow, uncertain, stop-go course ever since. In 1956 the contents of the secret speech had been cautiously passed on from the highest Party officials down the hierarchical ladder and revealed, at any rate partially, to members of the primary Party organisations. For the inhabitants of the Soviet Union the speech had marked a turning-point in their history – the uneasy beginning of a more liberal era, a hesitant relaxation of controls by men used to authoritarian and arbitrary rule, a difficult and faltering return to notions of human justice and legality disregarded for nearly forty years by those still in power; in fact, a renunciation of terror as a method of government.

The speech had also marked a turning-point in the history of the communist world and made the first breach in its monolithic unity. Indirectly, it encouraged dissenting elements in the Polish Communist Party to engineer a change of leadership and bring Gomulka to power against the wishes of the CPSU. It misled Imre Nagy into weakening his Party's control over the Hungarian intellectuals and very rapidly losing his hold over the country to the extent of yielding to nationalistic demands and withdrawing from the Warsaw Pact, a mistake Imre Nagy paid for with his life and the reoccupation of Hungary by Soviet troops. Perhaps more important than the tragic events in Hungary was the strong reaction which Khrushchev's speech evoked from Mao Tse-Tung. Although officially the Chinese Communist Party supported Soviet military intervention in Hungary, Mao Tse-Tung informed Khrushchev that it was the tactlessness of his de-Stalinisation campaign that was the root cause of the trouble. Khrushchev's denunciation of Stalin undermined the people's faith in communism and that of Communists in their leaders. In the course of the ensuing years other factors embittered Sino-Soviet relations, but the initial breach was over the wisdom (or rather the folly) of Khrushchev's de-Stalinisation policy and his demotion of Stalin as a world leader.

Ten years later, the speakers at the Twenty-third Party Congress were less inclined to dwell on past mistakes and more anxious to compete with the capitalist world in terms of economic progress. The country had just celebrated the twentieth anniversary of its victory over Hitler's Germany, a hard-won victory achieved after a devastating war during which over 20 million Soviet citizens had perished and the country had lost one-third of its national wealth. No colourful figure dominated the Congress, for Khrushchev had been retired eighteen months previously and his successors had none of his flamboyant brashness nor any of his illusions. The new First Secretary, L. I. Brezhnev, was essentially a Party organisation man, while A. N. Kosygin, the Chairman of the Council of Ministers, an engineer by training and a technocrat in outlook, was occasionally referred to as 'our chief accountant'.

The Congress was attended by nearly 5,000 delegates. It had been called according to the rules laid down in the Party programme, i.e. roughly four years after the Twenty-second Congress. In the early years of the Revolution, Congresses had been held more frequently;[1] the Sixth in August 1917, two months prior to the October uprising; the Seventh in March 1918; the Eighth a year later; and then annually until the Fourteenth in December 1925. The Twelfth, in April 1923, was the last to be held in Lenin's lifetime. At the Fifteenth, held in December 1927, the first Five-Year Plan was adopted; the Sixteenth met in June/July 1930 and approved the collectivisation of agriculture; the Seventeenth took place early in 1934, and the Eighteenth in March 1939. Then no

[1] Earlier still they had been small gatherings at which the Social Democratic Party, as it was then called, worked out its programmes and policies for the overthrow of the Tsarist regime. The first attempt at calling a Congress in 1898 was thwarted by the Tsarist police, who arrested most of the delegates. The next one, in 1903, met abroad in Brussels, but the delegates were expelled by the Belgian police and had to find a meeting-place in London. It was at this second Congress that the split occurred between the Mensheviks and the Bolsheviks. The next most important Congress met in 1917 as the tide of the Revolution was welling up and membership of the Party was said to be approaching 200,000.

THE TWENTY-THIRD CONGRESS OF THE CPSU 25

more Congresses were called until October 1952. That year Stalin, who was to die six months later, did not feel well enough to address the Congress. The interval between the Nineteenth (1952) and the Twentieth (1956) was much shorter, and since then Congresses have been held fairly regularly every four years.

As usual, the Twenty-third Congress was attended by delegates of fraternal foreign parties, but among the eighty-six delegations the most important – that from China – was conspicuously absent. The fall of Khrushchev had not appeased Mao Tse-Tung or allayed his worst suspicions; Khrushchev's successors continued his policy of appeasement towards the United States, his guarded, half-hearted support for liberation movements in underdeveloped countries, his wasteful allocation of resources to those countries, most of which were ruled either by their own feudal and bourgeois classes or dominated by outright 'lackeys of foreign capitalists', instead of using these resources to help China to industrialise and thus promote the greatness and prosperity of the communist world.

The make-up of the Twenty-third Congress, meeting eighteen months before the celebrations of the fiftieth anniversary of the Revolution, reflected the new social structure of the country. The 4,943 delegates represented a Party 12 million strong, its membership having increased by 23 per cent since the Twenty-second Congress, held about four years earlier. Only 11 per cent of the delegates came from the countryside. A quarter were full-time Party bureaucrats. There were among the delegates nine cosmonauts, including the only woman cosmonaut in the world, Tereshkova-Nikolayeva, 300 scientists, and some high-ranking military men. Well over half the delegates were graduates of some establishment of higher education. Somewhat less than a quarter were women. Perhaps more important was the fact that 92 per cent were over thirty years of age and that two-thirds of those present had joined the Party in Stalin's lifetime.

It was, then, a Congress of middle-aged men and women who remembered, if not the October Revolution, at least many events that had occurred since, and had witnessed the achievements of industrialisation, the hardships of the collectivisation campaigns, and the catastrophic devastation and loss of life incurred during World War II. The majority had joined the Party before de-Stalinisation had set in. Most were probably sincere in their conviction that the Party is the vanguard of the nation, its élite, armed with a scientific and, therefore, infallible theory of social progress; for them the idea that the Party could or should tolerate opposition groups or abdicate its unchallengeable leadership was tantamount to sheer mental aberration. They could have little sympathy or understanding with the writers Daniel and Sinyavsky, who were at that time standing trial on charges of anti-Soviet activities, namely the printing abroad of what was deemed to be anti-Soviet propaganda. The stories of these two *literati* had been repeatedly broadcast by the Voice of America and by Radio Liberty, the CIA stations in West Germany and one of its major means of psychological warfare against communism. These writers could only be regarded as CIA agents, like the traitor Oleg Pen'kovsky who had transmitted in 1961–62 information to the British 'businessman' Greville Wynne, about the missiles sent to Cuba, and whose treason and the ensuing events had nearly brought about World War III.

Many delegates, too, were not very happy about the new economic reforms discussed among planners and in specialised publications. The need for reforms was urgent to eliminate inefficiency in industrial enterprises, induce them to produce higher-quality goods, and adopt innovations, instead of seeking easily attainable targets so as to earn various bonuses and rewards for over-fulfilling plans. The provision of the new Charter of the Socialist State Productive Enterprise, passed in October 1965, had introduced a limited degree of decentralisation; it allowed enterprises within narrowly defined conditions to enter into market relations with others by selling them their products and in certain cases buying supplies direct from producers, instead of obtaining them from central allocation agencies as had been the case previously. The measure of plan fulfilment was no longer gross output of goods but the amount of goods sold. Even this limited degree of freedom of action by individual enterprises seemed somewhat incompatible with the concept of central planning, and aroused doubts among a considerable number of economists. In a multinational state any local initiative may trigger off dangerous centrifugal forces. Naturally, the Party felt it could ensure uniformity, conformity, and centralisation, but it had to be cautious and vigilant, considering the threat of direct attack or insidious subversion from capitalist countries which for so many years had done their utmost to stifle the first socialist state. Unable now to topple it by force, they were stepping up the ideological warfare, doing their utmost to undermine the faith of Soviet citizens in communism, sow discord among its nationalities, envenom relations between Party and non-Party citizens, rake up long-concealed blunders made by those in power, and practise every form of psychological aggression. The efforts of imperialists were doomed, because under communist leadership the country was obviously forging ahead, economically and scientifically. Whilst the Congress was meeting in Moscow, the first man-made vehicle had landed on the moon, transmitting its radio signals; another 'first' for Soviet science after so many others – the first artificial satellite in 1957 launched to coincide with the fortieth anniversary of the October Revolution, the first picture of the dark side of the moon in 1959, the first cosmonaut in orbit in 1961, the first man to walk in space in 1965. All the research, the calculations, the designing and building of the launching rockets and the ingeniously constructed vehicles, the training of the scientists who conceived the instruments, those who made them, and that of the cosmonauts themselves, had been planned, organised, and financed by the Party leadership. Soldiers without generals cannot win battles, nor can the scientific personnel of numerous research institutes and design bureaux win scientific victories without – according to the Party – its foresight, inspiration, and organisational powers. True, the Americans were catching up in the moon race, but the delegates to the 1966 Congress were still unaware that three years later the USA would win it by landing their first men on the moon.

Clearly science was not entirely and exclusively at the service of the communist cause, though the Party had always pinned its hopes for a better society on further scientific achievements. Moreover, it was becoming aware of some obverse aspects of scientific progress. Reluctantly it was being recognised that science, while enabling man to harness natural forces and put to use Nature's bounties, was also instrumental in helping him to destroy natural wealth.

In the same speech to the Congress in which the writer Sholokhov, author of *Quiet flows the Don* and 1965 Nobel prizewinner, harshly attacked writers like Daniel and Sinyavsky as traitors to their country, he also lashed out at those responsible for destructive overfishing in rivers, lakes, and even the Azov Sea, against those who bypassed legislation designed to combat water pollution and, having played havoc with Russia's most famous rivers, were now threatening with pollution the geologically remarkable Lake Baikal in Siberia, the deepest in the world, with its unique flora and fauna.

The subdued and unheeded voices of those who had been denouncing the predatory exploitation of forests, the slaughtering of wild-life, and the untold damage inflicted on the country's natural resources by planners incapable of seeing beyond the time-limits of a Five-Year Plan, have since become a mighty chorus. Yet urgent immediate needs or shortsighted financial considerations may sabotage the provisions of the 1969 decree on the preservation of natural resources designed to mitigate the damage done and forestall or curtail its further extension.

Many problems confronting the Soviet Union at present are those common to all advanced societies in the twentieth century, but because of her different political system, different solutions may be attempted and perhaps even found. Of these problems many have only begun to be recognised and have not yet been clearly defined or formulated. Nevertheless, they are implicit in the major topics touched upon in the report presented to the Congress by L. I. Brezhnev and in the resolution submitted to the Congress by the Central Committee of the CPSU for discussion and ratification.

Both documents deal with (*a*) international relations; (*b*) the development of the country's economy and the resulting rise in the population's standard of living as well as further progress in science and culture; and (*c*) last, but not least, the growing role of the CPSU in guiding 'communist construction', that is, promoting the economic, scientific, and cultural preconditions that would make a reality of communism, when every citizen would contribute according to his abilities and receive according to his needs.

In foreign relations the major concern continued to be the industrial and military might of the USA, whose stockpile of thermonuclear devices was already sufficient to annihilate all life on earth, and was still being increased. The danger was enhanced by the avowed policy of the USA of liberating the 'captive nations' of Europe and containing communism. The most forceful manifestation of this containment was the war in Vietnam. The fear of American aggression has for a long time been very real in the USSR. The dropping of two atomic bombs on Hiroshima and Nagasaki at the end of World War II (when Japan was already defeated and seeking for peace terms less onerous and degrading than 'unconditional surrender') had been interpreted as a show of military superiority which the Soviet ally had better heed. Having never experienced war on their own soil nor seen invading armies burn down their homes, nor witnessed their womenfolk fleeing across snowbound fields with children unlikely to survive in primitive, makeshift forest hideouts, Americans have always been suspicious of the sincerity of the craving for peace among Soviet people. Those who have not suffered cannot understand those who have. Soviet-American misunderstandings can be neatly summarised by quoting the old Russian saying: 'The rich do not believe the poor, the well-fed cannot understand the hungry.' Those who have not suffered war at home simply cannot imagine its horror.

The numerous military bases that the Americans established in various European and Asian countries after the war could only be regarded by Soviet leaders as an encirclement of Russia. West Germany soon became an arsenal of nuclear and other weapons, and with time a resurgent *Wehrmacht* backed by US technology emerged as the strongest army in Europe. There were missile bases in Turkey, their rockets trained on Moscow and other major industrial cities of European Russia; there were more rocket sites and bomber bases in Pakistan, threatening the Central Asian republics; and there were naval installations and yet further bomber bases in Japan for a possible attack on Siberia. Even the Arctic Ocean was no longer a safe barrier because of Polaris submarines lurking under its ice-cap. Further afield in Canada, Greenland, and the United States itself, there were more rocket sites and military installations. For years, day and night, hydrogen bomb-carrying aircraft went on flying along the borders of the Soviet Union and violating her air space. Giant B2 planes on spying missions intruded deep into Soviet air space and 'strayed' as far as the Urals, where one of them, piloted by F. G. Powers, was shot down by the Russians in May 1960. Since then, these rather primitive spying forays had been superseded by a round-the-clock watch effected by spy satellites over the entire territory of the USSR.

In response to the constant fears of thermo-nuclear annihilation, the Soviet Union devised, built, and stockpiled her own costly lethal weapons. Being by far the poorer of the two super-powers, the Soviet Union had more difficulty in shouldering the costs of the arms race. These costs were a heavy burden on Russia's economy and the greatest single impediment to any rise in the standard of living of the population. The arms race posed a military threat and was, moreover, economically ruinous. In an affluent society like that of the USA, where the market has reached saturation point, the manufacture of weapons is only another form of the general manufacture of waste. In the Soviet Union the position is different: the population is still short of essential goods and industrial capacity could be used more purposefully to alleviate scarcities.

Khrushchev had attempted to come to terms with President Eisenhower, but there was too much fear and mutual distrust to allow for talks on disarmament to get anywhere, and whilst they dragged on, ever more lethal weapons, 'conventional', nuclear, chemical, and biological, were being devised and manufactured as if the destiny of mankind was to be self-annihilation and the probable destruction of all forms of life on its fair planet.

On the brighter side, Brezhnev could report hopes of closer integration between the European allies of the socialist camp, not merely military, within the framework of the Warsaw Pact, but also economic. For the first time the individual plans of Poland, Czechoslovakia, East Germany, Hungary, Bulgaria, and Romania were being drafted in consultation in an endeavour to make better use of their pool of natural resources.

The development of the Soviet economy occupied the major part of both Brezhnev's report and of the final resolution. The report of Premier A. N. Kosygin dealt entirely with the draft of the new Five-Year Plan. An account of it will be found in the chapters on planning, industry, and agriculture of this book. Because of the paramount importance of the CPSU in directing communist construction and affecting the entire life and destiny of the country, priority will be given to an account of its organisation and ideology, for it is the Party that provides the dynamism and the organisational framework within which the country develops. The Party also provides a unifying doctrine which it disseminates and imposes on the masses, moulding their world outlook, cementing different nationalities through a single creed, and directing their energies towards a common goal.

Chapter 2

The Communist Party of the Soviet Union

Membership and Organisation
IN 1969 THE MEMBERSHIP of the Communist Party of the Soviet Union stood at 14 million (including 600,000 candidates) or roughly about 9 per cent of the total *adult* population. According to the rules in force, a person wishing to join the Party should be recommended for membership by three Party members of at least five years' standing. The new member is first admitted as 'candidate' for membership, the period of probation lasting for a year or possibly more. The recommendation of the three sponsors is no mere formality; they are personally responsible for the acts and behaviour of their nominee. Eminent citizens such as cosmonauts, outstanding scientists, and, in wartime, members of the forces who had distinguished themselves by their gallantry, were invited to join the Party in recognition of their services. In the case of an ordinary applicant, he can be admitted only if two-thirds of the Party primary to which he applies vote in his favour, and his acceptance as candidate or full member must then be confirmed by the Party committee of the higher echelon, i.e. the appropriate town or district committee. Although it is possible to be admitted to the Party at the age of eighteen, normally those aged under twenty-three must have first been members of the Communist Youth League (*Komsomol*).

Rates of admission to Party membership have fluctuated over the years. On the one hand, the Party has always sought to be closely linked with the masses, because it represents their vanguard, in particular the vanguard of the most progressive class, i.e. the workers. On the other hand, the Party must maintain high standards of ideological purity, devotion to the cause of communism, and qualities of leadership among its members. It must be an élite. High rates of admission were the rule during the war; thereafter a period of very restricted enrolment lasted until 1954; a considerable expansion in membership took place when Khrushchev put forward the idea that the Party had become the Party of the whole people (not only that of the proletariat, a word no longer applicable to Soviet workers in any sphere); in the 1960s there were again several years of reduced intake and consolidation.

Membership of the Party is an essential precondition for appointment to certain important posts in the state bureaucracy, the military forces, scientific institutions, etc., enumerated in a special list known as *nomenklatura*. It is also required for certain teaching posts, namely those of history-teachers in schools and universities. However, rank-and-file members do not necessarily occupy all the responsible positions, since in many spheres, e.g. science, industrial management, and the arts, fitness for the job may be of greater importance. For instance, there are still members of the Academy of Sciences who are not members of the Communist Party, though this is an increasingly rare occurrence.

Membership of the Party is a great asset for promotion in any field, but it also carries numerous responsibilities. Members contribute membership fees in proportion to earnings (0·5 to 3 per cent of their wages), thus providing the Party with considerable funds not directly derived from the state Budget; the other major sources of Party funds come from its publishing activities.

While bestowing many advantages, membership of the Party also imposes many duties and onerous tasks, such as assuming the chairmanship of a bankrupt collective farm or leading groups of *Komsomol* to bring semi-desert lands under cultivation, and, generally speaking, requires Party members to display great courage and devotion in the performance of assignments which, owing to the strictness of Party discipline, they are not entitled to refuse.

An analysis of the make-up of the Party shows that half of its members were over forty in 1968. About 18 per cent were graduates of establishments of higher education and, together with those who had had a secondary specialised education, they constituted about one-third of the membership. In other words, the percentage of specialists within the Party was much greater than in the population at large, where the ratio of specialists to others was one to ten. On the other hand, about one-quarter of the Party members had had only four years' schooling in their younger days. The majority of the Party members belonged to white-collar professions; workers or ex-workers came next in numbers; nearly 5 million members lived in the countryside; they were either collective farmers or workers on state farms or, more commonly, members of the rural intelligentsia, such as primary-school teachers, collective-farm agronomists, engineers, or veterinary surgeons. Women constituted one-fifth of all members, which is less than could be expected in view of the high proportion of women in the population (55 per cent women as against 45 per cent men, according to the 1959 census).

The organisation of the Communist Party is based on Lenin's principle of 'democratic centralism', i.e. free discussion of a question within the Party before a decision is taken, but iron discipline in putting the final decision into effect once it is made. In this way no minority opinions are allowed to undermine the authority of the Party, for it is considered that only a strongly centralised Party can exercise effective leadership.

Every Party primary organisation in a village, factory, military unit, or institution annually elects a committee known as 'bureau' and a secretary (usually not a full-time official) who serve as its chief officers. The election of the secretary has to be confirmed by the committee or bureau of the next higher unit, i.e. at the district level for primaries. Every two years the primary organisation (of which there are about 340,000) elects delegates to a conference at the next higher level, the district. The delegates of the several primaries of the district (larger towns have several districts, each of which may be responsible for several hundred factory and workshop primaries within its territorial boundaries) elect a committee which, in turn, elects a bureau and three secretaries. The latter are full-time paid officials of the Party apparatus. The district conference also elects delegates to the next higher level, i.e. the provincial conference or, in the case of large cities, the city, or, if the area is inhabited by a national minority, to the conference of that particular area. There are about two hundred such territorial units throughout the USSR. The provincial conference elects a committee which, in turn, elects its bureau and three to five secretaries every two years. Every four years the provincial conference elects delegates to a Union Republic Congress; these elect their central committees and bureaux and secretaries. Provincial conferences and those of the smaller republics elect delegates to the All-Union Congress of the CPSU. These Congresses are the highest authority within the Party.

An All-Union Congress elects the Central Committee and the Central Inspection Commission. The Central Committee then elects its General Secretary (also called First Secretary), his deputies, the Politburo (called Party Praesidium between 1952 and 1966), and the Party Control Commission. The size of the Central Committee has fluctuated considerably over the years and, on the whole, tended to increase. Its plenary sessions (plenums) called at irregular intervals, usually two or three times a year, have acted as a kind of Communist Parliament at which important measures concerning the country's economy have been taken. Occasionally these plenums have been attended, by invitation, by specialists in the field under discussion at that particular session.

The extent to which the leadership of the Party exerts pressure on elections at primary and district levels is not known, though it is common practice for high-ranking Party officials to address such meetings and possibly advise on nominations. According to Merle Fainsod[1] as far back as October 1923 Trotsky complained that

> appointment of the secretaries of Provincial Committees is now the rule. That creates for the secretary a position essentially independent of the local organisation ... The bureaucratisation of the Party apparatus has developed to unheard-of proportions by means of the method of secretarial selection.

Full-time Party secretaries and other paid officials of the Party machinery or *apparat* are sometimes known as *apparatchiki*. The principal institutions of the *apparat* are the Central Committee's Secretariat (i.e. the General Secretary's Office) and its various sections, each of which is responsible for supervising the activities in any one definite field, e.g. the Soviet government bureaucracy, the armed forces, and the economic agencies; other sections ensure liaison with either foreign communist parties or the Party organisations at the lower echelons. One of the most important sections is the one in charge of Propaganda and Agitation, which supervises the mass communication media and runs the system of Party schools.

The role of the Party in all fields is to guide without actually taking over the administration directly. This is possible because in all spheres the men in responsible positions are members of the Party, though not necessarily members of the *apparat*, and vice versa. The interlinking is ubiquitous. Thus the director of the Military Section of the Secretariat is also a general in the armed forces; conversely, directors of important industrial concerns may be rank-and-file Party members; all *nomenklatura* appointments are in the hands of men belonging to the Party. This method of indirect rule enables the Party to govern while maintaining in power local, republican, and supreme All-Union Soviets, composed of both Party and non-Party members elected by universal suffrage. This network of Soviets includes local village Soviets, district, province, republican, and, at the apex of the pyramid, the Supreme Soviet of the USSR which elects the President of the Soviet Union as well as the Chairman of the Council of Ministers. Thus large sections of the population are drawn into the orbit of administration and enabled to

[1] Merle Fainsod, *How Russia is Ruled*, Cambridge, Mass., 1954, p. 158.

partake in minor day-to-day decision-making concerning their daily life, while real power rests firmly in the hands of the Party. In the words of Article 126 of the constitution of the USSR,

> The Communist Party of the Soviet Union ... represents the guiding nucleus [*rukovodyashchee yadro*] of all organisations of toilers, both voluntary [*obshchestvennye*] and governmental [*gosudarstvennye*].

It was through his domination of the Party machine that Stalin, first appointed by the Central Committee as its General Secretary in April 1922, established his authority. He took on the status of Head of Government only much later. At the time of writing, L. I. Brezhnev is General Secretary of the Party, while A. N. Kosygin is Chairman of the Council of Ministers, but, of course, he is also a member of the Central Committee. The General Secretary of the CPSU is the most powerful man in the Soviet Union.

The Party and the Government

The Supreme Soviet of the USSR is elected for four-year periods by universal suffrage and consists of two chambers, the Council of the Union with well over 700 members, and the Council of Nationalities with a nearly equally large membership. All Soviet citizens aged eighteen and over are entitled to vote. To be elected they must be aged twenty-three or over. Constituencies are based on population, one deputy being elected from every 300,000 inhabitants to the Council of the Union. The procedure for election to the Council of Nationalities is somewhat different; the fifteen Union republics are each entitled to twenty-five deputies, autonomous republics to eleven, autonomous regions to five, and national districts to one.[2] Altogether fifty-eight nationalities are represented in the Supreme Soviet.

The right to nominate candidates for election to the Supreme Soviet of the USSR or, within each Union republic, to its republi-

[2] The fifteen Union republics are: the RSFSR, the Ukrainian, Belorussian, Latvian, Estonian, Lithuanian, Moldavian, Georgian, Armenian, Azerbaidzhanian, Turkmenian, Uzbek, Kazakh, Kirghiz, and Tadzhik Soviet Socialist Republics. There are twenty autonomous republics, sixteen of which are in the RSFSR (hence the name of Russian Soviet Federative Socialist Republic): namely the Bashkir, Buryat, Dagestan, Kabardin-Balkar, Kalmyk, Karelian, Komi, Mari, Mordovian, North Ossetian, Tartar, Tuva, Udmurt, Checheno-Ingush, Chuvash, and Yakut autonomous Soviet Socialist Republics. Of the other four ASSR, one, the Kara-Kalpak, is in Uzbekistan; two, the Abkhazian and the Adzhar, in Georgia; and one, the Nakhichevan, in Azerbaidzhan. There are furthermore five autonomous regions and ten national districts, most of them in the RSFSR. For population figures see below, Appendix B.

can Supreme Soviet or to the Soviets at provincial, town, district, or village level, belongs to 'public organisations', in effect to Party primaries and those of the Communist Youth League (*Komsomol*), trade unions, collective farms, and other co-operative bodies, but not to individuals. If more than one candidate is put up, arrangements are made so that only one remains to be voted for. Despite the provision of booths for filling in secret ballots, the electorate has no choice but to vote 'yes' or 'no', and few electors would have the guts to vote 'no' or spoil their papers. The whole exercise seems to be designed to enable candidates to address their electors at pre-election meetings and get the electorate to show its solidarity with the 'bloc of Communists and non-Party' candidates. In rural districts elections are said to be the occasion for public festivities, and additional supplies of scarce consumer goods, sweets, and vodka are timed to arrive at village shops to supplement the limited range of goods normally available there.

Meetings of the Supreme Soviet take place twice a year and last only a few days. Deputies retain their usual employment and draw their normal salaries at their place of work; as deputies they are paid travelling and other incidental expenses. Often both chambers hold joint meetings, especially to approve the annual state Budget or to hear the results of the past and the details of the forthcoming annual national economic plan. These annual plans are subdivisions of the Five-Year Plan, but are usually more precise and operative than the Five-Year Plan, which sets out only the major targets. As regards the Budget, it should be mentioned that revenue from major enterprises accrues to the All-Union Budget and only individual taxes and income from lesser enterprises are collected by the republics. The Supreme Soviet elects the President of the Soviet Union, a Praesidium, the Council of Ministers, the Supreme Court, and the Procurator-General. The Praesidium consists of a Chairman (who also acts as President of the Soviet Union), a secretary, fifteen deputy chairmen, one from each Union republic, and sixteen other members. Although the division of power is not adhered to in the Soviet Union, the Praesidium of the Supreme Soviet has mainly legislative functions, while the All-Union Council of Ministers has executive powers. This is a large body, since Ministers are in charge not only of the government of the country but also of its entire economy. The most important Ministries are the All-Union Ministries, that is, those which direct the most important branches of industry, such as the aircraft industry, civil aviation, foreign trade, merchant marine, railways, etc. Others are known as Union-republican and come under the dual subordination of their republican as well as the All-Union Supreme Soviet; such are ministers of agriculture, building materials, culture, home trade, etc. Within each republic there are ministries that are subordinate to their own republican Supreme Soviet only and administer less important branches of industry as well as education, health, and local transport.

The Supreme Court of the Soviet Union is elected by the Supreme Soviet of the USSR; republican courts are likewise elected by the Supreme Soviet of each republic and lower courts and judges are elected by the same method. All courts have both appellate jurisdiction and jurisdiction at first instance, except for the lowest courts in the hierarchy, known as People's Courts, which have first-instance jurisdiction only. There are no juries, but the People's Courts consist of one judge and two lay assessors, one of whom must be a woman. Trials are normally held in open court, but measures can be taken to hold them in such small courtrooms that only a handful of selected press reporters and public can crowd in, as was the case when the few protesters against the occupation of Czechoslovakia were tried for attempting to stage a demonstration in Red Square in 1968.

The duty of the Procurator-General is to supervise the observance of laws and he appoints or confirms the appointments of the subordinate procurators at all administrative levels from Union republics to districts and towns.

Apart from Ministries, there are several state committees directly subordinate to the Council of Ministers, such as the Committees for Labour and Wages, Planning, Prices, Science and Engineering, and until recently State Security. This organ is responsible for combating external espionage and for carrying out internal counterespionage and investigating anti-Soviet activities. Under various names like *Cheka*, OGPU, NKVD, it had, particularly in the days of Stalin, powers of deportation, confinement, and execution without trial; apart from agents, informers, and investigators with plenary powers, it had at its disposal internal troops armed with tanks and similar weaponry capable of crushing any large-scale uprising. After Stalin's death the powers of this secret police corps were drastically curtailed and it was made subordinate to the Council of Ministers.

At lower levels, each Soviet (provincial, district, town, or village) elects an executive committee which carries on local administration; its members become full-time paid officials. They are responsible both to the Soviet that has elected them and to the executive committee of the above-standing Soviet. Thus a district executive committee is responsible to its district Soviet and also to the executive committee of the provincial Soviet, and so on. Apart from executive committees, Soviets set up permanent commissions to organise and supervise local economic or cultural activities; these permanent commissions may co-opt members suitable to their functions; co-opted members of permanent commissions need not necessarily be members of the local Soviet. Local executive committees are responsible for general education, the health services, housing, local transport, urban utilities, employment agencies, supervision of industrial and agricultural enterprises, and the maintenance of public order within their locality. Since members usually lack legal training they are encouraged to study at higher Party schools or special courses.

Within this network of bodies elected by universal suffrage the Party naturally plays a very considerable role. In the elections carried out in 1967 to all Soviets, Party members gained 950,000 seats out of a total of 2,055,000. Party representation is greater in the more important bodies; thus in the Supreme Soviet Party members outnumber non-Party deputies in the proportion of 1,517 to 376. On local executive committees Party members account for 75 per cent of the total membership.

The Supreme Soviet passes all important laws, or rather ratifies the basic principles of such laws, thus leaving room for Supreme Soviets of Union republics to have the opportunity of introducing minor adjustments. Since 1927, when an effort was made at codifying the numerous enactments of the Soviet government and a *Systematic Collection of Laws of the USSR* was published, no attempt at codification was implemented until 1958, despite the huge number of decrees dealing with industrialisation, collectivisation, far-reaching alterations to labour laws, and secret instructions promulgated under Stalin. The present effort at codification has resulted in the passing by the Supreme Soviet of a spate of Basic Principles which are designed to introduce more legality into the life of the country and to reflect the present socialist relations which are or should be observed. Among the first to appear (December 1959) were the Basic Principles of Criminal Law, followed (in 1962) by those of Civil Law and (in 1965) by the law regarding the Socialist State Productive Enterprise; this was an important enactment, since many court cases are brought not by individuals but by one enterprise against another for late delivery or sub-standard articles supplied, or by the Procurator's Office for non-compliance with anti-water-pollution regulations. The Basic Principles of Labour Law have repealed many decrees passed in the late 1930s and 1940s and given trade unions many rights that they had enjoyed earlier. Legislation on land utilisation, health, and family will be discussed further. All that need be said here is that this legislation is prepared by a law commission of the Council of Ministers of the USSR, established in 1956 by a joint decree of the Central Committee of the CPSU and the Council of Ministers of the USSR, and that all major laws and decrees are always promulgated jointly by these supreme organs of the Party and the government.

Perhaps the most characteristic features of Soviet administration lie in the provisions to interest and involve the masses in the government of their country by election procedures, while the steering of the course is effected by the Party hierarchy; also in devolution of power to local authorities and national republics while overall control is retained by a centralised Party. The direct subordination of major industrial and other institutions to the central government, whatever their location, has yet another contributory centralising effect.

Lenin's Centenary

Whatever reservations the Party leadership may have today about Stalin's cult of personality, the greatness of Lenin has never been challenged. He is regarded as one of the most remarkable men who ever lived, and plans for the celebrations for his centenary were on foot since the festivities held to mark the fiftieth anniversary of the Revolution came to an end.

People who still remember the great leader have been encouraged to record their meetings with him, however brief or casual. The breadth of his interests has been enthusiastically emphasised and his contribution to every field of human knowledge brought to light. The forty-odd volumes of his collected works have been scanned for suitable quotations illustrating his prophetic insight into future developments and scientific discoveries. Every publishing house has brought out books about him and every imaginable aspect of his life and achievements. Workers have undertaken to complete special production targets and schoolchildren organised excursions to all the places in the USSR where he ever lived or spoke.

Stress on the timelessness of his teaching and the slogan 'Lenin lived, Lenin lives, Lenin will live', have been given great prominence to preclude the younger generation from dismissing as archaic the views of a man who had never travelled by plane nor watched television nor seen a computer, let alone a spacecraft. The centenary was a welcome opportunity to highlight the unity of the communist movement throughout the world. At the International Conference of Communist and Workers' Parties held in June 1969, and attended by representatives from seventy-five countries, a resolution was unanimously passed to organise centenary celebrations by every nation. UNESCO was asked to promote worldwide festivities. In December 1969 the CPSU published its *Theses* for the occasion of the one-hundredth anniversary of V. I. Lenin.

The document was no mere *pièce de circonstance* but an outline of the Party's present policy, and an account of it will help explain present aims and tribulations. The first section contains a tribute to the genius and achievements of the great leader, to his masterful analysis of the political situation in 1917, the brilliance of his tactics and timing, and the scope of his solution of fundamental social problems. He brought together scientific socialism and a mass workers' movement; developed Marxist theory to meet new conditions; forged the Bolshevik party into a fighting organisation; and eventually translated theory into the practice of a socialist revolution to be followed by socialist construction. He conceived the Party not as a conglomeration of groupings or as a discussion club, but saw that its strength lay in the monolithic cohesion of its ranks, and that any action directed to undermine its unity or weaken its iron discipline was utterly inadmissible.

The second part of the document, entitled 'Socialism – the embodiment of the ideas of Leninism', describes the early years of the Soviet regime, the need for and the meaning of the dictatorship of the proletariat and its present transformation into a 'political organisation of all the people under the leading role of the working class headed by its vanguard – the Communist Party'. In a veiled reference to Stalin's and Khrushchev's deeds, the document goes on to say that

> the Party rejects any attempts to direct criticism of the cult of personality and subjectivism against the interests of the people and socialism with the aim of blackening the history of socialist construction and discrediting revolutionary gains and the revision of the principles of Marxism-Leninism.

Describing the bonds of friendship between socialist countries, it refers in an even more cryptic allusion to the occupation of Czechoslovakia, stating that the community of socialist nations 'counters the imperialist policy of exporting counter-revolution with its invincible strength and determination to uphold the conquests of the people'.

After dwelling at some length on the benefits that socialism brought to the people by shortening working hours, and providing free educational and medical facilities as well as pensions and other welfare, it concedes that unresolved difficulties still exist, including such a major one, foreseen already by Lenin, as that socialism cannot yet give 'full equality in consumption and in material security to all people'.

Although the evolution of the world socialist system is a complex and multi-faceted process, connected with objective and subjective difficulties arising from unequal economic development, historical and cultural traditions, and social structures; and despite imperialists who exploit and fan the centrifugal forces of nationalism, revisionism, and local feuds and frictions, the co-ordination of economic plans is bringing to fruition Lenin's plan for an 'international co-operative of workers'.

The third part of the document, entitled 'Leninism – the banner of the struggle of the people against imperialism and for a revolutionary renovation of the world', reiterates the views expressed earlier in the resolution of the 1969 International Conference of Communist and Workers' Parties. The major obstacle to progress is imperialism. The bourgeoisie, by modernising its methods, has succeeded in retaining its hold over material resources; while bribing and misleading the proletariat by hypocritical assertions of social partnership, it makes enormous profits from military contracts, yet fails to avoid recurring economic and financial crises resulting in unemployment. The struggle against imperialism in emergent nations can only be successful if led by a Marxist-Leninist party. This is defined as a revolutionary party which directs and prepares the proletariat

> for the seizure of state power and its seizure in the form of a dictatorship of the proletariat ... a conscious vanguard of the class, closely linked with and leading the masses ... an international party for which the struggle with opportunist and petty-bourgeois pacifist distortions of the ideas and the policy of internationalism is the first and most important task ... a united militant organisation, built on the principles of democratic centralism, capable of rallying the working class and all toilers in the revolutionary struggle, irreconcilable to any form of opportunism and splinter-group formation.

There cannot be any neutralism or compromises in the ideological struggle between imperialism and socialism, nor any peaceful coexistence, let alone convergence of ideologies.

The last section, 'Along the Lenin path to Communism', is concerned with the transition from socialism to communism, that is, with the stage of development now reached by the Soviet Union. Thus it is in fact an exposition of the Party's present policy and the obstacles to be overcome. The preparation of the material and spiritual prerequisites for communism are lengthy and exacting, but the creation of material wealth to satisfy reasonable human needs is essential to allow for the full development of man's highest abilities and potential personality. In the expansion of the material and technical basis the greatest problem to be solved at the moment is the intensification of production. The conditions to achieve this are as follows: the creation of a modern and rational system for the organisation and management of production, ensuring comprehensive technical progress and the practical utilisation of the newest scientific data; the industrialisation of all branches of the economy (probably an indirect reference to agriculture); improvements in the structure of all branches of the economy and in their interrelations as well as in the proportions of their respective growth; a consistent and logical specialisation of production and an efficient use of material resources.

The scientific and technical revolution has brought about qualitative changes in the technology of production, particularly in that of energy, tools, and materials, and also in the organisation of management and the nature of labour itself. Science has become a productive force and a crucial factor in the competition between the two opposing social and economic systems.

Within the socialist society new social relations are evolving and Lenin's demand must become the norm, namely that 'a conscious worker should feel that he is not only master of his own factory, but also the representative of the country and that he should feel responsible for it'. One of the major obstacles on the road to progress is the need to divert resources to defence instead of using them to raise standards of living and culture. Furthermore, the formation of a new morality and philosophy of life is taking place within the context of a fierce ideological struggle. This requires precise and lucid thinking on ideological problems; a heightened revolutionary vigilance; continual struggle against apolitical indifference, survivals of a selfish acquisitive private-property mentality, 'manifestations of nihilistic attitudes to the achievements of socialism', and the infiltration of bourgeois and revisionist views.

The scale and complexity of the problems raise the role of the conscious organising vanguard in the life of our society – Lenin's party of Communists.

This brief summary of the *Theses* shows the importance the Party attributes to its own role, the pride it takes in its economic achievements, its fear of imperialism and of the subversive ideas that may undermine the authority of its doctrine; it shows too that the leadership understands that the Soviet Union dare not fall behind in the race of scientific progress, that she must modernise her economy and, in particular, her managerial techniques, and overcome the inertia of many citizens and their indifference to the official ideology. Despite their belief that the economic basis determines human thinking, the leadership has always attributed the greatest importance to political education.

Political Education

For the Party to be in Lenin's words 'the mind, honour and conscience of our epoch', each member of the Party in every walk of life must be superior to his fellow worker or non-Party colleague in knowledge, character, and devotion to duty, highly conscious of his calling, and well versed in the theory of Marxism-Leninism.

Because in the early years of the Revolution many people joined the Party on emotional rather than rational grounds, it was necessary to underpin their general revolutionary enthusiasm with a theoretical foundation. At the same time the new leadership was anxious to attract wavering left-wing professionals like teachers, scientists, and engineers, convert them to the new ideology, and persuade them to contribute their knowledge and skills to rebuilding the country. So the teaching of Marxism became a major function of Party members. The enduring strength of Marxism lay in its being an integral world outlook, a synthesis of philosophy, economics, politics, and sociology. Its philosophy, known as dialectical and historical materialism, claimed to be the science of the most general laws of development of nature, society, and human thought. A knowledge of the laws of nature enables scientists to influence and direct natural phenomena. Similarly a knowledge of the laws governing the development of human societies should enable the social scientist to act upon the course of their development. Prior to Marx, philosophers interpreted the world in various ways, but since his advent, social sciences – i.e. the knowledge of the laws governing the development of society – have enabled men to change social structures; in fact to take the evolution of societies into man's own hand. This is perhaps particularly relevant today, when mankind has gained such power over nature and is in search of a universal creed. Contrary to Nazism, Judaism, or white racialism, which favour the chosen and exclude the others, Marxism, like Christianity, Islam, or Buddhism, accepts all those who accept it. Like the great religions, it may give rise to different interpretations, but this cannot impair its fundamental universality.

Lenin decreed the introduction of a compulsory course of Marxism in all establishments of higher education in 1921, and it has remained to this day an integral part of any degree course. A special All-Union Communist University (named after Sverdlov) was set up in Moscow, as well as an Institute of Red Professors and scores of less well-known institutions and elementary schools of political literacy (*politgramota*).

At present the highest institution of the Party political education system (*politprosveshchenie*) is the Academy of Social Sciences of the Central Committee of the CPSU. At a lower level there are nearly three hundred evening universities of Marxism-Leninism, various study circles, and numerous lower-level Party schools known as *partshkoly*. These cater mainly for manual workers who have had little schooling in their youth, seldom read newspapers, and avoid listening to serious radio talks. Organisationally, the *partshkoly* are set up by the town or district Party Committees and are evening classes which meet regularly once a week or at least once a fortnight at the place of work of the students (factory, railway-yard, collective farm, etc.). The teaching is done by unpaid instructors who do it as a 'Party assignment' (*partiinoe poruchenie*). The course lasts two years and comprises the study of a simplified version of Marx's and Lenin's economic theories, the history of the CPSU, and current affairs. Students are set homework such as reading newspaper articles in preparation for discussion in class; they are taught to summarise data, to find illustrative material in fiction, and to express themselves in an articulate way; this will enable them later to carry on agitation (*agitatsiya*) among fellow workers. Occasionally an excursion to a museum, documentary film, or a particularly well-run factory may be arranged.

In Soviet parlance there is a considerable difference between the words propaganda and agitation. The latter is limited to explaining to workmates or inhabitants of the same block of flats, in general to small groups or individuals approached in face-to-face situations, the meaning and purpose of the latest decree or policy campaign, to exhorting fellow citizens to achieve higher productivity or vote at the next election, or strive to achieve standards of behaviour worthy of 'builders of communism'. Agitation is usually conducted by word of mouth, often enlivened by posters, slogans, caricatures, or by contributions to the local wall-newspaper. Propaganda, on the other hand, aims at communication on a higher level, involving cogently argued and well-documented presentation of the ideological or political aspects of any important political decision. It is effected by means of lectures attended by larger and more sophisticated audiences, or is disseminated by the mass media. The major Party newspaper, *Pravda*, had a circulation of 8½ million copies a day in 1969. Among other widely read Party newspapers are the agricultural publication *Selskaya Zhizn*, with a circulation of 6,200,000, and the women's magazine *Rabotnitsa*, with 10 million. The bi-monthly *Kommunist* has a wide coverage, with articles on economics, agriculture, education, and arts, while *Partiinaya Zhizn* is more concerned with matters relating to Party activities. At its most refined, propaganda becomes *partiinost'*, i.e. 'Party-mindedness', and *ideinost'*, i.e. faithfulness to principles – the two qualities that should permeate and inspire Soviet art and literature.

The circulation of the Party's provincial papers and those printed in the many languages of the non-Russian nationalities is also quite impressive. Incidentally, apart from the publications run directly by the Party as its 'organs', all forms of mass-communication media are under the indirect control of the Party owing to the vigilance of Party members who sit on the editorial boards of all publishing houses, printing organisations, broadcasting and television stations.

On completing the course of a *partshkola* the student becomes a politically conscious and articulate citizen and partakes as a volunteer agitator in mass campaigns in favour of measures initiated by the leadership; he may be entrusted with the production of the wall-newspaper at his place of work. More educated Party members are encouraged to study on their own, because all Communists are in duty bound to study and improve their understanding of Marxism-Leninism.

Most urban centres have 'homes of political enlightenment' where those who study individually obtain a syllabus, lists of recommended reading, advice on methods of study, books, and newspapers. Often they are drawn into study circles or regular seminars, or attend lectures by specialists. The syllabus of all Party schools (as well as that of social science courses given at establishments of higher education) comprises political economy, history of the Party, and philosophy. These subjects, philosophy in particular, can be studied at different levels and this depends much on the student's previous schooling. The study of the classics of Marxism-Leninism, Party documents, and other political literature should enable students 'to evaluate correctly the phenomena of public life and help them to master skills of political work among the masses'.[3] Most of those who complete their training by attending study circles or evening universities of Marxism-Leninism will then volun-

[3] N. Gents and V. Surov, 'Samostoyatelnaya rabota slushatelei', *Politicheskoe obrazovanie*, December 1965, p. 46, quoted by E. P. Mickiewicz, *Soviet Political Schools*, New Haven, 1967, p. 21.

teer to act as instructors at lower Party schools or as discussion leaders in study circles, this work ranking as Party assignments.

Highly educated Party members, i.e. scientists, doctors, teachers, and artists, usually attend theoretical seminars. The object of these seminars is to explore and relate Marxist dialectics to the students' professional field of knowledge. Thus the Institute of Automatic Mechanisms and Telemechanics organised a seminar on the philosophical implications of cybernetics, while a Laboratory of Helminthology held one on the history of biology seen as the history of the struggle of materialism with idealism. Theoretical seminars for actors, artists, and musicians deal with aesthetics, or the Leninist principle of Party-mindedness (*partiinost'*) in literature and art, or the creative method of socialist realism and its superiority over 'abstractionist formalist distortions'. Discussions at such seminars are designed to help mould a conformity of views compatible with Party doctrine. More practical topics may be discussed at seminars attended by technologists or factory administrators to prepare them for the advent of automation, the need to redeploy labour, to raise production norms, and find ways to mitigate or make more palatable any lowering of wages consequent on changed techniques by placing the fact within the broader context of technological advance. Occasionally, theoretical seminars may be called upon to organise a theoretical conference at which leading scientists read papers which are then published by the Society for the Dissemination of Political and Scientific Knowledge, now renamed 'Knowledge' (*Obschchestvo 'Znanie'*), as was the case with a book entitled *Philosophical Questions of Modern Physics.*

The most advanced students who have attended evening universities of Marxism-Leninism may be chosen to study full-time at a higher Party school. Such institutions exist in practically all Union republics and rank as establishments of higher education (VUZ). Apart from advanced courses in Marxism-Leninism they provide professional training for Party members who will be promoted to responsible posts in industry, transport, the health service, or agriculture, i.e. posts that require specialised knowledge from their incumbents. Thus they serve a somewhat different purpose than the dissemination of Marxism.

Since Stalin's death the content of political courses has undergone some changes. The *Short Course of History of the VKP (b)*, published in 1938 and probably written by Stalin, has ceased to be the standard basic text. Under the secretaryship of Khrushchev there was a considerable expansion of lower Party schools because of the large numbers of new recruits to the Party and also because of Khrushchev's policy of enrolling non-Party people into Party schools. This measure seems to have had a double aim. On the one hand it was designed to broaden the base of the Party and transform it eventually into a Party of the whole people. On the other hand, it brought large audiences in contact with 'concrete economics', i.e. the study of up-to-date concrete economic problems as they arise in a fast-developing planned economy. To a certain extent concrete economics were to supersede the theoretical approach to political economy, as expounded by Marx and Lenin, in favour of the appraisal of more practical problems set by present-day economic developments. To fulfil the new requirements those in charge of political education had to familiarise themselves with new fields of knowledge or call upon experts, such as directors of factories, chief engineers, specialists in cost-pricing, production planning, finance, technological innovations, agriculture, etc. In an endeavour to link theory and practice, students at a lower Party school who were studying Lenin's dictum that 'Communism is Soviet power plus the electrification of the country' were asked to perform practical assignments; for instance, one was to see whether the motors of his shop had enough power for the demands placed on them; another to check the electrical wiring system; while yet others were to find out whether lights were turned on earlier than necessary because of dirty windows or high wattage bulbs placed where lesser ones would suffice.

The expansion of political education under Khrushchev, coupled with emphasis on applied economics and the scrapping of Stalin's *Short Course*, made heavy demands on the teaching staff. The total number of people studying within the system of Party political education is said to have reached 36 million, of whom 25 million or 78 per cent were not even members of the Party. The fall of Khrushchev saw a sharp decrease in student numbers; in 1966 enrolment was down to 12 million, and three-quarters of those enrolled were, in fact, members of the Party.[4] At the same time there was a return to a more theoretical study of Marxism and much less emphasis on concrete economics.

Altogether the content of Party political education is somehow at the crossroads. The Party leadership would like distinguished scientists to participate more actively in theoretical discussions on dialectical materialism. In the past, specialists in dialectical materialism have often failed to bring their knowledge of science up to date. As a result, they failed to appreciate new theories that were revolutionising physics. They rejected Einstein's theory of relativity and Heisenberg's principle of indeterminancy on the grounds that these theories were incompatible with the notion of cause and

[4] Mickiewicz, op. cit., p. 10.

effect. Cybernetics were banned because the identification of the human mind with a machine was seen as a capitalist attempt to turn workers into robots. The most notorious case of Party obscurantism is associated with the name of Lysenko and his attack on genetics in 1948. The science itself was proscribed as justifying racialism and casting doubts on the overriding influence of environment as well as on the inheritance of acquired characteristics. If heredity was the determining and decisive factor, it followed that even a communist environment could not perfect human nature, and the emergence of a superior type of communist man could not be achieved. Geneticists were arrested on charges of anti-communist activities and some, like the distinguished biologist N. I. Vavilov, died in prison. The ban on genetics affected research work in animal and plant selection, and the after-effects of Lysenkoism are handicapping Soviet farming until the present day.

There seems to be no reason why dialectical materialism cannot be brought into line with modern science. Certainly the discovery of the genetic code has furnished genetics with a material basis acceptable to materialist thinking. Unfortunately, it appears that scientists are usually more interested in their own research than in philosophy. So it is left to the philosophers to study modern science. This is no easy task for men used to basing their arguments on quotations from authoritative texts. To overcome the theoretical gap, a Scientific Council on the philosophical problems of natural sciences has been set up by the Academy of Sciences of the USSR.

Philosophers who are responsible for organising theoretical conferences in scientific institutions and lecturers in charge of the compulsory courses in social sciences in establishments of higher education are in the same quandary. Major universities have special four-month post-graduate courses for the raising of qualifications of such lecturers; but some of these men are middle-aged and set in their ways, others lack adequate training in mathematics, and quite a number had chosen the subject because for a long time it was a soft option.

Another difficulty confronting Party political speakers is the unforeseen social consequences of technological change. In some ways their predicament is not unlike that of Western moralists and sociologists who had not foreseen that the affluent society would give rise to drug-taking, rising crime rates, 'contracting out', and, generally speaking, rejection of the hygiene, prosperity, and universal culture for which previous generations had striven so hard.

The spread of literacy and a better knowledge of the classics of Marxism-Leninism may lead to a more independent interpretation of their writings, just as a better knowledge of the Bible, when it became available in the vernacular, gave rise to numerous sects. A glaring case of inconsistency between Marxist theory and Soviet practice is the survival of the state. According to Engels, this instrument of class domination was doomed to wither away. Already Stalin in his speech to the Eighteenth Party Congress in 1939 had had to justify its survival by saying that the state was necessary to protect the only socialist country against a hostile capitalist environment. At present the organising and managerial functions of the state are adduced to justify its persistence.

Khrushchev made a first step towards its eventual withering-away by initiating a limited devolution of power to local bodies, such as 'comradely tribunals' set up by trade unions and some other organisations, and voluntary local para-police detachments (*druzhiny*) with considerable powers; they could forcibly bring people considered guilty of some misdemeanours to the militia, or initiate action to expel them from their dwelling or town under the anti-parasite laws. Apparently these powers led to considerable abuse and were later curtailed, though travellers to the USSR occasionally meet a *druzhinnik* (identifiable by his red arm-band) on a bus or suburban train, checking whether all transport-users are in possession of a valid ticket.

Another point obviously in need of comment is the forecast made by Marx that under capitalism workers would become increasingly poor. To explain why the opposite phenomenon is taking place, use is made of Lenin's argument, according to which only workers in imperialist countries do not become poorer because they share in the profits derived by the capitalists from the exploitation of the colonial proletariat or, in more modern terminology, the proletariat of under-developed countries.

Despite reductions in the unusually high wage differentials prevalent in the USSR, where equal pay was abolished by Stalin in the early 1930s, the gulf between the 'rich' who earn much and the 'poor' who earn little is too conspicuous to be denied. Therefore, Soviet citizens who have never read *The New Class* by Djilas are perfectly aware of great economic and social inequalities persisting in their country. Indeed, much is written to explain that under socialism (and the USSR has not yet reached the second phase of socialism – that is, communism), people are paid according to their work. 'Same as in capitalist countries' was the remark overheard by a baffled instructor of political economy.

Material and technical progress has brought the transistor set to Soviet youth. Coupled with a wider knowledge of foreign languages, it gives them the opportunity of listening, not necessarily to anti-Soviet broadcasts, but simply to hitherto inaccessible foreign programmes. It is now common to read in the more highbrow Soviet press, like the *Literaturnaya Gazeta*, adverse criticisms of foreign books or theories. If refutations are needed, there must be Soviet citizens who have at least heard about these alien and erroneous views. The major lure of the West lies probably in its greater material wealth and the permissiveness of its society. Comfort, luxury, lax morality, and easy life have naturally a great appeal for the masses. For the more thoughtful and highminded, the spontaneity of a really popular revolution may have more attraction; in any case, when Fidel Castro visited Moscow he met with a tremendous and genuinely enthusiastic welcome. The spirit of egalitarianism, anti-élitism, and revolutionary zeal in China might become contagious, though China's claims to a large slice of Siberia and an even larger one of Central Asia may antagonise Russians whose early civilisation was destroyed in the thirteenth century by the Mongol invaders, a bellicose, nomadic people who also conquered China under the leadership of Gengis Khan. It took the Russians two and a half centuries to throw off the Mongol domination. Only at the close of the fifteenth century did an independent, but weak and backward, Muscovy reappear on the map of Europe – a remote, semi-oriental state, bypassed by the great intellectual currents of the Reformation and the Renaissance.

Workers of successful and therefore profitable enterprises might become attracted by the syndicalism of Tito's self-managing producers' co-operatives, with their wide powers of sharing out profits. At any rate, there have been articles in the Soviet press to the effect that no group of workers can 'own' any factory because, according to Lenin, all industrial enterprises belong to society as a whole.

There certainly is great concern with ideology at the present time. On 22 August 1967 the Central Committee of the CPSU passed a resolution 'On measures for further developing the social sciences and heightening their role in communist construction'. It stressed the need for both a deeper analysis of social developments and a higher level of Marxist-Leninist education of cadres. An Institute of Scientific Information was set up to improve the quality and depth of philosophical generalisations of the latest discoveries in natural sciences and the study of problems of social psychology and social engineering. The Institute of Marxism-Leninism attached to the Central Committee and the Chief Administration of Archives were to be provided with modern means of reproduction and multiplication of documentary material, while the Academy of Sciences and the Central Statistical Administration were to work out a 'scientifically validated system of statistical data necessary for social research'. In 1969 the Academy of Sciences of the USSR set up an Institute of Concrete Social Research.

Indeed, there has been a proliferation of sociological surveys conducted by various institutions and mainly oriented towards practical goals: for instance, surveys of career aspirations among the young and opportunities or lack of opportunities to satisfy them; time spent by women on shopping and household chores, particularly in regions short of labour; the proper or wasteful employment of fully trained engineers; and other surveys on similar topics, though more general ones are to follow.

A truly scientific knowledge of social phenomena is essential for the Party to guide the people towards the goal of communism. Yet it failed to foresee quite a number of them, not merely the survival of 'negative' attitudes such as indifference to ideology, erroneous interpretations, unsocial behaviour, juvenile delinquency, and delinquency in general, but the unexpected and unaccountable fall in the birth-rate which is probably the most important consequence of social change. Demography has been a largely neglected field in Soviet social science studies, yet the economic and eventually military implications of a fall in the birth-rate cannot be underestimated, considering the 5,000-mile-long border with China, whose population is already three times greater than that of the USSR. Indirectly, the demographic factor may have prompted the present impetus to raise standards of living, though of course this is also the result of industrial expansion.

The meaning of 'standard of living' is affecting ideology in an interesting way. Marx's concept that wages cover the existence and the reproduction of labour has been given a new twist by trying to determine what a worker, under socialism, needs to exist and to beget and bring up children. It is being argued that 'to exist' a worker under socialism needs more than food, shelter, and clothing; he also requires cultural satisfactions, books, entertainment, tourism, etc. Because of its centrally planned economy, the Soviet government can decide which needs of the population are to be given priority, e.g. more and better medicines or more and better cosmetics; books on science or pornography; tourism to see the beauties of nature, historical monuments, modern constructions; or just to laze about on a beach.

Unlike private enterprise in capitalist countries motivated by prospects of financial gain, the Soviet government is in a better position to resist the tempting lure of exploiting vice because it is a profitable source of money. Some thinking on criteria of cultural policy and the meaning of high living standards is afoot, but it is a novel type of thinking and latterly the Party has not displayed the dynamic creativity called for by twentieth-century opportunities; rather the reverse. It still relies heavily on repressive measures to uphold its claims to infallibility. In June 1968 an All-Union Conference of heads of all social science departments in establishments of higher education discussed further improvements in the teaching of Marxism-Leninism and ways of protecting Soviet citizens from alien subversive ideologies. Since 1967 a marked tightening of censorship in the fields of literature and arts has been evident.

Apart from integrating scientific data into its doctrine, the Party is anxious to blunt the memories of what is euphemistically referred to in the USSR as Stalin's 'errors' and more outspokenly by Western sovietologists as the 'great terror'. When, after the death of Stalin and the execution of Beria, his Chief of the Secret Police, amnestied survivors began to return from exile, the long hushed-up truth about Stalin's 'errors' could no longer be concealed. Discreet behind-the-scene rehabilitations hardly satisfied victims or their families in the case of posthumous acquittals. The mere reappearance of thousands of concentration-camp survivors posed the question 'How could it have happened?' – a question that sincere and decent young Communists must have asked and which the poet Evgeny Evtushenko voiced so painfully in his early poems. According to Academician Sakharov,[5] a full-length book dealing with the subject from a strictly Marxist point of view has been in fact written in the Soviet Union but cannot be published, for there are still too many guilty people in power who hope that silence and time will bring oblivion. Their attitude is not without its parallel in West Germany, where those in power during the Nazi regime tend also to forget their cruel past.

The Purges

A ruling party is always in danger of being joined by careerists and even infiltrated by traitors. Hence the need for regular checks of its membership and for expelling, in Lenin's words, 'the rascals, bureaucrats, dishonest and wavering Communists, and Mensheviks who have repainted their "façade" but who have remained Mensheviks at heart'.[6] The first large-scale purge was carried out in 1921, but at that time expulsion from the Party, though naturally a disgrace, which may have led to loss of employment, did not entail any further penalties. Numerically the Party had grown by then to about three-quarters of a million, and nearly 20 per cent of the members were expelled on charges of passivity, careerism, failing to carry out Party assignments, drunkenness, corruption,

[5] Andrei Sakharov, *Progress, Coexistence and Intellectual Freedom*, English translation edited by Harrison E. Salisbury, London, 1968, p. 54.
[6] Lenin, *O chistki partii*, first published in *Pravda*, 21 September 1921.

practising religion, or even infiltrating the Party with counter-revolutionary aims. Among those purged, many were white-collar workers and peasants. Workers were either less suspect or measured up better to Party standards. In the early years the emphasis was naturally on recruiting working-class members. After Lenin's death there was an intensive recruitment campaign; a considerable influx took place again between 1929 and 1932, when the working class expanded with industrialisation. However, after 1930 preferential admission of workers was dropped because a new intelligentsia of proletarian origin, either promoted from the shop-floor or educated under the Soviet regime, was rising to important administrative or technical positions in the expanding industries. Between January 1933 and November 1934 admissions to the Party practically ceased because by 1933 Party membership had risen to $3\frac{1}{2}$ million and it was felt that many did not measure up to the standard required. In the following two years a large number of members, possibly over a million, were expelled from the Party. After the murder on 1 December 1934 of Sergei Kirov, a member of the Politburo and head of the Leningrad Party organisation, expulsion was followed by arrest and proscription. Mass arrests and the shooting of Party members, including Old Bolsheviks (i.e. Communists who had joined the Party prior to the Revolution and taken a direct part in the October insurrection), brought about the horrors of the great purges during which both Party and non-Party members perished in thousands and, possibly, in millions. Little is known about the numbers and fate of ordinary people arrested during those years, but in his secret speech at the Twentieth Party Congress in 1956 Khrushchev mentioned that of the 1,966 delegates to the Seventeenth Party Congress in 1934, 1,108 had been arrested and most of them shot. There was a bitter irony in the fact that this Congress had been referred to as the Congress of Victors, for those present had victoriously achieved the collectivisation of agriculture in the face of desperate peasant resistance.

The charges brought against prominent Party leaders in the late 1930s had probably little to do with reality; they were accused of counter-revolutionary activities aimed at the restoration of capitalism, of spying for Japan's militarist rulers, and similar unlikely offences. But if one believes in retributive justice, they paid with their lives for the part they had played in the ruthless liquidation of 'class enemies', inspired and directed by them when they were in power. Of more tragic consequence for the people of Russia was the purge of the Red Army High Command in 1937–38. Of the five marshals, only the two Party faithfuls, Budenny and Voroshilov, survived. Thirteen out of fifteen army commanders were shot, fifty-seven of eighty-five corps commanders were executed, and the purge affected the entire officer corps down to company commander level, leaving the Soviet army demoralised and deprived of military talent and know-how on the eve of Hitler's invasion of Russia. When on 22 June 1941 the German armies crossed the Soviet frontier, many officers who had not been shot but sent to concentration camps had to be released to take on the responsibility of holding the rapidly crumbling front. Later a few of them rose to fame, like the future Marshal Rokossovsky. Torture as a method of criminal investigation, abolished in the eighteenth century by Catherine II, was reintroduced under the name of 'physical pressure' for the purpose of obtaining self-incriminatory confessions and denunciations of other possible suspects. Informing became a legal obligation and 'vigilance', i.e. spying on one's workmates or co-lodgers in an apartment, the duty of every citizen.

The war, which revealed considerable disaffection among the population, exacerbated Stalin's maniacal suspiciousness and there were further post-war purges, the most notorious of which was the 'Leningrad affair', when leading members of the Leningrad Party apparatus were executed and N. A. Voznesensky, Chairman of the State Planning Commission (*Gosplan*) since 1938, disappeared without any statement regarding his fate. Shortly before Stalin's death several doctors, most of them of Jewish origin, were arrested and, according to Western observers, these arrests (known as the Jewish Doctors' Plot) foreshadowed yet another major purge. In each case, apart from Party members, many others were shot or sent to concentration camps in very great numbers. Indeed, prisoners-of-war returning from Germany were treated like traitors and sent to die in the concentration camps of Kolyma and Magadan in the far north-east of Siberia. Entire national groups had been forcibly evicted from their homes and transported under terrible conditions to underpopulated regions beyond the Urals during the war on the charge of having collaborated with the Germans, or on mere suspicion that they might have done so. This fate befell the Crimean Tartars, the Ingush-Balkars, a small Caucasian nationality, and the Volga Germans, i.e. the descendants of German immigrants who had settled in Russia in the eighteenth century – a total of nearly one million people. Any personal relations with foreigners became a treasonable act, and indeed an Iron Curtain descended between Russia and the West.

From its inception the Communist Party never shirked mass executions, nor did it hesitate to liquidate enemy classes such as the gentry, the clergy, and the bourgeoisie in the days of Lenin, and the kulaks or richer peasants during the collectivisation campaign directed by Stalin. To end the exploitation of man by man it condoned the physical extermination of the exploiting classes. Yet the scale and seeming irrationality of the Stalin purges, which hit the Party itself, resembled more a chain reaction of evil deeds beyond human control. The omnipotent dictator, extolled as superhuman by the adulations of his propaganda machine, surrounded by bodyguards, yet feeling unsafe even behind the mediaeval walls of the Kremlin, was unable to sleep until the small hours of the night and hardly ever dared venture outside. Occasionally, in great secrecy, under heavy guard, with endless precautions he would drive in a bullet-proof car to a country residence, or in an armour-plated railway carriage to his native Caucasus to live in houses protected by high walls and barbed-wire, himself a prisoner of his own terror. On his deathbed he was deprived of proper medical care, his personal physicians being in prison at the time.

It will probably take more than a generation for the Soviet people to recover from the traumatic impact of the years of terror.

A Single Party in a Multinational State

Apart from cleansing the Party of unworthy elements, purges were designed to enforce its monolithic unity. No opposition within the Party could be tolerated, since this could undermine its doctrinal purity as well as its ability to lead the masses. Time and again the choices confronting the Party and the decisions taken were of so fundamental a nature that wavering might have been fatal. Among these far-reaching decisions was Lenin's tactical retreat when he introduced the New Economic Policy (NEP) in 1921; this allowed small-scale private industrial and trade enterprises to exist alongside the nationalised sector and helped the country to overcome the economic collapse resulting from the Civil War. Again, Stalin's decision to 'build communism in one country' went against all earlier hopes of a worldwide revolution, to support which Trotsky would have committed what men, money, and materials were obtainable in Russia. No less bold was the decision to industrialise at top speed. How to finance industrialisation was yet another major decision which led to the forced and inhumanly cruel collectivisation of agriculture. To carry through decisions of such magnitude required great boldness, unity of purpose, and inflexibility of will.

There was yet another reason for the need of monolithic unity within the Party. Its membership was ethnically heterogeneous. Apart from Russians, many Jews, Poles, Georgians, Armenians, Hungarians (after the collapse of their short-lived Republic in 1918), and others held responsible posts in both Party and government.

Furthermore, the Party came to power in a multinational state. A unity of creed was a cohesive force essential to bind people of different origin and tradition, and to overcome the dichotomy between what Lenin termed 'Great-Russian chauvinism' and 'local nationalism'. In 1917 the country was not merely a multinational state; it was also a pluralistic society in the sense that its inhabitants, while contemporaries in time, lived culturally in different centuries.

The Russians, Ukrainians, and Belorussians formed the bulk of the population.[7] All three groups are of Slav origin, speak closely related languages, were christianised in the tenth century from Byzantium, and trace their early history to the mediaeval principality known as 'Kieven Rus'. All were overrun by the Mongol invaders in the thirteenth century. Thereafter the course of their history differed. The case of the Ukrainians is further complicated by the fact that, whereas the greater part of eastern Ukraine was united with Russia after 1654, western Ukraine (Galicia) remained under Poland until, with the partitions of Poland, it became part of the Holy Roman, later the Austro-Hungarian, Empire. Between 1917 and 1939 it was again part of Poland and was incoporated into the Soviet Union only in 1945. Under Polish influence west Ukrainians became Roman Catholic of the Eastern rite. The Austro-Hungarian Empire was more tolerant of local nationalism than Tsarist Russia and the setting-up of a Ukrainian university in L'vov contributed to the establishing of the west Ukrainian dialect as the literary Ukrainian language. Strong nationalistic feelings have survived in western Ukraine and its population has not yet been assimilated into the communist fold.

Along the western borders lie the three Baltic republics – Estonia, Latvia, and Lithuania – and, further south, Moldavia. Estonia and Latvia existed as independent republics only from 1918 to 1939. They differ mainly linguistically. Estonian, which is akin to Finnish, belongs to the Ugro-Altaic group, whereas Latvian (as also Lithuanian) is a very ancient and archaic Indo-European language. Contrary to her northern neighbours, Lithuania has had a long history as an independent powerful mediaeval state and dominated the Slav lands which now form Belorussia. She later formed a union with Poland and was converted to Roman Catholicism, being among the last nations of Europe to be christianised. Lithuania was annexed by Russia in the eighteenth century in connection with the partitions of Poland. From 1918 to 1939 she was an independent republic, though Poland occupied her capital, Vilnius.

Moldavia (also known as Bessarabia) was annexed by Russia from Turkey during the Napoleonic Wars and became part of Romania

[7] For population figures, see below, Appendix B, p. 246.

COMMUNIST PARTY OF THE SOVIET UNION 57

in 1918. Moldavian, which is practically identical to Romanian, is a Romance language with some admixture of Slav and Turkish words. Prior to 1945 the population of Moldavia, like that of Romania, was largely illiterate. Of the Union republics lying on the western borders of the USSR, all had been part of the Russian Empire prior to 1917 with the exception of western Ukraine.

The three Transcaucasian republics differ ethnically and linguistically. Armenian is an Indo-European language, Azerbaidzhani is a Turkish dialect, and Georgian is regarded as a cross between some Indo-European and semitic dialects. The history of both Georgia and Armenia goes back to antiquity. Both were converted to Christianity in the fifth century, and their scripts derive from Greek.

The five Central Asian republics were conquered by Russia in the nineteenth century and are sometimes regarded as Tsarist Russia's colonial empire. The population consists partly of sedentary agriculturalists of rather mixed origin – Iranian, Turkic, and Mongol. From time immemorial this sedentary population has practised irrigated agriculture around fertile oases and along the rivers that rise in the high mountains of northern India and Afghanistan, several of which then get lost in the sands of the dry steppes and deserts. Their history goes back to the days of the ancient Persian Empire; Samarkand was conquered by Alexander the Great in 338 B.C. In the seventh century the population was converted to Islam by the Arabs. Later their high civilisation suffered badly from the Mongol and other invasions. The other part of the population of Turkic origin were pastoral nomads until they were forced to settle by the Soviet authorities during the collectivisation campaign.

Apart from the Union republics, there are numerous smaller nationalities, some of which, particularly the Finnish and Paleoasiatic tribes of trappers and deer-breeders in northern Siberia and some of the sixty nationalities living in the mountains and valleys of Dagestan (Caucasus), had no written language before the Revolution. There are also other ethnic groups, some of which have been described as 'diasporas';[8] such were German immigrants who came to Russia from the eighteenth century onwards, Jews, and to a lesser extent Armenians and Kazan' Tartars.

The Germans came from or via the Baltic provinces as well as direct from Germany in the wake of German princesses marrying into the Russian Imperial family, as doctors, scientists, traders, or industrialists, and rose to high positions in the army and the Tsarist civil service. There were also larger groups who settled in the south

[8] John A. Armstrong, *Ideology, Politics and Government in the Soviet Union*, revised edition, New York, 1967, pp. 131–35.

and along the Volga in the eighteenth century. After the Revolution, Jews, whom Tsarist laws had tried to confine within the 'pale', i.e. within the former Polish territories annexed by Russia, rose to the highest positions in the Communist Party and the government and are still very numerous in higher education, among scientists, in the medical service, and in other white-collar professions. An attempt at providing a national home for Jews in Birobidzhan (southern Siberia) failed completely. Armenians, though they have their own republic, have spread into a variety of skilled occupations throughout the Caucasus and further north. Similarly, Kazan' Tartars who had achieved a high degree of literacy before the Revolution (the University of Kazan, founded in 1804, was the first to have a Faculty of Oriental Languages), migrated to Central Asian republics, first as middlemen acting on behalf of Russian merchants and later as teachers, interpreters, and Soviet officials.

The Soviet government's policy has always been to enable all national groups to achieve literacy in their own vernacular and to promote their culture.[9] It has also been its policy to convert them to Marxism. To be effective, propaganda had to be carried out in numerous languages, some of which had no writing and others no words to convey new political and scientific notions. The translation of current political propaganda, let alone the work of Karl Marx and Engels, involved the creation of an entirely new terminology in the case of many languages. Even at the Congress of Turcology held in 1926 in Baku, at which the main topic was the reform of the Arabic alphabet used by Moslems speaking Turkish, Tartar, and other Turkic dialects, the problem of terminology loomed quite large. A special committee was set up to elaborate new terminologies and compile dictionaries of new political and scientific terms. Its work was much hampered by the shortage of local trustworthy communist linguists. The two principal methods of word formation were the borrowing of international terms and the coining of new

[9] In the words of the Tenth Party Congress (1921): 'To help the toiling masses of non-Great Russian peoples to catch up with Central Russia which is ahead of them, and to help them: (a) to develop and consolidate their own Soviet state system in forms consistent with the national social conditions of these peoples; (b) to develop and consolidate their own courts, administrative bodies, economic organs, and government organs functioning in the native language and recruited from among local people acquainted with the customs and psychology of the local population; (c) to develop a press, schools, theatres, clubs, and cultural and educational institutions generally functioning in the native language; (d) to organise and develop an extensive system of courses and schools, both for general education and vocational and technical training in the native languages (first and foremost for the Kirghiz, Bashkirs, Turkmen, Uzbeks, Tadzhiks, Azerbaidzhani, Tartars, and Dagestani), in order to accelerate the training of native cadres of skilled workingmen and Soviet and Party workers in all spheres of administration and particularly in the sphere of education.'

words based on old vernacular roots. The main danger of flooding a primitive vernacular with international expressions lay in its becoming alien and incomprehensible to the masses. The main danger of coining new words from old roots could result in unforeseen un-Marxist overtones, as when the Tadzhiks translated the 'general Party line' as 'Royal road'. Moreover, old words used in a new sense often lacked precision; a single word would be used for price and value, or for capital, wealth, and property, or for people, nation, and state; 'production relations' became 'the division of people into classes during work'.

Marxist theory was not merely at the mercy of semantics, but could easily be misinterpreted by converts to Marxism coming from different cultural backgrounds. The case of Sultan-Galiev is very instructive. An early Marxist, he held an important post in the People's Commissariat of Nationalities, headed by Stalin since its inception. In the first turbulent years of the Revolution when ideas were still in a state of flux, this Tartar Marxist elaborated his own brand of Marxism coloured by the latent nostalgias of a once dominant race. For him the Russian Revolution was a mere prelude to far more fundamental liberation movements of the oppressed against the oppressors. According to him, Marxism was a Western ideology originating in and suitable to industrial societies, but further east it could become acceptable only if it were integrated into the Islamic tradition. The true Revolution would not be carried out by an effete Western proletariat but by the colonial peoples rising against their exploiters – the Western bourgeoisie. Sultan-Galiev advocated the formation of a Muslim republic between the Volga and the Urals (*Idel-Ural*) which would attract first the peoples of Turkic origin in the Caucasus and Central Asia and later the Muslims of Turkey, Persia, India, and Afghanistan. Eventually, somehow, colonial peoples throughout Asia and Africa would come to form a Colonial International and dominate the industrial countries which were holding them in subjection. The members of the Third International were too westward-looking to share or even understand Galiev's aspirations. In 1923 the majority of the Central Committee of the Communist Party declared Galiev's views to be more pan-Turkic than Marxist and he was expelled from the Party. He seems to have conducted a rearguard action in disseminating his ideas until 1930, after which date he was not heard any more. In the light of modern developments it can be seen that his call to integrate revolutionary and nationalistic liberation movements appeals to emerging nations, but would be quite outside present-day Soviet ideology.

The Party has made great efforts to attract natives of each

republic to join the Party and to make the latter truly representative of all the peoples of the Soviet Union. However, various nationalities are not equally represented within the Party and the percentage of Party members within each national group varies. According to recent estimates it is highest among Georgians (6·5 per cent of the population), Armenians (6·1 per cent), and Russians (5·8 per cent), and lowest among Moldavians (1·7 per cent), Lithuanians (2·4 per cent), and Tadzhiks (2·9 per cent). If other smaller nationalities are taken into account, the highest relative percentage (about 8 per cent) would probably be found among the widely scattered Jewish population of the USSR.[10]

Such a high percentage of Jews in the CPSU may seem strange at first sight in view of the anti-Israel policy of the Soviet government; yet the Soviet government is more anti-religious than anti-semitic; at home it enforces equally harsh measures against those who practise Judaism, Christianity, or Islam. As regards emigration, for a Soviet citizen to want to leave the USSR is nearly tantamount to treason; even girls who marry foreigners have the greatest difficulty in obtaining permission to emigrate.

The Komsomol

It is now increasingly common for young people to join the Party by first proving themselves worthy as members of the *Komsomol* (Communist Youth League). This is a much larger organisation than the Party itself. It was set up in October 1918 and now numbers over 23 million young people aged fourteen to twenty-six. Not all *Komsomol* members join the Party on attaining the appropriate age. Thus, between 1953 and 1963, 30 million young people joined the *Komsomol*, but only 2½ million proceeded to Party membership.

The organisational structure of the *Komsomol* is modelled on that of the Party. In 1966, according to S. P. Pavlov, the Secretary-General of the *Komsomol*, speaking at the Fifteenth Congress of this organisation, there were 348,000 *Komsomol* primaries scattered throughout the USSR. Top officers are usually Party members, since a young person who enters the Party can retain *Komsomol* membership until he is twenty-eight years old, and apparently even longer, as shown by an analysis of the Fifteenth *Komsomol* Congress,[11] if elected to office. Lower down the rungs the sprinkling of

[10] T. H. Rigby, *Membership of the Soviet Communist Party 1917–1967*, Princeton, 1968, pp. 378, 386, and 507.
[11] Of the 3,821 delegates to the Fifteenth *Komsomol* Congress in 1966, 371 members were under twenty, 2,476 between twenty and twenty-eight years, 589 were twenty-eight or thirty, and 371 were over thirty; S. P. Pavlov, the Secretary-General, born in 1929, was thirty-seven years old.

Party members decreases and only about 2 per cent of the *Komsomol* primary organisations are headed by members of the Communist Party. The close links of the *Komsomol* with the Party can be illustrated from the biographies of S. P. Pavlov's immediate predecessors, A. N. Shelepin and V. E. Semichastnyi. The former, born in 1918, was an active member of the *Komsomol* for eighteen years. His first appointment was that of a Moscow *Komsomol* instructor in 1940 and he rose to become the First Secretary of the All-Union *Komsomol* organisation in 1952. That same year he was elected a member of the Central Committee of the Communist Party at the Nineteenth Party Congress and re-elected again to the Central Committee in 1956 at the Twentieth Party Congress. During these years he was also in turn a member of the National Committee for Physical Culture, deputy chairman of the World Federation of Democratic Youth, and a deputy of the Supreme Soviet. In 1958, at the age of forty, he was replaced by V. E. Semichastnyi as First Secretary of the *Komsomol* and shortly after was appointed chairman of the Committee of State Security (KGB); in other words, he became the head of the secret police, a post he retained until 1961, when he was succeeded by the same V. E. Semichastnyi who had previously taken over from him the post of First Secretary of the All-Union *Komsomol* organisation.

Like Shelepin, Semichastnyi (born in 1924) began his career as a *Komsomol* organiser, joined the Party in 1944, was elected alternate member of the Central Committee of the Party in 1956 at the Twentieth Congress, and eventually replaced Shelepin as head of the secret police in November 1961. In this capacity he dealt with the Pen'kovsky affair. Pen'kovsky had revealed to Greville Wynne the presence of Soviet missiles in Cuba. He was arrested in October 1962 and sentenced to death in May 1963. Semichastnyi, like Shelepin, endeavoured to rehabilitate the secret police and build up its image as a security organisation whose activities were directed against foreign spies and traitors such as Pen'kovsky.

Membership of the *Komsomol* is practically a 'must' in secondary schools, establishments of higher education, and the armed forces. Admission is upon the recommendation of two members of the *Komsomol* or one member of the Party. Because so many young people are or have been members of the *Komsomol*, membership of the organisation does not carry the honorific status of Party membership.

The political activities of the *Komsomol* include the transmitting and disseminating of Party directives and the carrying-out of numerous urgent assignments, some of which may be very demanding and bound up with considerable physical hardships. Such was the work done by young enthusiasts on distant construction projects, in Spartan living conditions; for instance the ploughing-up of the dry steppes of Kazakhstan in the 1950s or, in earlier days, the building of the town now named in their honour, Komsomolsk-on-the-Amur (1932). More recently, the *Komsomol* took part in the building of the Bratsk hydro-electric power-station, the Abakan-Taishet railway in Siberia, the Bokhara-Ural gas pipeline, and the apatite combine on the Kola peninsula in the White Sea region. During the seven years 1959 to 1965, over a million young people went on special *Komsomol* assignments.

The *Komsomol* organises also leisure activities, provides sport and travel facilities, runs study circles, drama groups, summer camps, and, generally speaking, promotes a great variety of entertainment which individual youths could not afford financially on their own. Local *Komsomol* organisations have their representatives on the governing bodies of schools, universities, and factory councils. Their recommendation of entrants to establishments of higher education is as important as one from the school or place of work. They are expected to befriend teenagers who, on completion of a technical school, are directed to a place of work away from home; they should mark the occasion of his first pay packet or the day when he has achieved an adult's work norm. They should watch lest he come under the influence of some religious person, though that is not likely to happen nowadays, after half a century of anti-religious campaigns. Local *Komsomol* committees may dispense advice on personal matters, amorous involvements, and broken marriages, though how effective such advice may be is anybody's guess. However, it certainly creates a definite climate of opinion.

The *Komsomol* exercises its tutelage over the Pioneers, the mass children's organisation to which practically all Soviet children aged nine to fifteen belong. The Pioneer organisations resemble Boy Scouts in many respects, but are also regarded as a training-ground for future *Komsomol* and Party membership. Their role in the Soviet educational system is very considerable.

The *Komsomol* has its own publishing facilities, and brings out several papers and magazines. The most important is the *Komsomolskaya pravda*, with a circulation of 6,400,000 copies. Like other publications directed at a youthful readership, the paper aims at arousing interest in the surrounding world, in matters of concern to the Party and the nation, such as Marxist-Leninist theory, the economic problems confronting the country, the need and opportunities for further education, the heroism of labour, the moral satisfaction to be derived from joining groups of technical rationalisers, inventors, and 'brigades of communist labour'. The memory

COMMUNIST PARTY OF THE SOVIET UNION 63

of acts of courage, self-denial, and revolutionary zeal among young people of earlier generations is kept alive and the image of Lenin as both a historical figure or a mythological deity kept constantly present. Scientific topics are given wide coverage in *Komsomolskaya pravda*. Since 1956-57 the paper has endeavoured to move away from the 'teach and preach' attitude towards attempts at elucidating present-day needs and aspirations of the young and establishing a feed-back from its readers. It puts forward topics for discussion such as 'How to train willpower', 'What constitutes beauty in Man?', 'What leads Man to perform acts of heroism?', 'The honour of a worker'. In 1961 it initiated a special feature under the title of 'Institute of Public Opinion'. Letters to the Editor are encouraged, and extensive reviews of them published. These letters appear not to be heavily edited (as was the case earlier), but their selection may be designed to reinforce the opinions of the editorial board. Thus, when a letter was published calling into question the expense of the space programme while the writer of the letter was unable to buy simple articles of clothing which he badly needed, numerous letters refuting his views appeared in the paper, but none were published to support the initial argument. Opinion polls have been conducted by the paper within topical but limited fields, and occasional sociological surveys have been given a certain prominence.

Generally speaking, the Soviet leadership seems fully aware of a certain restlessness among the young and tendencies of which it disapproves. Such are an unhealthy interest in the Western way of life; bourgeois ideology; decadent Western fashions in art, music, and clothing; slothfulness in work combined with cynicism in respect of the lofty aims of communism; and also widespread attitudes described in Russian by the untranslatable word *meshchanstvo*, meaning petty and narrow-minded concern for No. 1, a restricted world view, indifference to major human problems, casual love affairs, lack of any redeeming deep emotions, and the shirking of any form of voluntary public service. More is heard nowadays about juvenile delinquency, drunkenness, and hooliganism; more is written about the causes of crime as well as methods of dealing with the criminal. The blanket explanation of 'survivals of capitalism in the minds of the people' is wearing thin after half a century of Soviet rule.

The fiftieth anniversary of the foundation of the *Komsomol*, celebrated on 29 October 1968, provided the occasion for a long statement by the Central Committee of the CPSU. Young people were reminded of the close links that have always bound the *Komsomol* movement to the Communist Party. The present generation was not to forget the heroic deeds of *Komsomol* members who had fought in the Civil War for a better future, taken part in the great constructions of the first Five-Year Plan, defended their country against the German invaders during World War II. It warned the present youth, which took so much for granted, of the dangers on the ideological front. Imperialist propaganda directed at youth was unrelentingly seeking 'to weaken its revolutionary enthusiasm, blunt its class consciousness, oppose it to the older generation, sow scepticism and indifference to politics, admiration for bourgeois *mores*, and morals alien to a socialist society'. Party organisations at all levels were to vary and perfect their methods of work with the present, more demanding youth; explain to them the laws of social development, the policies of the Party, the importance of the current economic reforms; and make full use of all media of mass communication. The quality and variety of programmes and publications for the young were to be given more attention. Interest in scientific discoveries and technical devices should be instilled by inducing them to attend extension courses and study groups. A reference was made in this Party document to para-military training, a feature related to the new law on military service. The Ministry of Culture, the trade unions, the Central Committee of the *Komsomol* itself were enjoined to improve the quality and variety of entertainment activities such as amateur theatricals, sport events, art exhibitions, and music festivals; to attract the collaboration of established writers, artists, and composers who should advise, direct, and judge events. Emphasis was laid also on the need to provide better club halls, stadiums, and swimming-pools.

A newer note was struck in the statement regarding the role of *Komsomol* members in organising these activities themselves, and the call to local Soviets, ministries, and trade unions to enlist the co-operation of and to consult local *Komsomol* committees in these matters.

Komsomol committees in factories were henceforth to participate fully with trade union and management in engaging and dismissing young workers, awarding bonuses, and allocating housing and hostel accommodation, and funds earmarked for culture and sport.

Permanent Commissions for Youth Affairs were to be set up by the Supreme Soviet of the USSR, those of the Union republics, and also by provincial, town, and district Soviets. As from 1969, *Komsomol* leaders, i.e. officials, were to undergo regular periods of further training at the Party Higher School of the Central Committee of the CPSU. A special *Komsomol* Higher School was to be set up by that body.

Finally, the jubilee statement of the Central Committee stressed the desirability of promoting well-recommended members of the *Komsomol* to responsible posts in management and administration, or as collective farm chairmen, and electing them more frequently as deputies to Soviets and trade union organisations.

The whole document conveys the impression that the latent desire of young people to run their own affairs is accepted, but the devolution of power is to be within the framework of the *Komsomol*; the yearning of the young to have a gayer life will be met by providing more amenities for sport and entertainment, but again within the same context; contributions coming from the young will be encouraged and appreciated in the fields of science; lastly, the most intellectually promising and reliable will be given better opportunities for rapid promotion. This should satisfy young people anxious to have a greater say in the running of the country, and reduce resentment at being kept out by an ageing and possibly less educated Establishment.

There is another aspect in the restlessness of youth not directly related to the political set-up but rather to the 'growing pains' of modernisation. Education has always been on the priority list of the Soviet government. Secondary education for all is now being implemented throughout the country. Yet one of the shortcomings of the Soviet economy is the amount of ancillary work still done manually in most primitive ways. Teenagers with a secondary education expect to handle complex machinery or supervise control panels in automated factories, and are reluctant just to fetch and carry, load and unload, goods, when they know full well that all this heavy work can be done by machinery. The point was brought out very forcibly by the girl who said, 'I have not completed a ten-years' school and learnt French and algebra to sweep streets with a witch-broom'. So it is for the *Komsomol* propagandist to explain that it is a patriotic duty to accept menial tasks while the cranes, trucks, and street-sweeping machinery are being built. But youth is by nature impatient and not prepared to wait meekly for things that 'ought to be there'.

The setting-up of a commission for the affairs of youth by the Supreme Soviet in December 1968 is a proof of the importance attributed to what obviously points to tensions between generations. Whether the adjustments envisaged within the present set-up are adequate is open to doubt. The make-up of the double commission formed by the two houses of the Supreme Soviet on 11 December 1968 can be gauged from the biographical data of some of the principal members of this commission. Its chairman, A. N. Aksyonov (not to be confused with the novelist), has been a Party member since 1945 and, after being a member of the Central Committee of the *Komsomol* in 1956–59, is at present Minister of the Interior of the Belorussian SSR and a member of the Central Committee of the Belorussian Communist Party. Another member of the new commission is N. A. Belukha who, although a Russian by birth, is Second Secretary of the Central Committee of the Latvian Communist Party. Two others, E. K. Ligachev and V. S. Paputin, are respectively First Secretary of the Tomsk Province Party Committee and Second Secretary of the Moscow Province Party Committee. Z. I. K. Guseinova is Minister of Higher and Secondary Specialised Education of the Azerbaidzhan SSR. The President of the Academy of Sciences, Keldysh, is also a member of the commission. To what extent these people are really in touch with present-day teenagers only time can show.

'We are the party of the future, and the future belongs to youth. We are a party of innovators, and youth is always more willing to follow innovators' said Lenin half a century ago. Is the Communist Party of the Soviet Union still a party of innovators? The future depends on the answer to this question. One thing that the Party cannot afford is to suffer from arterio-sclerosis.

Chapter 3

Economic Planning

Problems and Techniques

AS ALREADY MENTIONED, one of the major tasks of the Twenty-third Party Congress was to discuss and approve the draft of the Five-Year Plan for 1966–70.

The purpose of economic planning is to effect an orderly, rational development of a country's productive forces, in contradistinction to capitalism under which the economy is at the mercy of irrational market forces and the consequent chaos in production, culminating in cyclical economic crises. Economic planning was foreshadowed already by Lenin, who commissioned a plan for the electrification of Russia (known as GOELRO) to be drawn up in 1920. At the time, the country was just emerging from three years of civil war and economic ruin; nothing much could be done about electrification beyond restoring the power-plants left over from Tsarist days. The first new power-station, at Shatura, went into production after Lenin's death. However, many projects of GOELRO were taken over and incorporated into the far more ambitious first Five-Year Plan for the industrialisation of Russia.

At that time the notion of planning the national economy of a whole country the size of Russia for several years in advance was a novel, daring, unheard-of venture in applied economics. No one had yet attempted long-term planning of such magnitude and indeed, looking back, December 1927 should be remembered as a landmark in the history of mankind at least on a par with Colbert's first state Budget under Louis XIV or the Pharaohs' legislation on the Nile's irrigation system. Nowadays long-term planning on a national scale has been adopted by most countries and attempts at central government planning, though only of an indicative type, have been tried out in capitalist countries, mainly in France, but also in the United Kingdom by the Labour Party and even by the Johnson administration in the USA in its endeavour to create the Great Society – in the latter case with scant success.

There are more grounds for success in countries where means of production have been nationalised and production can be co-ordinated through a single planning organisation. In the USSR the state committee which (after various reorganisations) is in command of central planning is *Gosplan*. This is a very large organisation which co-ordinates the work of similar institutions in the Union republics, and translates into definite tasks and figures the targets set out in the drafts of National Economic Plans submitted to Party Congresses and later voted upon by the Supreme Soviet of the USSR.

The preliminary work is carried out by various departments of *Gosplan* and consists of a set of tentative studies, estimates, and preliminary draft plans setting out different options. These plans include assumptions expressed in figures on the overall growth targets for the national income, its division and utilisation for consumption and investment, and the distribution of investments among well over a hundred branches of the national economy. The share allotted to investment depends on the targets set for further industrialisation, while that set aside for consumption must take account of military expenditure, welfare provisions, outlays on science and education, and the balancing of the wages fund against the volume of consumer goods that will be made available to the population.

The consistency of draft plans for essential materials like fuel, metals, cement, machines, and for industrial capacities and their equipment is co-ordinated by means of a series of 'balances' for all major commodities established for the USSR as a whole; they have to be related also to 'balances' of manpower, i.e. numbers of workers and types of qualification, as well as to financial balances, particularly those concerned with income and expenditure incorporated in the state Budget.

Gosplan works in direct consultation with several economic research institutes, the State Prices Committee, the Council for the Study of Productive Forces, the Institute of Transport Problems, and local planning agencies employing all told an army of 35,000 men and women. Data obtained are processed nowadays by *Gosplan*'s computer centre and eventually the drafts and options submitted to the Party and government. In view of the growing complexity of planning methods, *Gosplan* has established courses in economic planning which are attended by its employees and those of local planning agencies. The importance of these courses is growing and they are being transformed into a Scientific Centre for Methods of Planning to cater for specialists requiring further training or refresher courses in new techniques.

The drafts received by the leadership are examined from the point of view of sound economics or from that of political and military exigencies. Thus, in the early years of industrialisation the Soviet government felt obliged to right the 'colonial relationship' which had developed in Tsarist days between the cotton-growing regions of Central Asia and the Moscow textile industry, a relationship rather similar to that of the Lancashire cotton-mills and their supply bases in India. To overcome this situation a huge textile *combinat* was built in Tashkent. It goes without saying that all the equipment had to be brought from central Russia as well as some of the labour force until local inhabitants, including women, came to be gradually recruited and trained as textile-workers. Later, engineering-works producing agricultural machinery were also built in Central Asia, for the same reason, though there were neither the raw materials nor the qualified manpower to justify locating them there and it would probably have made better economic sense to import agricultural machinery from the metal-working centres of the industrial Urals.[1]

Among the major constructions of the first Five-Year Plan was the linking into a single *combinat* of the iron-ore deposits near Magnitogorsk with the coal-mines of the Kuznetsky Basin (*Kuzbas*) in southern Siberia, well over 3,000 miles to the east. Trucks full of coal were sent from *Kuzbas* to Magnitogorsk and returned laden with iron ore. Blast furnaces were established at both ends of the rail journey. This bold venture had been dictated partly by economic and partly by strategic considerations. The iron-ore industry of Magnitogorsk, established in the eighteenth century, was in complete decline before the Revolution because the depletion of forests precluded the continued use of charcoal for smelting; coal was obtainable from the Donetsky Basin (*Donbas*) in the Ukraine, but, apart from being far away, the latter was the sole supplier of coking coal for all industry situated in the European part of the country. In spring 1918 the Germans occupied the Ukraine, and the Ural iron and steel industry came practically to a standstill. The German occupation proved shortlived in 1918 because of Germany's defeat on the Western Front, but the strategic lesson was not lost to the men in the Kremlin. Indeed, when during World War II vast areas of the Soviet Union were occupied by the Germans, the Ural metal industries became the country's major arsenal.[2]

[1] The draft for the first Five-Year Plan stated that 'The plan must pay particular attention to the problem of raising the economic and cultural level of backward borderlands and districts inhabited by national minorities and envisage the need for a gradual liquidation of their economic and cultural backwardness and, accordingly, to envisage a faster rate of development of their economy and culture while effecting co-ordination between the needs and requirements of these districts and those of the Union as a whole'.
[2] By that time a closer supplier of coke (Karaganda in Kazakhstan) had been discovered and linked by rail with the Urals and some iron-ore deposits, though less important than those in the Urals, were found nearer *Kuzbas*.

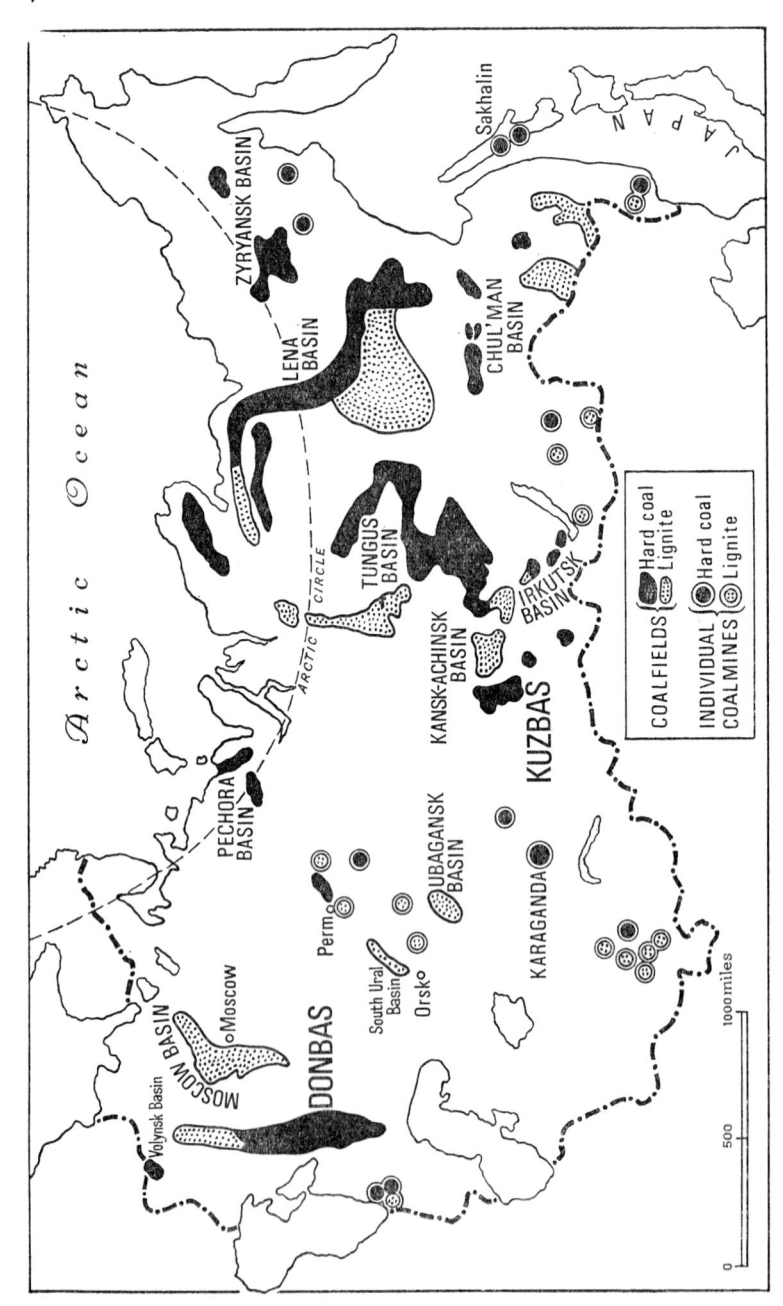

1. The Coalfields of the Soviet Union

Even when political or strategic considerations are not at stake, economic decisions may be difficult to arrive at. The very considerable mineral wealth of the USSR is scattered over great distances. Except for the European south where coal (*Donbas*) and iron (*Krivoi rog*) are located within a distance of about a hundred miles, the richest sources of raw material are all too often remote from each other and also from the most densely populated areas. These are – for climatic and historical reasons – central and north-west Russia, the Ukraine, the Baltic republics, Transcaucasia, and the oases of Central Asia; yet some of the most important mineral deposits are found in the least inhabited regions of the USSR. The complications connected with the dispersal of resources are well illustrated by the construction of large engineering-works at Cherepovets, hundreds of miles away from the arctic coal-mines of Vorkuta (along the Pechora river well beyond the Arctic Circle on the European side of the Urals) and nearly equally far from the Kola peninsula iron-ore deposits (west of the White Sea), on the grounds that these disadvantages were outweighed by the proximity of Leningrad which could supply skilled manpower as well as port facilities. Huge resources were allocated to the construction of the Bratsk hydropower-station (at the time of its construction in 1965–67, the largest in the world) in eastern Siberia; it is capable of generating enormous amounts of power which is not needed yet by local industry, but may promote the development of the region on the basis of an abundance of cheap electricity. On the other hand, it would have been perhaps wiser to concentrate resources on building smaller and more costly power-stations in the European parts of the USSR, where numerous fully developed industries, particularly in the south, are suffering from inadequate power supply.

At the moment one of the crucial dilemmas confronting planners is the further location of industry. The return per rouble invested in central Russia, the Ukraine, and the western republics of the USSR is greatest because of the plentiful supply of urbanised manpower in these densely populated regions, the good transport and communication network, the social amenities, and, generally speaking, the infrastructure already extant in these long-settled and well-developed areas; yet the subsoil of the frozen wastes of Siberia is one of the richest stores of minerals in the world. However, huge investments are needed for building there not only the actual mines and works but also transport facilities, housing, and social amenities, · capable of attracting and retaining settlers in those inhospitable regions, if their natural wealth is to be utilised.

An important aspect in the planning of new plants is to synchronise the erection of the factory with the arrival of its equipment; otherwise the latter may be left to rust in the open while the builders are still putting on the roofs. Conversely, the building must not be allowed to stand unproductively idle, waiting for some vital part of its equipment to arrive. Because the construction of new plants and their equipping is usually the responsibility of different Ministries (e.g. the Ministry of Construction and that of Light or Heavy Engineering), faulty timing is common, involving damage to equipment and delay in pay-off on investment. Presenting his Budget for 1970, the Minister for Finance, Garbuzov, complained that equipment to the value of 5·5 billion roubles, some of it imported from abroad, was not installed at the appropriate plants and was lying idle in warehouses and on construction sites.

Generally speaking, planning is becoming increasingly intricate because of the expanding range of industrial goods and the network of connections between industries involved in the production of components for complex items. The manufacture of a car can illustrate the point, for it involves making the chassis, the engine, tyres, electrical parts, and the body with its glass or plastic windows, internal upholstery, and external colourful finish. Yet this is a fairly simple affair compared to the building of supersonic jet aircraft.

Since resources are always scarce compared to needs, the allocation of resources to industries, regions, and eventually individual plants is a major exercise in co-ordination. In the words of R. W. Campbell,

> The intricacy of the interrelationship among different economic magnitudes staggers the imagination. The basic insight on which the science of economics is based is that almost all economic magnitudes depend on all other economic magnitudes... If one asks how much steel should be produced, the answer is seen to depend on how much it will be used by all the steel-using plants, and each of these magnitudes is in turn a function of many others.[3]

Crucial decisions have to be made affecting the future of whole industries. Thus the decision to replace steam-engines by diesel or electric traction had, as its corollary, a choice between giving priority to either the oil industry or to power production and here, again, choosing between hydropower-stations and fuel-burning plants. The present drive to provide personal motor transport,

[3] R. W. Campbell, *Soviet Economic Power*, 2nd edition, London, 1967, p. 36.

which has led to the purchase of whole plants from Fiat and Renault, will inevitably lead to a demand for better roads. Road construction on the necessary scale may turn out to be more expensive than the provision of repair facilities or even frequent replacements of cars whose span of life is shortened by atrocious road conditions. If road-building is preferred and hard-surface motorways are to replace the traditional mud tracks, the need for materials and road-building equipment will become acute. Priorities in the geographical location of roads will have to be decided. Going into further details, it has been estimated that higher-quality fuel and lubricating oil lengthen the life of an engine by anything from one and a half to three times. Should one spend funds on improving the quality of fuels and lubricating oils or on producing more engines? Even minor miscalculations may have disastrous effects, like the case of lorry tyres quoted once by Khrushchev: the planners had adjusted the production of tyres to match that of lorries, overlooking the fact that tyres wear out first; as a result, lorries which were otherwise still roadworthy could no longer be used. Incidentally, miscalculations in the production of spares is a recurring cause of stoppages in factories, and the major headache of rural mechanics.

During the early years when there was an overall shortage of everything, the fundamental question was: what commodities are most essential and should be given priority? More recently the question has become not merely *what* must we produce first at any cost, but a far more complex one: *how* shall we produce what we want most efficiently? This second question now preoccupies mathematical economists, working out their models with the help of a network of computers. The notion of optimisation is much to the fore. Any theory of an optimal plan poses acutely the problem of the criteria of optimisation.

For quite some time planners have had to envisage projects of such magnitude that their implementation exceeded the limits of a given Five-Year Plan. Only a bare outline of such long-term projects could be incorporated into any current plan, but this had to be done so that resources could be allocated and work started on the project. Initially the economic criteria in the siting of any major plant were the traditional ones, such as the availability of local raw materials, power, transport facilities, or labour. Later it became apparent that to make full use of the country's productive potential such a piecemeal approach had to be replaced by an overall appraisal of the country's resources. The advent of the computer made it possible to calculate increasingly comprehensive estimates. In the middle 1960s work was started on a most ambitious 'General Scheme for the Development and Location of the Productive Forces of the Country for 1971–80'. Nearly five hundred scientific-research institutes and design bureaux have been engaged in this mammoth exercise. The approach is two-pronged. The research institutes of the various industrial Ministries are studying the further development and location of their respective *industries* (including transport and agriculture), while the institutes of economics of the academies of science and the *Gosplans* of the Union republics elaborate plans concerning the productive forces of their own republics or *territorial* regions. The work of these numerous institutions is co-ordinated by the Council for the Study of Productive Forces attached to the *Gosplan* of the USSR.

Because of the quantity of unknown factors inherent in long-term forecasting, it was decided to draft at least three possible variants. Each variant should show the economic effectiveness of the location of the new plants of any given industry so that they could be classified in order of effectiveness. This should give some idea of the sequence in which plants should be built if one variant were replaced by another, and thus facilitate the integration of projects which will be inevitably affected by developments in other industries.

Estimates of effectiveness, in the sense of return on investment, start from an appraisal of the raw materials, fuel and power, and water resources of any one region, together with cost of transport to consumers and of the labour resources available locally or obtainable through migration. In a vast country like Russia, transport costs are an important item. For instance, the costs of mining coal in the Kuznetsky Basin (*Kuzbas*) in Siberia are far lower than in the Donetsky Basin (*Donbas*) on the eastern borders of the Ukraine, yet when transport costs are taken into account it becomes cheaper for the consumer in European Russia to use *Donbas* coal; in other words, it is unprofitable to haul *Kuzbas* coal further west than the Urals.

The optimum location calculated with great precision and rationality for one industry may be unsatisfactory from the point of view of the economy as a whole. A good illustration of this point is provided by the siting of chemical and aluminium plants at Volgograd. At first sight this was a rationally chosen place, for they were built there in conjunction with the construction of a large hydro-power-station on the Volga. Yet these plants now deprive other old-established power-consuming industries in European Russia of what could have been a welcome additional source of energy; this is unfortunate, because the demand for fuel and power in the European part of the Soviet Union exceeds supply.

There are considerable advantages in building several enterprises in the same locality, for they can share the expenses of building a branch railway, or a power-station, or river landing-stage facilities, or common water and sewerage installations. This type of 'production-territorial complexes' is particularly advantageous if one plant takes the processing of the initial material further (vertical integration) or if the industries are complementary (horizontal integration) or one of them uses the wasted by-products of another. On the other hand, excessive concentration of industries in one geographical spot may result in their competing for local fuel, water, or labour, unless they employ workers of the opposite sex. To mitigate the disadvantages of over-concentration and tap reserves of female labour still available in the smaller towns, the 1966–70 Plan enjoined the siting of new plants in smaller towns and envisaged deceleration in the growth of the large cities. Recent statistical and sociological surveys have shown that a fairly high percentage (up to 14 per cent) of the population of small towns are not gainfully employed; these 'unemployed' are married women who cannot find suitable work locally, but would join the labour force if jobs were brought to their doorstep. Another argument against the further expansion of large towns is the high cost involved in providing adequate local transport and maintaining roads in a good state of repair; the expenditure on these items is said to be three times higher in towns with half a million inhabitants than in those with 50,000 inhabitants.

From an analysis of factors favouring the building of certain new industries at certain geographical points, planners proceed by a sequence of approximations to find the optimum location or distribution of whole sets of industries, e.g. fuel and power (including coal, oil, peat, shale, and hydropower resources) or a complex embracing iron and steel, manganese, coke, and even some heavy engineering.

Technical innovation has to be taken into account, for it may render the exploitation of poor ores or thin seams more profitable than was first estimated. Major discoveries and innovations can play havoc with a plan. Earlier endeavours at expanding coal-mining as the major source of power have become obsolete with the discovery of natural gas, particularly of huge gas deposits in western Siberia and also in the region of Bokhara in Central Asia. Both forms of fuel may eventually be superseded by nuclear power-plants, several of which are already working. Another technological breakthrough, viz. the use of plastics which now replace steel in the manufacture of many articles, had not been anticipated in time, with the result that the chemical industry did not get adequate attention until the late 1950s.

The next step in the planning process is for disconnected estimates made by a large number of scientific and design institutions regarding whole ranges of industries to be co-ordinated into a single plan. The drafting of such a plan is possible only on the basis of very precise, reliable, and truly comparable data. Discrepancies in their comparability could lead to costly errors in the final plan, yet the methodology of devising adequate and comparable indices is still in its experimental stage.

Information regarding each *industry* or group of *industries* is then re-examined from the point of view of *territorial location* within any given republic or economic region with a view to its greater or lesser specialisation in certain branches of production and its greater or lesser diversification of industries. Effectiveness of production should lead to a growth of the national income in the country as a whole and also within each region. The contribution to the national income made by the different republics depends on their greater or lesser natural wealth and also on the Soviet price system. Prices for producer goods, although revised upwards in the 1960s, are still low and sometimes fixed at below costs. Consumer goods are priced very high, with the result that regions specialising in the production of consumer goods appear to be most productive. Agricultural prices are low, though an average rise of 28 per cent has been sanctioned for them since 1965. In its calculations the 'General Scheme for 1971–1980' will take into account both natural and man-made factors. At present in Estonia, Latvia, and the RSFSR (with its great industrial centres around Leningrad, Moscow, and the Urals) the national income per head of population appears to be well above the average for the USSR as a whole, while in the Tadzhik SSR and Turkmenian SSR it is well below average. These discrepancies are accounted for by differences in natural resources, the distorting effect of prices, and the considerable number of 'unproductive' women in Armenia and the Central Asian republics who stay at home and look after families, which are larger in those areas than elsewhere in the USSR.

An extremely important aspect of planning is the planning of manpower. It must satisfy the double requirement of ensuring full employment and providing expanding industries with adequate numbers of adequately trained men. Demographic, economic, and educational factors have to be taken into consideration.

The density of the population is very unevenly spread over the USSR and handicaps a rational deployment of labour resources. Migration to sparsely populated areas like Siberia and the Far East must be promoted and, at the same time, new jobs have to be created in the densely populated areas to ensure full employment without uprooting too many inhabitants. Therefore provision has to be made for labour-intensive industries with relatively low requirements in raw materials to be sited in these densely populated areas, which are also major consumers of services and can, therefore, provide employment in non-productive occupations such as trade, municipal utilities, educational establishments, and welfare services, most of which employ women.

Some recent studies have shown that in industries producing fairly homogeneous commodities (metals, cement, etc.) labour productivity increases with the size and capacity of the technical equipment; that in industries manufacturing and processing fairly similar goods (textiles, plastics, wooden articles, etc.) productivity increases with the speeding-up of the manufacturing process; while in industries producing complex articles, productivity increases with precise specialisation in the making of each component. Therefore, relatively small plants manufacturing small complex articles such as transistors, television sets, optical instruments, and the like, can be profitably sited and run in small townships.

Bringing new industries to people in densely settled areas or, conversely, moving people to work in areas rich in raw materials, is only one aspect of the problem. It is just as important to foresee the skills that will be required from the new workers and to educate and train them accordingly. This is the responsibility of a special section of *Gosplan* which deals with educational planning.[4]

Planners have to bear in mind the effect of scientific and technological progress both on production processes and on the types of skilled labour they will require. Attempts at planning science are a new feature of Soviet national planning. It is obviously difficult to forecast future scientific discoveries, but, on the basis of work in hand, a measure of prognostication is feasible in certain fields. In the USSR there are no private firms concealing their research activities from competitors and therefore all information regarding research is available to *Gosplan*. Consequently, certain developments can be planned, at least in the realm of the applied sciences, likely to benefit industrial production. The earliest attempt at what may become one day the planning of science started in 1949 when a plan was drawn up for introducing a definite number of technical innovations into production. In 1956 plans for scientific research work were incorporated into the general plan. In 1962 plans were drawn up estimating the finances and the supply of materials and equipment required for scientific research. More recently estimates have been made regarding the buildings needed for research and also the numbers and types of personnel to be trained. This is

[4] See below, pp. 143–6.

a particularly thorny problem because of the changing needs in the types of specialists connected with the emergence of new branches of learning. The Soviet government tends to promote research in applied sciences from which industry can benefit fairly quickly. Yet the progress of science is based mainly on research in the fundamentals of science. The allocation of funds to pure and applied science as well as between various sciences is bound to affect progress and have the greatest importance for the country's development. Much of the responsibility for the planning of science rests with the Academy of Sciences of the USSR.[5]

In long-term planning the demographic factor is crucial. The growth of population determines both future needs in consumer goods and the manpower that will become available to make them. Consumption is affected by the age, sex, education, and interests of the population. For instance, the neglect of demographic studies has led to the production of the wrong articles of clothing, books, and toys, and also of ill-designed household articles for newly-wed couples. The Soviet population has 'made do' for a very long time and now at last planners are beginning to take notice of consumer demand.

Raising Living Standards

Consumer demand is a term seldom used in the Soviet Union, where the more current expression is 'planning a rise in the population's standard of living'. It is a more comprehensive term since it embraces improvements in education, housing, medical services, sport and entertainment facilities, as well as provision for a growing supply of consumer goods and, more recently, for a wider choice and higher quality of these articles.

For many long years priority was given to investment and the expansion of capital goods industries or, to use the Soviet terminology, the production of means of production. This was the alpha and omega of industrialisation. The production of consumer goods expanded very slowly and allocations earmarked for the purpose were low. The position was similar in respect of housing, services, and, generally speaking, the so-called non-productive sphere of the economy. In the regions which had not been devastated during World War II, the building of new houses on a large scale got under way only in 1957–58 and, because of the crying need to make up for years of neglect, construction proceeded at great speed to the detriment of quality, with the result that hastily erected new blocks of houses are already in need of costly repairs. The inadequate thick-

[5] See below, pp. 207–9.

ness of their walls and consequent loss of heat in winter result in higher fuel consumption.

Education was given a higher priority because, in a sense, it is an investment in manpower. The same can be said – though to a lesser degree – about medical services, and indeed epidemic diseases such as smallpox, cholera, typhus, and more recently tuberculosis, have been stamped out and the expectation of life greatly increased. The care of the old, the incurable, and the mentally handicapped who can only be regarded as a liability on any society was provided hitherto on a very limited scale; for instance, in 1967 there were only 1,425 old-age homes for about 250,000 old people. It is true that workers and employees aged sixty years (fifty-five in the case of women) and war disabled were in receipt of pensions: the number of the latter after World War II was well over 7 million.

Before discussing living standards it should be made clear that the Soviet population derives its income from three sources, namely (a) wages and salaries paid by the state to all workers employed in both the productive sphere (i.e. industry, transport, state farms, etc.) and the non-productive sphere (education, medical services, etc.); (b) money and agricultural produce distributed by collective farms to their members; and (c) benefits from the social consumption fund. This comprises free or subsidised services provided by the state for the population, such as free education and medical treatment, certain pensions, students' grants, and various forms of welfare. Wages and salaries paid by the state to workers and employees, and income received by collective farmers from their enterprise, are related to their work, and highly differentiated rates of pay have been prevalent in the Soviet Union since the early 1930s. This makes for great inequalities which the social consumption fund is designed to mitigate, both high- and low-paid workers being equally entitled to free medical services, free education for their children, or further training for themselves if they wish to improve their qualifications. These services are financed from the state Budget and all Soviet citizens are entitled to benefit from them. Other welfare provisions, namely old-age pensions and maternity and sickness benefits, are financed not directly from the state Budget but from the social insurance fund. Contributions to this fund are paid by state enterprises for the men and women they employ. Employees do not contribute to the fund. Since collective farmers are not state employees, they were excluded from these benefits. Only in 1966 were old-age and other benefits extended to them, though the rates at which pensions were paid to collective farmers were lower than those fixed for workers, often not exceeding 12 roubles a month, instead of the minimum thirty. Since the end of 1969, a general contribution of 2·4 per cent of their respective payroll is paid by collective farms to the social insurance fund, and the benefit rates payable to farmers will eventually approximate those received by workers.

When planners envisage rises in the standard of living, they may therefore either increase wages or else expand the social consumption fund, with a resulting improvement of education and medical and other services available to the population.

Hitherto, in the planning of the production of consumer goods, the main factors considered were the productive capacities already available to manufacture them and the need to relate the volume and value of the consumer goods produced to the total wages fund. The result of keeping allocations to the consumer goods industries low was the chronic shortage of everything. The sight of long queues patiently waiting in front of poorly stocked shops struck every foreigner who visited Russia since the Revolution. However, things began to improve in the 1960s, and Khrushchev glibly talked of the younger generation coming to live under communism, when the slogan 'from everyone according to his abilities, to everyone according to his needs' would become a reality. In 1964–65 planners were instructed to devise new indices specifically designed to calculate rises in the standard of living and to incorporate them into the national economic plan for 1966–70. At this point some economists suggested that the overall criterion should be such a mix of consumer goods and services as would prolong man's active life at a minimum cost. The comprehensiveness of this criterion would allow for the integration of specific indices regarding medical care, nurseries, and other welfare provisions, improved nutritional standards as well as a better supply of consumer goods. Indices used hitherto in planning expenditure in the non-productive sphere were mere accounting devices; their reformulation was essential if they were to be used to measure rises in living standards and reflect improvement in the quality of goods and services. Thus, apart from the number of places in nursery schools, it is now necessary to plan details reflecting quality of child care, e.g. staff/children ratios; in the case of hospitals, the number of beds per thousand inhabitants must be supplemented by information regarding the diet provided, the medical equipment available, particularly that of a more modern and sophisticated type, as well as details of drugs and appliances supplied; housing can no longer be measured in square metres, and the availability of water-mains, sewerage, gas and electricity supply, central heating, and telephone installations, must be taken into account.

ECONOMIC PLANNING

The Institute of Nutrition of the Medical Academy of the USSR has established man's physiological requirements in calorie intake and also given a breakdown of the amounts of protein, fats, hydrocarbon, mineral salts, and vitamins needed by human beings according to age, sex, type of work performed, and climatic conditions. It published a list of foodstuffs indicating their nutritional value. The targets set for agricultural output in the Plan for 1966–70 were based on these physiological requirements, but hitherto the agricultural output of the Soviet Union has precluded a scientifically balanced diet for all her inhabitants. Only the need in calories is met owing to the high consumption of bread and potatoes – the staple food of poorer countries.

In the production of consumer goods more attention is to be devoted to quality, because with the easing of shortages consumers have become more difficult to satisfy. Indeed, the cluttering-up of warehouses with unwanted shoddy goods to the value of 2 billion roubles was one of the factors that hastened the introduction of the present economic reforms. These allow shops to enter into direct relations with their suppliers and it is hoped that the insight of retailers will help manufacturers to gauge consumer demand. It is now realised that demand for durable household objects may depend on both their price and their quality, that the production of poor-quality goods leads to an increased demand for replacements or for spare parts for repairs. At last it is admitted that articles like clothing are liable to fashion changes while others are affected by technical progress; thus radios are losing ground in favour of television sets and gramophones to tape-recorders.

While planners know the exact number of inhabitants from nationwide census data, they know family budgets only from sample studies. Yet demands for consumer goods depend not on the average wage for the country as a whole but on individual family budgets, and these depend on the earnings of the head of the family and also whether his wages are supplemented by those of his wife and/or older children or, on the contrary, depleted by the expenses of maintaining several dependants. Furthermore, questions of principle are involved in supplying individual families with domestic labour-saving devices. It has been calculated that owing to the scarcity of such utensils on the one hand and the dearth of public laundries, cleaners' shops, and various repair installations on the other, the population spends on domestic chores 150 billion hours annually, which is only a quarter less than the time spent in productive employment.[6] Domestic labour-saving devices would benefit

[6] V. N. Sergievsky, *Problemy optimal'nogo sootnosheniya proizvodstva i potrebleniya v SSSR*, Moscow, 1968, p. 127.

women, who spend twice the time men do on running their households. On the other hand, well-equipped households may foster too great an interest in the individual home. It would be more in the spirit of communism to provide laundries, laundrettes, and other maintenance and repair facilities catering for whole communities. This idea may eventually prevail. At any rate, *Gosplan* has now a Scientific Research Technochemical Institute of Domestic Services which has been estimating the demand for repairs of clothing, footwear, domestic appliances, and other durable goods for the periods 1970–75 and 1975–80. Union republics have been setting up ministries of this new home servicing industry, and the Scientific Research Technochemical Institute of *Gosplan* is to act as a central agency for this novel and, evidently, rapidly growing industry.

Thus planners are confronted on the one hand with problems of macro-economics, such as long-term plans to develop the productive forces of a vast country. In fact, they are looking beyond the borders to see whether a better economic integration of the Soviet Union and the East European People's Republics could not weld the socialist camp into a single powerful economic bloc. On the other hand, the growing variety and complexity of consumer industry micro-economics is setting so many mini-problems that a measure of market relations is going to be tolerated for some time to come, provided it does not threaten to undermine the principle of central economic planning.

So a certain degree of decentralisation of planning is accepted, concurrently with planning on an international scale, at any rate within the socialist camp, i.e. between countries who take part in the Council for Economic Mutual Assistance, known in Russian as SEV (*Soviet ekonomicheskoi vzaimopomoshchi*) or *Comecon* in English-speaking countries.

Comecon *Joint Planning*

The Council for Economic Mutual Assistance (*Comecon*) was set up in April 1949 and first comprised Albania, Bulgaria, Hungary, Poland, Mongolia, Romania, Czechoslovakia, and the USSR. It was set up partly as a substitute for the Comintern (the third Communist International, which had been dissolved during World War II to placate Great Britain and the USA) and partly to counter the temptation of accepting Marshall Plan aid by the war-devastated countries of eastern Europe.

Apart from highly industrialised Czechoslovakia and the USSR herself, the other members of the new grouping were essentially agrarian countries, with a low industrial potential. Most of them had suffered from the effects of World War II. In particular,

Poland's coal and textile industries had been damaged and Romania's major industry – her oil installations – had been bombed rather ill-advisedly by the American air force at the very last moment when the German armies were already hastily withdrawing from the Balkans.

The fact that the German Democratic Republic joined the *Comecon* organisation in October 1950 added little to the industrial potential of the group, because much of East Germany's industrial equipment had been carried off by the Russians bent on exacting reparations. The resignation of Albania in 1961 had a merely symbolic significance.

In the early 1950s bilateral trade or, rather, barter agreements were more or less the only effective joint arrangements. Furthermore, the actual idea of 'an international division of labour' allowed for very different interpretations in Bulgaria and Romania – anxious to industrialise at all cost – and Moscow, who would have preferred those fertile southern countries to continue in their old role of suppliers of agricultural produce, though exporting it no longer to Germany but to the USSR, whose own agriculture was in a very sorry state.

The first steps at collaboration were a few joint constructions such as the bridge over the Danube built in 1954 by Bulgaria and Romania, and the power-station at Novy Dvor (Poland) erected by Poland and Czechoslovakia to supply electricity to both countries. Things began to move in the later 1950s when the first attempts were made to co-ordinate the individual Five-Year Plans of the various countries; this involved calculating 'balances' of major resources and needs in fuel, iron and steel, non-ferrous metals, some branches of engineering, light industry, and agriculture. Wishful thinking rather than rational planning was still too prevalent in those days to make co-ordination truly effective. However, arrangements were made at least to rationalise rail haulage and shipping on the Baltic and the Black Sea. More far-reaching co-ordination was arrived at when mutual credit arrangements began to be negotiated. Thus the GDR agreed to supply 90 million roubles-worth of mining equipment to Poland, which the latter was to repay by increasing her coal exports to East Germany. On similar lines Poland obtained from Czechoslovakia mining equipment and various durable consumer goods repayable also by regular coal deliveries over a period of twenty-five years. Since 1960 Czechoslovakia has been supplying the USSR with equipment to expand the mining of iron ore and non-ferrous metals in the USSR, these supplies being also repayable in iron-ore deliveries to Czechoslovakia. It was again Czechoslovakia, the most industrialised country of the *Comecon* group, which helped set up the copper-refining works, 'Medet', in Bulgaria. The Soviet Union and Czechoslovakia collaborated in geological surveys and helped Poland to prospect and start exploiting the important Legnitsko-Glogolev copper deposits. Of particular importance was the construction of the huge 'Friendship' (*Druzhba*) pipeline which brings oil from the USSR to Hungary, East Germany, Poland, and Czechoslovakia. Each country was responsible for building and bearing the cost of its section of the pipeline.

Inevitably there were causes of friction. Thus it would have been to Poland's advantage to sell more of her coal for hard currency to Western countries like those of Scandinavia. Czechoslovakia was quite willing to pay for the section of the pipeline and pumping installations on her own territory, but considerably more reluctant to shoulder the cost of drilling oil-wells and providing equipment to expand Soviet oilfields east of the Volga; yet without an expansion of her oil production the Soviet Union would have found it difficult to meet the growing demand for oil in Czechoslovakia. In fact, recently the consumption of oil has rocketed so rapidly in both countries that although Soviet oil-production doubled between 1960 and 1967 it can no longer satisfy Czechoslovakia's total requirements and the latter is making arrangements to obtain additional supplies from Iran.

On the other hand, Czechoslovakia, being the most industrialised country of eastern Europe and therefore a major supplier of machinery, having been guaranteed a large and stable market for her engineering products, did so little to modernise her articles that the Soviet Union – her principal client – had to turn to capitalist countries for more sophisticated and up-to-date models.

Member countries are not equally endowed with natural resources: thus, only the USSR and Romania are oil-exporting countries. They differ in their manpower resources: East Germany has lost much of her able-bodied population to West Germany, because the young and enterprising moved westward in search of freedom and higher wages. In Czechoslovakia and the USSR the falling birth-rate is already creating labour shortages in certain sections of the economy. On the other hand, rural areas in Poland suffer from a certain agrarian over-population. Combined with initially different levels of industrialisation, these inequalities aggravate complex problems of costs and prices, making some items needed by one country too expensive to be bought from its neighbour. All *Comecon* countries are plagued by the inconvertibility of their currencies, and Western observers have accused the USSR of underpaying her partners. Endeavours to carry out transactions on

ECONOMIC PLANNING

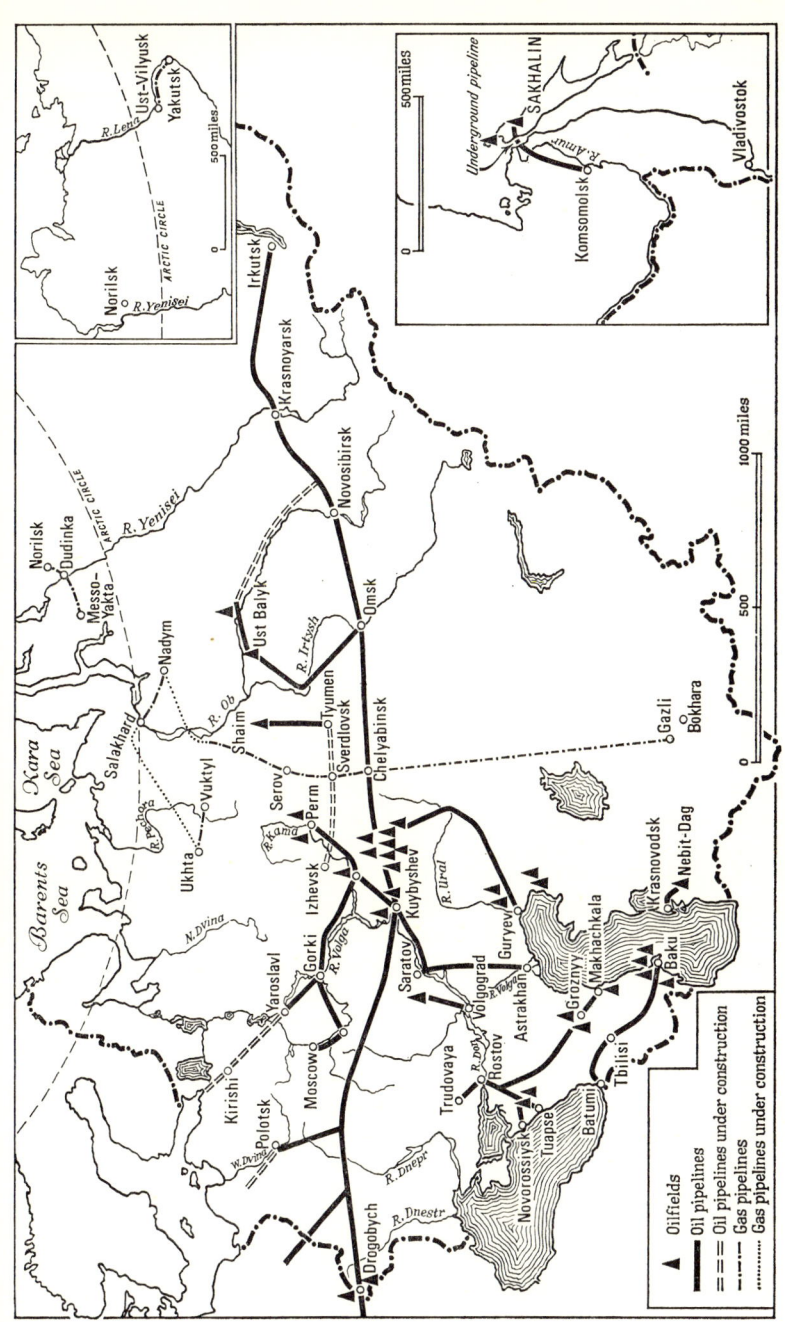

2. The Oilfields of the Soviet Union

the basis of world prices have not been very successful, and often misleading, because accounts are settled in 'transfer roubles', a paper currency used in multilateral transactions between *Comecon* countries. An International Bank (international in the sense that it services all *Comecon* countries) has been set up and schemes are preparing to transform the 'transfer rouble' into a convertible currency. This will become possible only if trade with hard-currency capitalist countries could expand. So far trade with the West has been expanding very slowly, partly because the quality and the after-service of goods manufactured in socialist countries have been inferior to those of advanced Western models and partly because of discriminatory measures originating in the USA to prevent trade in 'strategic goods' which included even ladies' swimming suits if they contained rubber) and block the formation of commercial ties between socialist and developing countries which come within the orbit of American neo-imperialism. An example of the difficulties experienced by the USSR in foreign trade is provided by New Zealand's commercial policy: while the Soviet Union buys from New Zealand up to 15 million dollars-worth a year (mainly wool), New Zealand's imports from the USSR average less than one million dollars a year, and New Zealand private firms may be refused import licences if goods similar to those offered by Soviet export agencies are obtainable elsewhere.

One of the promising fields of collaboration between *Comecon* countries is the exchange of technical and scientific information. The sharing of patents, blueprints, and specialised know-how was initially free, and greatly benefited Bulgaria, Romania, and Hungary in the early stages of their post-war industrialisation. Recently, however, the high costs of research and development have been taxing the generosity of the scientifically more advanced countries, especially the USSR. It is now proposed that the countries who use and benefit from a new invention or the manufacture of a new product should contribute an appropriate share of the initial outlay incurred on the research and development of the new item. A coordinated plan of joint research and development by two or several countries has been in force since 1966. Yugoslavia, though not a full member of *Comecon*, is taking part in this project as well as in several other joint ventures. In the scientific and technical fields, attention is directed mainly towards the production and transmission of electric power, geological prospecting, electronics and remote control devices, new synthetic materials, information science, and improvements in agricultural techniques, medicine, and the health services. There have been exchanges of personnel and, among the several international research centres, the atomic research centre

ECONOMIC PLANNING 87

at Dubna near Moscow and the laboratory of powerful magnetic fields and low temperatures in Wroclaw are the most important. An international centre of scientific and technical information was set up in 1969.

Plans for 1970–75 and more long-term forecasts for the community as a whole are being drafted in increasingly close consultation. They include the building of atomic power-stations in Bulgaria, Hungary, and East Germany, all of which are short of fuel and power. Plans are also made for greater specialisation, such as the production of different types of ball-bearings by different countries, or different countries supplying different parts for complex items like ships or aircraft, or, on the contrary, specialising in the building of different types of vessels, industrial equipment, or vehicles. For instance, whereas Hungary builds buses both for the home market and for export, the Werdau works in East Germany specialise in the manufacture of lorries.

A new field of collaboration is opening in manpower exchanges. To alleviate the labour shortage in East Germany, Polish workers have taken part in the laying of the oil pipeline between Schwedt-on-Oder and the petrochemical works Leina II. Two Bulgarian timber enterprises have been established in the USSR (in the autonomous Komi republic); the latter provides equipment and machinery, and Bulgaria has sent there some 3,000 workers, engineers, and technicians. The enterprises are to provide first-class timber for Bulgaria's furniture, woodworking, and papermaking industries.[7] In 1967 Hungary and East Germany concluded an agreement to recruit 30,000 temporary Hungarian workers for the East German electro-technical and machine-building industries.

Whether the member countries of *Comecon*, with a total population of 340 million, will be more successful than those of the Common Market in achieving integration, or less so, is difficult to foretell. They have all started from a much lower level of 'take-off' and have suffered from a good deal of unrealistic planning, dreams of economic autarky, misguided pricing practices, isolation, and hostile discrimination from the capitalist West, as well as from the centrifugal forces of their own intense nationalisms. Yet scientific and technical progress, a common ideology, and the realisation that the pooling of technical know-how, material, and even human resources increases prosperity could transform a group of pre-war Europe's poor relations into a community capable of emulating the Common Market's 'rich men's club'.

[7] *Manpower Aspects of Recent Economic Developments in Europe*, ILO, Geneva, 1969, p. 109.

Chapter 4
Industry

Overall Performance

IN VOLUME OF OUTPUT Soviet industry is second only to that of the USA. It took the country about five years of toil and privations to get back to pre-war levels of production and, after 1950, growth was very rapid. Within fifteen years the output of steel went up fivefold, that of rolled metal 5·5 times, oil 8 times, cement 13, tractors 11, and electricity 10·5 times.[1] Though growth began to decelerate in the 1960s and the return per rouble invested began to fall from about half a rouble of product to about one-third,[2] the Soviet achievement in getting back on its feet after the war was very remarkable when compared to the recovery of other devastated countries. For, unlike Germany whose *Wirtschaftswunder* received its impetus from massive American aid, Russia rebuilt her devastated areas without any outside help, apart from what reparations she extracted from Manchuria and the East German war-damaged industries. Both pre-war industrialisation and post-war recovery came about through the Soviet people's own 'sweat, toil, and tears'.

For quite a long time Western economists, rightly or wrongly suspicious of Soviet claims in general and Soviet statistics in particular, have indulged in complex and detailed calculations to arrive at estimates of the Soviet industrial potential expressed in terms which would be satisfactorily comparable to those used in capitalist countries. The distrust of Soviet statistics centres mainly on the monetary evaluation of the value of the goods produced and the weighting of indices. Like other countries, the USSR has been through periods of inflation and monetary reform. Thus in 1947 the rouble was revalued, one new rouble being made equal to ten old ones and in 1961 its parity to the dollar changed from 4 roubles to 90 kopeks. More intricate still is the assessment of various indices used by Soviet statisticians based on prices which are not dictated by market conditions but arbitrarily fixed by state planning organs. Prices charged for capital goods sold by state-owned enterprises to other state-owned enterprises, although they reflect costs of production, are accountancy devices rather than 'prices', as understood

[1] Brezhnev in *Pravda*, 30 March 1966.
[2] G. E. Schroder in *Soviet Studies*, July 1968, p. 2.

in a market economy. On ideological grounds the production of capital goods has always been given priority, initially to promote industrialisation, later to rebuild the industries, transport, and, in fact, whole towns in the war-devastated areas. The larger share of Soviet industrial output is the object of planned allocations rather than trade transactions. Even the prices of consumer goods may not directly relate to their cost of production. For instance, new articles, which are always expensive to make because of the expense incurred on research and development which has preceded their manufacture as well as teething troubles that may have plagued the initial stages of mass production, may continue to be highly priced even when their manufacture has become a matter of routine. In capitalist countries their price would come down in time, but in the USSR it may remain high, thus inflating the total value of commodities produced.[3] Furthermore, prices for agricultural produce vary according to whether they are valued at the price which state procurement agencies pay to collective farms, or state retail prices, or those charged by collective farmers at special markets (*kolkhoz* markets) where they are allowed to sell their produce direct to the consumer. In any case, turnover tax, which is very high on consumer goods, is included in their price, thus inflating the total. To complicate matters further, the Soviet Union has a method of calculating her national income different from that used in the West; Soviet statisticians include in their totals only the value of commodities obtained by extractive industries and agriculture, or manufactured by the processing industries, together with transport costs. They do not include services at all, which has the effect of reducing the figures for the GNP, while the Soviet pricing system tends to inflate it.

Precise and reliable comparisons, especially in monetary terms, are difficult to establish, whether in roubles (an unconvertible currency) or in dollars, at some elaborately calculated rate of exchange. In the final analysis the results obtained are widely discrepant and highly controversial.

On the other hand, data relating to physical output are perfectly credible and seldom disputed. Such are the figures quoted by Kosygin in his speech to the Twenty-third Congress and the figures set out in the new Plan:

[3] The 1964 Soviet Statistical Yearbook estimated the GNP of the Soviet Union to equal 60 per cent of that of the USA. Western economists assume lower figures, in any case not exceeding 50 per cent of America's GNP. See Abram Bergson, *The Real National Income of Soviet Russia since 1928*, Cambridge, Mass., 1961; A. Nove, *The Soviet Economy: An Introduction*, London and New York, 1961. The 1968 Soviet Statistical Yearbook seems to confirm the lower figure (*Narodnoye khozyaistvo SSSR v 1968 g.*, p. 146).

	1940	*1965*	*1970 (planned)*[4]
Steel (million tons)	18·3	91	124– 129
Rolled metal (million tons)	13·1	70·9	95– 99
Oil (million tons)	31·1	243	345– 355
Cement (million tons)	5·7	72·4	100– 105
Gas (billion cubic metres)	3·4	129·2	225– 240
Motor vehicles (thousands)	145·4	616·4	1,360–1,510
Tractors (thousands)	31·6	355	600– 625
Electricity (billion Kw)	48·3	507	830– 850

There is, however, an obverse side to this grandiose achievement. From the population's point of view it is the decreasing but still persisting shortage and poor quality of consumer goods. The shortage (though not the poor quality) is the result of the Party's deliberate policy which has always been to give priority to producer goods; indeed, it stands to reason that in the long run the more factories that are built, the more machines that are made, the more transport facilities that become available, and so on, the more consumer goods they will produce eventually.

Even in the 1966–70 Plan, which contains so many provisions to improve the standards of living of the population, the growth of group 'A' (capital goods) remains somewhat higher (49–52 per cent) than that of group 'B' (consumer goods). If a shortage of consumer goods is a consciously accepted position, the poor quality of both producer and consumer goods as well as the low productivity of labour have long been a source of worry to Soviet economists, planners, and managers. Poor quality is the result of many causes – unrealistic demands for quantitative output, absence of competition, inadequately qualified manpower, fear of innovation that might endanger the fulfilment of planned quantitative targets, and lack of responsibility for the sale of goods produced. Low productivity of labour was formerly due to inadequate equipment and poorly qualified labour, but more recently it has been caused by uneven mechanisation when the smooth running of the production process in highly mechanised and automated plants depends on ancillary activities still carried out by hand.

Numerous, mainly administrative, measures to overcome these shortcomings have done little to right the position. The purpose of the present economic reforms is to eliminate or mitigate them. The gist of these reforms is stated in the directives of the Twenty-third

---

[4] These very high targets were scaled down and the annual plan for 1970 set the production of steel at 115 million tons; oil, 350 million tons; cement, 94·5 million tons; gas, 195·8 billion cubic metres; motor vehicles, 875,000; tractors, 456,400; and electricity, 740 billion Kw.

INDUSTRY

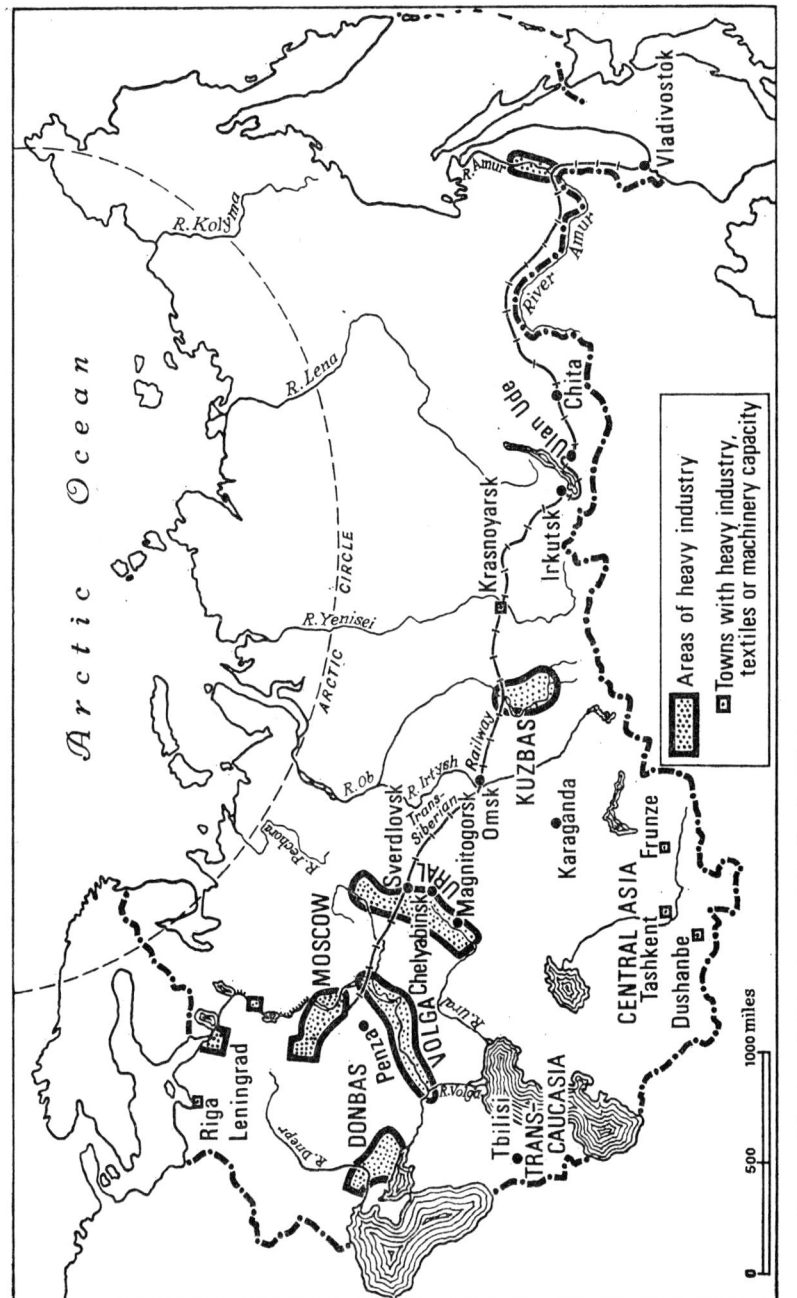

3. General Industrial Regions of the Soviet Union

Congress as designed to secure 'the correct combination of centralised planned guidance with the development of the economic initiative and independence of industrial enterprises', and somehow to combine the best of both worlds.

Planning has always been highly centralised and very detailed. The overall National Plan is broken down into smaller units, according to industries and regions. In their turn these units are subdivided and sent down to individual plants. Each enterprise is given a set of exact instructions or 'success indicators' to measure its performance. Hitherto the most important was the plant's gross output, while other indicators related to the assortment of articles, their quality, and the price at which they should be sold and which was related to the cost of production plus a certain margin of 'profit', most of which went to the state Budget, while a percentage was allocated to the Director's Fund to be used in bonuses for rewarding plan fulfilment; these bonuses were awarded jointly by the director of the enterprise and representatives of the local Party primary and the trade union, either to individuals for outstanding work or to groups, or else used to provide general amenities like housing, nurseries, or sports facilities for the employees of the enterprise.

Although every enterprise's plans and the attendant indicators were set centrally, individual plants had a say, too, in drafting their individual plans. They submitted their own 'counter-plan', which was discussed, amended, and eventually integrated by the planning authorities in charge of either the industry as a whole or of the region into more comprehensive plans, and these larger plans were finally co-ordinated by the central planning authority (*Gosplan*) into the overall National Plan.

Administratively, enterprises of the same type – i.e. extracting or manufacturing the same type of commodities – were brought under one authority, usually an industrial Ministry. This had the advantage of their sharing in the research and development carried out for the whole industry. On the other hand, the prevalence of the territorial principle, i.e. the co-ordinated development of various industries within a definite geographical region, had the advantage of cutting down on distant cross-hauls. Each organisational set-up had its advantages and drawbacks. The 'end-product' type of organisation gave rise to the powerful industrial Ministries of the Stalin era, each responsible for either coal production, or oil production, or heavy industry, aviation, instrument-making, etc. To ensure the timely deliveries of materials, fuel, or equipment, each Ministry tended to become self-sufficient by developing its own subsidiary enterprises, so that, for instance, the Ministry of Coal Industry owned not merely repair shops engaged on maintenance and routine repair of mining machinery, but entire engineering-works for the actual manufacture of the machines and tools it required, as well as sawmills to supply pit props, research institutes, and vocational schools for the training of miners. Because its engineering-works were of an ancillary nature, they were often small, inefficient, and their production methods contrary to economies of scale. Furthermore, their location often led to long hauls because it was quicker for the Ministry to obtain deliveries from its 'own' though distant ancillary enterprises than to undertake a lengthy correspondence and cut through the red tape of another Ministry whose works may have been located in the vicinity.

The regional principle tried out by Khrushchev, who dismantled the powerful industrial Ministries and transferred the administration of industrial plants to regional economic councils (*sovnarkhozy*), had its drawbacks too. It encouraged parish patriotism, and regional authorities were inclined to give priority to less urgent but local requests while postponing or neglecting orders from other enterprises, possibly of All-Union importance, which happened to be situated outside their own region.

Gradually, centralised Ministries superseded the regional economic councils, though their organisation has been rationalised very considerably to cope with the increasing diversification and sophistication of industrial production, the invention of synthetic materials, rapid changes in machine design, and improved manufacturing methods. For even basic commodities like steel can no longer be measured merely in tons; the variety of steel alloys has greatly increased with the diversification of instruments for which different types of steel are used.

The problem of quality became increasingly acute when delicate and complex articles, from television sets to giant computers, came into existence. In the consumer industries, once the acute shortage of everything and anything became less crying, shoddy goods no longer found buyers and enormous stocks of unsold goods accumulated in warehouses. Too often, in order to fulfil its plan or, better still, to over-fulfil it and qualify for bonus awards, it was to the plant's advantage to produce large quantities rather than high-quality goods. Cases have been quoted of factories producing unnecessarily heavy household goods because their output was measured in tons. Moreover, plants were reluctant to introduce new lines, since innovation was fraught with the danger of breakdowns, stoppages for retooling, delays, and other unforeseen and unplanned difficulties which jeopardised plan fulfilment. Managers and workers naturally endeavoured to secure an 'easy plan' well within the plant's capacity to fulfil, and one which did not require too much risky change. Numerous and detailed indicators regarding volume of output, range, quality, time of delivery, expenditure on raw materials, fuel and power, labour, production costs, 'planned profit', etc., somehow always failed to foresee all contingencies and constantly left loopholes for inefficiency and bad workmanship.

Slowly planners came round to the idea that profitability, the motive power of Western capitalism, could somehow be adapted to a socialist economy. To be profitable, i.e. to make a profit, the plant would have to produce goods that were essentially saleable and if its 'profit' (or at least a larger share of it than previously) were left at the disposal of the management, the latter could use its own initiative to make the enterprise pay its way, instead of relying on state subsidies in case of trouble. The profitability, or at least the viability, of an enterprise is defined as its observing *khozraschet* or economic accountability – in fact, balancing its accounts.

It should be borne in mind that a National Plan, once it is accepted and confirmed, is legally binding, and in Stalin's days failure to fulfil it could result in criminal proceedings being taken against the management. More recently, however, the status of juridical person has been conferred on individual plants, and non-delivery or late delivery of goods or their substandard quality is dealt with as breaches of contract under the provisions of the Civil Code. The October 1965 statute defining a state enterprise gives the latter somewhat more latitude in the execution rather than in the drafting of its plans. The main success indicator is no longer total gross output nor the reduction in the cost of production, but the sale of output and the resulting profit calculated as a percentage of the plant's fixed capital. The share of the profits payable to the state has been greatly reduced, but plants now have to pay interest (usually 6 per cent) on their fixed capital. Under the new regulation the enterprise obtains a limited freedom in setting its own standards of quality and the size of its labour force, but its total wages fund is incorporated in its overall plan and actual wages are fixed by law according to a scale of grades of skill. The new regulations enable a plant to cut down on its labour force, though it is still almost impossible to dismiss workers on grounds of redundancy; however, they may be transferred to other work; since wages are fixed by law they can be altered only by awarding bonuses. Savings on wages over one period may be used to supplement wages during a later period, which gives some flexibility in the hiring of temporary workers. It is hoped that a somewhat wider latitude in decision-making at the grass roots will stimulate the initiative of management and that of workers through their trade union.

Trade Unions

The role of trade unions in the USSR differs from that in capitalist countries. Since socialised industry belongs to the nation as a whole and, therefore, indirectly to the workers, it follows that workers toil for the nation and not for any private employer or for the shareholders of a capitalist corporation; in a sense, they work for themselves. Consequently, there can be no industrial disputes because – so the argument runs – workers cannot strike against themselves. Any difficulties that may arise can and must be settled by arbitration, in which trade unions take a direct part.

Each enterprise has its own commission on labour disputes on which management and union have equal representation. In very large factories every workshop may have such a commission. If one of the sides in the dispute is dissatisfied with the decision it may bring the matter before the factory trade union committee (*fabkom*), which has considerable powers in such matters as dismissal and reinstatement. If arbitration fails within the enterprise both sides may take the matter to court and there is a possibility of appealing from the lower court to that of the province and finally to the All-Union Supreme Court. If a dispute involves Party members, the factory Party primary may intervene. In any case the Party can make its influence felt indirectly through those members of the factory trade union committee who belong to the Party as well as through Party members among the managerial personnel.

Considering that in any industrial, trade, or transport enterprise, or in any institution in general, all the labour force belongs to the same union, one of the most common causes of labour disputes in the West, namely disputes between two unions arguing over whose work it is 'to bore the holes', cannot arise. A single union means also that members of the administration as well as rank-and-file workers may be elected to the factory trade union committee (*fabkom*). The collective agreement signed by the trade union with the management is binding in so far as many details of the enterprise's plan are incorporated into the agreement. As already mentioned, the enterprise's plan is not issued as a directive from the planning authorities straightaway. The enterprise is entitled to send up its 'counter-plan' and this is drafted by management in consultation with the trade union. Only after the final plan has been decided upon by the authorities does it become legally binding and, by signing the collective agreement, the workers in a sense accept to fulfil it. In the drafting of their counter-plan, management and workers are at one in their endeavour to secure an 'easy plan', the fulfilment of which (or better still its over-fulfilment) earns bonus awards to both sides. The only cause of friction that may arise in connection with collective agreements is of a very local type, such as the amount of money to be spent on housing or the date of opening of a crèche or cafeteria.

Another major cause of dispute in Western countries is over wages. In the USSR all wages are centrally fixed and not subject to bargaining. Local trade unions, together with management and representatives of the Party primary, are only concerned with determining the precise classification of jobs within given skill grades, or deciding whether any of them fall into the class of 'hot, heavy, or unhealthy work', payable at higher rates; in the case of piecework they are responsible for norm setting.

Piecework is still a widely used method of payment, though monthly wages are more common. These are set according to the type of industry, the nature of the job, and the geographical location. The minimum wage fixed on 1 January 1968 was 60 roubles per month. Other rates of pay are arrived at by multiplying the wage set for grade I workers of a given industry by certain factors. In most industries there are six grades of skill, though in some industries requiring higher specialisation, like the chemical and several extractive industries, there may be up to ten grades. The differentials between grades I and IV seldom exceed a doubling of the wage. Personnel employed in hot, heavy, or unhealthy work are paid 10–16 per cent above normal rates, and those working underground 25–30 per cent more.[5]

Overtime can be ordered by management only with the permission of the trade union committee (*fabkom*) and is allowed only in emergencies, e.g. in time of war or natural disaster and, by stretching the wording of the law, to fulfil planned targets on time. An individual worker is permitted a maximum of four hours' overtime for two consecutive days or 120 hours in the course of a year. No overtime is permissible in the case of women after the fourth month of pregnancy, nursing mothers, or juveniles. Time-workers are paid time and a half for the first two hours, and double rates

[5] In industries accorded priority, like engineering, rates of pay may be up to 18 per cent above those in less important consumer industries. The present drive to overcome the housing shortage as well as expand construction industries in general has prompted a 20 per cent rise in building-workers' wages and their minimum is now 76 roubles. Since 1 January 1968 the co-efficient used for raising the pay of people working in climatically unfavourable or remote districts has been fixed at twice the normal rate for the job in the islands of the Arctic Ocean and the Chukchi national district; 1·8 for Norilsk; 1·7 for Kamchatka and Sakhalin; and 1·2 for the Far East (i.e. the Maritime and Khabarovsk provinces).

for any additional hours or for working on Sundays (now also Saturdays); equivalent arrangements are made for pieceworkers. The factory union committee is responsible for organising shift-working, particularly in plants on continuous production where the seven-hour day caused some problems before the five-day week was universally adopted. Thus arrangements had to be of a three-weeks rotation type of shift : the day shift worked eight hours for six days; the evening shift eight hours for five days; and the night shift seven hours for five days; this gave two week-ends off out of three. At the time of writing the normal working week is forty-one hours or five days of eight hours twelve minutes. The factory trade union committee is also responsible for holiday timetables, though here again detailed legislation sets the guidelines. Juveniles are entitled to one month's holiday in the summer, others to from fifteen to eighteen days (according to industries and length of service at the same place of work) any time that can be arranged for them; those studying take their holidays prior to their examinations, pregnant women immediately before or after confinement leave.

Trade union permission is required for any dismissals of rank-and-file workers, but not in the case of engineering and technical staff. Apart from dismissals that can occur in connection with the closing-down of an enterprise or the arrest and conviction of a worker on a criminal charge, a worker can be dismissed either for inability to cope with the job or repeated absenteeism, or for 'loss of trust' in the case of employees handling money (like cashiers and taxi-drivers), or because of redundancy. The latter case is difficult to implement because any cut-down must be authorised by a higher administrative authority and the worker must be offered alternative employment; moreover, his personal circumstances are taken into consideration, such as being the only breadwinner in a family of two or more dependants, or a pregnant woman or a mother with a child under one year of age, or a war-disabled or an employee taking an evening course. A dismissed worker is entitled to two weeks' notice or pay. A claim for reinstatement can be brought before the courts and if the dismissal is found to have been illegal, the employee must be given his job back as well as up to twenty days' back pay. Security of tenure may be a blessing now, but this has not always been so. In 1940 a decree was issued forbidding a worker to leave his job without the management's consent, and even one day of absenteeism as well as lateness was made into a criminal offence punishable usually by the obligation to continue at one's place of work at two-thirds of the normal pay-rate. This law was designed to end high labour turnover, and was of particular importance during the war years when many industrial plants were evacuated to the Urals and beyond. In 1940 the length of the working day was also increased without additional pay, and overtime made compulsory. The fear of large numbers of workers leaving the evacuated enterprises (which remained in their new location when the war came to an end) to return to their home towns in the European part of the Soviet Union may explain the strange fact that although criminal responsibility for unauthorised leaving and absenteeism was revoked by a decree of the Supreme Soviet on 14 July 1951, it was not made public until all wartime labour legislation was repealed in April 1956, i.e. after the death of Stalin. Even today, repeated absenteeism[6] may lead to dismissal with an entry to that effect in the worker's labour book, which could deprive him of certain benefits contingent on continuous service at one place of work, such as length of paid holidays. An entry like 'leaving of one's own accord' is on the whole preferable when looking for a job.

The Soviet Union has not experienced unemployment on any scale since the introduction of the first Five-Year Plan. However, with increasing automation it will be necessary to provide alternative jobs possibly even for highly skilled categories of workers, and in 1967 special employment agencies were set up to deal with placements in a more centralised way. Hitherto Ministries and enterprises had recruited skilled labour direct by sending in applications for young specialists to the appropriate technical institutes and schools, and unskilled labour either locally or by arrangement with certain rural district executive committees. A decree passed in 1963 made it compulsory on enterprises to employ a definite percentage of juveniles aged sixteen to eighteen; the purpose of the decree was to overcome the reluctance of managers to employ juveniles, who are entitled to shorter working hours (six instead of eight) and longer paid holidays (a whole month). Special agencies were in charge of finding employment for war-disabled in suitable industries like textile design, wood decoration, watchmaking, technical drawing, or more intellectual work as librarians or archivists. Other agencies existed for placing demobilised soldiers and retired officers. In 1967 each Union republic set up a special committee with a network of agencies in cities and rural districts to deal with all placements. It is hoped that the new arrangements will also reduce 'frictional unemployment', i.e. the loss of labour to the community caused by workers changing jobs. High labour turnover leads to considerable loss of man-hours in the USSR.

A major function of the Central Committee of Trade Unions is the overall administration of the state insurance fund from which

[6] Absenteeism is defined as absence from work for a full day (or shift) and also arriving too drunk to do any work.

pensions and sickness and maternity benefits are paid, and over 3,000 rest-homes, children's and tourist camps, and hostels for workers and employees are subsidised. In 1970 this fund exceeded 16 billion roubles. At local levels, trade unions supervise social amenities provided by the enterprise, such as housing, nurseries, clubs, holiday and various cultural facilities. Apart from the money allocated under the collective agreement for such purposes, there used to be a director's fund formed from 6 per cent of the enterprise's planned profits and up to 60 per cent of any over-plan profits; in connection with the new reforms this fund, renamed the enterprise's fund, becomes more important. Expenditure from this fund is decided upon by the director of the enterprise in consultation with its trade union; however, they have not got an entirely free hand in the matter and must conform to certain rules: namely, 20 per cent of the fund must be spent on the introduction of new techniques, 40 per cent on housing and social and cultural activities, and 40 per cent on bonuses. The latter, supplemented by any premiums from the wages fund, seldom exceed 20–30 per cent of the basic earnings and can be awarded to individuals or groups or to all workers of a given enterprise for exceeding production targets.

Trade unions are responsible for doing their utmost to promote production and ensure the fulfilment of the plant's planned targets. In this connection they organise socialist competitions within the plant or challenge to a competition another plant producing similar articles. A socialist competition agreement is then drafted and the winning plant is awarded prizes by the appropriate Ministry or the All-Union Central Committee of Trade Unions. A distinctive feature of socialist competition – the word 'emulation' would be more appropriate – is the comradely help that the winning enterprise then extends to the loser by showing what methods or shop layout are preferable and giving any other useful advice to the less successful competitor. Apart from being a method to raise output and encourage rationalisation, socialist competitions between enterprises add interest to industrial work and enliven its monotonous drudgery.

Participation, Reforms, and Innovation

Over the years the authority of managements and that of enterprise directors has grown; the days when workers' councils ran the show have long passed. The director and senior staff are appointed by higher authorities, usually the Ministry to which the plant is subordinate, but it is the director who hires and fires the labour force. He has full control over the operations in the enterprise and is responsible for dealings with other agencies, including State Arbitration. He is usually a highly qualified executive and, probably, a fairly high-ranking member of the Communist Party.

Before discussing the present economic reforms and their prospects of success or failure, it is worth mentioning some fundamental difficulties inherent in any industrial society, namely the lack of personal interest or involvement of the rank-and-file workers in the improvement of manufacturing processes. Under capitalism, where enterprises are run for profit, workers are anxious to obtain part of these profits (or surplus value, in Marxist terminology) by claiming higher wages. They are little concerned with higher productivity, though this would raise profitability and should be in the interest of the workers as well as the shareholders. Various 'profit-sharing schemes' now endeavour to impress this point upon the workers. Their lack of success, the persistence of restrictive practices, and rivalry among trade unions about 'who does what' are entirely irrational; they are survivals of fears and attitudes harking back to the bad old days of the Great Depression in the inter-war years. They are slowly being overcome by various 'increased productivity' conditions incorporated into higher wage agreements, which may eventually surmount workers' indifference to the progress of their plant. This indifference is also caused by the complexity of modern manufacturing processes; rank-and-file workers are unlikely to have the competence to suggest improvements and rationalisations that have not already been thought of and introduced by the better educated and informed technical and managerial staff. Therefore the workers of an enterprise are no more concerned with the running of their plants than passengers in a train are in the running of the country's railway system. It is just beyond them. The inability to influence modern industrial processes, together with the historically conditioned demand for a larger part of the cake through strike action, are bound to affect detrimentally and even disrupt production and lower the plant's earning capacity. Although capitalists have come to realise that they must share more equally with the employees, they still find it difficult to enlist workers' participation. Meanwhile a third claimant to profits – the state – is siphoning off through taxation an increasingly large share to spend on its military needs and the maintenance of a growing class of 'unproductive' workers such as doctors, nurses, scientists, teachers, and bureaucrats.

In the Soviet Union, workers' control proved an ephemeral phenomenon. It was killed by the complexities of modern manufacturing techniques even before being finished off by the authoritarianism of Stalin's efficiency drive. In the early days of the Revolution workers felt that factories had become theirs, that they had wrested them from the grasping hands of the exploiting capitalists, and that they were going to run them for their own benefit and that of the whole country. They flocked in thousands to evening classes and short courses to improve their education and come to understand production techniques. The more able became the *praktiki* whom the Soviet government promoted to run the factories and keep in check the engineers and specialists who had been in charge before the Revolution and whom it employed but did not trust. Workers gave of their free time on Saturdays and Sundays to perform all sorts of jobs to restart production, to load and unload trains and restore the transport system brought to a standstill by the Civil War. Later they devised various forms of friendly and comradely socialist competition to achieve better results; they partook willingly of the great experiment of industrialisation, joined the Party, and contributed their energy to modernise the country. Industrialisation caused a tremendous social mobility and created unprecedented opportunities for the able, the ambitious, and the hard-working enthusiasts. Later, what had started as spontaneous mass movements became institutionalised; discussions at meetings or criticism of managerial decisions became cramped by the fear of becoming politically suspect. With more Party men coming to occupy managerial positions, the directors of enterprises were given greater powers at the expense of the trade unions and even of local Party primaries. Meetings of the factory committee became increasingly formal and eventually their role was reduced to rubber-stamping appeals for harder work and higher output. Eventually, as mentioned already, before the outbreak of World War II, workers were forbidden to leave their jobs without the consent of management, and absenteeism and lateness for work became criminal offences. Though these draconian laws were repealed after the war, the new generation of workers had lost any proprietary interest in their places of work (to which they might even have been directed in their younger years) or the quality of their output. Like the management, their only concern was to fulfil the quantitative plan and secure the attendant bonus awards.

One of the aims of the present economic reform is to enlist the active participation of the workers and managers while preserving overall central planning. Can this be done? If employees come to regard their plant as their own concern, they will seek to put its interests first, forgetting those of others, and they will resent levies on their profits appropriated by the state to maintain its apparatus, or the non-productive third sector, or to develop industries in remote regions. This is the danger inherent in syndicalism and the Yugoslav type of socialism. In Yugoslavia it has led to the closing-down of non-profitable industries that had been started earlier in the more backward regions of the country, like Macedonia and Montenegro, under state sponsorship. To alleviate widespread unemployment, Yugoslavia grants travel documents to workers seeking jobs in capitalist countries; the money they send home is a useful source of foreign exchange and their wages abroad are probably considerably higher than their earnings would have been at home; but losing its most active manpower to foreign countries does not help a country to solve the long-term problems of its underdeveloped regions, and exacerbates local nationalism. Furthermore, in many industries the managing committees have been tempted to accept foreign loans, which may have been an easy way to inject new life into these industries, but which may prove to be a piecemeal sell-out to foreign capitalism (mainly German and American) and the death knell of rational central planning.

To return to the USSR, the recent economic reforms give an enterprise somewhat more independence, while retaining overall central control. The reform was first introduced in the clothing industry, which had been particularly unsuccessful in selling its goods. In 1966 it was extended to other consumer goods industries, some railway lines, and motor transport enterprises. The main success indicator is to be the profitability of the enterprise, proved by its ability to sell its goods. There are reasons to believe that a growing number of other indicators will be retained. Profit is defined as the residue of the plant's earnings after it has met its outlays on power, raw materials, repairs, wages, and also paid an interest on its fixed capital, which is a new departure from the former practice when no charge was payable on these assets. Another aspect of the reform is the reduction in the number of commodities to be allocated centrally; now enterprises will be able to buy many items direct from suppliers and enter into regular supply and purchase contracts with each other.

By the end of 1968 the reform had been introduced into 25,000 enterprises which accounted for 70 per cent of the total volume of industrial production. However, the new system is in its experimental stages, and it will probably take time to find a point of equilibrium between the orderly planned development of the country and the creative, and possibly individualistic, initiative of workers and management.

The introduction of the 'profit motive' is on the whole half-hearted because it is contrary to the principle of the 'service motive', which is the hallmark of socialist industry, and also because many economists argue that with the broadening of information-flow and computers capable of processing far more data than was possible ever before, planners will be able to find the most rational and optimal solutions to economic planning without resorting to market relations. However, for the time being, whilst mathematical economists formulate and solve their intricate sets of equations and construct models with an increasing number of variables arising in an unmanageably large and complex economy, a limited play of market-type relations will be tolerated as a kind of temporary rule-of-thumb regulator. This will also give time to construct a network of improved computers – still in short supply – and design more satisfactory economic indices to be used for programming, as well as to instil a more scholarly approach to planning among those who tread the corridors of power.

Another stumbling-block in the path of the reform is the cost of innovation. The purpose of the reform is to increase efficiency and improve the quality of goods by enlisting grass-root initiative, but so long as prices and wages are centrally fixed there is little room for financial manoeuvring at factory level. In the second half of the twentieth century improved quality usually means not merely a better-made article but a new model, whether it is a thermostatically controlled washing-machine or an entirely automated production line. In a country which has reached the industrial and technological level of the Soviet Union, innovation is a crucial factor for further progress. Long gone are the days when the Soviet Union relied on Western know-how or bought foreign patents. It is her turn now to sell patents abroad and compete, in some fields at least, with the most advanced Western countries in the export of complex machinery, though the latter still accounts for only about 20 per cent of her total exports.

Central planning has enabled her to concentrate on industries regarded as a first priority and to achieve spectacular successes in certain cases. Yet other industries not given the same attention have been neglected and remain backward. Altogether, development has been very uneven.

Science, particularly applied science, has received much encouragement, and the scientific achievements of the USSR will be discussed in a separate chapter. The topic dealt with here is the introduction of the results of discoveries made in applied science and of technical devices perfected by research and development institutes into industry. Apart from selected fields such as high-speed aviation, rocketry, and certain sections of the machine-tool and the iron and steel industries, innovation has been handicapped by the reluctance of enterprises both to experiment with new products and to embark on their manufacture on a large scale. Thus Kosygin[7] cited transistors, polyprene, and high-pressure working of metals

[7] Kosygin in *Pravda*, 28 September 1965.

with liquids as examples of impermissible lags in the practical application of Soviet ideas. Because of this resistance to innovation and the ensuing delays, the 'lead-time' has been so great that occasionally new products were out of date by the time they became available, as was the case with the Ural-4 computers and the Zaporozhets small passenger-cars. Another cause of delay is the long time it takes to build additional workshops often required to manufacture new products or to introduce new technical processes. This affected the chemical industry in particular. Of the 230 new models of agricultural machinery approved for manufacture in recent years, nearly half are still not being made.[8]

On the whole, the drive for technical progress comes from government agencies and not from a competitive market as in capitalist countries. Of these government agencies, by far the most important is the State Committee for Science and Technology. In the case of priority items the government either provides research institutes – where applied research is carried out – with pilot plants, or sets up for them experimental factory laboratories. In an ordinary, production-oriented factory, an experimental workshop or laboratory could easily be diverted into assisting with normal production, while frequent re-equipping of a major kind which is a necessary part of the work of an experimental factory may be cut short or even prohibited by *Stroibank*, the bank which deals with credits for building purposes, on the grounds that excessive credits are contrary to the regulations governing its crediting system.

Apart from direct government action to promote innovation in priority industries, innovators, when seeking modernisation in non-priority industries, can obtain the backing of numerous voluntary societies, such as the Scientific Technical Societies (*nauchno tecknicheskye obshchestva*) and Councils of Innovators, often acting in conjunction with the local trade union. They either exert moral pressure on the senior officers of a Ministry or organise competitions and displays and enlist the help of Party representatives on various bodies. In enterprises where Scientific Technical Societies are well supported, they are sometimes given the status of a permanent technical-production council to advise the director and chief engineers. Councils of Innovators act through their headquarters, the All-Union Society of Innovators and Rationalisers. The latter, together with the Central Directorate of Scientific Technical Societies, carry out annual inspection of all plans for scientific research and technical innovation throughout the country. The function of these inspections appears to be both a check on the implementation of existing measures and a source for suggesting new ones. During the

[8] *Voprosy ekonomiki*, 1969, No. 12, p. 66.

third public inspection in 1965, over a thousand republican, regional, and city directorates of Scientific Technical Societies participated, together with 35,000 primaries, representing 1,600,000 people, and over a million useful suggestions were said to have resulted from this inspection. The general climate of enthusiasm for science among wide sections of the population is probably the best channel for obtaining the participation of the workers in the implementation of the national economic plan, the object of which is in the long run to raise their own standard of living.

To support innovation financially, a Fund for the Assimilation of New Technology was set up in 1961, initially for engineering-works, and in 1964 its help was extended to many consumer industries. This fund is formed by a levy from all enterprises under a Ministry or regional council (*sovnarkhoz*); this levy amounts to from one per cent to $3\frac{1}{2}$ per cent of their cost of production; payments from this fund are allocated to enterprises for expenditure on designing new products and processes, on purchasing special equipment to manufacture new products, and on manufacturing and testing industrial prototypes and small first batches. These allocations alleviate considerably, though they may not cover entirely, the financial losses initially incurred by progressive enterprises, for losses can be quite substantial; for instance, a 1963 survey of fifty engineering enterprises in Moscow and Leningrad showed a fall in profitability from an average of 32·7 per cent to 8·9 per cent when the proportion of new products in their total output rose from 20 to 60.[9]

Suggestions have been made that, to encourage innovation, industries should be entitled to charge higher prices for new products, but this right may weaken the principle of centrally fixed pricing.

Speaking at the Twenty-third Party Congress, Academician Keldysh said:

> The decisions of the September Plenum of the Central Committee have established the prerequisites for the economic interest of enterprises in technical innovations. So far, however, material incentives to work on technical innovations are lagging behind the incentives to produce, and they must obviously be increased. The need to reward the manufacture of technically more advanced production must also be taken into account when the new price system is worked out.

The principle of centrally fixed prices will probably also have to be applied less rigidly, for it leads to absurd situations. A curious case was reported from the Latvian SSR, where the price of a new

---

[9] *Ekonomicheskaya Gazeta*, 1965, No. 48, p. 5.

brand of ladies' nylon stockings had to be confirmed not only by the Latvian ministry of light industry but by the State Prices Committee of *Gosplan* in Moscow.[10]

Ignorance of modern managerial techniques is also blamed for the poor performance of whole sections of Soviet industry. Latterly, Soviet economists have been drawing attention to the success of American schools of business management, especially to American techniques of obtaining and processing large volumes of information and using the computerised data to estimate quickly and with great precision the various courses open to maximise sales and profits. Similar techniques, it is argued, could be used by socialist enterprises to achieve more socially-oriented aims of either maximising output or reducing costs, or raising quality without increasing inputs.

The industrial achievement of the Soviet Union was summarised by the authors of a detailed survey on science and industry in the USSR in the following words:

> In some important respects the USSR is technologically one of the two world super-powers. Largely as a result of the size and quality of her defence and aero-space industries, she is the only serious rival to the United States, both as a military power and as a competitor in the space race. In certain other industries, such as iron and steel and machine-tools, the USSR has also on the whole a high level of technical performance...
>
> The Soviet Union has, however, been able to reach this high technical level only in a few priority fields. In the computer and chemical industries and in almost all consumer products, the USSR is a long way behind the United States, and in some major industries she is less advanced than the industrial countries of Western Europe. While in certain respects a super-power, the Soviet Union is therefore in general, like the countries of Western Europe, looking across a substantial gulf at United States science and technology.[11]

It is in respect of technology that the gulf is greatest and it affects almost all branches of the economy, in particular the backward and long-neglected Soviet agriculture.

[10] *Kommunist*, 1968, No. 17, p. 74.
[11] R. Amann, M. J. Berry, and R. W. Davies, *Science and Industry in the USSR*, part 5, p. 576, in E. Zaleski *et al., Science Policy in the USSR*, OECD, Paris, 1969.

Chapter 5
Agriculture

The Causes of Backwardness

AGRICULTURE REMAINS THE WEAKEST spot in the Soviet economy. Yet without a rise in the production of foodstuffs and other agricultural produce there can be no improvement in the standard of living. The total volume of Soviet agricultural production for 1959-63 was estimated at 70-75 per cent of that of the USA and at 85 per cent on the average for 1964-68.[1] Considering that the population of the USSR was somewhat greater than that of the USA, this means that there was a smaller quantity of food produced per inhabitant, irrespective of its quality. If quality is taken into account the comparison is even more unfavourable because of the shortage of high-protein foods in the USSR. Meat, dairy produce, and fruit are still scarce commodities, less noticeably in Moscow but very definitely so in the small towns and the remoter northern regions. The Institute of Nutrition of the Medical Academy of the USSR has put forward as a desirable minimum the following *per capita* average consumption of high-protein foods: meat – 62·3 kgs.; milk and dairy products – 551 kgs.; and 307 eggs per annum. The actual average figures for 1966 worked out at 43 kgs. of meat, 259 kgs. of milk and dairy produce, and 130 eggs *per capita* per annum. On the other hand, the consumption of potatoes, bread, and farinaceous foods has been higher than that recommended by the Institute of Nutrition.

The target figures for food production in the present (1966-70) Plan are based on the findings of the Institute of Nutrition. However, planned results in agriculture have repeatedly fallen short of the mark. Thus, during the previous Seven-Year Plan (1959-65) gross farm output increased by only 14 per cent instead of 70 per cent as planned, just about keeping ahead of population growth. In years of crop failure, particularly in 1963, the Soviet Union had to import large quantities of wheat from Canada, and after the exceptionally severe winter of 1968-69 has done so again. The causes of recurrent crises in agriculture are probably threefold, though the relative importance of each factor is difficult to assess.

First, there are the geographical conditions. Of the huge area of

[1] *Narodnoye khozyaistvo SSSR v 1963 g.*, Moscow, 1964, p. 69; and *Nar Khoz. SSSR v 1968 g.*, Moscow, 1969, p. 143.

the USSR only 10 per cent (2,224 thousand sq. km.) is arable land. This works out at roughly 0·94 hectares (or a little over two acres) per head of population. Twenty per cent of this area lies in regions frost-free for less than 120 days per annum; nearly half is in regions liable to drought and therefore in need of irrigation, while in the north and north-west extensive drainage is badly needed.[2] Other large-scale land amelioration schemes require also adequate, i.e. substantial, investment: such are the liming of acid soils and the removal of boulders in the north-west; these boulders are relics of the glaciation age and their presence is becoming particularly obnoxious with the introduction of machinery. The severity of the climate in most regions makes agricultural work a seasonal occupation and turns farmers into 'unemployed' during the winter months. Machinery, too, stands unproductively idle. Large quantities of animal feed have to be stored for the animals to survive until they can be put to graze out of doors; this makes for a lower animal/acre ratio and for costlier dairy and meat production, particularly in the central and northern regions.

Over the years, agriculture has been starved of investment and this persistent neglect constitutes the second factor of the endemic crises. In 1928, when the first Five-Year Plan was inaugurated, the country possessed a total of 28,000 tractors, most of which were still privately owned. Although by 1940 their number had risen to half a million, many were put out of action during the war years, when no replacements and practically no spares were available. By 1969, i.e. nearly twenty-five years later, the total reached 1,800,000, but experts estimate that at least 2·9 million are needed to approach anywhere near the area/tractor ratio prevalent in the USA which, incidentally, possesses something like 4½ million tractors.[3] They should be replaced by new ones more frequently too. The position with trucks and lorries is not much better. Their numbers were reduced during the war, when they were often requisitioned and used for other purposes. In 1945 only 62,000 remained to service the entire rural community. Their state of repair at the time is anybody's guess. In those days machinery was concentrated in Machine-Tractor Stations (MTS), and both during and several years after the war the MTS were short of spares and technically

[2] *Voprosy ekonomiki*, 1968, No. 7, p. 51.
[3] *Voprosy ekonomiki*, 1968, No. 7, p. 49; R. W. Campbell, op. cit., p. 155. Of the total number of tractors, 905,000 belonged to collective farms and the others to state farms. The figures given for tractors in Soviet statistics are often misleading because it used to be customary to convert the actual numbers into 15 h.p. units; therefore the more powerful tractors accounted for more than one physical unit, thus swelling the total figure. The number of trucks in 1969 approached the million mark, of which collective farms owned 530,000; it was planned to produce another 155,000 p.a.

trained personnel. Much agricultural work was done manually by peasant women and older children. Men aged eighteen to forty-five had been called up and, because of heavy war losses, more than half never returned.[4] Owing to the shortage of machinery and male manpower, the village folk were often unable to complete autumn ploughing and sowing before the onset of the long Russian winter, and similar delays occurred in spring, adversely affecting crop yields. At harvest time students and urban workers came down to help. Even today, in the eastern cotton-growing republics, urban schools and universities close down for several weeks to set students free for work in the fields. Similar arrangements exist in central and northern regions to help collective farmers to lift the potato crop before the onset of frosts. Special machines are now coming into use, particularly for cotton-picking, but they are still in short supply and often too bulky to be used on smaller fields, so that much cotton-picking is still done by hand.

In general, apart from overall shortage of machinery, there is inadequate differentiation. One often reads about the wrong type of cultivators which were designed for certain regions or soils and are not appropriate under different conditions. Many models still in use are obsolete and inefficient.[5]

Lack of machinery calls for the use of greater human labour resources. Nearly one-third of the work force is still engaged in agriculture;[6] this is a very high percentage compared to the 5–15 per cent in the USA, France, Canada, and Sweden. The sex and age composition of the rural population is unfavourable because of the high proportion of older people, particularly older women. Hitherto the demographic factor has not been a major one, but, as will be shown further, it is becoming increasingly ominous.

Machinery increases output per man rather than per acre, whereas soil amelioration techniques and the use of fertilisers raise output

[4] Yu. V. Arutyunyan, *Sovetskoe krest'yanstvo v gody velikoi otechestvennoi voiny*, Moscow, 1963, p. 318 gives the following figures for able-bodied males on collective farms: in 1940 – 16,873,400; in 1945 – 6,519,000; and in 1946 (after demobilisation) – 8,161,800.
[5] *Voprosy ekonomiki*, 1968, No. 8, p. 15, and 1969, No. 12, pp. 63–6; according to *Pravda*, 13 November 1969, of the 1,400 types of machines, trailers, and other equipment, only half are being manufactured, though the others have passed tests and been certificated.
[6] According to the statistical yearbook *Narodnoye khozyaistvo SSSR v 1968 godu*, Moscow, 1969, p. 446, the numbers on collective farms were estimated at 18·1 million and on state farms at 9·1 million. However, of this total of 27·5 million people only 24·6 were actually employed in agriculture. On the other hand, if members of their families working solely on private plots were included, the total figure would approximate 30 million; the total labour force (less agricultural workers) was 76 million in 1969 (ibid., p. 548). See also Philip Grossman in *Soviet Studies*, January 1968, pp. 398–404.

per acre. The replacement of draught animals by machines and the decrease in the number of livestock at the time of collectivisation, a decrease which it took decades to make good, reduced the use of farmyard manure, while industry was not yet geared to the production of fertilisers. As a consequence, in the north-west and central regions of Russia where graincrop yields had averaged 7·2 to 7·3 quintals per hectare in Tsarist days, they were down to 5·3 to 6 quintals in 1949–53.[7] Peasants who owned cows (and nearly half of all cows were until quite recently in private hands) naturally used their manure on their garden plots, the productivity of which contrasts so strikingly with that of the collective-farm fields.

Since 1953 the Soviet government has taken various measures to raise agricultural output. Apart from the human incentive of higher purchase prices for farm produce, it hastened the development of the chemical industry. The annual production of fertiliser, which amounted to only 3 million tons in 1940, increased to 30 million tons in 1966 and should have reached 47 million tons in 1969.[8] But the use of fertilisers requires soil science experts and a wide range of fertilisers adapted to local needs. Here, as in the case of machinery, a wider choice and greater sophistication are required than the Soviet chemical industry is able to offer and, furthermore, to offer at lower prices to make them economically worth using. Discussions on quality and the appropriateness of certain remedies to particular deficiencies is only now beginning to loom large in Soviet specialised publications and it will probably take some time to translate theoretical considerations into effective practical measures.

Both the geographical factor and even the economic factor can be regarded in a sense as 'objective constraints'. Without indulging in science fiction, it may be assumed that, given time, modern science with its resourceful and powerful technology may eventually overcome drought, excessive moisture, and the barrenness of sandy or leached-out *podzol* soils. The task of transforming a marginally agricultural country into a land of plenty was unthinkable before the advent of the technological era and the building-up of a powerful industry. Yet the actual building of this industry had to be financed from the resources of agriculture. To understand the third, psychological, factor adversely affecting agricultural production, one has to look back to the prehistory of collectivisation.

In Tsarist days the greater part of the Russian peasantry and that of the present Union republics lived by subsistence farming. Surplus

[7] *Voprosy ekonomiki*, 1968, No. 8, p. 94.
[8] Brezhnev in *Pravda*, 31 October 1968. Apparently this target was not achieved, since N. K. Baibakov, chairman of *Gosplan*, spoke of 46 million tons as the 1970 target (*Pravda*, 17 December 1969).

grain to feed the towns and for export came from the large estates. These were broken up and the landowning class eliminated immediately after the Revolution. A few particularly well-run estates were transformed into model state farms (*sovkhoz*) to promote better methods of farming. When the Civil War (1918–20) came to an end, primitive peasant agriculture got back on its feet fairly quickly, but urban industry was slow to recover. The supply of manufactured goods from the towns was less than in Tsarist days and the prices were three times as high.[9] Yet the Soviet government insisted on maintaining fixed and relatively low prices for agricultural produce, with the result that peasants ceased supplying the towns with adequate quantities of foodstuffs and reverted to a mediaeval spinning-wheel economy. The Soviet government attempted to promote co-operative farming, and supplied tractors and machinery to such undertakings, but because of the inability of industry to provide machinery very few model collective farms could be organised. A way had to be found to obtain larger surpluses from the peasantry both to feed the towns and for export so as to pay for the plant equipment needed to industrialise the country.

During the economic debate which preceded the adoption of the first Five-Year Plan and centred largely on how to finance industrialisation, Bukharin suggested that the richer peasants, the so-called *kulaks*, be allowed to become well-to-do productive farmers and, through taxation, contribute to a gradual and slow industrialisation. However, this policy was too reminiscent of the measures taken by the Tsarist Minister Stolypin who, between 1906 and 1912, the year of his death at the hands of a revolutionary terrorist, had assisted some 5 million peasants to leave the village commune and settle on independent individual farms. Stolypin's aim was to create a numerous, stable, conservative-minded class of well-to-do farmers, a project which infuriated Lenin and his followers because this policy was an alternative to the revolution they were promoting; the success of Stolypin's plan would have deprived them of the support of rural masses, who were being seduced by the opportunities of becoming petty capitalist farmers.

Research carried out by a group of economists headed by Chayanov in the 1920s seemed to support the viability and satisfactory prospects of a prosperous peasant-farmer economy. However, Chayanov's findings were dismissed and Bukharin's proposals rejected as too dilatory and, above all, as contrary to the aims of socialism. They would have led to the re-emergence of the Stolypin-type petty rural capitalism, something the Party could not tolerate.

[9] V. T. Chuntulov, *Ekonomicheskaya istoriya SSSR*, Moscow, 1969, pp. 214, 237.

So forced collectivisation, 'a revolution from above' as Stalin called it, was decreed. A revolution – whether from above or below – is always directed against someone. In 1930 the 'someone' was the peasantry. The richer peasants (*kulaks*) were deprived of their homesteads and stock and deported. The others – the majority of the population – despite stubborn resistance and occasional armed rebellion, were forced into collective farms and became, as will be shown later, the depressed class of the new society.

In theory a large-scale, mechanised, scientifically-run agricultural enterprise is more productive than many small peasant holdings worked by a family and such implements as they can afford. Inevitably these implements are cheap and inefficient, such as horse-drawn ploughs or simple harvesters. That collective farming can be economically profitable and psychologically satisfying is shown by the success of truly voluntary, prosperous *kibbutzim* in Israel, though even there the younger men are said to drift eventually to more rewarding urban jobs, and the *kibbutzim* themselves are increasingly indulging in non-farming activities such as catering for tourists.

Despite allegations to the contrary, collectivisation in the USSR was merely a device for extracting the largest possible share of produce from the rural community without adequate compensation in either manufactured consumer goods or capital goods for the farms. Peasants were made to pool their land-holdings and livestock, thus forming a collective farm (*kolkhoz*). As a concession, each family was allowed to retain the land on which their cottage stood with its outbuildings and a plot not exceeding an acre. They were also allowed to keep one cow, a few pigs or sheep, and fowls. When the harvest was brought in the farm delivered a certain quota of it (usually about half) at fixed prices to state procurement agencies. Prices were low already in 1930 and were never changed until 1953, despite pre-war and wartime inflation. By that time the price paid for compulsory deliveries by the state procurement agencies had dropped to about 10 per cent of their value. The effect of inflation can be illustrated by the price of a ZIS-5 truck expressed in tons of wheat. Prior to 1941 it was equivalent to 99 tons of wheat, in 1948 to 124 tons, in 1949 to 238 tons. After the prices for agricultural produce had been raised in 1953–54, its price was equivalent to 53 tons of wheat and, after further price rises in 1958, to 20 tons.[10]

Farms could sell the rest of the produce harvested and distribute the money to the farmers as dividends, but only after having paid agricultural and income taxes, and insurance premiums, and after

[10] I. Lukinov, *Kommunist*, 1968, No. 4; English translation in *Current Digest of the Soviet Press*, 1968, Vol. 20, No. 25, p. 19.

footing the bills of the MTS, and contributing to an investment and depreciation fund. Only when all these payments had been met could the farmers share out the residue in cash and/or kind in accordance with the work done on the farm and measured in 'labour days'. The labour day was not necessarily a day's work; some types of labour being worth more, others less, than the unit. The payment for the labour day depended on the value of the harvest left over after all other obligations had been met. Peasants paid also an individual income tax on their labour-day earnings and also an agricultural tax in cash and kind on their plots and individually owned stock.

After collectivisation one of the major sources of state revenue was the difference in the price at which the state obtained produce from the collective farms and that at which it sold that produce to the urban population. Since most items underwent processing, e.g. grain was milled, sugar-beet was made into sugar, animals were slaughtered and skinned before being sold as meat, the state imposed a 'turnover tax' on each article at the time when it left the mill or the slaughterhouse, amounting to anything up to 100 per cent, if not more, of the initial outlay. Turnover tax, though levied on industrial goods, was triflingly low on producer goods, higher on consumer goods, but nothing like the tax levied on foodstuffs. In the Budget returns all revenue from turnover tax was given as a total, so that the exact share of the revenue arising from the re-sale of agricultural produce obtained from collective farms at fixed prices, which became in fact lower and lower with inflation, cannot be precisely ascertained.

In 1930 the state could provide hardly any machinery and relied on that confiscated from the *kulaks* alongside their draught animals and other stock to be the mainstay of the new farms. What machinery was available was concentrated in Machine-Tractor Stations, which undertook to do ploughing and harvesting for the farms in return for a share of the crops. The concentration of machinery in MTS served a treble purpose: (*a*) it kept essential means of production in the hands of the state; (*b*) it ensured a fuller use of machinery since MTS serviced several farms in turn; and (*c*) by charging payment in kind for the work done on the farms it secured for the state a considerable amount of agricultural produce over and above the compulsory state deliveries.[11]

[11] Payments in grain to MTS averaged 30 million tons annually and accounted for nearly half all state grain procurements. Farms which dispensed with the services of MTS had their compulsory deliveries raised by 25 per cent. See V. A. Morozov, *Trudoden', den'gi i torgovlya na sele*, 1965, p. 31; also A. Nove, 'Rural taxation in the USSR', in *Was Stalin really necessary?*, London, 1964, p. 173.

During the pre-war decade, investment in agriculture was very limited and, inevitably, more or less ceased when Germany invaded Russia in June 1941. For several years after the war all efforts were directed to repairing the devastation caused by the fighting. Whole towns with their houses, schools, factories, and power-plants had to be rebuilt; the rehabilitation of the transport system included thousands of miles of track to be made good and rolling-stock to be replaced. The country had to shoulder the astronomical costs of the armaments race resulting from the Cold War. All this expenditure took priority over agriculture.

Out of the meagre production of their low-yielding fields and underfed livestock, farms had to supply fixed quotas of compulsory state deliveries assessed in advance by provincial and district authorities, irrespective of actual results. By making assessments prior to harvest on the basis of what was known as the 'biological yield', the authorities forestalled any attempts by farmers to deliver less produce on the true or false grounds of damage to crops by weather conditions before or during harvesting. All losses were borne by the farms. The urban population and the men in the forces had to be fed and the war-devastated areas restocked with animals and seed. During the late 1940s in some districts compulsory state deliveries absorbed the entire output of collective farms and peasants subsisted somehow on the produce of their individual plots. In the north in particular there were cases where villagers were reduced to going without ordinary black bread and living on potatoes from their plots and occasional fish from local rivers.[12] Peasants fortunate enough to keep a cow struggled to obtain fodder from the farm in payment for their labour days; others could afford to keep only a goat. Private holdings and stock were taxed and, since the tax on a privately owned goat was smaller than on a cow, goats came to be known as 'Stalin's cows', for in Tsarist days goats were practically unknown in central Russia. The burden of these taxes on private auxiliary farming can be gauged from the importance of

[12] A vivid description of rural poverty can be found in Soviet fiction, for instance in F. Abramov, 'Two Winters and Three Summers', *Novy Mir*, 1968, Nos. 1–3, and in an earlier story translated into English under the title *The Dodgers* by D. Floyd, London, 1963. In a story by B. Mozhaev, 'Iz zhizni Fyodora Kuz'kina', *Novy Mir*, 1966, No. 7, p. 43, a husband and wife receive in 1953 only 62 kgs. of buckwheat for a year's work and nothing else; V. Soloukhin in a story entitled *Kaplya rosy*, 1959, mentions 46 kopeks and 3 lb. of grain per labour day in 1955 as an improvement on earlier remuneration; 46 old kopeks being equal to 4·6 present-day kopeks, i.e. something like just over 5d. Although stories describing rural poverty have been criticised as unduly pessimistic, no one has disputed the facts described as untrue or unlikely. The earliest stories revealing both poverty and arbitrary excessive demands made on collective farms were *Rayonnye budni*, written by V. Ovechkin as early as 1952.

their share in state compulsory deliveries; in 1950 they accounted for 31 per cent of all meat deliveries, 43 per cent of milk, 61 per cent of eggs, and 15 per cent of wool.[13] The outcome of the harsh conditions which persisted in rural areas was twofold. On the one hand, it led to rural depopulation; although peasants, unlike urban dwellers, are not normally issued with passports, they managed to obtain these documents, without which no one can settle in a town or obtain employment. Thus older children obtained them on the pretext of attending technical training courses in the nearest towns and in the hope of either eventually settling there or finding employment in an industrial undertaking or in transport where they would be certain of earning regular wages. Soldiers of peasant origin did not return to their villages on completing their period of military service; girls sought to marry urban workers. On the other hand, peasant families got into the habit of relying on their individual plots as a source of livelihood and shirking work for the collective as an unprofitable occupation imposed under threats of penalties. The most dreaded of the latter was the loss of the plot. The term *barshchina* (labour service formerly exacted from serfs by their lord) crept into usage. The exhortations of Party officials to work harder fell on deaf ears. Administrative measures, such as the merging of smaller *kolkhoz* into larger units, did not result in improved management. Ambitious plans to 'change nature' by widespread shelter-belt planting failed because the saplings died from drought before growing into shelter-belts. Specialists trained in agricultural sciences shirked the responsibility of work in the countryside and sought refuge in any urban office, where they were prepared to accept the most menial tasks rather than face intolerable rural conditions, responsibility for crop failure, and the risks inherent in unpredictable weather conditions such as early frosts, spring drought, and heavy rains at harvest time.

After Stalin's death, reforms were introduced to find a way out of the impasse. A dramatic rise in prices for agricultural produce decreed by the 1953 September Plenum had an immediate effect. Within five years, helped by two bumper crop harvests, total pro-

[13] I. F. Suslov, *Ekonomicheskie problemy razvitiya kolkhozov*, Moscow, 1967, reviewed in *Novy Mir*, 1968, No. 7, p. 266. Since the abolition of taxes on privately owned animals, peasants pay only individual income tax on their earnings from labour days and an agricultural tax on the plots allocated to them. In 1968 this agricultural tax varied in different republics from an average of 85 kopeks for 0·01 ha. (about 40 roubles per acre) in the RSFSR to 2 r. 20 k. on irrigated lands in the Uzbek and Tadzhik SSR (D. V. Burmistrov, *Nalogi i sboy s naseleniya v SSSR,* Moscow, 1968, p. 55). Collective farms and individual farmers have always been entitled to sell what produce they had left after all other obligations had been met on collective-farm markets, subject to a tax which in the late 1960s varied from 10 kopeks per basket of produce to one rouble per lorry-load (ibid., p. 101).

duction nearly doubled. Compulsory deliveries were replaced by agreed purchases, with excess deliveries paid at higher prices. In 1958 the machinery hitherto concentrated at the MTS was sold to the *kolkhoz*. For the first time farms were trusted with means of production other than land. The measure was a mixed blessing. The collectives had to find the money to pay for the machines and some were unable to do so. The latter were eventually transformed into state farms (*sovkhoz*). The state took over their assets and debts, consisting usually of tax or delivery arrears. For the collective farmers this meant that they now became state employees, entitled to a regular wage equal to about 60 per cent of the average industrial worker's wages, and to various welfare benefits such as old-age pensions. However, it also entailed a reduction in the size of the plots to which they were entitled. The greater part of the state's investments in agriculture in 1960–65 went to refloat the economy of these bankrupt farms. As a result, the number of collective farms (*kolkhoz*) declined by 46 per cent to 36,900, while the number of the state farms (*sovkhoz*) increased by 94 per cent to 11,700. As state farms are usually larger than *kolkhoz* nearly half of the agricultural land is now worked directly by state enterprises.

The richer farms which had bought the MTS machinery were now masters of their own fate, no longer at the mercy of the director of the local MTS, but they were not always large enough to make full use of the machinery, which sometimes stood idle. Troubles also arose over spare parts and fuel because the state, having lost the revenue from the MTS, attempted to make up for this loss by increasing the price of spares and fuel to the rural consumer.

Although with better prices for their produce collective farms were now in a position to pay farmers more for their labour days, the peasants continued to cling to their dwarf holdings and give them first priority. To induce farmers to spend more time working for the collective and less on their plots, Khrushchev initiated his campaign against these individual holdings. He claimed that collective farms were now in a position to pay adequately in money and kind for labour days, that many could make regular 'advances' instead of paying out 'dividends' only at the end of the year, or even go over to regular cash payments; therefore there was no longer any need for the peasant to have a plot or livestock and waste his time at home instead of working on the *kolkhoz* fields. From 1958 to 1961 Khrushchev made a number of speeches advocating the advantages of collectively owned herds, and appropriate pressures were put on the farmers to sell their stock, particularly the young animals, to the *kolkhoz*. The land area under plots was reduced from a total of 7·4 million hectares to 6·3 million and the number of cattle decreased from 29·2 million head to 24·1 million. As usual, there were great publicity campaigns; impossible promises were made by ambitious bureaucrats in charge of collective farms, culminating in cases where thoroughbred bulls were slaughtered to fulfil the promised norms of meat deliveries, with the consequence that cows went barren the following season. The final result of this campaign against individual agricultural activities was a fall in the production of meat, milk, and eggs, nearly 40 per cent of which had hitherto come from that source. Farmers suffered a loss of income, since they were less and less in a position to sell surplus vegetables or dairy produce on *kolkhoz* markets, while townsfolk suffered from being no longer able to purchase foodstuffs there in order to supplement those available in state-owned shops. Particularly hit were the older, retired members of the community for whom the plot was a major, if not the sole, source of income; according to the 1959 census they numbered nearly 10 million, of whom 90 per cent were women. Collective farmers, not being state employees, were not entitled to old-age pensions, with the exception of war widows whose claim to a pension was on the grounds of the husband's death on active service.

After Khrushchev's downfall his agricultural policies were reversed. All taxes on privately owned animals were repealed, workers in industrial settlements were again allowed to keep stock, and farms were ordered to include cattle-feed in payment for labour days. The new permissiveness towards individual ancillary farming contributed to the more successful production levels achieved in agriculture since 1965. The right to a plot and even help to cultivate it have been incorporated into the new Model Collective Farm Charter adopted in November 1969. Apart from the importance of subsidiary farming to every peasant family, it is now recognised that it is valuable to the urban population as well. Indeed, all towns have markets where agricultural produce brought on behalf of a *kolkhoz* or by individual peasants can be sold at uncontrolled prices, and where townsfolk buy fresher eggs, perishable vegetables, and, occasionally, better varieties of fruit grown with care and understanding by untutored but keen local gardeners.

The present drive to introduce specialised farming, even to practise monoculture on some farms, may make the produce of the plot of even greater importance to the peasant; for if he is no longer to receive payment in kind for his labour days, he will find it very difficult to obtain foodstuffs elsewhere, considering the well-nigh non-existent shopping facilities in the countryside.

The adoption of the law on land utilisation in December 1968 and a new Model Collective Farm Charter a year later must be described as a rescue operation, and one can only hope that it is not coming too late to redress forty years of mismanagement and excessive squeezing of the peasantry, with the resulting psychological rift between the peasantry and those in authority. The cause of the rift lies in the inevitable divergence of interest between two classes – an urban proletariat in need of food and a peasantry unwilling to provide it without adequate recompense – which has been exacerbated by the nature of Party dictatorship. Conflicting economic interests have been magnified into a deep psychological antagonism which for decades opposed an autocratic, arbitrary, ruling bureaucracy wielding enormous powers and a peasantry denied a say in matters concerning its livelihood and literally its survival. The bureaucrat needed speedy and spectacular results to achieve personal promotion as well as to prove the correctness of Party policy and therefore its right to leadership. To this the peasant opposed a stubborn and slothful inertia, amounting to a form of semi-conscious passive resistance, because he understood that the measures decreed from above were often agriculturally unwise, unremunerative, and even downright detrimental to his interests.

The mutual distrust began long ago in the days when the famous 25,000 industrial workers volunteered to go to the countryside to organise collectivisation. Their aims were twofold – to socialise the countryside and also to obtain food for an urban population which since the days of the Civil War was still incapable of producing an adequate amount of consumer goods to establish economically fair exchange relations with the peasantry. Devoted to their cause, the 25,000, who became chairmen of fairly large agricultural enterprises, were usually ignorant of even primitive agricultural techniques. In the hands of experienced and intelligent peasants applying their native wit and knowledge of local conditions, traditional techniques had yielded tolerably efficient results, yet a local successful farmer was the last person to be trusted by Party officialdom. Indeed, he might attempt to favour his fellow villagers, conceal part of the harvest in order to allocate more generous payments for labour days, or put the interests of the farm before those of the state. It was therefore deemed preferable to have reliable Party men from some industrial centre to act as *kolkhoz* chairmen. To remedy their ignorance, orders to plough, sow, and reap at the right time and in the right way were sent out by Party and government authorities from district and provincial towns, by men with bookish knowledge often unaware of actual local conditions. Some, indeed, were better versed in Marxist theory than in soil science and agricultural techniques; others may have graduated from agricultural institutes situated in Moscow, Leningrad, or some other major town far removed from the countryside which they controlled from afar.

There came thus into existence a bureaucracy completely divorced from the daily life of the peasants, anxious to carry out orders even when those orders were detrimental to the peasant communities. Such were 'voluntary supplementary deliveries', or the wholesale and indiscriminate enforcement of changing fashions in agricultural science. Two notorious cases may serve as examples. A well-known agricultural specialist of American extraction, V. R. Williams (Vil'yams), had advocated ley farming. In a country short of fertiliser the periodic sowing of fields to perennial grasses helps maintain soil fertility. Evidently this is not an intensive method of farming, for every so often high-yielding cereal crops must give way to less valuable grasses usable only for cattle-feed. In fertile black-soil regions the system was somewhat wasteful. In an endeavour to increase the production of cereals, ley farming was banned throughout the country, even in districts where it had proved its worth. More modern intensive forms of cultivation were decreed, but no provisions were made for the supply of fertilisers which are an essential and integral part of intensive farming. In many regions the results of the changeover proved very disappointing.

In the late 1950s and early 1960s Khrushchev launched his campaign for the growing of maize. Maize is an extremely productive crop; its yield per acre may be six times as high as that of wheat, provided conditions are favourable. In central and northern Russia maize failed to mature or even to grow; at best it had to be cut green to be made into silo; at worst the fields had to be hastily reploughed in the middle of summer and sown to low-yielding spring rye. Despite the obvious waste of human labour and land area, the bureaucrats enforced this ill-considered measure until the downfall of Khrushchev.

There is yet another area where Party principles and the Party's mistrust of the peasantry affected adversely, if not actual production, at least a better use of the produce and, more generally, the standard of living of the peasants which, in its turn, is now reflected in an ominous flight from the land. In many parts of the USSR the winter is long; peasants are in a sense unemployed. This is the reason why in bygone days peasants turned to various crafts in wintertime. Apart from a variety of wooden household articles from spoons and buckets to carts and sleighs, pottery and home-woven textiles, some regions were famous for other articles. Thus the villages of the Tula province, south-west from Moscow, were renowned for locks, cutlery, and samovars; villages of the province of Vladimir for lacemaking, woodcarving, and ikon-painting;

Mstera and Palekh were especially famous in this respect.[14] On ideological grounds the Soviet government has always discouraged cottage industries as a survival of the past, considering that they should be replaced by modern large-scale industries.

Immediately after the war, when destruction on a colossal scale had to be made good, many collective farms ran small brick-works, pottery kilns, and woodworking, and even canning and milling, enterprises. Often these proved more profitable than agricultural work, and farms sold some of their manufactured goods to cover losses incurred in their agricultural activities. The authorities began to fear that industrial enterprise might deflect farmers from their task of producing food for the country. Furthermore, a proliferation of small-scale local industries could give a measure of economic self-sufficiency to the countryside and weaken central control. In the late 1950s and early 1960s these enterprises were closed down one by one. Recently, however, opportunities for allowing small-scale local industries have been reconsidered. Food-processing industries are now to be set up in rural areas and owned jointly by the state and one or several local farms, which would supply the produce for processing. Such arrangements might reduce the acute need for adequate storage facilities in urban areas. Annually in the Caucasus and the Central Asian republics delicate fruit, like peaches, goes bad for lack of canning and refrigerating facilities or adequate transport to carry them fast enough to the densely populated areas of European Russia.

Measures to 'overcome the contradiction between town and country' are certainly on the agenda, but the backlog is tremendous, both in the economic and psychological fields.

Thus, in the economic field, the directives of the Twenty-third Congress envisaged a sum of 41,000 million roubles to be invested in agriculture by the state over the period 1966–70, while some economists speak of a total of 220,000 to 250,000 million roubles, of which 95,000 million should come from state funds and the balance be found by the farms themselves.[15] So even today the needs of agriculture outstrip resources available for investment. Moreover, inadequate allocations are not being properly used, and plans for the manufacture and delivery of machines and fertilisers during the 1965–70 period, after lagging behind schedule, have had to be officially reduced in 1970.

The new mood, too, of obtaining the best return per rouble

[14] Their craftsmanship was eventually recognised and they now specialise in the production of miniature decorated, black lacquer boxes and cigarette cases for export.
[15] V. Venzher, *Kolkhoznyi stroi na sovremennom etape*, Moscow, 1966, p. 84.

invested may also have some undesirable side-effects. The best returns are likely to be from investment in the better farms, and since the latter are in a position to invest more themselves, there may arise an even greater discrepancy between richer and poorer farms, with the richer growing richer and the poorer growing poorer. The present differentiation in prices, with higher prices paid to farms in climatically less favoured zones, is apparently not adequate. In March 1965 the USSR was subdivided into six zones, but, within the same zone, soil, moisture, and other natural conditions vary substantially and zonal prices are far too crude a method for equalising earnings. It was suggested that it might be preferable to draw up a detailed cadastre of lands and charge differential rents for use of land instead of levying revenue by underpaying farms for their output, as has been done for so long. However, recent legislation has reiterated that collective farms are granted land free of charge for agricultural use.

The problem of agricultural prices is an extremely thorny one the world over. It has been much abused in the past when, for instance, the Central Asian republics were made to grow cotton and were paid for cotton in wheat on a ton for ton basis. Even Stalin protested against such 'terms of trade', and later the Central Asian republics benefited considerably from better and eventually even very favourable prices for cotton. Since 1953 prices for agricultural produce have been raised several times, yet were still not economically adequate in dairy-farming and stock-raising. A paradoxical situation arose, therefore, on state farms. Their sales of produce to the state procurement agencies did not cover their costs – which included regular wages to their workers and employees – and these agricultural enterprises had to be subsidised by the state. Only in recent years have measures been taken to make them adopt *khozraschet* methods, i.e. make them balance their accounts so that even if not profitable they are self-sufficient. Indeed, prices paid for excess deliveries to both state and collective farms approximate world prices. As a consequence of the new policy towards agriculture, revenue from the resale of agricultural produce has decreased and the state is actually making a loss on the resale of meat and dairy produce to the urban population. It has also given up its policy of overcharging collective farms when selling them machinery and fuel, and abolished all rural surcharges on industrial goods sold to the peasantry; this was a kind of additional indirect tax which brought the state 400 million roubles per annum.

In 1966, collective farmers became entitled to a guaranteed, though unspecified, wage, which the peasant can supplement by earnings from his plot. These are said to provide him with approximately one-third of his income. Wages are no longer paid out of the residue left after all other charges, such as taxes, insurance premiums, and payments to the accumulation and social security funds, have been met, but are regarded as the first priority on the collective farm's gross income. To pay a guaranteed wage to their members, collective farms are entitled to borrow money from banks. Cases have been reported of farms unable to meet their obligations and of banks refusing further credits to those which had already run up large overdrafts. The government has had to accept a situation in which the earnings of collective farmers rose faster than those of urban workers, despite the former's low productivity. Between 1958 and 1968 daily rates of pay doubled, reaching an average of 3 roubles 25 kopeks. There is a possibility that the target of 3 roubles 60 kopeks set for 1970 may be further raised and that on both state and collective farms the daily pay will reach 4·5 to 5 roubles. At the moment, owing to geographical conditions, discrepancies in pay are still considerable. In several national republics collective farmers have been earning more than state-farm workers, while in other regions their earnings were still only 50 to 60 per cent of the average state-farm wages. The complexity of the problem of remuneration can be illustrated by the fact that bonuses established for industrial workers in the far north-east have been extended to state-farm workers in those regions. Furthermore, averages are apt to conceal wide pay differentials. Thus a contributor to *Literaturnaya Gazeta* in December 1967 described a collective farm where the chairman was paid a monthly salary of 300 roubles, the chief agronomist 170 roubles, a milkmaid 90 roubles, and the lowest paid members of the farm received only 30 roubles per month. It should be borne in mind that the tax system favours higher-paid workers. Wages below the state minimum of 60 roubles per month are exempt from income tax, while the upper rate of taxation is 13 per cent, payable on incomes of 100 roubles and above. Recent sociological surveys of rural districts show very marked differentials in income between rural state employees, skilled manual workers in agriculture, and the still large section of very poorly rewarded unskilled *kolkhozniks*.[16]

Apart from better pay, working conditions are to be improved by introducing two-shift work in stock-raising. This should compensate for the physically heavy labour involved in the carrying and distribution of feed and water, and the milking and other activities still done by hand on the majority of both collective and state farms. In the long run it will be necessary to face the expense

[16] Yu. V. Arutyunyan, *Opyt sotsiologicheskogo izucheniya sela*, Moscow, 1968, pp. 49–50.

involved in laying on water supplies and extending the electricity grid to the countryside. Although nearly 80 per cent of Soviet farms have access to electricity, it is usually available for lighting purposes only. Much of it comes from very small and inefficient local plant. This was partly inevitable because of long distances between widely scattered villages, but is also the result of Stalin's policy of deliberately prohibiting collective farms from drawing on industrial power supplies.

On the Road to Modernisation

Recent legislation such as the law entitled 'Fundamentals of Land Legislation of the USSR and the Union Republics', enacted in December 1968, and the 'Model Collective Farm Charter', adopted at the end of November 1969 by the Third[17] Congress of Collective Farm Representatives, as well as the setting-up of an All-Union Collective Farm Council, are the culmination of the piecemeal measures taken since 1965 to improve agricultural production and also raise the standard of living of the peasantry.

Both Acts reaffirm provisions already present in the directives of the Twenty-third Party Congress regarding land amelioration measures designed to mitigate adverse geographical conditions such as drought, soil acidity, or excessive moisture. Both are also concerned with the conservation of natural resources and the protection of land from wasteful deforestation, soil erosion, damage by water pollution, and the encroachment of industries, transportation (including roads and airfields), and urban construction, which have been taking over agricultural land at a disquieting rate. Thus in the course of the last ten years 1·5 million hectares of arable land were expropriated for building purposes. Particularly wasteful was the flooding of vast areas to form lakes for regulating water-supply in hydropower construction. Henceforth the expropriation of agricultural land for industry, transport, construction, and other needs unrelated to agriculture will be allowed in exceptional cases only; expropriation of irrigated as well as arable lands, or land planted to orchards and vineyards for non-agricultural uses, will require express permission from the Council of Ministers of the individual republic. The detailed land cadastre in the process of completion is designed to give information on land use, the quality of the soil, any amelioration work done, and the economic value of each area. Enterprises obtaining land from other users must pay compensation, and in the case of collective farms any land transfer must be agreed to by a farm's general meeting.

Both enactments are designed to ensure that good use is made of

[17] The previous Congress of Collective Farmers was held in 1935.

land, and its fertility increased by appropriate agronomic techniques. Both confirm that land is granted to users free of charge but on certain conditions, one of which is land amelioration by users. Other provisions of recent land legislation are concerned with raising food production and defining the rights and obligations of land users in general and collective farms in particular. The importance of ancillary farming on individual plots gets full recognition and henceforth, apart from collective farmers and state-farm workers, other employees are entitled to small plots of land for personal use, including rural doctors, teachers, veterinary staff, railway-workers, various other employees, and pensioners. Without contributing to the marketable surplus of foodstuffs they are likely to satisfy the needs of their families in vegetables, eggs, and milk, instead of drawing on the national food pool; this will alleviate indirectly the shortage of shopping facilities in rural areas.

As already mentioned, collective farms are granted land free of charge on certain conditions; the two major ones are their obligation to partake in land-amelioration work, such as irrigation, liming, draining marshland, or clearing scrub and undergrowth, according to local conditions; and to deliver on a contractual basis specified quotas of agricultural produce in amounts and at prices negotiated for several years in advance within the requirements of the national economic plan. No arbitrary demands for additional deliveries are to be made, though farmers will be cajoled and encouraged to supply over-plan quotas payable by the state procurement agencies at higher prices.

The Model Collective Farm Charter puts on a more secure legal basis both the relations of collective farms to the state and those of collective farmers to their enterprise.

Considerable autonomy is granted to farms in the conduct of their farming activities. Provided they meet their delivery quotas, district authorities are no longer to send detailed instructions as to how much land is to be sown to what crop or what numbers of cattle the farm is to keep. Very considerable powers are vested in the general meeting or, in the case of large farms comprising several villages, meetings of representatives. These must be held regularly, perhaps four times a year, or otherwise, at the discretion of the meeting itself. Special meetings can be called if two-thirds of the members request it. The general meeting adopts its own charter which must conform to the Model but include details deliberately left unspecified in the Model; some of these are extremely important but difficult to implement, namely those relating to welfare provisions. The general meeting elects the chairman (for three years), the board of management, and the inspection commission, and is entitled to revoke these officials if they do not prove satisfactory. It ratifies important decisions made by the chairman or the board, such as the hiring and firing of specialists, admitting new members, accepting resignations, or expelling an idle or troublesome member. Team leaders (*brigadir*) are also to be elected, not appointed by management. On the important and much abused way of conducting elections, the Charter gives no definite ruling and allows voting at the discretion of the meeting by secret ballot or, as previously, by open vote. A charter, once drawn up, must be sent up for registration to the executive committee of the district Soviet.

The Charter endorses the right of a member and his family to a plot of land not to exceed 0·5 hectare (or 0·2 hectare of irrigated land) and to a guaranteed monthly wage in cash and kind in accordance with the quantity and quality of work done. Norms of work and rates of pay are to be fixed by the farm management. Payments for labour days are a first charge on the farm's gross income. Article 43 details the maximum of livestock allowed (one cow, two hogs, etc., small variations being permitted according to regions); a member of the farm, especially if disabled, is entitled to obtain help from the farm to plough up his plot, and also fodder for his animals (in payment for labour days) and pasture rights. Additional premiums for good work, holidays with pay, and leave for pregnant women are mentioned, though no fast rules are laid down for their implementation. Rewards and punishments for loafing or damage to property are also largely at the discretion of the collective farm. In this respect the provisions of the Charter may be described as indicative planning, for they leave considerable latitude to individual farms. Not all farms are rich enough to implement generous welfare provisions, so in this respect the Charter merely reflects the aspirations of the rural community. However, an important additional decree makes it mandatory on farms to contribute 2·4 per cent of their pay-roll to a central fund from which old-age pensions and other benefits will be payable at a flat rate to all collective farmers entitled to them. This is an improvement on the 1966 scheme which, while granting old-age and disablement pensions to collective farmers, made the actual rates dependent on the contributions of individual farms towards the central fund. Collective farms are also to encourage further education among their members, which may mean that managements will have to release members and provide them with passports on request.

Most important is the right of collective farms to run enterprises for processing their produce. They can do so on their own or jointly with one or two other farms, or by creating a mixed enterprise in partnership with the state. In each case the share of the capital invested remains the property of each partner. This is an important measure in several respects. First, it will rationalise the use of labour because, as already mentioned, in winter peasants often have nothing to do. It will channel local initiative and collective-farm funds into building small canning, refrigerating, milling, cheesemaking, or other enterprises. Apart from providing work in the off-season to farmers and becoming an additional source of income, a proliferation of local plants will decentralise and augment the provision of storage and refrigeration facilities, which are generally inadequate in towns. The 'agro-industrial enterprises' envisaged are a form of vertical integration of farm and industry and, by bringing industry, even if on a small scale, they will contribute to the urbanisation of the countryside. Ever since collectivisation, Party leaders have cherished the dream of 'overcoming the contradiction of town and country' by replacing small, scattered, old-fashioned villages by what Khrushchev in 1951 called agro-towns (*agro-gorod*). In the 1930s, at the time of collectivisation, or even in the 1950s, the Soviet Union was not sufficiently industrialised to extend urban facilities to rural areas. This would have meant building multi-storeyed houses, laying on water supplies, sewerage, electricity, public transport, as well as erecting school buildings, hospitals, clubs, and libraries. A precondition for such a transformation of the countryside would have been the concentration and resettlement of the population in semi-urban centres. When Khrushchev put forward his plans for agro-towns, all he could suggest was just herding peasant huts together away from their cowsheds and garden plots without compensating them for the move by any tangible advantages; moreover, they had to travel longer distances to the fields in the absence of good roads and adequate transport. The project was soon abandoned, though it has been recurrently discussed since.

At the time of collectivisation, every village was usually transformed into one collective farm. Later, collective farms were amalgamated and most of them nowadays encompass several villages. Naturally, the largest in any one group of villages has become the seat of the farm's management and when farms bought the machinery, formerly held by Machine-Tractor Stations, hangars, sheds, and tractor repair shops tended to be built there. A better case exists now to increase these settlements at the expense of the other villages. The idea of multi-storeyed houses is unlikely to appeal to villagers, who prefer to live in one-storey or two-storey houses with their plots and cowsheds close at hand, but the increasing numbers of the rural intelligentsia – teachers, doctors, nurses, planners, and accountants – might prefer the urban type of blocks of flats. Soviet urban blocks of flats are designed to be self-contained communities of 2,000 to 6,000 inhabitants, with a nursery, a first-aid post, and some communal utilities like a laundry on the premises. If an industrial enterprise, run fully or partially by the collective farm, is also situated within the boundaries of the settlement, the latter is likely to grow and become an agrotown.

The major stumbling-block on the road to rural industrialisation, modernisation, and urbanisation is the shortage of equipment and construction materials, as well as the absence of good roads between villages. Complaints have been voiced that even when processing plants are built they run into difficulties with the supply of tins or glass jars for bottling. So it will probably take many years to achieve the transformation of the countryside. However, measures taken since 1965 and consolidated by recent legislation are in line with many desiderata of the peasantry and should transform it from a depressed semi-serf class attached to the glebe into a class of rural citizens of a new type to which the word 'peasant' would no longer apply.

The delay in convening the Third Congress of Collective Farmers (its calling had been expected for the last four or five years) and the number of foreign guests from *Comecon* and developing countries, as well as from Finland, France, Italy, and Yugoslavia, who attended it, testify to its importance as a breakthrough in the intended modernisation of the countryside. Of the 4,541 delegates to the Congress, 48 per cent had secondary or higher education; more than half were members of the CPSU; ministers of agriculture of all the Union republics were present; there were 859 chairmen and 2,250 members of collective-farm management boards; over half the delegates were members of the local Soviet, and 349 were members of the Supreme Soviet of the USSR or of their own republic. A few belonged to the rural intelligentsia and were by profession accountants, librarians, and nursery-school teachers; among the rank-and-file collective farmers many, at one time or other, had been awarded the title of Hero of Socialist Labour. This hand-picked élite reflected the shape of things to come – a countryside no longer inhabited by traditional peasants, but one of large-scale farming enterprises; indeed, enterprises which were aiming at becoming agricultural-industrial *kombinats*.

Yet the difficulties in the path of such a radical change are numerous and the present Soviet leadership, with its pragmatic approach to economic affairs, is prepared to tolerate and even encourage any small-scale private initiative that can make a contribution to help feed the country; thus by granting plots even to people not otherwise directly concerned with farming, it is making use of their leisure-time as well as their initiative.

In all advanced countries where a considerable peasant population has survived, as in the case of France, it is becoming evident that its complete elimination is only a matter of time. To become efficient and remunerative, farming must be transformed into an industry. It will require a much smaller labour force, but one intent on innovations, skilled in the handling of machinery, expert in the use of the right fertilisers for a given soil, and expert in the choice of scientifically selected seeds, as well as in the degree of moisture needed on irrigated lands.

The exodus of the younger and more educated in search of secure wages and a socially more satisfying life may thwart the plans to modernise, specialise, and industrialise agriculture. The traditional outflow of labour from rural areas is more disquieting in the USSR than elsewhere because of the recent steep fall in the birth-rate and the demographic problems that it may bring in its wake.

Chapter 6

Demographic Trends

THE SOVIET POPULATION CENSUS scheduled for 1969 was postponed until 1970 on the grounds that in drafting the return-forms the statisticians in charge had not included certain items of great importance for the forecasting of demographic trends.

Demographic projections are essential to improve the planning of labour resources and, in this connection, the provision of educational and training facilities; they are no less essential for the planning of welfare services, in particular old-age pensions. The charge of old-age pensions on the state Budget rose sharply after 1966 when collective farmers were granted pension rights. This suddenly swelled the previous total of 21 million pensioners by an additional 11 million, bringing the total to 32 million, or 14 per cent of the population, and the overall figure increased to 41 million in 1970, of whom 12,300,000 were collective farmers.

The present preoccupation with demography, the study of which had long been neglected in the Soviet Union, has arisen in connection with a disquieting fall in the birth-rate. For the first time in her history, the USSR is confronted with the problem of an ageing population. The decline in the birth-rate began in the early 1960s for reasons that are still obscure, and there is little likelihood, if any, that the trend will be reversed in the 1970s, when the larger post-war cohorts will reach the age of parenthood.

Formerly, fluctuations in the birth-rate were always the result of well-defined disastrous events; such were – closely following upon each other – World War I, the Revolution, the Civil War, and the 1921 famine, which they brought in their wake. After increasing between 1924 and 1929, when the country was getting back on its feet and material production was rising to pre-Revolution levels, the birth-rate fell again from the figure of 4·2 per cent, which it had reached, to under 3 per cent as a result of collectivisation, the liquidation of the *kulaks* as a class, and the ensuing famine years. It rose once more in the late 1930s to about 3·5 per cent, possibly as a result of the ban on abortions, and dropped very sharply during World War II. Demobilisation did not bring about any 'baby boom' similar to that in Britain and the USA, because too many potential fathers did not return from the battlefields. Nevertheless, a fairly steady 2·5 per cent birth-rate persisted even after 1955 when abortions were legalised. However, after 1960 the decline set in.

The decline is disquieting because the small cohorts born in 1942–46, who should now be the most fertile groups of the population, seem to be having very small families for no obvious reasons. Indeed, the standard of living is rising, there have been no widespread famines since 1946–47, and vast rehousing schemes are being steadily implemented. Admittedly, the new housing-blocks are not conducive to large families because of the smallness of the standard two-room accommodation, but other factors may be also at work. With the death-rate remaining fairly stable, the overall natural increase of the population has fallen from an average of 1·76 per cent in the 1950s to 1·07 per cent in 1967 for the Soviet Union as a whole. It is lowest in Moscow, Leningrad, and the Baltic republics (0·5 per cent), not much higher elsewhere, and fairly high only in Azerbaidzhan and the Central Asian republics (3·5 per cent), where Muslim tradition still favours early marriage and large families.

The overall sex structure of the Soviet population is unsatisfactory. Since the early days of the Revolution the number of women has exceeded that of men. The first census taken after the Revolution, in 1926, revealed that there were 5 million more women than men in the USSR, mainly as a result of World War I and the Civil War. The next census taken in 1939 showed an even greater discrepancy, with an excess of 7 million women. These figures may reflect the loss of life during collectivisation and the political purges of the late 1930s. The greatest discrepancy – 20 million more women than men – shown in the 1959 census was a direct result of military losses during World War II.[1] The balance is being slowly restored, with more elderly women dying off, while among children born since 1945 the proportion of boys and girls is fairly equal.

Increased longevity, combined with a falling birth-rate, involves the state in a proportionately increasing outlay on pensions. Expressed in more general terms, it means that at the present time every hundred productively employed adults (men and women) support eighty-six non-productive dependants (children and old people), as compared to seventy-four in 1954. Hence a growing desire to make use of the labour of older people, particularly since retiring age in the Soviet Union is sixty for men and fifty-five for women. Moreover, there are reasons to believe that quite a number of old folk are, in fact, at work, but in an individual capacity, and

---

[1] It was also a result, though obviously to a lesser extent, of the high death-rate among the deportees and labour camp inmates whose numbers remain a strictly guarded secret, but may have run into several millions.

so do not contribute to the general pool of labour. This is certainly happening in the countryside. So one of the questions in the January 1970 census return-forms seeks to find out the conditions that would enable people working in their homes or on their plots to join the labour force. Another question is designed to help elucidate the size and directions of internal spontaneous migration, which is disrupting governmental plans for transferring labour resources to the areas particularly short of manpower.

Owing to the historical development of the country, the population of what is now the Soviet Union is spread very unevenly. Sixty per cent of the population occupy only 10 per cent of the land area. At the other end of the scale, 30 per cent of the total area is inhabited by 1·2 per cent of the population. The most densely populated regions are in and around Moscow and also the Ukrainian part of the *Donbas* and the Fergana valley (Uzbekistan), renowned for its fertility and mineral resources; these areas add up to only 0·5 per cent of the country, yet contain 10 per cent of the population. At the same time 80 per cent of the country's mineral wealth appears to be in Siberia and the far north-east, i.e. the provinces of Magadan, Kolyma, and the Chukotka. Governmental endeavours to channel migration to accord with planned development of this natural wealth are being thwarted by unrelenting individual initiative to move in the opposite direction. The northern regions of the European part of the RSFSR and even sparsely populated western Siberia are losing inhabitants to the more attractive and already over-populated south, in particular the Ukraine, northern Caucasus, Moldavia, and the Central Asian republics. Administrative controls designed to prevent the unplanned growth of towns are circumvented. The great cultural and industrial centres, such as Moscow, Leningrad, and Kiev, are irresistible magnets of attraction. Rural youth is leaving the countryside to the tune of one million a year. Indeed, nearly half the school population in urban lower vocational schools consists of pupils from rural areas.

The phenomenon of mass migration is not new. Much of the history of Russia can be explained in terms of migration and colonisation. Migratory movements are currently observed in western Europe, where the south-east of Britain and the Midlands are attracting migrants from Scotland, northern England, and even from India and Pakistan. In Italy the movement is from the eroded south to the Po valley and the industrial centres of Milan, Turin, etc. The millions of East Germans who moved to the Ruhr and the Rhineland were motivated by economic as well as political reasons. But in a country with a planned economy, spontaneous large-scale migration disrupts the planned development of natural resources, particularly when the latter are located in climatically unfavourable regions, often north of the Arctic Circle, such as the Norilsk nickel-mines, the Kolyma gold-fields, or the diamond-mines of Yakutiya.

The concern over demographic trends is threefold. First of all, an ageing population places a heavier burden on a decreasing number of breadwinners who have to support a growing number of elderly dependants. If the cohorts of teenagers who annually join the labour force go on diminishing, the position may further deteriorate at a time when new automatic factories seek to engage younger workers because the young are better educated and also because work in such plants, while physically less demanding, requires a more sustained effort of attention and a faster speed of perception, understanding, and reaction, all of which decline with age. Secondly, the problem of adequate labour supply in less favoured regions may become even more acute and the development of the natural wealth of Siberia and the far north-east will be further hampered by shortage of manpower. Thirdly, the persistent flight from the land is draining the countryside of its most productive age-groups, which are only too readily absorbed by industrial enterprises unable to recruit adequate numbers of urban school-leavers.

In order to stabilise or reverse the present decline in birth-rate, Soviet demographers are attempting to discover the causes which are bringing it about. Research on the problem has been started by the University of Moscow setting up a department (*kafedra*) of demography under the chairmanship of V. Perevedentsev, the author of several studies on Siberian manpower problems. One of his suggested remedies is to replace the present very inadequate family allowances by full-scale wages payable to women who withdraw from productive work to rear a family.[2]

The financial cost of such drastic measures would be very high indeed, though they would certainly create a new attitude to parenthood. The Research Institute of the Central Statistical Administration of the USSR has made rough estimates of the loss incurred by the country when a woman withdraws from work to rear a

[2] Family allowances are paid only to larger families in accordance with a decree passed in November 1947. A lump sum of 20 r. is payable on the birth of the third child; 65 r. for the fourth child, followed by a monthly allowance of 4 r. for the following 4 years; 85 r. and a monthly allowance of 6 r. for the fifth child; 100 r. and a monthly allowance of 7 r. for the sixth; 125 r. and an allowance of 10 r. for the ninth and tenth; and for the eleventh and any following, 250 r. and a monthly allowance of 15 r. Since the monthly allowance comes to an end when the child is five years old, a large family seldom benefits from more than two or three allowances simultaneously. For the sake of comparison, it should be remembered that the minimum wage of an adult worker is 60 r. per month.

family or, conversely, the expenditure sustained by the state if she has her children brought up in a state-subsidised nursery while staying at work. In the case of the very qualified and, therefore, valuable work of highly educated mothers, it would apparently pay to retain their labour, whereas in the case of less specialised female labour the state's outlay on places in child institutions would cancel out the value of the labour contributed. The adoption of extremely generous child allowances in France after World War II reversed the nearly century-old decline of the French birth-rate. However, the USSR could hardly afford a similar scale of allowances, for this would absorb 25 per cent of the monies earmarked in the Soviet Budget (in 1965) for all cultural and welfare measures.[3] On the other hand, less generous allowances might have little impact on parental behaviour.

At the other end of the scale, various proposals are being made to retain older workers in production. Some institutions, in particular the Institute of Gerontology of the Academy of Medical Sciences of the USSR, have been conducting research into the physical capacity for work among older people, the frequency of absenteeism due to ill-health, growing time-reaction, and consequent loss of speed and dexterity in manual operation, and other aspects of senescence. The economic aspect has not been overlooked. According to present legislation, old-age pensioners lose their pension if employed full-time for more than two months per year. However, in some industries suffering from labour shortages, pensioners are entitled to draw up to 50 and even 100 per cent of their pension when gainfully employed; as a result their income may be greater than that of their younger workmates, who come to feel that *they* are underpaid, which causes friction in enterprises employing young and old. As is usual in other countries too, highly-paid people prefer to continue working as long as possible, since retirement may mean a considerable loss of income – in fact, anything up to two-thirds of their former earnings – while the loss to low-paid workers retiring on the average standard pension may be no more than 10 per cent of their former wages.

The shortage of labour which may eventually result from the present decline in the birth-rate will affect the two areas where such a shortage is already being felt, namely Siberia and the far north-east, and also the agriculturally marginal rural areas of European Russia, i.e. the northern and central non-black-soil regions.

Since the middle 1950s when convict labour-camps were dis-

[3] V. Perevedentsev in *Literaturnaya Gazeta*, 20 November 1968. A. Ya. Kvasha in *Izuchenie vosproizvodstva naseleniya*, 1968, pp. 73–6; this is Vol. 14 of the series 'Uchenye zapiski po statistike'.

banded and deportees began to return home, the number of people leaving Siberia has exceeded that of new arrivals. Western Siberia was particularly affected. In the period 1956–60, for every hundred people going to western Siberia the following numbers moved out:

To –
The Ukraine	128	Kazakhstan	163
Transcaucasia	141	Moldavia	194
Central Asia	141	Baltic republics	230[4]

Various calculations have been made regarding the number of immigrants needed to develop the vast resources of Siberia and the north-east during the 1961–80 period; a fairly conservative estimate by the Institute of Economics and Organisation of Industrial Production of the Siberian branch of the Academy of Sciences of the USSR puts the number at 5 million.

At present nearly a quarter of new arrivals to Siberia are graduates from various establishments of higher education or from technical and vocational schools, who are compelled by law to spend three to four years in any job to which they may be assigned. These years of work, though paid at normal rates, are regarded as a kind of repayment for the training and education received at public expense. These types of immigrants seldom settle for good in the places to which they have been posted. At the end of the appointed time they either return home or make their way to one of the climatically more attractive national republics (excepting Belorussia). The growth of Siberian towns has been made possible not by any influx of immigrants from other regions of the USSR but by that of villagers from the Siberian countryside, which is increasingly losing its sparse population to the growing towns of Siberia. Immigrants from southern regions such as the Ukraine, Moldavia, Transcaucasia, and the Central Asian republics find acclimatisation extremely difficult. Usually they return home, and sometimes induce natives of Siberia to seek better economic and climatic conditions under the milder skies of the southern and western national republics. Considering that the state spends anything from one hundred to 500 roubles on costs of transport and settlement per migrant,

[4] According to M. Ya. Sonin in *Struktura narodnogo khozyaistva SSSR*, edited by A. I. Notkin, Moscow, 1967, p. 250. Apparently these figures are taken from a study by V. Perevedentsev, *Sovremennaya migratsiya naseleniya Zapadnoi Sibiri*, Novosibirsk, 1965, p. 38. In a more recent book by Perevedentsev entitled *Migratsiya naseleniya i trudovye problemy Sibiri*, Novosibirsk, 1966, p. 93, table 41, slightly different figures are given, but the overall trend is the same.

the financial losses occasioned by failure to retain the newcomers have been variously estimated at 2–3 billion roubles per annum.[5]

In the present state of human civilisation harsh climatic conditions are unlikely to be altered, but standards of living might be improved by the provision of housing, modern heating systems, educational and cultural facilities such as nurseries, schools, libraries, cinemas, theatres, and medical services. It is now admitted that they should be provided on a more generous scale than the usual 'norms' per head of population. With people scattered over huge distances the 'norm' of hospital beds per thousand population may mean in fact travelling hundreds of miles to the nearest hospital or maternity home.

The decree of 26 September 1967 has reinstated and extended the system of bonus payments above normal wages for workers in remote regions; formerly a 15 per cent bonus was paid to workers only in the Far North, and this was abolished in 1960; now workers in many parts of Siberia and the Far East will be entitled to bonuses, which can amount to considerably more than 15 per cent for workers staying over longer periods at the same place.

Unfortunately, much of the extra pay is absorbed by expenditure on fuel, warm clothing, and the higher price of foodstuffs imported from more southerly regions. In other words, pay increases do not remove the need for state-financed housing as well as medical, educational, and cultural facilities. Actual building is difficult and costly because, apart from the shortness of the building season, any construction under permafrost conditions raises numerous problems. Metals at low temperatures become brittle, and in the laying of pipes for sewerage or water supply one has to reckon with the stresses and strains to which pipes are subjected by seasonal swelling and hardening of the soil. Building materials and machinery have to be hauled over long distances in the absence of railway or road communications. Transport is mainly by river craft or on sleigh as in former days. Air transport is developing, but liable to be disrupted by the severity of winter frosts, gale-force winds, and snowstorms.

The usual answer to a shortage of labour is the mechanisation of work processes. However, much of the machinery used for mining and road-building, having been designed for the more temperate climate of European Russia, is unsuited to arctic conditions. Furthermore, it suffers all too often from being handled by inadequately skilled workers, many of whom have volunteered to come to the unhospitable north because they are by nature drifters

[5] S. G. Prociuk, 'The manpower problem in Siberia', *Soviet Studies*, October 1967, pp. 190–210.

and flitters who have not adapted to their former occupations or have been repeatedly dismissed from their jobs, or even, without being actual convicts, have been banished from their home towns for drunkenness and hooliganism under the anti-parasite laws.

Since 1961 the Siberian branch of the Academy of Sciences of the USSR has been conducting surveys of migratory movements to and from Siberia and also within Siberia, i.e. between its various regions and between its rural and urban areas; it has made estimates of the high cost occasioned by excessive labour turnover, characteristic of Siberian industries, and the effect of wage differentials. A number of sociological studies have been published testifying to a desire to put the manpower problems on a rational basis instead of resorting to forcible Stalinist measures.

Essentially these rational measures amount to raising the standards of living of immigrants both by higher wages and even more by providing the population with better housing, more nurseries and schools, and cheaper food (subsidising its transport instead of charging the cost of transport to the consumer); and by setting up as far as possible light industries which could employ female labour in towns where men are employed in mining and heavy metallurgy. Hitherto the lack of jobs for women on the one hand and that of nurseries on the other has resulted in women spending their time looking after their own children and households, which includes growing vegetables on private garden plots. This is an important activity, because fruit and vegetables are practically unobtainable in Siberian state shops. Merely to raise wages might not be conducive to permanent settlement; it would simply encourage men to come as temporary workers, save on their wages (which they have little opportunity to spend anyhow, because of the scarcity of consumer goods in these remote places), and return home with their savings.

The cost of a vast and elaborate programme for improving living conditions is obviously very great. According to some economists it could be achieved by diverting a fraction of the GNP allocated to the overall rise in living standards and concentrating that fraction on a vast Siberian programme. Can the Soviet government delay the improvement of living standards nearer home in the long-settled, densely populated regions, including the national republics, for the sake of developing Siberia? In any case, nowhere will the development of the oil industry in Alaska be watched with greater interest than in the USSR, though the powerful industrial base of the USA can probably face up to costs of exploitation unthinkable in the Soviet Union. It is, at any rate, gratifying to see that proposals for the development of the Soviet north-east are based no longer on coercion but on economic incentives.

The other area where a shortage of labour is apparent is the countryside in the marginally agricultural areas, particularly Siberia itself, more exactly in western Siberia, which is agriculturally more important than eastern Siberia. Here the ratio of land per worker is high, with an average of 12–15 hectares of arable per collective farmer compared with 4–5 hectares per man in most European parts of the USSR. Because the warm season is so short and Siberian collective farms particularly ill-equipped with machinery, hundreds of thousands of seasonal workers have to be sent annually from the western regions to help with the ploughing, sowing, and harvesting. In fact, hardly any winter rye is sown, and mainly spring crops are cultivated, because ploughing is usually not completed before the onset of frosts. The labour position is deteriorating also in the north-west and central regions of European Russia as well as in the districts east of the upper reaches of the Volga (the Volga-Vyatka region). Cases have been reported of expensive drainage projects being implemented in localities where, owing to shortage of labour, peasants were unable to cultivate fully their old fields or keep their meadows free from alder scrub and other undergrowth. In some northern and central areas of European Russia this has caused the cultivated area to shrink by 15 per cent.

Even greater than the overall manpower shortage is that of rural specialists. The present policy of transforming farming into a modern, highly mechanised industry, adequately supplied with fertilisers, chemicals for pest control, and additives for cattle-feed, and the selection of high-yielding animal breeds and better seeds of cereal, vegetable, and technical crops, requires educated and competent manpower. Yet in April 1967, 58 per cent of all engineers on state farms, 54 per cent of men in charge of repair shops, and 64 per cent of veterinary surgeons were people without special training.[6] The position on collective farms was equally lamentable. Tractor-drivers were so scarce that often machines could not be manned for one shift, whereas in the summer they should work two shifts. Unskilled mechanics damaged new machinery, and its wear-and-tear losses were the highest in the world. There is also a shortage of economists and accountants, who are badly needed to fix bonus payments and calculate the profitability of crops; such personnel is essential if farms are to use their rights of decision-making.

A number of very expensive proposals are being put forward, such as holidays with pay for both state-farm workers and collective farmers. The former have been granted an annual twelve days'

[6] I. Sal'nikov in *Kommunist*, 1968, no. 4, p. 54.

holiday; this is less than the present fifteen days for industrial workers which, since the introduction of the five-day week, gives them three weeks' annual holiday. For the collective farmers, holidays with pay will be a novelty. They could hardly be expected to take them in summer, so trips to the south may have to be laid on. No estimates have yet been made, and it will take a very long time to implement such generous plans. Indeed, the new Model Charter has cautiously left most welfare provisions at the discretion of the collective farms, which will have to find the money to transmute pious statements into actual facts.

The fall in the birth-rate seems to have brought to a head economic and social problems that have been shaping for a long time. Human resources – like natural resources – are not inexhaustible; they have to be husbanded and attracted by high wages and costly incentives if the natural resources of the north-east are to be exploited for the benefit of the community as a whole; they have to be lured back to agricultural work and the latter made less physically hard and financially more rewarding.

Even wider issues are involved. According to Marxist views, geographical factors are of secondary importance as compared to social structures and the level of development of productive forces. Scientific discoveries, technical advances, and communist organisation of society can defeat harsh natural conditions. However, the economic costs of overcoming adverse environmental factors are high. If the present mood of investing in enterprises which yield the higher return persists, an increasing reluctance to face up to the costs of developing Siberia and the Far East may tempt the Soviet planners to give preference to the densely populated western and southern regions capable of satisfying more quickly the pressure of consumer demand.

In recent years some Western geographers interested in Soviet affairs have been taking a look at the map of the world from two different angles. Without fully accepting the implications of Mackinder's controversial and outdated theory of the continental 'heartland', they have nevertheless considered the two different courses open to the Soviet Union.

Throughout her history Russia has sought for an outlet to the sea, not merely to the coast of 'closed' seas like the Baltic or the Black Sea, but beyond – i.e. a foothold on the Mediterranean, symbolised by the *Aia-Sophia*[7] of Constantinople to be wrenched from the Turks and returned to Orthodox Christianity. However, in 1878, when her armies were in sight of Constantinople after their costly victories over Turkey, the Western Powers thwarted her of

[7] Hagia Sophia.

the glittering prize. Once more she found herself to be, as one author puts it, a marginally European country on 'the eastern fringe of Europe in an east-west Atlantic centred Mercator projected world', and her endeavours brought her only 'conflict, frustration, disillusionment and backwardness'.[8]

On the other hand, developing the Volga-Baikal zone with the rich deposits of iron ore, gas, and oil of western Siberia, would result in a powerful industrial heartland. This would be the first case in history of the emergence of a truly continental heartland civilisation, for hitherto all civilisations have arisen along coastlines – with smaller or deeper hinterlands – prospering on the basis of sea communications and international trade. But, says the same author,

> Soviet difficulties in industrialising the continental heartland are not limited to the economic liabilities of unfavourable physical geography and distance from the sea. There are human problems as well ... Siberian industrial development has been slowed down because the migration of labour to new areas has not kept pace with the installation of capital equipment. To persuade skilled men to leave Russia and endure the hardships of the Siberian heartland ... higher pay, longer leave, earlier retirement ... [are required]. The burden falls upon the whole nation in terms of deprivation and sacrifice. The unpopularity these cause may constitute a threat to the security and permanence of the authoritative government upon whose existence such plans for conquering Nature depend. For competing political parties would be unlikely to succeed with policies involving austerity and hardship.[9]

A compromise solution for the Soviet Union might be to steer a middle course, straddling the Urals rather than trying to develop her remotest north-east.[10] Further scientific progress could make possible the exploitation of these areas with a minimum labour force, a solution still remote but already envisaged. Short-term economic calculations favouring European areas may postpone indefinitely costly long-term schemes for developing the north of Asia. Strategic considerations may influence decisions. The Soviet Union has 4,500 miles of land frontier with China, and the population of China is three times that of the USSR. Across the frozen

[8] W. H. Parker, *An Historical Geography of Russia*, London, 1968, pp. 378–9.
[9] Ibid.
[10] D. J. M. Hooson, *A New Soviet Heartland?*, Princeton, 1964, pp. 113–26, and by the same author, *The Soviet Union*, London, 1966, pp. 344–5.

Arctic, no longer a barrier against missiles and nuclear warheads, lies the North American continent, with a population equal to that of the Soviet Union. The industrial potential of the USA alone far exceeds that of the USSR. This tremendous American industrial might seems to thrive on defence contracts to such an extent that any relaxation in the armaments race could lead to large-scale unemployment and affect, if not endanger, the prosperity of the USA. How Soviet joint ventures with Japanese capitalist firms to develop industries in the Far East will fare, time alone can tell.

No easy choice lies before Soviet planners, whether they are inclined to be Westernisers or Eurasians in their outlook, but what demographers have discovered and are at long last bringing to the notice of those in power is that human resources are a country's most valuable asset.

Chapter 7

Education

Organisation and Planning

THE LONG-TERM AIMS OF Soviet education envisage the emergence of the New Communist Man who would be the product as well as the creator of the New Society. The expanding boundaries of science, combined with technological progress and a rationally planned economy, are creating the material basis essential for the life of such a society. Scientific research will eventually become the major social activity of Man and he will at long last be freed from the curse of dull and exhausting daily toil.

While scientific knowledge will allow the New Man to transform nature, his understanding of the laws that govern human society will enable him to enter into more rational and humane relations and evolve a new progressive communist morality. In the evolution of man, environmental factors are believed to be decisive. Together with the material conditions of his existence, education – in the sense of both formal schooling and the informal influence of mass-communication media – moulds a child's personality.[1] The administrative reforms of the late 1960s, such as the setting-up of an All-Union Ministry of Education to co-ordinate the work of the republican ministries; the reorganisation of the Academy of Educational Sciences of the RSFSR into an All-Union institution; the holding of a Teachers' Congress in June 1968; and the 1969 decree regarding higher education, are further manifestations of the concern of the Soviet government for raising the standards of attainment of the young and instilling into them the ideas and ideals of communism.

Soviet educationalists, like their Western counterparts, seek to

[1] Belief in the power of environmental factors explains the persistent Soviet hostility towards Freud's and especially Jung's psycho-analytical theories with their rediscovery of primitive subconscious urges. It explains the persecution of geneticists in Stalin's day, because the views of geneticists on heredity had been used by politicians like Hitler and the South African propounders of apartheid to justify racialism. More recently, the discovery of the chemical foundation of the genetic code has helped to integrate genetics into the general study of nature and brought it into line with other natural sciences whose discoveries enable man increasingly to dominate his environment.

give a child the opportunity of developing all his potentialities, but in addition they aim at making him into a productive worker and good citizen of his communist homeland. The implementation of these three closely integrated aims is carried out by three types of organisations. General education is the responsibility of schools run by the ministries of education of each Union republic. Training for employment is that of technical specialised schools, institutes, and universities, subordinate to republican ministries of higher and secondary specialised education or directly responsible to the All-Union Ministry of Higher and Secondary Education in Moscow; on the lower level there are vocational schools organised by the appropriate industrial ministries (including transport) under the general supervision of the State Committee for Vocational and Technical Education. Education for citizenship in a communist society is effected through the collaboration of all members of society and, in particular, by the Pioneer and *Komsomol* organisations under the overall direction of the Central Committee of the Party.

Administratively, general education is decentralised; eight-year and secondary schools, evening schools, and teachers' training institutes (at both secondary and higher levels) are organised, controlled, and financed by republican ministries and local authorities. Such decentralisation ensures that children are taught in their own vernacular and that schools are sited within reasonable distance of their homes, i.e. not further than 3 kilometres in rural areas. In sparsely populated regions, transport or boarding facilities must be provided. In 1967, however, in view of the imminent introduction of secondary education for all and the expansion of educational technology, an All-Union Ministry of Education was set up in Moscow to co-ordinate the administration of republican ministries of education.

Higher education has always been more centralised and an All-Union Ministry of Higher Education (later renamed Ministry of Higher and Secondary Specialised Education) has long been in existence.[2] This tighter integration is dictated by the closer connections of professional manpower-training with national economic planning. Plans are made usually for periods of five years, and this makes it possible to forecast the types of specialists that will be required and, conversely, the types of openings that will exist for

[2] Many establishments of higher education come under both the Ministry of Higher and Secondary Specialised Education and the ministry which will later employ their students; for instance, pedagogical institutes are the responsibility of the republican ministries of education; medical institutes that of the ministries of health; and various higher technical institutes, of the appropriate industrial ministry.

the graduates of various higher and secondary specialised institutions. Economics and training become integrated into the planning of labour resources, a major item of the national economic plan.

General education is naturally also planned, but in a different sense. Demographic estimates of the size of cohorts of children entering school are the basis for estimating the needs in accommodation, teachers, teaching aids, and materials, which in their turn have to be co-ordinated with available resources.

The planning of education, both general and specialised, is of course becoming increasingly common in the Western world. Since the early 1960s several studies on engineering and technical manpower of the OECD countries have been published. Closely connected with such planning are various estimates of the types of schools to be built, equipment to be provided, teachers to be trained, etc. Neglect of forward estimates may bring about situations like those in France in 1968, where enrolment of students exceeded in numbers the facilities offered by educational establishments, to the extent that in Paris students had to stand during lectures because of a shortage of seating accommodation in the overcrowded lecture-rooms and one professor was responsible for supervising the research work of up to two thousand post-graduates.

The importance of forward planning was recognised by UNESCO and in 1963 it established in Paris an International Institute for Educational Planning. The first publication of this Institute devoted to the subject was *Educational Planning in the USSR*, because IIEP wished to examine and make known the experience

> of those countries which were the first to undertake the establishment of plans for the developments of their educational systems and especially those in which that effort was a part of their general economic and social planning.[3]

In the Soviet Union educational planning is handled by two subsections of *Gosplan*'s department for culture and education. One of them deals with the planning of general education, which starts from an estimate of the child population and then examines the material and human resources that can be allocated to educational purposes, bearing in mind certain priorities. Among the latter is the desirability of doing away with the shift system which persists because of the shortage of school-buildings. In the middle 1960s about 30 per cent of Soviet schools still operated on a two-shift basis and in some places there were even three shifts using the same school.

[3] *Educational Planning in the USSR*, Paris, 1968, foreword.

Compared with 1914, the school population had increased fourfold, whereas the number of buildings had only doubled. A large proportion of the new schools have been built in Central Asian republics, where schools were few in Tsarist days and where the birth-rate is still fairly high. Another priority is the provision of boarding facilities in rural areas where distances between villages are considerable and the child population in each village too small to justify the maintenance of an eight-year school. In fact, most villages have local primary (four-year) schools, often with a contingent of less than twenty pupils in all four grades. Eight-year schools are sited in larger settlements and some kind of boarding arrangements are made for children from the outlying villages; even these eight-year schools often have less than a hundred pupils, which makes them expensive to staff (high staff/pupil ratio); they are often understaffed, ill-equipped, and inefficient. Yet another priority that planners must bear in mind is the need to provide 'prolonged-day' groups or schools for children whose parents are at work, so that pupils can stay on at school, get a meal there, and do their homework under supervision until at least one of the parents returns home.

The planning of professional manpower-training is effected by a different subsection of *Gosplan*. It starts with an analysis of the needs of the economy and the compilation of a balance sheet of labour resources. This balance sheet includes estimates of the population by age-groups, an analysis of the utilisation of labour resources in different branches of the economy, data on any surplus of labour in densely populated areas, and the opportunities for transferring definite contingents of able-bodied workers from such areas to regions short of labour, as well as numerous provisions for ensuring full employment. Apart from manpower already employed in the national economy, overall estimates of additional numbers of workers and employees required by various branches of the economy are computed in order to replace those who retire, and to man new enterprises or fill jobs requiring higher qualifications than the practical skills possessed by their present occupants, who had acquired the necessary know-how through practice and are known in Russian as *praktiki*. On the basis of these data the student intake by various establishments of higher and secondary specialised education is calculated, as well as the intake of lower vocational and technical schools.

One of the greatest difficulties of long-term manpower planning is to forecast the type of specialists that will be required by the time school entrants complete their training; in this connection it is also difficult to foresee and co-ordinate the respective proportions of

1 Malozemel'skaya Tundra (Nenets National area), north of the Arctic Circle, south of Novaya Zemlya

2 Reindeer-racing at a collective farm in the Olekminsky region, Yakut ASSR

3 Landscape in the Daghestan SSR, North Caucasus, on the Caspian coast

4 A branch of a canal dissecting the steppe in the Uzbek SSR

5 Leningrad. View of the Winter Palace from Strelki, Vasilievsky Island

6 The Kazan Cathedral, Leningrad, built in 1810–11

7 The fifteenth-century Registan Square in Samarkand

8 The Bratsk hydropower-station on the Angara river: capacity 5 million Kw; height of dam 126 m; length along crest 1430 m.

9 A section of the Bokhara-Urals gas pipeline

10 The Kremlin, seen from the Moscow river embankment

11 The Moscow television tower, 533 m. high

12 Derricks of the Neftyanye Kamni oilfield over the Caspian Sea near Baku in Azerbaidzhan

13 Norilsk (69° latitude North), a 'black blizzard'
14 Lenin Avenue, Norilsk

15 The factory district of devastated Stalingrad, 1943
16 Leningrad under siege, 1942

17 Russian ballet—*Cinderella*, the ball scene

18 Photograph of the earth from about 70,000 kilometres, taken on 8 August 1969 by Zond-7 automatic station

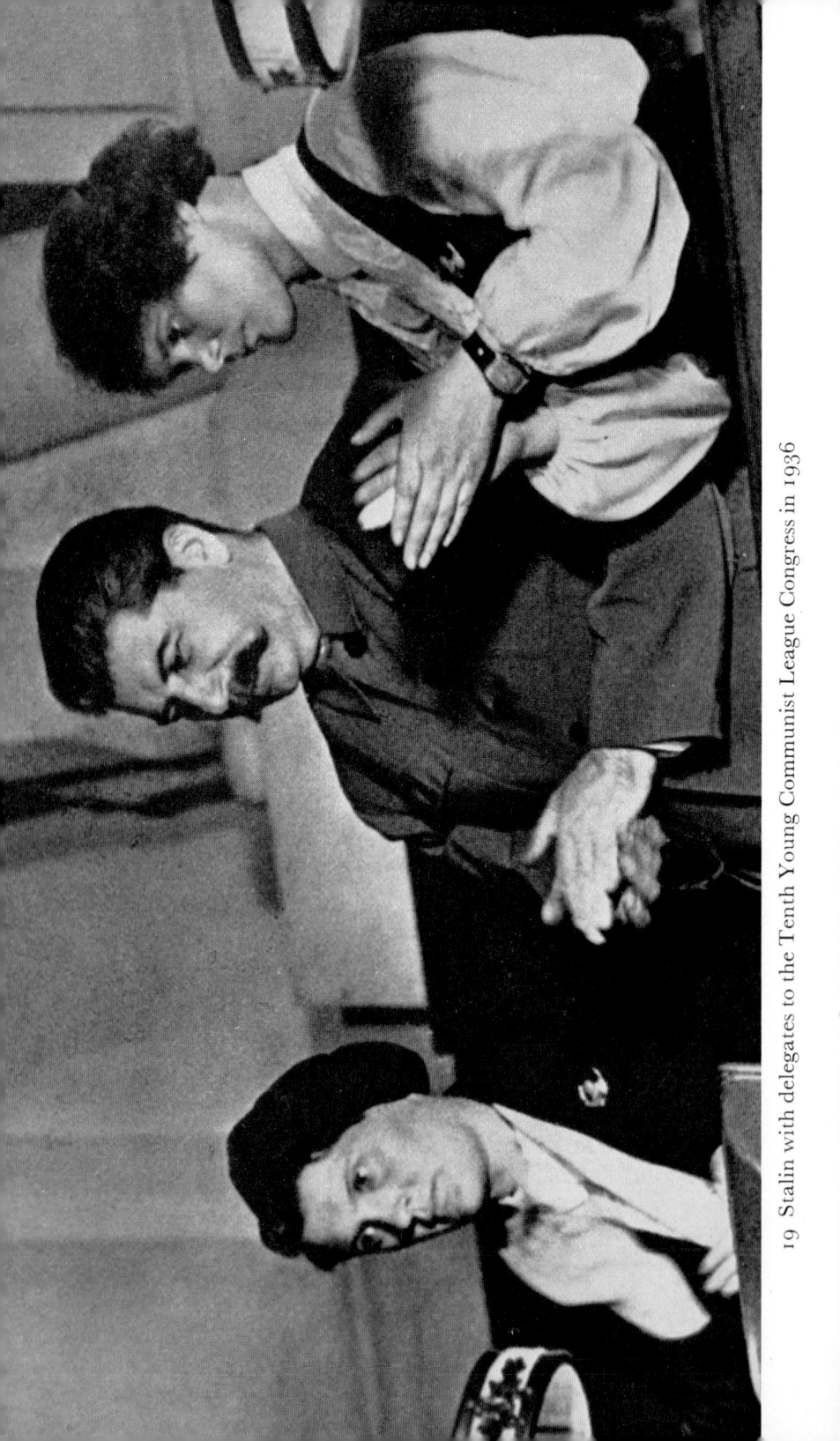

19 Stalin with delegates to the Tenth Young Communist League Congress in 1936

20 Moscow, May 1960. Nikita Khrushchev addresses the USSR Communist Work Team Conference

21 Leonid Brezhnev speaking at the unveiling of the Lenin Memorial at Ulyanovsk, 16 April 1970

22 Alexei Kosygin meets representatives of Scottish sports organisations in Kilmarnock during his visit to Scotland in February 1967

23 May Day celebrations in Moscow, 1966

24. Moscow, monument to the first sputnik
25. A TU-144 supersonic passenger plane

professionals to semi-professionals. Inadequate co-ordination has often resulted in a shortage of semi-skilled personnel and this in turn has affected adversely the work of highly qualified specialists. For instance, the USSR trains more and possibly better engineers than the USA; yet, as a whole, they are less productive because of the shortage of draftsmen, typists, and telephone operators, as well as of equipment such as calculating machines, photocopying facilities, and computers. As a consequence highly qualified men, whose training represents a considerable capital investment, waste time on work which could be done by less qualified ancillary staff whose training would involve less costs.[4]

Long-term planning of specialist training began in 1927 with the adoption of the first Five-Year Plan. In the words of A. V. Lunacharsky, then People's Commissar of Education,

> One cannot construct a plan of industrialisation, take into consideration the quantity of machines, raw materials, lubricating oils, trade opportunities, etc., and not take into consideration the quantity of skilled hands which will be employed – right up to the top engineer – or even simply of people possessing one skill or another necessary for this huge task. On the contrary, every thing must link up.

The first calculations of qualified manpower were based on 'specialist saturation factors' for major industries and individual plants. The saturation factor was the number of specialists per 100 or 1,000 workers employed in various industries in preceding years. There was at that time a vast discrepancy between the number of specialists that could be trained in existing institutions and the requirements of the projected industrial expansion. It was therefore decided to shorten the periods of training and limit the training itself to narrow ranges of specialisation. A very detailed classified list of staffing requirements was compiled, specifying the number of specialists needed to fill each type of post in model enterprises and workshops in each industry, making allowances for proposed technical and organisational changes in production. However unsatisfactory such crash courses may have been, they did help at that time to overcome the crying need for specialists. Later, when the staffing position became somewhat less acute, the curricula of specialised institutes were broadened and the periods of training lengthened. Already by 1935 the initial 950 narrowly specialised courses were replaced by 275 broader ones. The legacy of those days has persisted in the preference for specialised institutes, though ob-

[4] *Literaturnaya Gazeta*, 10 September 1960, p. 10.

viously their present syllabuses are considerably more comprehensive and advanced than they were initially. As late as 1969, out of a total of 794 establishments of higher education (VUZ), only forty-two were universities with a full range of faculties covering law, arts, journalism, and pure science, while others were either specialised institutes or polytechnics providing a wide variety of courses in education, medicine, applied science, and engineering.[5]

The techniques of manpower planning, though refined and perfected in the course of time, are still based on detailed assessments of types of specialists that will be required to replace natural wastage arising from death and retirement, and also to meet the needs of industrial expansion.

At present the requirements of the productive sphere (industry, transport, construction, agriculture, communications, etc.) are planned separately from those of the non-productive sphere (culture, health, education, etc.). In the latter case planning starts from estimates of existing staffs and proceeds from there to the proposed targets for further expansion or upgrading of jobs. These estimates are indirectly dependent on the productive sphere, which provides the buildings, instruments, and materials for the expansion of service industries, including education itself.

Apart from the usual complexities of planning, where one item is dependent on practically every other one, the size of the age-groups presents an additional constraint. This limiting factor was particularly acute in the immediate post-war period, when the student body not only decreased by more than half but consisted mainly of women.

The post-war years saw a large expansion of evening and correspondence courses; they enabled the economy to retain its depleted labour force while promoting specialised education and thus making up for the heavy losses of qualified manpower suffered during the war. Shortages in specialists persisted until the early 1960s. Extension courses, which had been regarded at first as an emergency measure or a second chance given to those who had missed the opportunity to study in their younger days, began to be regarded as valuable in their own right. They seemed to constitute a cheaper alternative to full-time study; the major saving was on students' grants, which are the second largest item (after staff salaries) of the higher education budget and ran to 300 million roubles in 1961. Part-time students are wage-earners and do not, therefore, qualify for grants. Furthermore, they can use the existing premises either in the evening or during vacation time, in the case

[5] *Vestnik vysshei shkoly*, 1969, No. 3, p. 3.

of correspondence students coming for three weeks of intensive pre-examination coaching.

In 1958, steps were taken to expand extension courses by granting extension students time off for study. The 1958 Education Act (described further) laid great stress on labour education before and during the academic year and even envisaged the possibility of merging the two streams of students, i.e. those coming from production via extension courses and those registered as full-time students but spending their first and often their second year in production. Eventually the number of part-time students exceeded those enrolled in full-time courses. However, it soon became apparent that the wastage rate among part-time students was much greater than among the others. Depending on subjects and institutions, wastage among full-time students varied from 15 to 20 per cent of intake, while among part-timers it averaged over 50 per cent. Moreover, the former achieved higher standards, the only exception being in the case of part-time students raising their qualifications within the same field of knowledge, of the kind known in France as *promotion du travail*, e.g. technicians becoming engineers, or nurses qualifying as doctors.

At the present time the Soviet Union is confronted by problems very similar to those which beset advanced Western countries, namely the growing volume of knowledge, the rising costs of education, and the desire to educate not merely highly skilled personnel to run present-day complex production processes, but also, and increasingly, research scientists able to extend the frontiers of knowledge.

General Education

In the Soviet Union, children start school at the age of seven and should complete the universal eight-year school by the age of fifteen or sixteen. Like the advanced Western countries, the USSR is committed to introducing secondary education for all from 1970 onwards. This will mean ten years of schooling from the ages of seven to seventeen. In some republics where pupils have to learn Russian in addition to their own vernacular, as well as satisfy the foreign language requirement, secondary-school education lasts eleven years.

Pre-school education is not compulsory and is only indirectly supervised and financed by the ministries of education. Nursery schools fall into two categories, i.e. crèches for infants under three years old and kindergartens for children aged three to seven, at which age free and compulsory education begins. Nursery schools are maintained by trade unions, collective farms, and other institutions, but receive subsidies from the state through the budgets of local authorities. Parents contribute small fees proportionate to earnings. Subsidies to crèches form a part of the National Health Service, while grants to kindergartens come under the heading of educational expenditure. Between 1955 and 1965, the years for which a detailed breakdown of appropriations has been published, allocations to crèches from the state Budget have doubled, while those awarded to kindergartens have increased fivefold, reaching a total of 1,824 million roubles, with urban institutions getting the lion's share as compared to the rural nurseries. This allocation grew to 3 billion roubles by 1970, and accommodation is to be provided for $9\frac{1}{2}$ million infants and children under seven years old. The increasingly large share allocated to pre-school institutions is partly designed to free mothers for work in the public sector. A decree passed in 1965 makes it obligatory for every new block of flats and every new enterprise employing women to allocate space and funds for the building of a nursery and a nursery school.

Compulsory education was introduced in 1930–32; in 1949–50 the seven-year school for children aged seven or eight to fourteen or fifteen became the obligatory minimum; in 1958 the length of schooling was extended by one year, and gave rise to the universal eight-year school for pupils aged seven to fifteen. That year was marked by a lively controversy regarding the purpose of secondary education, a topic under debate for the last half-century. Was the purpose of secondary education to prepare for entrance to tertiary education, or was it a gateway to adult life and productive work in and for the community? A good grounding in mathematics and science and the mastery of one's own language, a *sine qua non* to clear thinking, are essential for prospective university students; a more vocational bias would benefit the others.

In 1958 the Education Act 'On the strengthening of the bonds between school and life', introduced by Khrushchev, was designed to combine the two. It may have also aimed at mitigating social stratification through educational attainment. Essentially it was yet another attempt, like several earlier ones, to combine formal schooling with productive work and physical education as advocated by Karl Marx in his *Kapital* and by Lenin in his drafts on polytechnical education, though neither had elaborated on the subject. According to the 1958 Act, pupils in the upper grades spent one-third of their school hours training for productive work in factories or on farms or, at least, learned some crafts in school workshops. To maintain academic standards the total length of schooling was raised from ten years (for pupils aged seven to seventeen) to eleven years (aged seven to eighteen). However, practical work-training soon ran into both organisational and psychological difficulties. In 1965, i.e. after the fall of Khrushchev, the amount of time spent on productive work was halved and the length of secondary schooling shortened to ten years.

The November 1966 decree on education envisaged the ten-year school as still providing 'polytechnical education', though the teaching of manual work was limited to two hours per week. Time freed from factory work was to be given to optional subjects; training for a craft could be one of them. Only schools which had successfully organised training in useful and fairly advanced trades were encouraged to retain this option.

The organisation of vocational training on a mass scale for all pupils of secondary schools, attempted several times and in particular in 1958, has always proved extremely difficult to implement, because of the reluctance of factory managers to allow inexperienced teenagers to handle expensive machinery and alternatively because many schools lacking good workshop facilities could provide a training only in the simplest, and therefore relatively useless and out-of-date, crafts. For instance, schools unable to obtain enough typewriters trained girls as seamstresses in towns where there was a crying need for typists. Boys were taught carpentry in the vicinity of new factories which were desperately trying to recruit mechanics, etc. Pupils felt that the training they were getting at school was irrelevant to their future occupation, whether they proceeded to a VUZ or sought employment in an up-to-date factory. A very critical attitude developed among pupils and parents *vis-à-vis* the 1958 Act. This was not entirely justified. Some schools succeeded in establishing links with industry and provided useful forms of apprenticeship. When the 1966 decree abolishing compulsory labour training came into force, one-third of the schools in the RSFSR expressed their willingness to continue with vocational training as an optional subject. Furthermore, the 1958 reform broke down the rigidity of the academic and rather old-fashioned curriculum introduced in the 1930s as a reaction to the extravagances and inefficiency of the experimental schools of the 1920s. Endeavours to find links between school subjects and actual work forced educationalists to give much thought to the content of the secondary-school syllabus. A commission was set up jointly by the Academy of Sciences of the USSR, the Academy of Educational Sciences of the RSFSR (later promoted to the rank of an All-Union institution), and the ministries of education of the Union republics to draft new curricula. With its subject subsections the commission brought together some 500 scientists, educationalists, and officials. Evidence was obtained from another 10,000 people. As a result of this scrutiny the curriculum was drastically overhauled and new textbooks were commissioned. The first, on biology, reached the schools in 1968; others were to follow. No less a man than Academician Kolmogorov was in charge of the mathematics syllabus.

Modernisation of the Curriculum and Educational Research

The heart-searching discussions that preceded the promulgation of the 1958 Act and its later repeal have focused the attention of educationalists on the need to modernise both teaching methods and the curriculum. Modernisation in the Soviet Union has meant, first of all, cutting out dead wood left over from the Stalin era, such as the study of naïvely propagandistic novels regarded earlier as gems of Soviet literature, or Lysenko's questionable theories on hybridisation and the transmission of acquired characteristics. More important were the efforts for a genuine modernisation of the science syllabus. Schooling cannot be lengthened indefinitely, so the problem confronting educationalists the world over is to increase the efficiency of teaching methods and instructional aids and to streamline the curriculum in a way that would develop the child's reasoning powers and ability to observe, thus preparing him for a life of constant adaptation in a changing world and for recurrent training, or what is sometimes called permanent education.

In the teaching of biology, pupils are now introduced to the notion of the chemical basis of heredity; in physics, to modern ideas on the structure of matter, the theory of relativity, and quantum mechanics, treated not as an addendum to the traditional course in classical physics but by means of a broadly generalising approach; the wave theories are examined as a single complex and not split between mechanics, optics, acoustics, and electro-magnetism. In chemistry there is a greater emphasis on the understanding of general principles, the role of chemical bonds and their importance for chemical properties and structures, rather than on the descriptions of individual reactions and compounds. Work on the teaching of mathematics has been going on in the specialised mathematical schools like the now world-famous one in Novosibirsk and several less known and less specialised ones connected with computer centres. In each case pupils are taught to apply principles to the solution of practical problems and to learn to think for themselves in coping with novel situations. Learning is no longer assimilating and regurgitating information but approaching new knowledge in a spirit of enquiry, as an attempt at personal discovery. This is what is coming to be known as 'the didactics of creative activity'. There is considerable opposition to this from more conservative-minded educationalists who fear for the stability of the curriculum;

they demand that the school be shielded from changing and possibly ill-proven though fashionable scientific hypotheses; on the other hand, innovators insist that the school must cease being the place where 'children are taught to live and think in terms of an obsolescent and fast-disappearing world'.

Educational research is carried out by the Academy of Educational Sciences, which consists of forty-eight academicians and seventy-nine corresponding members. It has eleven scientific research institutes and a network of experimental schools or schools where members of the Academy are entitled to carry out teaching experiments. Most of the work of the Academy is focused on general education and child psychology, but it also has more specialised institutes, such as the Institute of Defectology, to study and devise methods of educating blind, deaf, and otherwise handicapped children; and an Institute of Evening and Correspondence Schools, which studies methods of teaching in such schools which are attended both by teenagers and adults, who need different types of instruction, even if they cover the usual school syllabus. In 1967, an Institute of School Equipment and Technical Teaching Aids was set up. Like many other things, teaching aids are in short supply; there is a shortage of laboratory equipment, chemical reagents, films, projectors, tape-recorders, and, of course, teaching-machines. The high cost of educational technology, together with that of secondary education for all, is now involving the Academy in yet another field of research, namely the economics of education.

Programmed learning and machine teaching are bringing new notions of algorithms, feed-back, and model-building into the classroom. The pioneers in this field have been the higher technical institutions, particularly in the Ukraine : namely the Kiev Institute of Engineering and Radiotechnology, the Kiev Institute of Engineering and Construction, and also the Moscow Power Institute, some of the military academies, and others. The University of Kiev has established an Institute of Teaching-Machines and Programmed Learning in which specialists in electronics collaborate with professors in arts subjects, including those teaching Russian to foreigners. In Moscow, the Interdepartmental Scientific Council for Programmed Teaching has inaugurated a Faculty of Programmed Teaching at the Polytechnical Museum. The first All-Union conference on programmed teaching and the use of technical appliances in education was held in Moscow in the summer of 1966. One of the aims of the conference was to overcome the gulf which separated the specialists in radio-electronics, cybernetics, and operational research from members of the teaching profession. The former are handicapped in devising suitable programmes by their lack of training in child psychology, their ignorance of didactic methods, and their inability to assess a child's capacity for sustained effort, while teachers have an inadequate knowledge of modern computational techniques, technical refinements, and information theory. The demands made on programmed learning in the USSR are very high because the aim is to find forms of programming which require more independent thought on the part of the learner than is needed in multiple-choice answers; programmed learning should stimulate rather than blunt the creative powers of the child.

Polytechnical education has come to be regarded as an awareness of the working of modern industries, their interlinking, and of the major technical processes they use; in a sense, an understanding of the application of science to the daily life and toil of a modern society. It is now conceived with a minimum labour content. A certain degree of manual dexterity and a 'feel for machinery' will still have to be taught in schools because it cannot be taken for granted that every Soviet child can pick it up from a machine-saturated environment, as urban children often do in western Europe or the USA. So two to four weekly periods are set aside for labour instruction; but polytechnical education is increasingly *knowing about* the broader issues of production rather than *knowing how* to perform a relatively narrow range of operations.

Although less urbanised than other advanced societies, the USSR has changed very considerably over the last half-century. Many children now learn to read while still at nursery school or simply because they come from literate families. A general acceleration of physical and mental development is induced by a more cultivated environment, better child care, and the stimulus of mass-communication media. Therefore the four-year course of the primary school (grades I to IV), designed for children of previous generations whose parents may have still been illiterate, is now being compressed into three years (grades I to III). Henceforth ten-year-olds will be introduced to elementary science and algebraic notation as early as grade IV. Arguments backed by experiments are put forward to the effect that intelligence can be developed by suitable practice, that a child's mind can be weaned from sensory perceptions of concrete objects and trained to reason in abstract concepts. With an earlier start, a more streamlined curriculum designed to develop reasoning powers rather than memorise facts, the elimination of the time-consuming repetitiveness inherent in the 'concentric circles' approach to learning, and a wider use of audio-visual aids, youngsters should be able to assimilate more of the overwhelmingly expanding knowledge and, above all, train their minds to handle information more rationally, to reason and generalise at an earlier age, and come to think in the abstract terms characteristic of present-day science.

Optional subjects are taking the place of practical work-training in secondary school, though a month of practical work is still scheduled for those completing grade IX. The advocates of specialisation in the upper grades have repeatedly failed to breach the principle of the single syllabus, but its rigidity is mitigated by a choice of optional subjects in grades VII to X; they should not, however, take up more than one-seventh or even one-tenth of the total thirty-six-hour school week. It is hoped to foster a great variety of options, possibly as many as forty, though obviously the full range will not be available everywhere. Many optional subjects are used for vocational guidance and others are designed to give an impetus to physical training and aesthetical appreciation. A completely new departure was the introduction in 1968 of military training in schools. In addition to the general secondary-education schools, there are a small number of music and ballet schools for artistically gifted children, and a somewhat larger number of schools where a foreign language is used as a medium of instruction; most of these specialise in English, French, or German, but a few use Chinese, Hindi, or Arabic; lastly, there are four schools for young mathematicians attached to the Universities of Moscow, Leningrad, Kiev, and Novosibirsk, which select by means of countrywide olympiads promising pupils from grade VIII. The provision of boarding schools on a large scale, envisaged by the 1958 Act, proved too expensive and their numbers remain limited.

Optional subjects will require new types of teachers and this, together with the modernisation of the curriculum, will make it imperative to retrain many of them. This retraining will mean bringing teachers up to date in their subjects as well as instructing them in new teaching techniques involving a better understanding of child psychology and of the use of technical appliances.

The retraining of teachers will have to be on a vast scale, particularly among the older generation, not merely because of advances in sciences and educational theory but because many Soviet teachers are still poorly qualified, especially those employed in rural schools. Many of them joined the profession when the four-year primary school was the only one available in the countryside, and they themselves have had only seven years' schooling followed by two years (later extended to three or four) of further specialised education (*pedagogicheskie uchilischa*).[6]

[6] When in 1949–50 the seven-year and in 1958–60 the eight-year school became the compulsory minimum, primary-school teachers had to raise their qualifications by means of evening and correspondence courses. In fact, the

Since the late 1960s teachers are given opportunities to attend courses every five years to keep abreast with scientific discoveries, programmed learning, and educational psychology. The organisation of such courses presents a formidable problem because the staffs of the Pedagogical Institutes, which are responsible for the training of teachers and rank as institutions of higher education (VUZ), are said to be inadequately qualified. Few members of their staffs have higher degrees and fewer still are engaged in research in the much-neglected fields of didactics. The Academy of Educational Sciences has therefore organised special post-graduate courses to train experts in the educational sciences. New syllabuses in pedagogy and the history of education have been published. Considering that the army of teachers numbers 3 million, their retraining is a costly and formidable proposition.

Research schemes are to be so devised as to bring together educationalists, workers in the fields of literature, art, sociology, and philosophy, and those concerned with the practical day-to-day running of the schools. A long-term study is in course of preparation to determine the qualities that make a good teacher. Entrants to several selected Institutes of Education fill in a questionnaire regarding their own interests and the motives for choosing teaching as a career. Their progress, first as students and later as young teachers, will then be collated and it is thus hoped to establish a better vocational selection of teachers and reduce wastage of fully trained teachers turning to other occupations.

The Cost of Education

Out of a total state Budget expenditure estimated for 1970 at some 144,656 million roubles, 24,500 million (approximately 17 per cent) were allocated to culture, science, and education. Of these 24,500 million roubles, 3,000 million were to be spent on pre-school education, 4,500 million on professional training, and 6,100 million on general education. The balance, plus some extra funds for building purposes, was allocated to science and amounted to 11,000 million roubles.

The sums allocated from the Budget for educational purposes are less than the total bill for education, considering that collective farms and industrial enterprises contribute to the building and equipment of schools, while outlay on pre-school education is also

---

expansion of extension courses in the 1950s was largely in response to the needs of teachers anxious to retrain as 'subject teachers'. Later still Institutes for Improving the Quality of Teachers (*instituty usovershenstvovaniya uchitelei*) were set up to improve both the teachers' knowledge of their subjects and their 'pedagogical craftsmanship'.

financed from trade union and co-operative funds, parents' fees, and other non-governmental sources, totalling something in the range of 4,000 million roubles. Nor is on-the-job training included, because outlays on skill-training are incorporated into a given factory's production costs. Furthermore, military schools and academies are financed from money allocated to defence. (The total defence expenditure amounted to nearly 18,000 million roubles or 12·4 per cent of the total state Budget in 1970.)

A comparison of the figures for the ten years 1955 to 1965, for which a fairly detailed breakdown is available, shows a steady growth of the state Budget's contribution towards primary and secondary education, reflecting the growing length of the period of schooling, while the cost of professional training, including establishments of higher education (VUZ), secondary specialised schools (*srednie spetsial'nye uchebnye zavedeniya*), and vocational trade schools (*professional'no-tekhnicheskie uchilishcha*) had risen less steeply over the same period.

However, bearing in mind the growing GNP and the consequent expansion of Budget allocations in general, the outlay on general education can be said to have remained fairly static, fluctuating between 20 and 25 per cent of the monies allocated to culture, science, and education, while the share of professional training actually declined slightly. This slower growth (or relative decline) may be partially accounted for by administrative changes; for instance, expenditure on teaching hospitals was transferred in 1960–61 from the heading 'professional training' to a subsection of the national health accounts. More important may be the fact that VUZ are now obtaining resources earmarked for science which formerly accrued to scientific research institutes alone, because since the late 1950s VUZ have ceased to be regarded merely as teaching institutions. In the course of the last few years they have been setting up their own research laboratories or participating in joint research projects with the scientific research institutes. That science is generously supported from Budget funds is a well-known fact, illustrated by the rise in the appropriations to science from 807 million roubles in 1955 to 4,265 million in 1965, 7,200 million in 1967, 9,000 million in 1969, and 11,000 million in 1970.

Lastly, some VUZ, particularly the larger institutions of the RSFSR and the Ukrainian SSR, undertake research for industrial plants and, in 1965–66, obtained as much as 160 million roubles in this way. Usually the Budget grants are far in excess of any income from industry, but things are changing; for instance, in 1967 the University of Leningrad received three-quarters of a million roubles for research from Budget funds and over 3 million from industry. This money was entirely spent on scientific projects financed by the appropriate ministries or plants in accordance with detailed estimates submitted by the university. The new regulations allow VUZ to make a profit and retain 75 per cent of their outside earnings. This should stimulate research work, but may prove a temptation too; namely, it could encourage VUZ to concentrate on applied rather than on pure science, a tendency which is in any case widespread in the USSR.

Some economists go even further in their search for more efficient methods of forecasting the need for definite types of specialists, calculating the outlays of educational establishments, and for financing them more rationally. In an article published in 1967 Professor V. Zhamin[7] (Director of the Institute of Economics of the Academy of Sciences of the USSR) suggested that ministries engaged in the sphere of material production should enter into 'accounting' (*khozraschetnye*) relations with educational establishments which train the types of specialists (scientists, engineers, technicians, etc.) required by the enterprises of the given ministry. For each specialist successfully completing his course, the ministry would pay a certain sum and this would be included in the costs of production of the enterprises subordinate to that particular ministry. Furthermore, the sums payable to the educational establishments should be calculated so as to show a profit from which the VUZ or specialised school would pay a kind of rent on its fixed assets and accumulate funds for incentive payments, housing, and social-cultural amenities for its staff and students. For the purpose of calculating the outlays of educational establishments whose graduates go into production work, Zhamin proposed the following formula:

$$P = \frac{(A+O+Z+R) \cdot T}{K}$$

where P is total expenditure, A – depreciation, O – circulating capital, Z – wages and salaries, T – length of course in years, K – average number of students, and R – profit. The latter is to be related to the wages fund because wages are the major outlay and also because this fund is normally calculated in relation to the number of students.

In an earlier article the same author had pointed out that expenditure on the training of personnel for the productive sphere is bound to be more effective than money spent on training personnel for the non-productive sphere, since the former would contribute more immediately to a rise in production and, consequently, to

[7] *Voprosy ekonomiki*, 1967, No. 2.

national income. On the other hand, no education is possible without teachers and, of course, the economy of a civilised country cannot function without officials, clerks, doctors, etc.

Without going as far as Zhamin, the Soviet government seems to be inclined to view at least capital investment in specialised education as partly the responsibility of industry; the September 1966 decree allowed and encouraged industrial ministries, with the sanction of the state planning authorities, to spend up to $2\frac{1}{2}$ million roubles per annum on buildings and equipment for the VUZ which are subordinate to each of them. Surveys made in the 1960s regarding the cost of training a full-time student showed that, depending on the duration of his studies (four to six years), the total cost amounted to from 5,000 to 7,500 roubles, whereas in the case of a part-time evening student the cost was 900 to 1,500 roubles, and in the case of a correspondence student only 750 to 1,200 roubles.[8] Moreover, in the two latter cases students still contributed their labour to the community during their years of study, although they were given some time off, which could, under certain circumstances, amount to nearly two months because of day-release and the three weeks' leave granted to attend pre-examination coaching and actual examination sessions.

If expenditure on science is excluded, the total outlay on education in the USSR, although rising over the years, has not been growing ahead of the GNP, as it has in many other advanced countries. Studies on the returns from investment in human resources have been scarce hitherto in the USSR, particularly on the relationship between labour productivity and better health, nutritional standards, and housing conditions. On the other hand, a few statistical studies designed to correlate labour productivity to educational attainment have been attempted. As far back as 1924, S. G. Strumilin, in a paper entitled *The Economic Significance of National Education*, sought to assess

> not only the gain for an individual who receives education at the expense of the state, but also... the cheapest and... most effective way of creating a productive labour force. Any amount of education may be extremely desirable and useful for a worker if it is free. But the state which has to pay for education wants to know whether all amounts of education are equally useful in raising the country's productivity. If all amounts are not equally useful, what is the most profitable length of education for each worker, and how much should be spent on it in order to spend

[8] L. I. Tul'chinsky, *Finansovye problemy professional'nogo obrazovaniya v SSSR*, Moscow, 1968, p. 117.

the national revenue in a way most likely to increase it in the future?

Using a sample of machine-tool operators, he endeavoured to correlate skill to age, length of service, and education. He found that returns were greatest on the initial stages of education and decreased steadily with the years of schooling. In other words, he found that a literate or even semi-literate worker learns a skill and achieves high efficiency in his trade far more quickly than an illiterate by on-the-job training.[9] Similarly, E. F. Denison convincingly demonstrated the existence of a definite correlation in the USA between growing productivity of the labour force and length of schooling over the periods 1909–29 and 1929–57. On the other hand, despite the very similar average of years of schooling in Great Britain and the USA in the latter period, the productivity of American workers measured by their earnings and reflected in the national income of the USA is considerably higher. Evidently geographical, historical, and social factors are no less important to the productivity of a nation than the educational average of its population.[10]

[9] Strumilin also made some calculations about higher education to show that indirectly 'teachers increased the nation's productivity' and that although it was even 'more difficult to evaluate the work of doctors in lengthening the working lives of the many hundreds of workers treated by them, yet, generally speaking, the economic effect of doctors' work is not impossible to calculate and is no doubt sizeable'. Strumilin's method has been used more recently by V. Zhamin (Jamin) in a paper based on the 1959 census returns and presented by him at a conference on the economics of education held in Menthon St Bernard in 1963 by the International Economic Association; he used similar methods in his surveys of several Leningrad factories.

[10] Costs of education are accounted in different ways in different countries. In the USSR subsidised meals and hostel accommodation come under educational costs. So, naturally, do teachers' salaries, but not teachers' pensions as in some countries. The effect of including maintenance costs is reflected in the different share of teachers' salaries in different types of schools. Thus in general education they account for 85 per cent of a school's expenditure, but in nursery schools where outlays on ancillary personnel, food, laundry, etc., are considerable, teachers' salaries represent only 39 per cent of all costs, and 32 per cent in vocational schools, many of which are residential and provide uniforms as well as materials for use in workshops. Textbooks and writing appliances are not supplied free, but the publication of textbooks is subsidised partly by the ministries of education and partly, in the case of technical literature, from the accounts of industrial ministries. Workshop tools and materials are often supplied by local industries. The loss to the economy of the labour of full-time older pupils and students is not usually taken into account, though foregone earnings to the student and loss of taxes by the state are included by some American economists in their calculations. Hardly any information on losses connected with student dropout is available, yet it must be considerable since large numbers of evening and correspondence-course students fail to complete their course, having wasted a lot of their own and their teachers' time (as well as other resources) to no gainful purpose.

The difficulty of calculating the return on educational investment is bound up with the multiplicity of factors affecting both the measurement of any increases of labour productivity that can be attributed to better education and that of total educational costs. If labour productivity is calculated in terms of wages it should be borne in mind that the latter are fixed by Soviet authorities, who take into account educational attainment, but also manipulate wages so as to attract workers into certain geographical regions short of manpower, or to more essential industries; and, in any case, actual productivity depends greatly on the machinery and equipment available to the worker as well as on the rather elusive effects of health standards, motivation, and personality. Studies now being carried out, mainly at the Institute of Labour of the Academy of Sciences of the USSR, are designed to see whether output levels do in fact correspond to the levels of qualification of the workers concerned and what are the respective shares of living labour and of embodied labour (or capital) in contributing to output. It has been argued by Zhamin that in 1960–64 nearly 30 per cent of the increase of the Soviet national income could be attributed to investment in education and the resulting higher qualifications of workers.[11]

Increasing material wealth makes possible the training of a highly skilled labour force which in its turn contributes to economic prosperity and further scientific advance; knowledge and wealth go hand in hand, each conditioning the expansion of the other. The quantitative assessment of their intricate mutual relations is still debatable, yet the slowing-down of the growth-rate of the Soviet economy in the later 1960s has been attributed to shortages of skilled manpower, capable of making full use of modern sophisticated capital equipment reaching new industries.[12] There are also cases of wrong utilisation of professional manpower when, for instance, fully trained engineers are employed on technicians' jobs because of planners' miscalculations arising from the changing demands of production and the appearances of novel professions (e.g. programmers); such unforeseen innovations make manpower-planning particularly difficult, even at the lower levels of skill. To adapt to rapidly changing techniques and cope with the growing complexity of industrial processes, recurrent retraining becomes inevitable. This can be achieved only on the basis of a fairly high general education, which thus becomes essential for flexibility of

[11] V. A. Zhamin, *Ekonomika obrazovaniya*, Moscow, 1969, p. 313. For a more detailed discussion, see V. A. Zhamin and G. A. Egiazaryan, *Effektivnost' kvalifitsirovannogo truda*, Moscow, 1968, pp. 113–43.
[12] I. E. Kurakov in *Voprosy filosofii*, 1966, No. 5, p. 97.

employment. Hence the introduction of universal secondary education.

The implementation of secondary education in rural areas is fraught with problems. Until the late 1960s, and despite the closure of a number of smaller schools, of the total of 77,400 primary rural schools, 70 per cent catered for less than forty children each and nearly 30,000 for fewer than twenty. Even eight-year schools had often less than a hundred pupils. This made them both costly and inefficient; costly, because allocations are calculated on the number of forms in a school and not on that of pupils in the form, so the expense of teaching a village boy may be over 200 roubles per annum, while in a large urban school with thirty pupils per class it may be less than 40 roubles. Small schools are also inefficient, lacking laboratory facilities and specialist teachers, with the result that subjects may be taught by people without any qualification in the given discipline, for the sake of making up the statutory eighteen hours per week teaching-load fixed for subject teachers in grades V to X. (In primary schools, i.e. grades I to IV, the teaching-load is twenty-four hours per week.) Small schools are also wasteful in their outlays on heating, lighting, repairs, and other incidentals, calculated per pupil. Considerable work has been done to improve the siting of rural schools in order to enlarge their catchment areas as far as possible and also to calculate their most economic size, so as to ensure full utilisation of classroom-, laboratory-, and workshop-space; latterly in the Ukraine computers have been used for this purpose. The proliferation of small schools is due to their being erected by collective farms at their own cost, for their own village children.

In non-Russian republics pupils are taught in their vernacular and Russian is introduced as the first foreign language, usually in the second or third year of schooling. In rural schools the teachers of Russian are usually not proficient in the language and, later in life, teenagers who have had a bare smattering of Russian at school are handicapped by their ignorance of the *lingua franca* of the country if seeking employment in towns or on large construction sites, or if proceeding to higher education. This handicap particularly affects women in the Central Asian republics. The rural areas in these republics are overpopulated, yet much female labour is lost not only because women in these republics have large families that prevent them from going out to work and leaving their villages, but also because their very poor knowledge of Russian puts further education and gainful industrial employment practically outside their reach. It is a well-known fact that in advanced countries rural youth is educationally at a disadvantage as compared with their urban contemporaries, but this disadvantage is particularly marked in the Central Asian republics and affects girls even more than boys. In the long run it affects the GNP of these regions, in particular Tadzhikistan.

Professional Training

Professional training takes place on three levels. At the lower level there are the vocational schools (*professional'no-tekhnicheskie uchilishcha*), at secondary level the secondary specialised schools, and at higher level the universities, polytechnical, medical, pedagogical, and other specialised institutes (VUZ).

Vocational schools are naturally very diversified and their curricula are narrowly utilitarian. Organisationally they come under the appropriate industrial ministry and the general supervision of the State Committee for Vocational Training. Formerly they used to enrol teenagers from primary and eight-year schools and train them for periods of six months (for lumberjacks) to two years (for railway mechanics). On completing their course, teenagers were directed to the enterprises for which they had been trained, and had to work there for a period of four years. The obligation to work at places to which they are directed is universal for all youngsters completing any specialised institution in the USSR. In the case of graduates it is three years, while in the case of those who complete secondary specialised and vocational schools it is usually four years. These young workers are paid the appropriate wages and, since the latter are higher than those of unskilled workers, in a sense the young people pay off the educational advantages that society has bestowed upon them.

Vocational schools have greatly improved of late, partly because entrants now come from the universal eight-year school (though drop-outs from grade V upwards are also admitted) and also because the skills they are taught are more modern and advanced. However, these schools still remain somewhat of a blind alley because they are outside the educational ladder; a former pupil of a vocational school cannot proceed further unless he completes his secondary education by attending evening classes or taking a correspondence course that will bring him up to the level of a secondary school-leaving certificate.

Vocational schools are said to be popular with the sons of workers whose ambition is to become skilled workers and to start earning wages as soon as possible. For the same reasons vocational schools attract the children of widows and pensioners, and also children from rural areas whose ambitions are curtailed by the relatively poor schooling obtained in their village schools, and whose main wish is to settle in a town.

Many vocational schools are boarding institutions and pupils get free uniforms as well as board and lodging. Sometimes they get pocket money from articles made for enterprises in the course of their practical work lessons. The prospects of employment of pupils from vocational schools are much better than those of teenagers who complete secondary general education, because employers regard the latter as unskilled labour. There is at the moment a crying need for more vocational schools, secondary specialised schools, and also for short vocational courses for secondary school-leavers, particularly for the hitherto despised but expanding service occupations. Because of the shortage of vocational schools, of the 4½ million young workers who joined the labour force in 1964 two-thirds had had no professional training. In 1965 the position was similar; some 5 million young people entered employment. Of these one million came from vocational schools; there were, furthermore, 600,000 coming from secondary specialised schools and 400,000 from VUZ. However, an allowance must be made for the two latter categories, since half of the graduates had studied at extension courses and were already employed in the national economy.

According to a statement by the Chairman of the State Committee for Vocational Training, made in March 1966, 'for every worker trained at a vocational school there are at present three workers who obtained an elementary qualification on the job'. The planned intake of vocational schools in 1970 was set at 1,700,000 or 1,800,000.

Educational planners consider that the optimal proportions to be aimed at are: 20 per cent of any age-group to receive higher education; 30 per cent to be trained in secondary specialised schools; and 50 per cent at vocational schools or by means of short courses following upon ten years' schooling.

Secondary specialised schools usually enrol pupils who have completed the ten-year school, though some of them take pupils from grade VIII. The length of courses varies from eighteen months to two and a half years. The majority of these schools train technicians for railways, hydropower-stations, mines, and every imaginable industry, including the petrochemical and the pharmaceutical; others prepare junior medical personnel, dentists, nursery school-teachers, and also teachers of handicrafts, sports and games, singing and music; some are arts schools, while yet others train rural club organisers. Like vocational schools, they come under the dual supervision of the appropriate industrial Ministry (or the Ministry of Culture) and, at the same time, under the republican ministry of higher and secondary specialised education. Some are boarding schools, but usually they are day schools; in this case pupils get small grants of 20 to 30 roubles per month. As with vocational schools, work done for an industrial enterprise may bring a small profit which is either distributed among pupils or, preferably, spent on a collective outing or musical instruments if the school has an orchestra or some other collective form of entertainment. If the school is of a type where fairly expensive articles are made, income from pupils' work may be substantial enough to be used to expand workshops or laboratories and generally help with the upkeep of the institution. In 1970 they were planned to enrol 1,300,000 pupils.

Higher educational establishments (VUZ) also often come under the double supervision of the appropriate republican industrial ministry or that of culture, education, or national health, as well as under the republican ministry of higher and secondary specialised education. Twenty-five of the country's most outstanding institutions are directly subordinate to the Ministry of Higher and Secondary Education of the USSR. Enrolment is by competitive examination, with many candidates for each place in the case of the best institutions like the Universities of Moscow, Leningrad, Kiev, and Novosibirsk, and hardly any competition for small provincial pedagogical or narrowly specialised technical institutes. Apart from passing the entrance examination, each applicant must present a reference from either his Party or *Komsomol* primary, school, or place of work. No fees are chargeable. Students' grants are very small for freshers, but increase by 25 per cent annually if examination results are satisfactory. The length of studies varies from four years to six in the case of medical institutes. Apart from full-time day courses, practically every VUZ has an extension department for evening and correspondence students. Evening students are a minority, but study by correspondence is on a vast scale. The expansion of this type of education is partly due to the vastness of the country and the impossibility of siting VUZ in every small town. It is also a cheap form of education, since extension students earn wages at their place of work and are not in need of grants, nor do they need accommodation in student hostels, which are heavily subsidised by the state. It is also considered that one tutor can cope with fifty correspondence students, whereas the normal staff/student ratio is ten to thirteen students to a member of staff. However, although the duration of extension courses was lengthened by six months to a year, the numbers graduating were for a long time less than 50 per cent of the initial enrolment.

In more recent years various methods of achieving personal contacts with extension students have been devised. Apart from the three-week initiation course at the beginning of their academic studies and the annual three weeks of intensive pre-examination coaching periods, various devices have been used to improve teaching. In the densely populated Ukraine, faculties of general science have been set up in smaller towns under the auspices of a larger provincial VUZ. Correspondence students living within a reasonable radius attend courses there several evenings a week. These faculties of general science prepare students in maths, physics, and chemistry for two or three years and then arrange for promising students to leave their jobs and continue full-time at larger and more specialised institutions situated in major towns. Trains with coaches transformed into laboratories have been organised to bring staff and equipment to students living in small towns situated along a railway line; the train is shunted for a week or a fortnight at the station and students come in the evenings to perform their practical work in these laboratories on wheels; then the train moves on to the next town. Radio and television have naturally boosted correspondence courses. In Moscow one of the television channels is used solely for educational purposes; in other towns considerable viewing-time is allocated to similar broadcasts. Factories now often set aside a special room equipped with a television set for their worker-students.

In 1969 over half of the 4½ million students were studying part-time, either attending evening classes or by means of correspondence courses; they accounted also for 47 per cent (272,000) of all those who graduated at the end of that year.

It has often been pointed out that social stratification through education was becoming apparent in the Soviet Union. The larger towns had better schools than the smaller ones, and very much better than the rural ones. People in more important jobs lived in the larger towns, could afford better housing facilities, and could encourage their progeny to study more, with the result that children from better-off families were educated at better schools, passed their entrance examinations with greater facility, studied at the better VUZ, and eventually got the better jobs. It has even been alleged that these privileged children benefited more than the less fortunate ones from the social consumption fund – designed to mitigate wage differentials – since they benefited from one of the most expensive items paid from the social consumption fund, namely higher education.

Some of the provisions of the 1958 Education Act were designed to preclude further stratification. Already an earlier Act had given priority to entrants who had either worked in production for two years or had been demobilised after their period of national service. The idea of sandwiching two years' work in production between completion of secondary education and enrolment to VUZ was bitterly opposed by scientists on the grounds that creativeness, particularly among mathematicians, is at its height roughly between the ages of seventeen and twenty-four. Therefore, apart from delaying graduation and entry into productive employment, it deprived most gifted young people of opportunities to use their faculties at the time when they were at their height. Under the pressure of academicians, VUZ were allowed to admit 20 per cent of their total intake from among school-leavers. With the fall of Khrushchev, the initial 20 per cent quota was allowed to become so elastic as to include all freshers entering faculties of pure science or other departments with many courses in mathematics and physics, such as engineering.

At present the two-year period in productive work is no longer an absolute condition of enrolment, though preferential treatment is given to applicants coming from production. Priority is also given to young people coming from rural areas to study at agricultural and biological institutes if they have done only one year's practical work, and this condition is completely waived and priority is still given to rural youngsters applying for entry to pedagogical and medical institutes.

Apart from state student grants (payable through the VUZ where the student is enrolled), industrial enterprises and collective farms are encouraged to award special grants (usually larger than state grants by about 15 per cent) to their young workers or collective farmers who are willing to come back later to their respective enterprises as highly skilled specialists. It is hoped that children born and bred in the countryside will retain the nostalgia for the old home and return to the native village and contribute their new skills to agriculture, which needs them so urgently.

During the two years spent in production or in the army, young people forgot much of what they had learnt at school. It was felt also that intelligent young peasants, because of the low standards of instruction in the rural ten-year schools, were unable to pass the competitive entrance examination to VUZ; therefore many institutions had been running preparatory courses for prospective applicants; these courses lasted from three to ten months and were usually on a part-time basis. In September 1969 the Soviet government issued a decree making it mandatory on all VUZ in the country to provide preparatory courses of eight to ten months' duration for workers, collective farmers, and demobilised servicemen. These courses are to be either full-time or evening or by correspondence; full-time students will receive grants on par with first-year VUZ students. Enterprises, trade unions, and collective farms are called upon to provide accommodation and equipment, as well as travelling and maintenance allowances for those whom they send to study.

This measure should enlarge the catchment area of higher educational establishments and help prospective students who have either forgotten much of what they have learnt at school or who have received a very unsatisfactory education in rural schools; it is also designed to help those who have attended part-time schools for working and rural youth, which have existed since the war to provide further education for people who, because of the war or the remoteness of their village, never studied beyond the three Rs provided by primary four-year schools.

Like others, these students will have to have a recommendation from a Party or *Komsomol* primary, or from their trade union or the management of their collective farm.

The Statute of a Higher Education Establishment adopted by the Party and Soviet government in January 1969 seems to be concerned with three issues: to define the rights and duties and the organisation of the institution itself; to raise the standards of attainment of students; and to train fervent and convinced Communists.

The rector is given very considerable powers in academic matters, such as the syllabus and the research work undertaken within the VUZ, and also in financial matters concerning expenditure on staff, materials, equipment, and maintenance, as well as in dealings with industrial firms for which his VUZ may undertake research work connected with their production plans. Rectors are appointed by the Ministry of Higher and Secondary Specialised Education and so are their deputies, one of whom is usually responsible for academic matters and the other for finance and the running of the plant. Deans are elected by members of their faculties. Staff appointments are made by appropriate commissions chaired by the rector and are normally for a period of five years, after which the appointment can be extended for further five-year periods or come to an end.

The timetables of both students and staff are very heavy. The load of compulsory courses and laboratory periods has been cut from thirty-six hours per week to thirty to give students a chance to do some independent reading, but this still seems exorbitant. The six-day week remains in force, though some VUZ have cut it down to five on the understanding that the sixth day will be used by students for individual study.

The normal teaching-load of staff is not fixed except for those responsible for the compulsory courses in social sciences, which consist of dialectical and historical materialism, the history of the

CPSU, and philosophy, which includes scientific communism and atheism. For the lecturers in these subjects the annual teaching-load is fixed at 550 hours, and at 420 hours per annum if they are heads of departments. Surveys carried out in the 1960s to ascertain how staff members spent their time revealed that, together with preparation for lectures and administrative work, staff members usually work 58 or 59 hours weekly. Senior members tend to spend about one-third of their time on teaching and two-thirds on research and administration, while junior members spend up to two-thirds of their time on teaching. In both cases the work-load could be reduced if more secretarial and technical assistance was available, particularly in the preparation of experiments and the assembling of documentation. Some economists would like norms of work to be set centrally, and suggest a total work-load of 1,560 hours per annum, of which professors should spend 600 on teaching, lecturers 720, and assistants 780.

Even major universities still feel the effects of the long period during which they were regarded merely as teaching institutions, indeed just glorified schools, while all research work was concentrated in scientific research institutes. This division of functions was not the result of any ideological bias but was caused by the shortage of scientists, whose numbers had been depleted by the Revolution. On the other hand, the adoption of the first Five-Year Plan called for a tremendous expansion of education. In order to enable leading scientists to concentrate on research and, to a lesser extent, on writing textbooks, they were relieved of teaching duties, while much less qualified staff did the teaching with the help of their textbooks in rapidly proliferating VUZ, with their mounting numbers of students.

As the supply of more or less qualified specialists rose and became more or less adequate to meet the requirements of industry, including education itself, it was recognised that truly higher education cannot be achieved unless staff keep abreast of the latest developments in their field and, moreover, become themselves capable of original research. So the idea of a VUZ as both an educational and a research institution gained ground in the late 1950s.

One of the first and most successful cases of symbiosis between research institutes and VUZ took place when the Siberian branch of the Academy of Sciences of the USSR was established in Novosibirsk in 1957, immediately followed by the foundation of the Novosibirsk University. These institutions developed in close collaboration. Since then many departments of other VUZ have established joint research laboratories with appropriate research institutes; in other cases research institutes were established jointly by two related VUZ with similar departments, e.g. the physics department of a university and a physics department in an institute of engineering joining forces to work on a common project. Some larger VUZ have set up interdepartmental research laboratories, for instance when an engineering and a geological department in Tomsk collaborated on some complex construction problems in Siberia.

Apart from attracting better staff, opportunities for research have enabled senior students to partake in some projects. As a consequence, the very aim of higher education is being transformed from merely assimilating available knowledge to learning methods and discovering techniques for expanding the frontiers of science.

The development of research work in VUZ is probably one of the most promising features of the Soviet educational scene, for it affects not merely institutions of international standing, but many smaller ones in their endeavours to break new ground, even if within narrow fields. It also helps to direct students towards future careers in the sense that those endowed with gifts for research discover their abilities before they graduate, whereas others will be content to undertake later more routine jobs or be persuaded to take up school-teaching. The volume of VUZ research work is becoming so important that they have been invited to submit plans which will be included in the general plan for the development of science drafted by the Academy of Sciences of the USSR.

Consulting and experimental work for industry is growing very considerably. It both promotes innovation in industry and brings income to VUZ. As usual, the material basis of all too many VUZ is quite inadequate. Student numbers have outstripped available library and laboratory facilities and even classroom accommodation. Many impressively large, well-equipped, new universities have been built, for instance in Moscow, Kharkov, Novosibirsk, or the new polytechnicum in Irkutsk on the banks of the Angara; yet many others are still housed in very old buildings, some of which were never designed for the purpose; for instance, in stately town houses built by aristocratic families on what was a large scale for housing one family and its retainers, but not at all adequate to accommodate a VUZ catering for several thousand day and evening students.

Work on the building site chosen for the new 'university city' in Leningrad started only at the end of the 1960s. There are similar shortages in student hostel accommodation, in furnishing and equipment. However, where there is a will there is a way, and there certainly is a will to learn among the population; in the past students have put up with and are still undeterred by considerable hardships confronting them in their pursuit of tertiary education.

Another important development is the provision of special courses at major VUZ for retraining lecturers and instructors from smaller and more backward institutions.

Since 1966 special faculties for the raising of qualifications of VUZ staffs have proliferated, and in 1968-69 the number of specialists attending them had reached a total of 17,000 (out of a total VUZ staff of 272,000). Half of these courses were in highly specialised subjects in the rapidly developing natural sciences, but there were others in general science, economics, and physical culture. Some lecturers from provincial engineering schools were attached not to faculties for the raising of qualification but to large modern industrial enterprises to enable them to gain practical experience in new technologies. One of the methods used at these refresher courses was to make these student-lecturers prepare and read papers to be discussed in class; another was to instruct them in the use of computers and other modern 'hardware', or else to partake in a research project being carried out at the major VUZ to which they had been seconded, or to mark and comment on the written work of undergraduates at a major institution. These courses, initially designed to last four months, have been extended to cover a whole academic year. Many student-lecturers take advantage of their study-leave either to start or to complete a thesis. In the USSR completing a course at a VUZ entitles the successful student to a diploma, not a degree; there are, however, two types of higher degrees – that of 'candidate', roughly equivalent to a Ph.D., and that of doctor, awarded on the basis of important or numerous publications.

Small VUZ are apparently reluctant to grant study-leave to members of their staff, since the teaching-load of the absentees has to be shared out among their overworked colleagues. Nevertheless, it is hoped to expand these refresher courses to cater for 30,000 or 32,000 lecturers annually. As already mentioned, similar refresher courses for lecturers in pedagogical institutes are organised by the Academy of Educational Sciences. As regards lecturers in social sciences, i.e. in Marxism-Leninism, their subject is regarded as so important that six special institutes for raising the qualifications of specialists in social sciences have been set up.

Yet another new development is research into the didactics of higher education and the psychological and physiological factors affecting academic success. A council for scientific methods of education in higher schools has been set up by the Ministry of Higher and Secondary Specialised Education of the USSR. Interest in the subject seems to have been sparked off by the introduction of programmed learning. Among the major problems on the agenda are those of intensifying the assimilation of knowledge and at the same time presenting it in a less time-consuming form. There is no point in expanding curricula, raising standards, and increasing the learning-load before first assessing the amount of information that can be mastered by a student within a given period of time and before investigating how this information is perceived, digested, remembered, or forgotten, and how it affects further thought-processes. Indeed, it must be first ascertained to what extent thought-processes can be reduced to algorithms. Educational psychology has still no definite assessments of the relationships of the physiological acuteness of sensory perceptions and their relation to the thought- and learning-processes. Questions now raised are: what subjects can be programmed and to what extent; or should programming be limited to a testing device? Does its value lie primarily in the obligation it puts on the instructor to analyse precisely what information is essential and what is merely illustrative and secondary? Is illustrative material, educationally speaking, really superfluous, or can it be aesthetically or emotionally important and, therefore, even necessary? Apart from cognitive factors, others affect the learning process, e.g. motivation. What makes some students set their target no higher than the pass-mark and display no deep interest in their subject? What are the causes of drop-out? In the first year drop-out may result from a realisation of lack of ability to master the subject or wrong choice; but what causes drop-out in later years? While directing the course content at the average student, how can opportunities for individual studies be made available in Soviet mass institutions to promising young men capable of research activities? Strong arguments are put in favour of technical devices, but how shall radio, television, and recorded lectures fit in or alternate with the traditional lecture and seminar work, since their respective effectiveness is still a matter of opinion and has not been quantitatively assessed?

Another aspect of the 1969 Statute of a Higher Education Establishment is the stress laid on *vospitanie*, that is, on character formation and the building-up of firmly held convictions. The aim of higher education is seen as twofold: on the one hand it is to educate a scholar and a scientist, preferably one capable of doing original research work and advancing human knowledge, and on the other to mould him into a staunch supporter of communism. The obsessive concern with ideology has been mentioned already in connection with the *Komsomol*. If the aim of communism is the establishment of a scientifically organised society to which everyone would contribute according to their ability and from which they would receive according to their needs, the goal in itself should be sufficiently desirable not to require a continuous verbal reassertion of its superiority over that of a capitalist society motivated solely by material gain. In any case, if the economic basis determines ideology, the latter should be directly conditioned by it. So either the material and technical basis is still inadequate for the emergence of a truly communist superstructure and, therefore, indoctrination is a manifestation of voluntarism – in fact, a substitute for the genuine superstructure – or else the superstructure affects the basis to a greater extent than is usually admitted. In the latter case, material development, if not rationally directed to a predetermined goal (predetermined not by productive forces but by ideological concepts), may lead simply to a type of affluent society. Although desirable in itself, the affluent society should not be allowed to develop the consumer mentality prevalent in Western post-industrial societies. To possess more and more things should not be the aim of life, but only a means to a higher aim – a fully developed human personality.

Education for Leisure

Leisure-time is increasing with a shorter working week and the improvement of trade and service facilities for the population; hence education for leisure is beginning to be envisaged. The 1966 decree on secondary education set up a special post of deputy headmaster (or headmistress) in charge of out-of-school activities. It also enjoined *Komsomol* and Pioneer organisations to go all-out to make children's lives interesting, active, and healthy.

Sport

More is being done for sport. Organised games are not part of the normal school curriculum, but for many years Pioneer and *Komsomol* organisations have been running a great variety of circles for children interested in music, drama, making things (from embroidery to aircraft models), as well as organising excursions and sport events. Both youth organisations have at their disposal considerable funds, Pioneer Palaces and Houses, children's railways, and facilities for lending or hiring out sports-gear and providing instructors.

For centuries displays of physical fitness were a part of traditional folklore connected with combat games and acrobatic horse-riding, for which Cossacks, Kirghiz, and other steppe horsemen became world-famous. During the early years of the Revolution life was too chaotic, intense, and tragic for sports and games to gain widespread appeal. Mass sport organisations slowly expanded after World War II, but facilities remained scarce and scant. Suffice to say that in 1952 there were only three indoor swimming pools in the whole of the country. That year was also the one in which Soviet athletes made their debut at the Olympic Games.

Among the games gaining increasing popularity is (soccer) football. It came to Russia at the beginning of the century, and it has been reported that Khrushchev told businessmen at the British Trade Fair in Moscow in 1961 that he had played left-half in a football team organised by the British-owned engineering firm where he had worked as a fitter in his youth. Certainly since those far-off days football has become a national game, and stadia to seat thousands of spectators have been built in all major cities. Volleyball, basketball, swimming, and water polo are also immensely popular. Winter sports like skiing and skating can be easily enjoyed anywhere during the long Russian winter, and the Soviet ice-hockey team has repeatedly come out top in winter olympics, though not in 1969 when it was beaten by the Czechs, an event highlighted by the anti-Soviet rioting in occupied Prague.

The connection between sport and military training is fostered by an association known under the initials GTO, corresponding to the Russian phrase, 'ready for work and defence'. Training includes hurling a 700 gm. grenade 35 metres and firing a small-bore rifle at 50 metres. There has also long been in existence a voluntary association known under the initials DOSAAF, standing for the Russian equivalent of Voluntary Co-operation with the Armed Forces. It is now called upon to expand its facilities and organise para-military summer camps for older boys, both those still at school and those already at work. The introduction of pre-conscription training in schools as well as at enterprises and institutions (through DOSAAF and the *Komsomol* primaries) originated with the passing of the Law on Military Training and Conscription in October 1967. Conscription has always existed in the Soviet Union, but the present preoccupation with pre- and post-conscription military training is a result of strained relations with China. The danger from the USA has always been nuclear annihilation, not conquest in the old sense; occupation by American ground forces of an utterly devastated and biologically lethal area after the nuclear strike would be too irrational to be even considered. A war with China, on the contrary, would be an invasion of incalculable human hordes across land frontiers thousands of miles long.

Organisationally, local sports clubs form larger associations with the Union of Sport Societies and Organisations at the top of the pyramid. This union ranks as an autonomous social organisation somewhat on the lines of the All-Union Trade Union Congress or the Union of Writers of the USSR.

More expensive forms of sport like yachting, riding, and horseracing, are gaining ground as the country becomes materially better-off, increasingly consumer-minded and pleasure-loving. The government and Party are fully aware of the importance of sport for the health of the nation and for providing harmless outlets for aggression and socially harmful impulses, as well as for the military value of physical fitness and the international prestige that winning teams confer on the country and the Party. But interest in sport is not limited to a narrow circle of semi-professional athletes trained to win gold medals at international events. On the contrary, sport in the Soviet Union is characterised by its *massovost*; indeed, it is a mass movement, and in recent years up to 55 million people have been taking part in local sports events, republican competitions, and nationwide *spartakiads*. Calisthenics or artistic gymnastics bridge the gap between sport and ballet, which is one of the most flourishing forms of art in the USSR. Indeed, sport is backed by science and there is in Moscow a scientific research institute where the anatomical adaptation of the human body to the strains imposed on it by physical effort is studied. Even old people are increasingly attending keep-fit classes.

Tourism, camping, and mountaineering are also gaining ground. In June 1969 a decree was passed to promote tourism, extend hotel-building, and expand camping facilities. Hotel accommodation in the Soviet Union is very limited and, apart from Intourist hotels,[13] much of it rather primitive. It is now planned to build accommodation of various types which could cater for 200,000 persons at a time, half of which would be usable all the year round, not only in the summer. In Moscow and Leningrad the Trade Union Council will build compounds to provide accommodation simultaneously for 10,000 and 5,000 tourists respectively. The expansion of private motoring will call for the setting-up of service stations. The number of trains with sleeping accommodation and steamers for pleasure trips are to be increased. More maps are to become available for motorists, mountaineers, and ramblers.

Geographical conditions complicate the organisation of tourism. Sunny riviera-type summer resorts are limited to the strips of land along the southern shore of the Crimea and the Black Sea coast,

[13] Intourist is a special travel agency for foreigners. It lays on tours and provides transport, accommodation, interpreters, and other services payable in foreign currency. Intourist hotels are open to all, but priority is given to foreign travellers who pay their expenses with Intourist coupons. This arrangement serves a treble purpose: (*a*) to earn foreign currency for the USSR; (*b*) to spare foreigners who do not speak Russian trouble with time-tables, porters, taxis, etc., and protect them from the usual mishaps to which foreign travellers are prone; and (*c*) to shepherd them to places and hotels where their comings and goings can come if necessary under surveillance, for in Soviet eyes an alien is likely to be a potential spy.

south of the Caucasus range. Climatically less attractive, but within easy reach of Leningrad, are the Baltic coast resorts with better tourist amenities, communications, and traditions of service going back to the nineteenth century. The Caucasus could, with more roads and hotels, become a second Switzerland; in fact, with its higher peaks and the sub-tropical climate of the Rion valley, into an even finer playground with a fairly long tourist season. Further east the Tian-Shan mountains are still so remote and inaccessible that mountaineering there is like climbing in the Himalayas, something for the specialist, but not a place for a Moscow fitter or textile-worker to take his family to for a three weeks' holiday. A vast project to turn a large area around Lake Baikal in Siberia into a national park may save this unique lake from the pulp- and paper-mills, one of which is already poisoning its pristine waters. Young and hardy tourists may find other austere and unspoilt beauty spots along the huge Siberian rivers and even the geyserland of the Kamchatka, but all these remote places require expensive development. Nearer home there are many mediaeval towns in European Russia that are becoming centres of attraction and where works of restoration have been going on throughout the 1960s. Some, like Novgorod and Pskov, have suffered very badly at the hands of the German armies; others nearer Moscow, like Suzdal, Vladimir, Rostov, and Yaroslavl, at the hands of the builders of communism who thought that to build the future one had first to destroy all memories of the past. Thus, in the 1930s, the Chudov monastery within the walls of the Moscow Kremlin was blown up to make room for the yellow and white, classical-style building of the Supreme Soviet. Fortunately, the shortage of housing and the thickness of mediaeval walls saved many churches from destruction; they were turned into cinemas or warehouses and survived, though naturally their frescoes peeled off and the ancient ikons were chopped up for firewood. A similar fate befell the ancient monuments of Central Asia, though the restoration work carried out in Samarkand is quite remarkable. It was speeded up for the celebration of the 2,500th anniversary of the town, mentioned already as one of the places conquered by Alexander the Great during his military campaigns.

Tourism is a sign that affluence as well as culture is spreading to increasingly large numbers of the population. Those in power recognise its value for the health of the people, and also its cultural and patriotic importance. Well-informed guides are to be provided in places of historical interest. Since 1969, treks to 'Lenin's memorial places', including the remote village of Shushenskoe where Lenin was exiled and where he wrote one of his major works, *The Devel-*

opment of Capitalism in Russia, published in 1899, have been particularly encouraged as part of the worldwide celebrations of Lenin's centenary.

Culture

Alongside sport, aesthetic appreciation is given more attention, and the teaching of music in schools is being promoted. Usually schools provide only one singing lesson a week if they can find a suitable teacher. In 1969 there were just under 22,000 trained music-teachers, and of these less than 3,000 had completed a *konservatoriya*, i.e. an academy of music. The others had been trained in singing and playing an instrument at specialised secondary schools. Further opportunities to perform are, however, provided by Pioneer and *Komsomol* organisations, which have musical instructors and lend instruments to their members. Balalaikas, accordions, and seven-string guitars are among the most popular instruments, and are often used for accompaniment to singing. Russian folk-songs, as well as songs from other republics, are widely appreciated. Jazz, long looked upon with disfavour as a manifestation of Western decadence, has been smuggled in under the label of folk-art. The major handicaps are the usual material shortages: shortages of instruments, of scores, and often of notepaper. Even selections of popular songs are printed in editions of only 50,000, and scores of classical music in editions of one thousand to 3,000 copies. On the credit side, it must be noted that scores and records are very cheap. Apart from schools, Pioneers, and *Komsomol*, trade unions often have their own song and dance groups. The Baltic republics – Estonia, Latvia, and Lithuania – boast the best children's choirs and the most outstanding youth festivals; these are held annually in many parts of the Soviet Union, but in the Baltic republics with particular success, for they are thus given an opportunity to assert their national identity.

There are many theatres 'for the young spectator' in the Soviet Union, where plays for children are performed. In Moscow there is also a children's musical theatre which stages light operas that can be performed not only by professionals but by the children themselves. Pioneers also have drama circles. In smaller towns and larger villages there are 'culture workers' attached to the local club; often they act as librarians, but many are trained as organisers of amateur theatricals. Several well-known song and dance ensembles have come into existence in the course of musical festivals arranged by competing *Komsomol* and trade union artistic groups. The famous Soviet Army Choir came into being in this way during army-unit singing competitions. The best singers were then selected, discharged from the army, and sent for training to academies of music; naturally they eventually became professionals, but they did not start as professional singers who then donned uniforms.

The arts of singing and dancing are the most popular and widespread among the population of the Soviet Union, both old and young. However, drawing and painting are growing in popularity and children's work exhibitions are held regularly in many towns; some of these trials of the brush have even been on world tours.

Like sport, cultural manifestations in the USSR tend to be on a mass scale, which inevitably means that standards are not always outstanding. It is both a blessing and a curse that the spread of high-quality records, colour photography, and the replacement of live theatre by easily available highly artistic films leaves less and less room for the minor talent unable to compete and discouraged by comparisons with the performance of great musicians, singers, dancers, composers, acrobats, and other artists, whom obviously he cannot emulate. On the other hand, modern technical devices do spread culture and enable a growing public to appreciate and enjoy art forms, formerly the exclusive privilege of small élites.

Not all Soviet culture is very highbrow or inspiring, but it is on a mass scale. One should remember that, not in Victorian England, but in the affluent 1960s in the large industrial cities of the Midlands, children during the summer holidays had literally nowhere to go and nothing to do. It took years for municipalities, egged on by private initiative, to lay on youth arts centres and children's playgrounds. Seen from this angle, Soviet urban Parks of Culture and Rest have much to be said for them. The culture may not be very refined, the plays in the open-air theatres may be naïve and moralising, the open-air concerts may not be up to the London Philharmonic Orchestra standards, but they are there for anyone who wishes to come; for the children there are rowing-boats on the pond, luna-park attractions, rows of chessboards for old and young, and a dance floor where one can take one's girl-friend out for the evening. In winter there are skating on the pond and artificial slopes for children's toboggans.[14]

The major maintenance work in Parks of Culture and Rest is done by gardeners, scavengers, and other municipal employees, but *Komsomol* and Pioneer organisations are expected to help by send-

[14] Under the circumstances it may seem strange and even shocking that museums should charge an entrance fee; but in a country where for so long housing was in a desperate state, with one room in a communal flat to accommodate a whole family, a well-heated museum in winter would have soon become more like an overcrowded wartime air-raid shelter than a sanctuary of culture.

ing detachments of volunteers who give up a Saturday or Sunday to sweep the snow off the paths or help with digging and planting in spring or tidying the place in the autumn. Meanwhile, other volunteer groups of *Komsomol* and Pioneers may go off to gather wild-growing medicinal plants or scrap-metal. The value of such manifestations of public spirit and of labour given freely, willingly, and collectively, is regarded as an important part of education for citizenship. It is assumed that there is more satisfaction in constructive than in destructive activities. Creativity is surely more gratifying than vandalism. Indeed, it may be less tempting to destroy things which one has helped to make; they embody some of your own toil and time, they create a bond between the maker and the thing made. In a much wider perspective, self-service creates a bond between the citizen and the country to which he contributes his labour; indeed, the service he renders to the community benefits him as much as the community at large.

Chapter 8

Literature and the Arts

The Origins of Socialist Realism

SINCE 1932 ALL SOVIET WRITERS who wish to have their works published have belonged to the Union of Writers and subscribed to the method of socialist realism. The exact definition of the term is elusive. It came into usage in the early 1930s. Essentially, socialist realism postulates that art should not be obscure and esoteric, but accessible to the masses; furthermore, it should reflect reality, although the attention of the artist or writer should be focused on the progressive socialist aspects of reality and convey an optimistic message of hope and faith in man and in the bright destiny of his planet.

The concept of socialist realism took many years to evolve. It crystallised in the 1930s under the impact of political events and social changes due to industrialisation, collectivisation, and the disappearance of whole classes together with the emergence of a powerful totalitarian state-structure. It was midwifed by bitter polemics between competing literary groups. Most of them sought to discard all traditions and create a truly proletarian culture in accordance with the Marxist view that art is part of the superstructure and that the latter changes in accordance with changes in the economic basis. To understand the purpose and method of socialist realism and its connection with nineteenth-century traditions, something must be said about the search for new concepts and novel forms, which makes the literature of the early years of the Revolution fascinating until the present day. In those early days, politicians (Lenin in the first place) had little time to devote to art and literature. Indeed, their energies were absorbed by the struggle to establish and consolidate power over the vast expanse of the old empire, to fight a bitter civil war against disunited but determined opponents, to subdue national minorities, and to overcome the economic chaos into which the country had sunk, with the concomitant famines and epidemics that ravaged it.

Though censorship was imposed immediately, its prime object was to silence political opposition – not to legislate on literary matters about which the new leadership held vague and often

LITERATURE AND THE ARTS 179

divergent views. Admittedly, as far back as 1905 Lenin had declared that writers belonging to his Party were in duty bound to write in a way that promoted Party aims. He had praised Gor'ky's novel *Mother*, which came to be regarded later as a prototype of socialist realist novels. Lenin did not like Mayakovsky's poetry, and was critical of the endeavours to create a proletarian culture (*Proletkult*) because he suspected Bogdanov, one of its major proponents, of 'god-seeking' propensities and distrusted any type of organisation outside direct Party control.

Most writers who had made their name before the Revolution welcomed it, but were soon overtaken by the magnitude and harshness of events. Few of them were Marxists, and fewer still understood the implications of what was to come. For many, like Aleksandr Blok, the Revolution was the mighty wind of freedom blowing away the shackles of past bondage, or an apocalyptic snowstorm cleansing the earth of its old sins. Esenin mistook the Revolution for an awakening of the mythological peasant hero, Ilya Muromets, and the dawn of a peasant millennium. Though many intellectuals had hailed the Revolution, its violence and the setting-up of the *Cheka* a few weeks after the Bolshevik seizure of power to co-ordinate mass executions turned a number of writers away from a Party whose propaganda appealed to savage mob instincts. Bunin, Kuprin, L. Andreyev, Merezhkovsky, and others emigrated. Some remained. A few like Blok and, to a certain extent, the old 'populist' Korolenko, perished from sheer physical exhaustion, malnutrition, and cold during the hard Civil War years. The poet Gumilev, a one-time husband of Anna Akhmatova, was shot as a counter-revolutionary. Yet others, including A. Bely, Bryusov, Chukovsky, and later Aleksei N. Tolstoy, tried to come to terms with the new reality, and depicted in their work the questioning, hesitations, suffering, and final acceptance of communist rule by the old intelligentsia.

Most consonant with the mood of the Revolution were various avant-garde poets, in particular the youthfully aggressive groups of Futurist painters and writers. They had been active in word and deed for several years before the Revolution. Their provocative manifestos, such as *A Slap in the Face of Public Taste* (1912), called for the emancipation of words from the shackles of grammar, syntax, and normal semantic usage. Poets should invent their own words and use words with no concrete meaning in evocative combinations and suggestive associations. Rhymes, if any, should be placed indifferently at the beginning or the end of the line. Printed lines should be such as to allow them to be read from right to left as well as from left to right. The ballast of classical literature should be thrown overboard from the 'steamship of modernity'. A genuine concern for the value and power of sounds, and a mood of impatient and irrational rebellion against the obsolescent world into which these young men had been born, destined them to be the literary forerunners of cataclysmic upheaval. They greeted the Revolution with enthusiasm. 'To the streets, Futurists, drummers, poets, the streets are our brushes, the public squares are our palettes!' cried Mayakovsky, their most gifted spokesman. His powerful voice thundered in halls, bohemian cafés, and workers' clubs where he read his poetry (his *Left March* in January 1919, his *150,000,000* early in 1920), or at literary meetings organised by the People's Commissariat of Education. There he argued that art must not be concentrated in dead museum-temples but should live everywhere – on streets, in tramcars, factories, and workers' dwellings. His *Mystery Bouffe*, with its crudely blasphemous, absurd, and magnificently strident lines and irrepressible phantasy, is a play designed to be performed in the streets, using all the artifacts of an urban industrial setting to symbolise the end of the old world and the triumph of a new dispensation. (Actually it was staged in a theatre by Meyerhold and Bebetov early in 1921.)

As a champion of the Revolution, Mayakovsky fought for it from October 1919, day in and day out, by drawing posters for ROSTA (Russian Telegraphic Agency) windows. The posters illustrated the latest news, and he composed rhymes and slogans for them. The rhymes were usually parodies of well-known fairy-tales, songs, and proverbs; they enhanced the vigorous sketches, and made their point with coarse wit. On one poster, for example, a caricature pictured Mayakovsky shouting to a Red Army man, 'This is what the Powers bring to the people'. It was accompanied by four sketches – a grave with the caption 'Land for the people'; gallows, 'Freedom for the Workers'; a gaol, 'An Abode for the Homeless'; and a blow in the face from an enormous fist, 'Food for the Hungry'.

Mayakovsky's lasting fame rests on his early poetry and later plays (*The Bedbug* and *The Bathhouse*), but in all his post-1917 activities he led the struggle for a new art which would combine words, sounds, colours, and movements to serve, educate, and appeal to the masses. It was in that spirit that he formed the LEF (Left Front in Art) and began editing a journal of the same name. Mayakowsky and his Futurists were unimpeachable revolutionaries, but they were not of proletarian origin.

Nor, strictly speaking, were the founders of the *Proletkult*. The origins of this movement went back to 1909 when Bogdanov, Lunacharsky, the historian Pokrovsky, and Gor'ky founded a Party school for workers at the villa which Gor'ky owned on the isle of

Capri. After October, genuine factory-workers, anxious to enter the literary field, found support in Lunacharsky, now People's Commissar of Education, as well as in Bogdanov, the main theoretician of the *Proletkult*. According to the latter, proletarian art perceives and reflects the world from the point of view of the labour collectivity, and therefore the spirit of this art is that of labour collectivism. The 1918–19 events in Austria, Germany, and Hungary held out the promise of an imminent world revolution, and both Party members and workers expected it to sweep the entire planet. The Revolution was apprehended as a cosmic conflagration, and proletarian writers sought for a language and imagery that would convey the overpowering greatness of the most crucial event in human history – the victory of the long downtrodden masses led by the urban industrial proletariat over their capitalist oppressors. Henceforth poetry, like industry, could no longer be the task of individual craftsmen poets but, like industry, it would be manufactured by the masses.

> The poetry of the collective principle and the joy of labour as creation, the poetry of the technically organised world, a world subjected to the creative will of man set free from material dependence – man the cosmist – is the pulse of proletarian culture.

The pronoun 'I', so much used and misused by individualistic poets, was replaced by 'we', reflecting the collective, group endeavours.

> We are the countless, dread legions of labour,
> We have vanquished the expanse of seas, oceans and dry land,
> We have lit towns with the light of artificial suns,
> Our proud souls are burning with the fire of rebellion.
> (V. Kirillov)
> . . .
> We will find a new dazzling road for our planet!
> . . .
> We will plant the stars in rows and put the moon in harness.
> . . .
> The world itself will be a new machine, where the cosmos will, for the first time, find its own heart, its heartbeat.[1]
> (A. Gastei)

[1] Quoted in *Istoriya russkoi sovetskoi literatury*, Moscow, 1958, pp. 23–5. Hence the ironical implication of the title of Zamyatin's novel, *We*, which was never published in the USSR, but influenced considerably George Orwell's *1984*.

Appropriately, a Leningrad group was known as *Cosmists*, while a Moscow group voiced its aspirations to forge a new civilisation by calling itself the *Smithy*. Most proletarian writers were poets. There was no time for writing leisurely novels. Indeed, the shortage of paper in those days of economic collapse precluded bulky publications.

The new civilisation was not to be cramped by the old one, so 'in the name of our tomorrow we will burn Raphael, destroy museums, and trample underfoot the flowers of art'. The old culture, a cherished privilege of the idle rich, was doomed like their coats-of-arms, top hats, and other insignia of social and intellectual superiority. In any major social upheaval there is always an unconscious craving to eject old occupants and make room – room at the top – for newcomers. By emigrating, well-known living writers had vacated the front stalls of literary fame, but the dead still clogged library shelves and school textbooks. Destruction was in the air. Yet Lenin and other Party intellectuals like Trotsky and Bukharin held the view that the proletariat was heir to *all* human culture created by previous generations. It should be sifted and adapted, not rejected wholesale. Lenin lent a favourable ear to Maxim Gor'ky's pleading for help to save libraries, works of art, anything that Gor'ky's devotion to culture could salvage from annihilation in those hectic days of crumbling values. To him many scholars, writers, and artists owed their physical survival. In September 1918, to enable them to qualify for ration cards, he initiated a state publishing house, *World Literature*, and set them to work on translations. A year later in Petrograd, in the luxurious town residence of a merchant who had fled the country, Gor'ky opened a House of Arts, which was both a meeting-place for artists and a hostel for those in need of food and shelter.

In December 1919, together with Lunacharsky, he set up a literary section at the People's Commissariat of Education

> to regulate the relations between the state and the literary, artistic life of the country, render support to living literary forces, unions, clubs, and circles, and strive to discover literary talents latent in the nation.[2]

Among the nine members of the board were Blok, Gor'ky, two representatives of the *Proletkult* central committee, and others.

Smaller groupings like the *Constructivists* and the *Imaginists* came together in 1919. For a while Esenin was one of the latter.

[2] Quoted op. cit., p. 561.

Although the most active and vocal were the Futurists and the *Proletkult*, neither held any literary monopoly.

Early in 1921 the disastrous economic situation led Lenin to put forward his New Economic Policy, which was approved by the Tenth Party Congress. This was a temporary retreat from the totalitarianism of the Civil War policies. Peasants were no longer forced to give up all their surpluses of agricultural produce, but, after paying a tax in kind, were free to sell whatever was left on the open market. Small-scale private commercial and industrial enterprises, employing less than twenty workers, were allowed to open. In December 1921 this right was extended to privately owned and cooperative publishing houses. The proliferation of the latter mainly benefited those writers who were dubbed 'fellow travellers' by Trotsky. Without opposing the regime, fellow travellers remained unattached and rather independent in outlook. Chance had it that they were the most talented of their contemporaries. The existence of private publishing facilities gave them the opportunity to have their works published in Russia and occasionally even abroad, since several of the small publishing houses had branches abroad, namely in Germany, where in pre-Hitler days the left-wing movements were still strong.

Fellow travellers did not form groups, apart from the so-called Serapion Brothers. The Serapions had first met in the Translators' Studio of World Literature, where Kornei Chukovsky and Evgeny Zamyatin were in charge of the Anglo-American section. In the autumn of 1919 the critics Viktor Shklovsky and Boris Eikhenbaum joined the group. Both promoted the formalist approach to literature; they were solely concerned with analysis of form in a work of art, its structure, plot, and literary devices, irrespective of the social or moral content of the work analysed. Students who had been helping with the translation work now began to write themselves and became deeply interested in problems of literary techniques. In February 1921 several of them formed a group, taking for their patron saint St Serapion, or rather deriving their name from a cycle of tales by the German Romantic novelist E. T. A. Hoffmann. They proclaimed that politics and ideology were irrelevant to art.

> Art lives its own life and has no ultimate goal. Art is meaningless to politicians. Men of politics want only an art which works upon society – that is journalism. We, the Serapions, will not be journalists. We demand one thing – that the voice should not ring false.[3]

[3] Quoted by Max Eastman, *Writers in Uniform*, New York, 1934, p. 76.

The best known of the Serapions were M. Zoshchenko, Lev Lunts (who died at the age of twenty-two on a trip to Germany to see his parents), N. Nikitin, V. Pozner (who later emigrated and became a French novelist), M. Slonimsky, V. Kaverin (Silber), Vsevolod Ivanov, and K. Fedin.

In October 1921 Gor'ky, who had done so much for the cause of Russian culture as well as for individual writers, fell out with Lenin and left the country. A year later, in December 1922, Zinoviev, the Petrograd Party Secretary, ordered the Serapions to vacate the House of Arts. Although they continued to meet, they were now evolving each in his own way, and their initial enthusiasm for independent art slowly waned.

Meanwhile, at a congress of proletarian writers held in October 1920, an association first known as VAPP (All-Russian Association of Proletarian Writers), later, in 1928, renamed RAPP (Russian Association of Proletarian Writers), was formed to overcome divergences of opinion, such as, for instance, whether proletarian literature meant literature about the proletariat, by proletarians, or championing the proletarian cause. A splinter-group known as *October* attacked the cosmism of the *Smithy*, demanding that the dawn of the future be shown in living people, for example 'in some chairman of a lumber commissariat'.[4] However, most of them were agreed that proletarian literature must be organised like any other branch of the working-class movement,

> and in any organisation at least two things are necessary: unity of views and unity of action. The particular advantage of this is that it makes a particular systematic outlook obligatory upon every proletarian writer.

In an agreement between MAPP (Moscow Association of Proletarian Writers) and LAPP (Leningrad Association of Proletarian Writers) both associations undertook to oblige other members to carry out the policy agreed upon. 'Executive boards will take the sternest measures, including expulsion, against those members who fail to carry out the orders of their respective executive boards.'[5]

Subsections of VAPP ran study groups and literary circles for newcomers to literature from factory workshops, the *Komsomol*, or Red Guard detachments. Like Dmitry Furmanov, the author of *Chapaev*, leading proletarian writers felt that without guidance and organisation relatively uneducated proletarians would be at a dis-

---

[4] A. Bezymensky, quoted E. J. Brown, *The Proletarian Episode in Russian Literature, 1928–32*, New York, 1953, p. 15.
[5] Ibid., p. 17.

advantage in competing with fellow travellers and other near-bourgeois writers, who possessed a long literary and cultural tradition. In August 1923 they founded a journal, *Na Postu*, designed to promote a proletarian literature more closely concerned with daily life than with the cosmos, and to denounce fellow travellers and other dissenters allegedly exerting a baneful, baleful, and petty-bourgeois influence on the reading public. The moving spirit of the journal, Leopol'd Averbakh, was a nephew of Sverdlov and brother-in-law of Yagoda (Yahuda), later to become head of the *Cheka* (renamed GPU). He was also a relative of Yaroslavsky, who headed the anti-God campaigns. Not being of genuine proletarian stock, Averbakh and his co-editors (Lelevich and Gorbachev) interpreted the term 'proletarian literature' as one organising the consciousness of the readers in the direction of the ultimate goals of the Communist Revolution. Those literary productions which do not organise the consciousness of the reader in this direction cannot be counted as proletarian even though the authors are workers, members of the Party, etc.[6]

In the face of insistent requests for the enforcement of ideological conformity voiced by the proletarian writers, the Party's Central Committee issued a resolution in 1925 to the effect that until genuine proletarian literature reached a certain level of quality, the Party could not allow 'any legal monopoly of literary production on the part of one group or literary organisation' and could not 'grant this monopoly to any group – not even to the proletarian group'.

This short account of some of the literary trends in the 1920s shows that demands for the regimentation of literature arose not from the Party leadership as such, but from among ideologically committed writers confronted by the subversive success of more talented fellow travellers.

Although the first attempt to stifle ideologically dubious competitors and monopolise the literary scene failed, things began to change with the introduction of the first Five-Year Plan and the elimination of private enterprise, including private printing facilities. A genuine enthusiasm for industrialisation swept the country, and RAPP proposed that literature be geared to the economic plan. It became the patriotic duty of writers to make economic construction and the heroism of labour the subject-matter of their work. Suitable subjects for literary treatment were put forward under the expression *sots-zakaz* (social order) and paper and printing facilities became available only to those who by their pen contributed to the implementation of the Plan. In June 1931 censorship was

[6] Ibid., pp. 62–3.

tightened by the setting-up of a principal administration for the affairs of literature and publishing (*Glavlit*), with a network of local organs; no publication, apart from those emanating direct from the Party, could legally appear without its sanction. The purpose of literature was to keep the public informed and enthusiastic about building communism and to inspire an all-out effort. Artistic communication was a channel for 'public relations' on a vast scale. In their striving for analogies between economic progress and literary endeavours, theorists spoke of 'blueprints for literary production', or of 'literary Magnitogorsk'. Stalin is alleged to have referred to writers as 'engineers of the soul'. Even the concept of 'mass production' was extended to hundreds of men and women from all walks of life who had shown minor literary talent and were signed on to augment existing stocks of writers and encouraged to contribute *collectively*. A group would visit a new industrial enterprise or construction site, and each member of it would agree to write so much towards a general account of what progress was currently being made there.

How did writers react to the demands to confine their work to the contemporary economic scene? The issue was possibly one of individual artistic standards – one thing for the journalist but quite another thing for the serious artist. For if a journalist's choice of subject-matter is determined by what happens day by day, and if his treatment of it is subject to his editor's discretion, it should make little difference to him whether he reports on a construction project or a flower show. Likewise in the case of the author of popular fiction who writes for a living. It should hardly matter to him whether, in order to get his work published, he must satisfy the popular palate or the Party's exhortations – whether in fact he bases his next novel on the prescribed theme of the heroism of socialist construction and 'the hero of labour', or simply writes something which will sell. On these grounds it seems probable that the majority of writers had little difficulty in adjusting to the new requirements. However, for the serious artist who wants to nurture an original work of art and present an independent critique of the society in which he lives, the case is different. Yet throughout history artists have always been trammelled by restrictions of various sorts, and the greatest artists have repeatedly conquered them. As things turned out, the output of established serious novelists (Pil'nyak, Sholokhov, Leonov) during the Five-Year Plan period spoke much for the enthusiasm of the era. They gave to the task the full depth of their talent and imagination. Leonov wrote two novels on industrial themes (*Sot'* and *Skutarevsky*), and Sholokov interrupted work on his masterpiece, *Quiet flows the Don*, to write one of the best books about collectivisation, *Virgin Soil Upturned*; even so staunch a supporter of the regime had some difficulty in getting the work published without the censor's cuts, because he could not avoid showing that resistance to collectivisation was not entirely due to counter-revolutionary plots. At the time, in 1931, only part I of the book was published. The second part appeared thirty years later, and nowhere approaches the standards of Sholokhov's earlier work.

Didactic literature, *roman à thèse*, and *littérature engagée*, are not a uniquely Soviet phenomenon. Russian nineteenth-century writers seldom remained indifferent to contemporary social problems, and literary critics used fiction to preach social justice or denounce the plight of the underprivileged. The artistically less gifted and ideologically more involved like Chernyshevsky attempted even to create a positive hero (the fearless and highly principled Rakhmetov in the novel *What should be done*, 1862) and depicted the success of a Fourierist association.

Indeed, Maxim Gor'ky let it be known that he had no time for Marcel Proust's endless monologues about himself; a speaker at the First Congress of Soviet Writers in 1934 criticised Joyce's *Ulysses* on the grounds that the novel set in Dublin in 1916 failed to mention the political uprising of that year.

In 1932 the RAPP and all similar groupings were dissolved and all writers invited to join a new Union of Soviet Writers. The 1932 Party resolution assumed that all writers, even those who had not contributed any production novels, were now on the side of the new order; all were invited to the First Congress of Soviet Writers (1934) at which the method of socialist realism was adopted as the fundamental aesthetic doctrine of socialism. Perhaps more cramping than the doctrine was the corollary of *partiinost'* or 'Party spiritedness'; that is, the ability to see things from the Party point of view. This obliged the writer to accept Party policy as the ultimate source of truth about life. More cramping still was the effect of the purges that started shortly after the First Congress of Writers and during which many fellow travellers disappeared, as well as others, including Averbakh himself. The more fortunate, like Boris Pasternak, turned to translating Shakespeare and Georgian poets; others died of poverty and malnutrition, like M. Bulgakov, in whose play about Molière, Stalin or one of his censors sensed an implied criticism of downgrading an artist to the role of court jester. Bulgakov's fantastic story *The Master and Margarita* was published posthumously in 1966–67 and took Moscow by storm because of the novelty of its symbolism, the beautiful lucidity of its prose, and the bitter irony of its humour.

In discussing socialist realism one should bear in mind the tremendous increase in literacy consequent upon the introduction of universal compulsory schooling in 1930–32. The new reader could understand better the plain language and direct statement of Tolstoy or Gor'ky than the stylistic novelities of the 1920s. Soviet literature could not afford to 'serve sweet delicate biscuits to a small minority, while the worker and peasant masses needed black bread'.[7] If Gandhi had qualms about literacy for India on the grounds that Western literature was not fit for Indians to read, the Party's prescriptions ensured that Soviet literature was at least black bread for the masses, supplying educative, intellectual nourishment well within their understanding. Under Soviet rule the masses undoubtedly enjoyed more 'culture' than ever before. In addition to the steps taken against illiteracy, activities such as theatre-going and amateur dramatics were encouraged. However much the poor quality and monotony of many Soviet plays and stories of this period may be lamented, the workers and peasants were admittedly more enlightened by the mass literature of their own day than their forefathers had been by the internationally acknowledged masterpieces of the nineteenth century.

Literary Straitjacket

Probably the most depressing period of Soviet literature came immediately after World War II. There had been a great surge of patriotism during the war, and no one knew better than Stalin that the Soviet people had fought not for communism or the Party but for the survival of their country. If some of the most celebrated American war novels treat us to the sight of discontented GIs engaged thousands of miles from home in military operations which make no sense to them strategically, in a war whose origins they do not understand, alienated from and bullied by their superiors (who often seem to evoke more hatred and fear among them than the enemy) and finding their only relief from the brutality of the battlefield and the tedium of barrack life in desultory sex and homemade alcohol, Soviet war novels like Leonov's *Chariot of Wrath* or Viktor Nekrasov's *In the Trenches of Stalingrad* need hardly embellish or exaggerate unduly to present a picture of troops united in their will to resist foreign invaders who have razed their homes, cast lots for their womenfolk, and annihilated the hard-won industrial progress of the past decade.

The horrors of war had only just come to an end when Andrei Zhdanov, commonly tipped then as Stalin's likely successor, made

---

[7] Lenin's words quoted by Clara Zetkin in her article *My recollections of Lenin*, first published by the Institute of Marxism-Leninism, Moscow, 1924.

his notorious attack on Zoshchenko for a light-hearted short story entitled *The Adventures of a Monkey* (1946) and on the poetess Anna Akhmatova for her preoccupation with intimate poetry which had no bearing on the work of reconstruction.

The war had been won at great cost by the people's steadfastness and courage, despite Stalin's blunders. One of these was the arrest and execution of hundreds of Soviet army senior commanders in 1938 on trumped-up charges, including forged documents supplied through the Czech President Beneš by the German High Command; another was lack of preparedness resulting from Stalin's trust in Hitler's promise of non-aggression written into the Molotov–Ribbentrop pact (1939). The war had been won by the sacrifices of the people who had fought at the fronts and those who had worked and starved in the rear; starvation in towns in the rear was largely caused by the chaotic state of transport and general mismanagement. Yet after the war the Party wished to establish and perpetuate the fiction that it alone had been responsible for directing the efforts of the people towards victory and winning the war. Aleksandr Fadeev, a writer with a long record of Party service, was made to rewrite his novel *The Young Guard*, because his young heroes showed too much initiative and insufficient reliance on Party leadership.

Since in the course of years the Party had remodelled society, Soviet citizens were deemed to be no longer capable of displaying the vices that enable works of art to centre around conflicts between good and evil. If a writer wished to create a villain, it was at least prudent to trace his wickedness back to his upbringing in an imperfect pre-revolutionary era, as did Leonov in his *Russian Forest*, to the detriment of its psychological insight. Conflict could arise only between 'good' and 'better'. In case of disagreement, an all-wise Party secretary could always be called upon to intervene. The Party secretary became an important figure in post-war Soviet fiction. He was uniquely qualified to give advice on anything from long-term economic planning to marital tiffs. Not only was he (or she) a sort of local medicine man who could work miracles of economic development through propaganda or personal example if production was lagging; he was also a 'father confessor' possessed of rare insight, and open to consultation on a variety of personal and family problems. (Babayevsky's *Light over the Land*, and Kochetov's *The Zhuzbins.*)

The pressures on writers to glamorise and idealise during a period when material conditions were miserable and nearly every family had lost one or several killed in battle, threatened to lead to almost complete disassociation between life and literature. However much trouble Soviet collective farmers may have actually had in restoring their livelihood after the devastation of the war, their literary counterparts were apparently back to normal and flourishing within no time at all. (Babayevsky's *Knight of the Golden Star*.) Such characters seemed to live in the world of television advertising, to eat well, dress well, and have ample time to admire the beauties of the countryside and prognosticate about the bright future of mankind. Adulation of Stalin became a perennial feature of Soviet literature, and this swelled to a climax for the celebration of his seventieth birthday in 1949.

The severe restrictions on writers in their choice and treatment of themes alienated readers and audiences to the extent that the Party was forced to renounce the demand for *bezkonfliktnost'*, i.e. lack of conflicts which deprived drama of tension and interest. The public was reacting to the mediocrity and monotony of current literature by turning to the past. Measured in box-office receipts, the most successful plays were those of the nineteenth-century Russian playwright Ostrovsky, followed by Shakespeare.

Various Party and government controls instituted in the 1930s were rigorously applied. The Union of Writers of the USSR,[8] which had been set up ostensibly to give writers a useful medium for the exchange of creative ideas, became an instrument for the enforcement of the official literary credo and its senior executives, chosen for Party allegiance rather than for any outstanding contribution to literature, acted (and still act) as the Party's watchdogs. The state monopoly on publishing proved (and still proves) the main check on literary output, for nothing can be published without the sanction of *Glavlit*, and illegal publication is hardly possible when paper and ink are allocated centrally; moreover, in Stalin's day it was far too dangerous to voice, let alone write, anything that could be construed as deviating from the Party line.

More insidious and extremely effective (then and possibly more so now), given the failings of human nature, were the lavish royalties, prizes, and welfare benefits available to writers, which make conformist literature a very lucrative occupation. Sholokhov, Simonov, and A. Tolstoy are reputed to have made fortunes from their writing. Rates of pay were generous. They are still calculated in a truly bureaucratic manner on the number of pages in the case of novels or that of lines in a poem or of acts in a play. Established

[8] In the course of time, Union republics set up their own Unions of Writers, the last to do so being the RSFSR. It is, of course, the ambition of every writer to belong to both the Writers' Union of his own republic and that of the USSR. Membership is on application; applicants must have had two books published to be recognised as suitable for admission.

writers are entitled to higher rates.⁹ Other benefits include direct financial aid from the Literary Fund and trips to country resthomes run by the Writers' Union. It has been rumoured that some writers made applications for aid from the Literary Fund a regular part of their income.

The Thaw

None of these controls or baits has been altered since the death of Stalin, though a certain amount of freedom to speak the truth has been tolerated. The more liberal attitude to literature and art in general has come to be known as the 'Thaw', from the title of a short novel written by Ilya Ehrenburg in 1954, depicting a factory director boosting the production of his factory and his own reputation at the cost of substandard housing for his workers. A sudden thaw leads to flooding and the collapse of the jerry-built workers' flats. But the title also implies a thaw in the rigidity of controls and the story depicts a real conflict in industrial relations, and contrasts the art of a well-paid official painter and that of a sincere and poor individualist. A number of novels and short stories on life in the countryside depicting peasant poverty and officials' highhanded arbitrariness were allowed to appear. Among the best are those of F. Abramov, V. Soloukhin, and some later stories by V. Tendryakov.[10]

Though slightly older than the others, Tendryakov came to literature after World War II. One of his earlier stories, *The Miraculous Ikon* (1958), affords a good example of the cramping effect of narrow-minded *partiinost'* and the attendant lack of literary culture. The story centres on a small boy finding in the mud of a stream an ikon which had been reputed miraculous but had been thrown into the river when the village church was desecrated in some earlier anti-God campaign. The boy's pious grandmother regards the discovery as a miracle and her little grandson as God's chosen saint. She makes him repeat prayers and wear a small cross tied to his neck. Wearing a cross was a universal Russian custom, but is very much looked down upon in an atheist society. The child suffers from being teased for it by his playmates and chided by a teacher whom he loves. The division of loyalties between family affection and concern for the opinions of his age-peers and teacher

[9] In 1969 the rates for fiction in the RSFSR varied from 150 to 400 roubles per sheet, i.e. 16 pages, and 0·7 to 2 roubles per line of poetry. New impressions were paid 60 per cent for the first and second and decreased to 20 per cent of the initial sum for the eighth. The usual minimum size of an edition is 15,000 copies in the case of fiction. Until 1969 the author was not entitled to royalties on translations of his work.
[10] For instance, *Ephemeride—a short lifetime* ('Podenka vek korotky', *Novy Mir*, 1965, No. 5), and *The End* ('Konchina', *Moskva*, 1968, No. 3).

within a bewildered child's mind could have been emotionally tragic and deeply moving. However, *partiinost'* prevents the author from picturing a loving and loved grandmother either as truly religious or, like that of Gor'ky, as a primitive, poetic, and infinitely attractive pantheist; so we get a crudely superstitious old hag who beats the child to make him say his prayers and submit out of fear, leaving no room for emotional choice or agonising inner tensions. An external factor is brought in to reinforce superstitious fear, namely the mysterious midnight ringing of the church bell, which impresses the child until his enlightened teacher explains to him that it is the effect of resonance produced by the passing of the night train. Despite its lack of psychological depth, the story was made into a play and a film, showing the defeat of religious obscurantism and the triumph of science in accordance with the tenets of socialist realism. Tendryakov's later stories are psychologically far superior to this conformist little tale.

In the freer atmosphere of the Khrushchev era, K. Simonov allowed himself to allude in his war novels to the decimating effect of the purges on the Soviet army and showed the lamentable lack of preparedness for the German invasion of 1941. Yury Bondarev's novel *Silence* described the war from the point of view of those who found that the courage and initiative which they displayed on the battlefield were no longer welcome in the crushing political atmosphere of post-war Russia.

Younger writers, like Vasily Aksyonov or Viktor Rozov, seem more concerned with personal human problems. Their youthful heroes drift through life, unconcerned with ideology and indifferent to the calls of duty; they would sooner 'go west' for holidays in the European environment of the Baltic coast than heed the Party's call to go east and work on the new Siberian industrial construction sites. Culminating in this crescendo of stories, which depicted life as it was and not as it should be, came the publication of Solzhenitsyn's *One day in the life of Ivan Denisovich*, in the journal *Novy Mir* (in November 1962), with the express authorisation of Khrushchev, then bent on dissociating the Party from Stalin's regime of terror. This story of life in a concentration camp was the most outspoken ever to have been published in the USSR; since the fall of Khrushchev nothing but fleeting references to the terror is allowed. Solzhenitsyn fell into disfavour and in November 1969 was expelled from the Writers' Union for failing to prevent the publication abroad of his novels *Cancer Ward* and *In the First Circle*. Contrary to Pasternak, Daniel, and Sinyavsky, who deliberately sent their work abroad for publication, Solzhenitsyn has never sought publicity outside his own country and is solely concerned with reviving a truthful, sincere, and thought-provoking literature at home. *Cancer Ward* was accepted for publication in the monthly *Novy Mir*, and its publication was expected until January 1968, when its inclusion was finally stopped, although the proofs had already been printed. The typescripts of both parts of *Cancer Ward* and the first part of Solzhenitsyn's other major and obviously unfinished novel, *In the First Circle*, were apparently sold by agents of the KGB (Soviet secret service) in order then to charge the author with collusion with foreign agents.

Solzhenitsyn is probably the greatest writer to be born in Russia since the death of Leo Tolstoy and, like the latter, he is more than a fiction writer. The reasons for his rejection in the Soviet Union go deeper than resentment of his vivid depictions of concentration-camp life, and will be discussed in the last chapter of this book.

Perhaps the most encouraging feature of Soviet literature in the late 1950s and early 1960s was the resurgence of poetry and the fantastic vogue for public verse-reading by authors; crowds filled the largest halls to hear them, culminating in the huge crowd of 14,000 at the Luzhniki sports stadium in 1962, when the authorities began to take umbrage at such large and possibly explosive gatherings. In his autobiography, Evgeny Evtushenko relates how these gatherings started when a Day of Poetry was first organised in Moscow with poets reading their verse in one or two bookshops, first inside and then outside as the crowd increased. In the following years poetry-readings took place in Mayakovsky Square, by the statue erected to the great proletarian writer.

Disregarding some youthful attempts at versification, Evtushenko's first thought-provoking poem, *Zima*, was published in the magazine *Oktyabr'* in October 1956. 'My poetry', says Evtushenko in his autobiography,

> is the expression of those new moods and ideas which were already present in Soviet society but had not yet been poetically expressed. Had I not been there, someone else would have voiced them.

On his own admission Evtushenko is not one of those creative geniuses who bring ideas to society and fire their contemporaries with them. He is not the prophet-type poet of Pushkin's vision, but the echo-type of another Pushkin poem. However, it is no mean achievement to echo certain aspirations of the more questioning type of Soviet citizens or to mirror certain aspects of their harsh reality.

For those who, like Evtushenko, were still teenagers when Stalin died, what followed was a concatenation of bewildering events. First the Doctors' Plot was revealed to have been a frame-up, engineered by Stalin and his henchman Beria; then the first amnesties brought back thousands of deportees describing the horrors of labour-camp conditions and the magnitude of their population. Finally, Khrushchev's famous secret speech at the Twentieth Party Congress denouncing Stalin's crimes slowly percolated down to the rank-and-file Party members. The shock was traumatic.

The overthrow of the idol created a moral crisis among thoughtful young citizens. Evtushenko was one of them. His was the voice of the new anxiety, that of a poet who could put into words the bewilderment, the disorientation, and the craving for truth and justice of less articulate multitudes of young people whose faith in the Revolution was in danger of being shattered. The Revolution which they had been taught to regard as the crucial event in human history, the turning-point in man's evolution, had somehow gone astray, taken somewhere a wrong turning, a turning that had led to the abominations of Stalin's regime, with its callousness, its iniquities, mass deportations, and crimes which far too many men of the older generation had covered up out of fear and cowardice and concealed with unfathomable hypocrisy under sanctimonious dirges to the Revolution.

Evtushenko speaks of the uncertainty, anxiety, and craving for truth which he shared with so many others:

> Oh, those who are my generation
> We're not the threshold, just a step,
> We're but a preface to a preface,
> a prologue to a newer prologue.[11]

Those who had been blinded by decades of propaganda began to ask questions. 'They stopped being silent in their homes and began to talk to each other about the most urgent controversial problems.'[12] The greatest danger became the loss of faith, and to save the younger generation from lack of faith the ideals of the Revolution had to be restated and purified. This belief in the purification of revolutionary ideals, Evtushenko shared with Bella Akhmadulina, the young poetess who became his first wife. Purification meant rejection of evils and exposure of past 'mistakes'. This was a difficult task, for it was bound to bring all the old Stalinist

---

[11] *There is something I often notice*, translated by George Reavey, *The New Russian Poets 1953–1968*, bilingual edition, London, 1968, p. 71.
[12] Evtushenko, *Avtobiografiya*, London, 1964, p. 105.

clique to clamp down on the exposure of the evils which they had concealed, even if they had not condoned them. The years of thaw and freeze brought in turn fame and disgrace to Evtushenko. In 1957, for defending Dudintsev's *Not by bread alone*, Evtushenko was expelled from the Institute of Literature on the grounds that he was missing too many lectures (he had done so for the last four years). Later he was reinstated and even elected secretary of the *Komsomol* primary of the same institute. His popularity was to be reckoned with.

In 1960–63 he was allowed to travel abroad. His journeys took him to England, France, Bulgaria, Ghana, Liberia, Togo, and the USA. He had already travelled far and wide throughout his native country. It was in 1961 that he became internationally famous for his poem *Baby Yar*. The poem is about a spot near Kiev where, during the occupation, the Germans exterminated thousands of Jews. No monument was erected to mark the place or commemorate the massacre, a negligence which Evtushenko attributed to deliberate anti-semitism fostered by Stalin.

In his *Autobiography*, Evtushenko tells how he wrote the poem immediately upon returning to Moscow from Kiev. It took him two hours. That same evening he read it to a spellbound audience of 1,500 at the Polytechnical Institute. A standing ovation followed. A member of the Party since 1905 came forward to offer Evtushenko his support for admission to the Party. From the meeting at the Polytechnical Institute, Evtushenko took the poem to the office of *Literaturnaya Gazeta* and read it to a friend there. The latter called his colleagues and they all began asking to be allowed to copy the poem. 'Why copy?' asked Evtushenko, 'I have brought it to have it published in your paper.' They looked at him in amazement. It had never occurred to them that such a poem could be printed. However, it was taken to the editor-in-chief. Evtushenko waited for two hours. An old compositor came to express his admiration, but the order to print was still not forthcoming. Rumour spread that the editor-in-chief had telephoned his wife to come. Although most journalists had finished their day's work, they stayed on. It was getting on for midnight. The editor's wife arrived. There was another wait. At last Evtushenko was called in. Husband and wife were smiling. Together they had taken the risk. The next morning the paper was selling so fast that the issue looked like becoming a bibliographical rarity before the day was over.

Baby Yar is also the title of a novel by Anatoly Kuznetsov, who defected while in London in 1969, complaining bitterly of the cramping tyranny of Soviet censorship which made cuts and alterations to the text of manuscripts and thus distorted published work (his own and that of other authors, too).

Evtushenko's next political poem was *The Heirs of Stalin*, and it had to obtain Khrushchev's personal approval to be published. It was printed in no less a paper than *Pravda* itself on 21 October 1962.

The Heirs of Stalin
Mute was the marble.
      Mutely glimmered the glass.
Mute stood the sentries,
      bronzed by the breeze.
Thin wisps of smoke curled over the coffin.
      And breath seeped through the chinks
as they bore him out the mausoleum doors.
Slowly the coffin floated,
      grazing the fixed bayonets.
He also was mute –
      he also! –
        mute and dread.
Grimly clenching
      his embalmed fists,
just pretending to be dead,
      he watched from inside....
He was scheming.
      Had merely dozed off.
And I, appealing to our government,
      petition them
to double,
   and treble,
      the sentries guarding this slab,
and stop Stalin from ever rising again
    and, with Stalin,
      the past.
I refer not to the past,
      so holy and glorious,
of Turksib,
    and Magnitka,
      and the flag raised over Berlin.
By the past, in this case,
      I mean the neglect
of the people's good,
     false charges,
       the jailing of innocent men.

We sowed our crops honestly.
Honestly we smelted metal,
and honestly we marched,
     joining the ranks.
But he feared us.
    Believing in the great goal,
he judged
   all means justified
      to that great end.
He was far-sighted.
     Adept in the art of political warfare,
he left many heirs
    behind on this globe....
Some of his heirs tend roses in retirement,
thinking in secret
    their enforced leisure will not last.
Others,
  from platforms, even heap abuse on Stalin
but,
  at night,
    yearn for the good old days.
No wonder Stalin's heirs seem to suffer
these days from heart trouble.
     They, the former henchmen,
hate this era
   of emptied prison camps
and auditoriums full of people listening
     to poets....
While Stalin's heirs walk this earth,
Stalin,
  I fancy, still lurks in the mausoleum.[13]

With the fall of Khrushchev, de-Stalinisation was halted. It had been rumoured that Evtushenko's stay in Bratsk was not entirely voluntary. The message of the long poem *The Bratsk Hydropower-station* is unassailably orthodox. Slaves worked on pyramids for the personal glory of the Pharaoh and their labour was sterile. The work that goes into the erection of the hydropower-station will benefit humanity. Some sections are more ambiguous, and can be interpreted in several ways.

However, in the late 1960s Evtushenko was again allowed to travel. He went to Australia and to the Middle East. His style is

[13] Translated by George Reavey in *The Poetry of Yevgeny Yevtushenko, 1953 to 1965*, bilingual edition, London, 1966, pp. 160–65.

becoming more involved, the language more complex. This may be due to his desire for greater sophistication, an attempt at 'modernism'; it may be due to the desire to convey a hidden meaning and to disguise allegorically what cannot be said outright.

But Evtushenko is not merely a political protester. Much of his verse is very personal, lyrical, and delicate in feeling. Among his early poems is the moving *Weddings*. In another he compares the glamorous funeral of the poetess Anna Akhmatova to that of an unknown old woman, whose life must have been all toil and devotion and whose funeral is as inconspicuous as her hard and inconspicuously useful life.

The poetry of both Andrei Voznesensky and Bella Akhmadulina is more modernistic and sophisticated. Unlike Evtushenko, who could be described as a waif and received little formal education, Voznesensky is the son of a distinguished engineer, and an architect by training. The imagery of Voznesensky is extraordinary in its originality, conciseness, and use of twentieth-century vocabulary, from airports to antiworlds and to downright mathematical formulae. The symbolism is provocatively baffling and a challenge to the reader's own imagination. Alliterations, assonances, and other sound-effects abound. Outrageously crude coarseness mingles with great depth of feeling. The allegory is often involved and obscure, and the world is seen upside down.

His longest poem, *Oza*, written in a mixture of prose and verse, is both a love poem about Oza, a beloved woman, the cyclotron at Dubna atomic-research station, human destiny, and other topics liable to grow exponentially with the reader's imagination. The following passage from section II can be used as an illustration:

... I did not recognise my surroundings.

Things were just the same, but their particles, flashing, changed their shape, like the neon sign on top of the Central Telegraph Office. The connections between things were the same, but their direction was different.

Trees lay flat on the ground like leafy lakes, but their shadows stood upright like paper cutouts. They tinkled slightly in the wind, like silver bonbon wrappings.

Now the shaft of a well shot upwards, like a black beam from a searchlight. A sunken bucket and bits of slime lay in it.

It was raining from three clouds, plastic combs with teeth of rain (two with teeth pointing downward, the other with teeth pointing upward)....

The pages of history have been shuffled like a pack of cards. The Mongol invasion came after industrialisation.

There was a line of people in front of the cyclotron, waiting to be serviced, to be taken apart and put together again. They came out transformed. One had an ear screwed to his forehead, with a hole in the middle, like a doctor's mirror. 'Lucky devil', people consoled him, 'very convenient for keyholes: you can look and hear at the same time!'

One lady asked for the manager. 'They forgot to put my heart back. My heart!' With two fingers he pulled out her chest, like the right drawer of a desk, put something in it, and slammed it shut again. The Scientist sang and danced with glee.

'E-9-D4,' murmured the Scientist. 'Oh, great mystery of life! The whole does not change if its components are rearranged, as long as the system as such is preserved. Who cares about poetry? We shall have robots. The psyche is a combination of amino acids...'[14]

Concealed behind suchlike displays of verbal fireworks, a message is implied, at times very personal, at times a bitter attack on philistinism, at times – as in *I am Goya* – saturated with universal pity and a pantheistic sense of brotherhood. The Soviet literary establishment, suspicious of Voznesensky's linguistic agility and his success, has accused him of formalism, to which he replied that he preferred that to reeking of formalin, and warded off his attackers with:

> Ah, my critics, how I love them
> Upon the neck of the keenest of them
> Fragrant and bald as fresh-baked bread
> There shines a perfect anti-head.[15]

In a simpler poem to Bella Akhmadulina he asserts the unrestrainably dynamic power of the poets, although they are a minority:

[14] *Oza*, part II, translated by Max Hayward in *Antiworlds and the Fifth Ace*, bilingual edition, ed. by Patricia Blake and Max Hayward, London, 1968, pp. 205–7.
[15] *Antiworlds*, translated by George Reavey, op. cit., p. 193.

To B. Akhmadulina

We are many. Four, perhaps, altogether,
spinning along in our car devil-may-care.
The girl at the wheel flaunts her orange hair,
the sleeves of her jacket yanked up to the elbow.

Ah, Bela, though your driving leaves me limp,
you look angelic, out of this world;
your marvellous porcelain profile
glows like a white lamp. . . .

In hell they bang their frying pans
and send their scouts up to the gate to watch,
when you, as the speedometer runs wild,
lift both hands off the wheel to strike a match.

How I love it, when stepping on the gas
in your transparent tones you say,
'What a mess!
they've taken my licence away. . . .

'I swear they got me wrong!
You'd think I was a reckless driver!
Why, I was just poking along. . . .'

Forget it, Bela. To argue with a cop,
you know, is a losing proposition.
He can't appreciate your lyric speed –
it's past the power of his transmission.

A poet owes it to himself
not to be trapped in miles-per-hour;
let him resound at the speed of light
like angels choiring in the stratosphere.

No matter, taking light-years as our measure,
if we should vanish like a radiant star,
with not a creature left behind to earn the prize.
We were the first to crack the sound barrier.

Step on it, Bela, heavenly friend!
Who cares if we're smashed to bits in the end?
Long live the speed of poetry,
the most lethal of all speeds!

What if the maps ahead are enigmatical?
We are only a few. Four, perhaps, altogether;
hurtling along – and you are a Goddess!
That makes a majority, after all.[16]

1964

Who are the four? Himself, Akhmadulina, perhaps Evtushenko, and Bulat Okudzhava. Or are the names still unknown? In his essay on socialist realism, smuggled and published abroad, Sinyavsky makes the rather obvious point that socialist realism could be more correctly described as classicism, in the sense of the seventeenth-century French classicism or, better still, its eighteenth-century Russian imitations. One can go further and ask why people liked such a type of literature; why did they like ceremonial odes, tragedies where characters were motivated by the noblest sentiments which they express in alexandrine verse, and idylls where clean and happy shepherds fell in love with sweet and simple shepherdesses? Probably because readers and viewers longed to be transported into a world of refinement and make-believe, escape from a coarser reality, and admire models of what they should be like. The Cinderellas of the world dream of Prince Charming.

Each period has had its ideal type : the knight in shining armour; the saint of the mediaeval legend; the perfect lover of courtly romance; the noble kings and princes of tragedy; the Romantic hero in his superb rebellion against the philistinism of his bourgeois environment; or, on a lower plane, the eternally appealing, youthful dare-devil, from d'Artagnan to James Bond. Soviet society is yearning after its own glorious image, the elusive positive hero that Soviet critics have been demanding for so long. But the tradition of realism is too strong. Russians do not seem to be much good at myth-making. The district Party secretary fails to reach the dimensions of Prometheus. There is a dichotomy between the lofty ideals demanded from the writer and his traditional keen sense of reality, and, under the thin veneer of his first-generation atheism, a deeply Christian compassion for human misfortune and fortitude in adversity. The positive hero has appeared, but Soviet critics have failed to accept him. He, or rather she (again this is so very Russian), appeared in Solzhenitsyn's story *Matryona's home*, and more fleetingly in Evtushenko's poem alluded to above; and the same feeling of pity for the helpless and downtrodden inspires Voznesensky's *Hunting a hare*. Yet if the desperately fleeing hare exists, this means

[16] Translated by Stanley Kunitz in *Antiworlds and the Fifth Ace*, op. cit., pp. 255–7.

that there is a hunter, powerful, armed, and cruel, in a cruel, senseless world. Such imagery has nothing to do with socialist realism. The tradition of humility, compassion, and truthfulness comes into conflict with the demand for a make-believe world of steadfast and righteous builders of communism. There is another curious feature about Soviet literature: although written in a proletarian country, it seldom deals with factory life. Novels are set in the countryside, research institutes, on geological expeditions, occasionally on the premises of a provincial or district Party committee. Even the production novels were and still are usually set on some construction site against a backdrop of forest, river, or semi-desert steppe. The valiant efforts of Party stalwarts like V. Kochetov are somehow the exceptions that confirm the rule. The common explanation of stressing the social origins of many writers who inevitably come from peasant stock, which was a more numerous class than that of factory-workers, does not hold water. For surely the landowning class that gave so many creative artists to nineteenth-century Russia was numerically no larger than the Russian working class in the twentieth century. Why can a small country like New Zealand produce an unbeatable All-Blacks football team? Or the small Greek city-states a culture that much larger modern nations cannot emulate? The numerical basis obviously cannot be the decisive factor in human affairs. Is it because the worker at the conveyor-belt has no time for thought? Is he still what he was in the words of Karl Marx – an appendage of the machine? Is industrial work in a socialist enterprise as soul-destroying as in a capitalist one?

Despite the tightening of censorship after the 1968 occupation of Czechoslovakia and the increasingly strident campaign of literary critics for vigilance and ideology, there has been mounting interest in and reprinting of the experimental writers of the 1920s, a revival of M. Bulgakov, a posthumous reappraisal of Pasternak and Anna Akhmatova, as well as a wealth of translations from Albert Camus, Natalie Sarraute, R. P. Warren, and many others – even Kafka. Articles about many Western writers show that they are known in the original by a considerable readership, particularly the younger generation which has been taught foreign languages much better since the introduction of technical devices like tape-recorders, radio lessons, and one more dangerous technical device that is becoming more common with industrial progress, namely the typewriter. Novels and short stories unacceptable to the censor, and poems too long to be memorised, circulate in typescript, apparently on a scale that has led to the expression *samizdat*, self-published. As yet editions are naturally very small, though when

Solzhenitsyn wanted delegates to the Fourth Congress of Writers to read his protest letter against censorship he managed to circularise 250 copies. Anatoly Kuznetsov kept microfilms of his manuscripts and thus smuggled them out when he defected to London. Microfilm readers and duplicating machines and photocopying are bound to become more common and, therefore, more accessible and more difficult to supervise. Vigilance may perhaps protect Soviet youth against hostile foreign propaganda, but only a revival of monstrous Stalin-scale purges could silence dissenting voices within.

There is one aspect of Soviet literature that has been little studied. It is the effect of cross-fertilisation of Russian literature by that of Soviet national minorities. Translation of foreign literature into Russian by writers from Pushkin and Lermontov to Blok and Bely has never been looked down on as lack of personal creativity, but regarded rather as a challenge to the translator's verbal mastery. To wit, there exist no less than thirty-five versions of *Hamlet*, one of them by Boris Pasternak.

Translations are not made from Western languages only, but from practically all tongues spoken by Soviet minorities. Some writers have become famous far beyond the boundaries of their republic, like the Kirghiz Chingiz Aitmatov, now on the editorial board of the Moscow monthly *Novy Mir*. The little attention paid hitherto to any possible effect of cross-fertilisation in literature is due simply to the ignorance of languages less common than Russian among Western sovietologists. That a cross-fertilisation must exist is shown quite obviously by the plastic arts, music, and, above all, the art of dancing and ballet. One of the best Soviet companies, the Moiseev group, specialises in character- and folk-dancing and makes a point of performing non-Russian dances and recruiting its cast all over the USSR. On a smaller scale, other companies revel in the interplay between classical and folk-dancing, and this has certainly diversified and enriched one of the most successful art forms in the Soviet Union. Non-Russian companies have emerged and triumphed on the international stage – as, for instance, the now world-famous Georgian dancers. Every summer major Moscow companies go on tour, and Ukrainian, Tartar, Uzbek, and other song and dance companies perform in Moscow.

Among Soviet composers many non-Russians are outstanding, and the Armenian Khachaturyan is one of the most famous. While insistence on socialist content may have an impoverishing effect on art, the encouragement given to the national forms of culture has certainly enriched art forms such as music and ballet.

A most successful blend of different cultural traditions is embodied in the building of the Tashkent Opera House. It was designed by the Russian architect A. V. Shchusev (who built also Lenin's mausoleum in Moscow), and combines the monumental outlines of a traditional European theatre with the delightful and intricate arabesque pattern-work characteristic of the mosques of Central Asia. However, architecture will probably be less and less influenced by any traditions, since it is becoming increasingly functional and dependent on completely novel building materials. So it is more likely to develop as an international art rather than retain traditional forms.

The canons of socialist realism apply also to painting and sculpture. Indeed, the great debate on art between the Party leadership and the abstractionists took place in connection with an art exhibition at the Moscow Manege in 1963, when Khrushchev described the modernistic pictures displayed as having been painted with a donkey's tail by an ass. His wrath was also directed against the contortions and ugliness of the distorted figures of the sculptor Ernst Neizvestny, one of the leading Soviet experimental artists.

Because all too often socialist realism has been marred by facile optimism, bombastic and truculent heroics, and the concealment of harsh and unpalatable truths, it is contemptuously dismissed by Western critics as so much rubbish. But Western critics are hardly competent to judge art forms engendered by conditions outside their experience. They lack the insight, sensitivity, and imagination bred by suffering and distress. Art appeals to deeply-felt, inarticulate emotions. Those who have neither experienced nor shared them are not attuned to this particular wavelength. The profoundly moving figure of the Motherland towering over Piskarevo cemetery, where 600,000 inhabitants of Leningrad lie buried, cannot arouse compassion among those who have not lived through the horrors of a 900-day siege and watched in despair their nearest and dearest die slowly from starvation and cold. There is an old Russian tradition to bury the dead in their best clothes. During the battle of Berlin a German nurse at the Charité Hospital was astonished that the wounded Russian soldiers brought in were wearing clean shirts. Later, one or two explained the reason. The storming of Berlin they knew would be one of the fiercest battles of the war; they had 'dressed for death'. In the memorial garden to those who fell in that battle, figures of warriors kneeling in memory of the killed, sculptures on the concrete blocks along the path that leads up to the giant statue of a man holding a sword in one hand and shielding a child with the other, convey no vainglorious sense of victory and triumph but only grief and sorrow for those who suffered and gave up their healthy, hopeful, young lives to save their homes and families from a ruthless invader. Can the secure, the sheltered, the affluent tourists who visit perfunctorily the East Berlin memorial garden, imagine what it is to 'dress for death'?

There *is* censorship in the Soviet Union; there *are* guilty men stubbornly suppressing the memories of the abominable deeds that go under the blanket term of Stalinism; there *are* in the Union of Soviet Writers envious and despicable scribblers bent on crushing men of genius like Solzhenitsyn. But in the free West there is far too much self-righteous arrogance, and lack of concern for the masses. Abstract art, the theatre of the absurd, poetry to be read by other poets, is fare for the leisured, the sophisticated, the satiated minority. For the others, it is the commercially churned-out detective story, the bedroom-scene love-novel, which in the good old days of Queen Victoria would have been labelled pornography, and tales of crime and violence that sell best. Viewed from this angle the present output of Soviet writers and artists compares favourably with both Western experimental and mass fiction produced for women's magazines, Playboy-type journals, television shorties, and X-certificate films. At least it does not exploit so shamelessly the vulgar taste of its readers, nor does it appeal so blatantly to their sadistic instincts. After all, it may be better to 'serve a cause' than Mammon, and black bread is more wholesome than the spicy biscuits of Western sensationalism.

Moreover – who knows – perhaps deep down in the obscure and illogical regions of the unconscious, creative artists in West and East and their audiences, too, are closer to each other than could be expected for, whether they seek to escape from a terrifying reality or to embellish it out of all recognition, they share in the same predicament of living under the constant threat of nuclear annihilation, in a state of bewilderment and spiritual confusion, confronted by forces unleashed by Man himself but over which he has lost control.

Chapter 9
Science

Men as Gods

SCIENCE HAS ENDOWED MAN with such a knowledge of the laws of nature that his present creative and destructive powers make him master of his planet, provided he does not blow it up for 'defence' purposes, nor renders it uninhabitable for the living, himself included.

The expansion of scientific research in the Soviet Union has been as spectacular as in other advanced countries. Allocations to science from the state Budget were estimated at 3 per cent of the country's GNP in 1965. In 1967, the number of scientists and supporting personnel employed in scientific institutions and establishments of higher education had risen to 2·9 million, of whom 770,000 were graduates, and of these 25 per cent were holders of higher degrees (i.e. doctors or 'candidates' of science). The number of scientists has been doubling latterly every six or seven years.

There are 'futurists' or, as the French say, 'futuribles' in the USSR as elsewhere in the world and they forecast that by the year 2000 A.D. the whole working population of the Soviet Union will be engaged on scientific research. The bewildering accumulation of information is only partially mitigated by the publication of *referativnye zhurnaly* for various sciences, equivalent to what is known as 'Abstracts' in the Anglo-American world, and by the setting-up of an All-Union Institute of Scientific and Technical Information on the lines of the USA Institute of Documentation. Scholars, particularly those specialising in descriptive sciences, spend a quarter of their working time just searching out information about already published facts.

Whilst on the one hand each specialist 'knows more and more about less and less', the reverse tendency is becoming manifest through the interlocking and integration of diverse fields of knowledge at unexpected points of convergence. Because the range of knowledge required exceeds the capacity of one man's mind, research is becoming a group activity. Making the work of a collective more rationally and productively organised leads to the 'organisation of science'. For instance, it is often preferable to carry out research on some problem involving several branches of knowledge not within the most appropriate existing scientific institutions, but to create – possibly even on a temporary basis – centres where specialists brought in from different disciplines work together on a specific complex problem. Hence the proliferation of 'problem laboratories' in the Soviet Union. Incidentally, this term is often given to a group working on a problem not necessarily involving any 'laboratory', except in the etymological sense of the word.

There are still no criteria to determine the optimum ratio between the amount of research in fundamental and applied science that yields the most productive results. If the value of research in applied sciences can be measured by economic effect, no yardstick has been devised as yet to assess the importance of a breakthrough in fundamental science. Indeed there are discoveries remarkable for depth of insight, like Newton's formulation of the law of universal gravitation, and others remarkable for their practical consequences, like the discovery of gunpowder in an experiment that failed to achieve its purpose (the transmutation into gold of a mixture of saltpetre, charcoal, and sulphur). Chance may be a minor factor in the more rationally purposeful world of twentieth-century science, but a casual observation may still spark off unexpectedly far-reaching consequences.

For a government to choose the fields of science that are potentially most promising and allocate resources to research in these fields is a decision of national and possibly global importance. In capitalist countries crucial decisions in the fields of scientific research may be taken individually by big corporations as well as by the official government of the country concerned. In the Soviet Union decision-making in matters of policy rests squarely with the Party leadership. It must find criteria for making its choices and determine the sequence of its priorities to achieve the aims it has in view. It cannot, like a capitalist enterprise, base its decision merely on the profit motive and promote research for the sake of selling its product. It has to envisage the social consequence of scientific progress.

As in other countries, among the more thoughtful and responsible citizens, there is a growing interest in the 'science of science' (*naukovedenie*). The aim of this new discipline is to study the organisational and social aspects of science. According to one Soviet author, the aim of the new discipline is

> to elaborate the theoretical foundations for the organisation, planing, and managing of science, i.e. devising a system of measures, based on the objective logic of the development of science to secure the optimum tempos of scientific research and its increas-

ing efficiency.... What is needed is not just.... a synthesis of knowledge about logical, social, economic, psychological, structural, and organisational aspects of the development of science and technology, but a science which will study the *interaction* of the different elements, which determine the development of science as a complex integrated system.[1]

A first step is to determine the scientific potential of a country. This is largely conditioned first by the number of its scientific personnel and their qualifications; and secondly by the instruments and apparatus at their disposal, both of which are easier to estimate than some other factors such as the innate ability of individuals for original ideas and the information available to them in their respective fields of knowledge from world literature.

Several detailed studies of the numbers and standards of attainment of Soviet scientific manpower have been made in the West. As far back as 1955, i.e. before the launching of the first sputnik made people first aware of Soviet scientific progress, the American sovietologist Nicholas de Witt pointed out that the output of fully qualified engineers in the Soviet Union was exceeding that of the USA. His major study, *Education and Professional Employment in the USSR*, was published by the National Science Foundation in 1961 and was followed by another detailed study, a book by Alexander Korol, *Soviet Research and Development: its organisation, personnel and funds*, also published by the NSF in 1965. A more recent and very competent study on Soviet science policy, resources, and personnel has been carried out under the auspices of the OECD.[2]

In the Soviet Union, a group of four authors[3] sponsored by the Ukrainian Academy of Sciences investigated the number, age, location, and specialities of holders of higher degrees; the study was based on records of these scholars in the archives of VAK, the commission which officially confirms or rejects the degrees awarded by the establishments of higher education entitled to provide postgraduate tuition. It was noted that the number of theses submitted for the degree of candidate (roughly equivalent to a Ph.D.) was greatest in the fields of technology, physics and mathematics, chemistry, and medicine; fewer dissertations had been presented in the fields of philosophy, history, law, biology, geology, mineralogy, agriculture, education, philology, and economics, though in recent

[1] S. P. Mikulinsky in *Organizatsiya nauchnoi deyatel'nosti*, Moscow, 1968, pp. 148–9.
[2] E. Zaleski *et al.*, *Science Policy in the USSR*, Paris, 1969.
[3] G. M. Dobrov, V. N. Klimenyuk, L. P. Smirnov and A. A. Savel'ev, *Potentsial nauki*, Kiev, 1969.

years economics has come much more to the fore. The smallest number of dissertations was in the fields of veterinary sciences, geography, architecture, and the history of arts. The number of scientists qualifying for a doctorate is much smaller and they usually obtain this higher degree much later in life, nine or ten years after qualifying as candidate, and possibly even later. Within the most favoured groups of disciplines, technology came first, a quarter of all doctorates and nearly a third of all candidates' degrees having been awarded for work in the field of technology.

If one compares the number of holders of higher degrees with the population at large, the highest number is to be found in Armenia (53·1 for every 10,000 inhabitants); next come the RSFSR with 44·8 and Georgia with 39·5. The lowest number (16·3 for every 10,000 inhabitants) is in Moldavia. The major training-centres for those qualifying for higher degrees are Moscow, Leningrad, and Kiev; although in absolute numbers higher-degree awards are mostly from Moscow and Leningrad, the highest relative increase in the numbers preparing for higher degrees is in Kiev and more recently in Siberia, which is now catching up with Leningrad.

The age-structure of scientists with higher degrees is somewhat worrying, considering that scientists are reputed to be at their most inventive and productive between the ages of twenty-five and forty. The average age of all scientific personnel in the network of institutions of the Academy of Sciences of the USSR is about thirty-eight, but doctors of science are usually over sixty and latterly every fourth scientist appointed to a chair with the rank of professor was already sixty years old, which is the normal age of retirement in other professions.

The high cost of scientific research has prompted several studies in the economics of science. Their main concern has been to make research-work more effective. Indeed it has been calculated, though less than approximately, that over the last half-century the doubling of the quantity of new scientific results is accompanied by an eightfold increase in the volume of information, a sixteen-fold increase in the number of scientists, and an increase in financial allocations to scientific institutions and design bureaux that has grown thirty times. In other words research is becoming increasingly expensive, complex, and time-consuming. This state of affairs can be remedied only by a more efficient organisation of science, a subject of great concern to both Party and government in the USSR.

The Academy of Sciences of the USSR

Of the 4,500 institutions carrying out research work in pure and applied sciences, in industrial design, and in the humanities, the most important are probably those subordinate to the Academy of Sciences of the USSR, known sometimes as the Headquarters of Soviet Science. The Academies of the Union republics are somewhat less important. VUZ are still essentially teaching institutions whose research activities, although expanding, are a novelty of secondary importance. On the other hand, applied sciences and the development of new products and machines are carried out in an impressive number of scientific institutes and design bureaux (*opytno-konstruktorskie buro*) of various All-Union and republican Ministries.

Historically, the Academy of Sciences of the USSR is a direct descendant of the St Petersburg Academy of Sciences, the brainchild of Peter the Great, who with uncanny foresight, and probably the first among eighteenth-century European monarchs, perceived the potential power that science and technology would deliver into the hands of those who mastered the knowledge of man's material environment. In the course of the ensuing two centuries the St Petersburg Academy remained a rather isolated community which carried on disinterested and somewhat esoteric studies into the natural and philological sciences. World War I brought the academicians out of their ivory tower to confront the harsh realities of the applied sciences, which were tilting the balance of military power in favour of a science-conscious Germany on her eastern front. A committee for the study of Russia's natural productive resources was formed, with special emphasis on geological surveys, including studies of the mineral-salt deposits of the Caspian Sea.

Immediately after the Revolution, Lenin entrusted the People's Commissariat of Education with the task of establishing relations with the Academy, for he, too, appreciated the paramount importance of science for human progress. In April 1918 he drafted a short plan of work, listing the types of contribution the Academy could make to the economic development of the country. This draft seems never to have actually been sent, but it was published later and is often quoted as a proof of Lenin's plans to build economic progress on scientific foundations.

Until the end of the 1920s the character of the Academy's work did not change fundamentally, but in 1927 its statutes were altered and in 1929 it elected its first Marxist members, most of whom were social scientists, including Lunacharsky, the People's Commissar of Education. In 1932 it opened its doors to technologists, thus adding a Division of Technical Sciences to its two former divisions, namely the Division of Mathematics and Natural Sciences and that of Humanities. It was now pulling its full weight in the implementation of the first Five-Year Plan. Its geological exploration work expanded in connection with the accelerated search for new mineral deposits; its technical experts visited factories, addressed workers' meetings, and helped solve technological and engineering problems related to the major construction projects. The number of the Academy's research institutes increased. Many were founded in remote regions, such as the Kola Peninsula of the White Sea, in the Urals, the Far East, and in the Union republics, where they were designed to promote prospecting and to encourage the growth of local scientific cadres. Later, these institutions became in their turn fully-fledged republican Academies of Sciences. Those of the Ukraine and Belorussia came into existence as early as 1919 and 1928 respectively, the others during or after World War II, the last (in 1961) being the Moldavian Academy of Sciences. (It should be remembered that between 1918 and 1945, Moldavia was part of Romania.)

Increasingly, the Academy formed links with industry and with research institutes set up by various industrial Ministries (or People's Commissariats as they were then called); these research institutes specialised in applied science, often of a fairly narrow type, dealing with problems of electric welding, the construction of blast furnaces, the technology of heat-resisting materials, the metallurgy of iron and steel, and various aspects of crop rotation.

In 1934, the Academy moved from St Petersburg – renamed Leningrad – to Moscow. In 1936, it was amalgamated with the Communist Academy of Social Sciences, which had been set up as a separate institution in 1918 to promote a Marxist approach to social science. This amalgamation brought into the Academy a strong pressure-group of men, anxious to exert influence over the less politically committed natural scientists.

Other learned societies were merged with the Academy or, to put it more correctly, with what had become a network of institutions. Among them were associations started as separate entities in the nineteenth century, like the Geographical Society, and others founded after the Revolution, like the Gor'ky Institute of World Literature and the Central Institute for the Study of Language and Writing of the Peoples of the USSR.

Since establishments of higher education had become mere teaching institutions where no post-graduate work was done, the Academy undertook post-graduate training, known in Russian as *aspirantura*. Altogether the Academy became a huge organisation with hundreds of research institutes, experimental stations, observatories, specialised libraries, museums, and presses for the publication of scholarly journals. Only its senior members had the status of full members of the Academy and elected its governing body, i.e. the Praesidium, its President, and its Learned Secretary, as well as new full or corresponding members. The latter drew smaller salaries than the full members and had only limited voting rights. All other scientific workers within the network of the Academy system are known as senior or junior scientific fellows (*nauchny sotrudnik*) and their status is that of highly qualified employees within their respective institutions.

The history of the Academy in Stalin's days, particularly between 1948 and 1953, was not a happy one. It was financially well supported and its members enjoyed substantial salaries and high social status. On the other hand, its activities were closely controlled from within and without. Many talented people were diverted from their research if it did not fit into the general economic plan and set to work on urgent practical problems. Decision-making was vested in the Praesidium, to which under Party pressure some very second-rate scholars – turned bureaucrats – had been elected over the years. Party prejudices interfered with the acceptance and spread of new scientific ideas coming from the West. Outside opinion was imposing the strange notion that there existed a superior Soviet science which somehow differed or should differ from bourgeois science. Bogus theories like those of Lysenko, if backed by Party support, had to be accepted as true. There were ugly cases of vitriolic denunciations by mistaken if sometimes honest scientists against their opponents and even more vicious ones arising from envy and personal feuds.

Fortunately for the Soviet Union in general, and for her scientists in particular, scientific theories cannot be proved or disproved by quotations from Marx–Engels–Lenin or Stalin; they have to be substantiated by experimental results. If the country was to develop, the work of the Academy could not be stifled, like that of poets, playwrights, and other expendable scribblers. Even so, the atmosphere was far from healthy in the scientific community. At the time of Stalin's death, the genetecist N. I. Vavilov was dead, the aircraft designer A. N. Tupolev was in prison, and the physicist P. L. Kapitsa was under house arrest. The fate of many others remains unknown.

A story told about P. L. Kapitsa is a good illustration of the causes that hampered Soviet science in Stalin's day and yet enabled scientists even then to hold in check Party interference and further strengthen their position in more recent years. In 1946 Kapitsa was dismissed from his post of director of the Institute of Physical Problems (according to rumour, for refusing to work on the atomic bomb). In 1955 he was reinstated, and on arriving at the Institute he enquired about the work done by the very considerable personnel and accounts departments. 'They select staff and finance the work of the Institute,' was the answer. 'I see,' said Kapitsa, 'they should all pass an examination in experimental physics. I will set the questions; L. D. Landau will see to the exam in mathematical physics.' Those reluctant to face the examination ordeal were allowed to resign of their own accord, but those intending to remain in charge of staffing and fund allocation were henceforth expected to understand the scientific work done at the Institute.[4] A Party membership card was no longer the sole or even the essential qualification to work there.

In 1961, in order to enable the Academy to concentrate on fundamental research in pure science and the humanities, it was decided to reorganise its work and transfer its institutes of applied sciences and technology to the appropriate industrial Ministries. The reorganisation was further streamlined in 1963, but although the network of the Academy's institutions was reduced, its standing remained equivalent to that of a Ministry. It is directly subordinate to the Council of Ministers of the USSR and responsible for the planning and supervision of research in its own institutions, and also for co-ordinating the research plans of the republican Academies of Science and those of VUZ. These plans are drawn up independently of, though in consultation with, the State Committee for Science and Technology, which is the body that co-ordinates and, in fact, strongly influences all research and development carried out in the research institutes and design bureaux subordinate to various Ministries. This relative independence of the Academy enables it to concentrate more on fundamental research, which is of tremendous importance, considering that the present aim of the Soviet leadership is no longer to borrow and improve on foreign inventions, but to place the Soviet Union in the forefront of world scientific achievement. It is appreciated that for too long emphasis was on applied science, on inventions that could yield economically tangible results, on discoveries that would pay off quickly; this attitude, although quite understandable in the earlier phases of industrialisation, affected adversely research in fundamental science.

Another proof of the Academy's prestige is its right to elect its own Praesidium, its President (for a period of four years), and its Learned Secretary, who is, apparently always or at least usually, a member of the Central Committee of the CPSU. More pedestrian but very important for its personnel is the fact that all Academy institutions are included in the top categories of research institutions. All research institutions in the USSR are classified into three categories, according to the importance of their research and develop-

[4] *Novy Mir*, 1969, No. 8, p. 284.

ment work. Their respective status is reflected in the salaries paid to their staff. Thus a senior research fellow (*starshy nauchny sotrudnik*) is paid 280 roubles per month if he works in a top-category establishment, 230 roubles if he works in a second-category institution, and 200 roubles in the third.[5]

In 1964 the number of scientific establishments belonging to the Academy system was 194, the number of full members was 181, and that of corresponding members 368. Scientific workers totalled 23,563. Of the republican Academies by far the largest was the Ukrainian Academy of Sciences with 54 institutions, 222 members, and just over 6,000 scientific workers.

Among the most outstanding institutions of the USSR Academy are those centred around its Siberian branch, situated in a specially built and now world-famous little township, *Akademgorodok*, 25 kilometres from Novosibirsk. Apart from its President, the mathematician M. A. Lavrent'ev, and a few senior academicians who went with him to head the first institutes, only scientists under thirty years of age were recruited as research fellows. The Siberian branch works in close collaboration with the University of Novosibirsk. Among its many privileges is that of receiving a lump sum from the Council of Ministers of the RSFSR without any detailed schedule from *Gosplan* as to how the money is to be spent. The dynamism, the spirit of innovation, and the general success of the Siberian branch have prompted the creation of other similar centres. One is already under construction near Sverdlovsk, a town of a million inhabitants at the heart of the industrial Urals; two others are being planned, one at Irkutsk in Siberia and the other probably at Vladivostok on the Pacific coast, where there is already a major Institute of Oceanography.

Not belonging to the Academy of Sciences of the USSR, yet collaborating with it in many ways, are the following important institutions, each of which heads research in its own field. They are :

the Academy of Arts of the USSR;
the Academy of Medical Sciences of the USSR;
the Academy of Educational Sciences of the USSR;
the All-Union Lenin Academy of Agricultural Sciences and six republican agricultural academies;
the Academy of Construction and Architecture of the USSR and a similar institution in the Ukraine; and
the Academy of Communal Economy of the RSFSR.

[5] L. Potekhin, I. Rozenfeld, and N. Itin, *Planirovanie raskhodov na sotsial'no-kulturnye meropriyatiya*, Moscow, 1962, p. 195, quoted in E. Zaleski et al., *Science Policy in the Soviet Union*, Paris, 1969.

Apart from research done on a large scale by the network of the Academy system and that carried out on a much smaller scale in VUZ, research-work in applied sciences and design, or what is sometimes known as R and D, is carried out in the scientific research institutes and design bureaux subordinate to All-Union and republican industrial Ministries. The research plans of these institutions are co-ordinated by the State Committee for Science and Technology. Institutions bearing a number instead of a descriptive name work on military projects and naturally little is known about them.

One of the problems confronting present-day research-workers, which has already been alluded to in the chapter on industry, is to overcome the obstacles and delays in the practical utilisation of new inventions. Essentially this is due to the lack of suitable workshops and pilot plants in which a new model can be tested; but even in the earlier stages of research there are the usual material shortages to contend with, namely the dearth of precision instruments, chemically pure reagents, and specialised apparatus, as well as paper and printing facilities to publicise results. As in other fields, qualified staff is diverted from research to ancillary work designed to overcome deficiencies. This problem is further aggravated by shortages of supporting personnel, like technicians, laboratory assistants, and secretarial staff trained in modern office routines. One sociological survey found that 36 per cent of the scientists of its sample had no help whatever and another 26 per cent relied on part-time or casual assistance.[6]

In October 1969 a resolution was passed by the Central Committee of the CPSU and the Council of Ministers 'On measures to raise the efficiency of the work of scientific organisations and to accelerate the utilisation of scientific and technical achievement in the national economy'. The provisions of the enactment, while enlisting the help of the Academy of Sciences, are more concerned with R and D and the modernisation of production than with fundamental research. Top priority is to be given to improve the supply of equipment and chemicals required by scientific institutions; they are to be provided with experimental workshops or given access to facilities specially set aside for the purpose in industrial enterprises, so that by 1972 major experimental centres will be able to test their projects within a year.

On the organisational side the resolution allows for the commissioning of two or more institutions to work in competition on the same project, so that the best solution can be chosen from various submissions. Material incentives for individuals and whole institu-

[6] N. Konchalovskaya and M. Murov in *Literaturnaya Gazeta*, 18 February 1970, p. 10.

tions will be directly tied to the advantages gained from putting their invention into practice; indeed, research institutions will be held responsible for supervising the introduction of their innovations into production. Another highly acceptable source of gain for them will be the sale of patents and licences abroad. Institutions whose research leads to no useful results may be closed down.

Possibly with the Kapitsa case in mind, it is proposed to hold inspections of the institutions every three years or so and to recertificate individually members of their staff, apart from those whose appointment has been by competitive procedures, as in the case of senior VUZ personnel. The certifying commissions are to consist of top-ranking scientists and also to include representatives of the Party and trade union organisations, so that the measure is somewhat double-edged. Whether regular bureaucratic inspections combined with material incentives based on the financial success of inventions will achieve a real upsurge of technical progress, time alone can tell. One can only say that they are a far cry from Mao Tse-Tung's reliance on the creativity of untutored working masses.

The list of priorities reflects the urge for modernisation; it includes highly productive machinery for industry, transport, agriculture, the building trades, and consumer servicing; mechanised and automated processes, and new materials; better utilisation of raw materials and of waste products; improvement in quality of articles and reduction in costs; better layout, ventilation, and general concern for working conditions; the use of mathematical methods and computerised data in management; and also measures designed to improve public health.

The perennial comparisons between Soviet and American scientific achievement are usually rather desultory. In a general way the USA is endowed with many natural advantages that are lacking in the Soviet Union, such as a milder climate, shorter distances, and easy access to two oceans. Within the narrower field of scientific endeavour the USA has been able to provide more and better equipment for her laboratories, including equipment of a labour-saving type from office furnishing to giant computers. Apart from training her own scientists, America imports highly qualified specialists from all over the world, mainly from the famous seats of learning of western Europe, but also from under-developed countries. In 1966 immigrants constituted 10 per cent of the new recruits to the American supply of engineers and 26 per cent of the supply of physicians.[7] It has been calculated that the benefit that accrues

[7] N. Calder, *Technopolis, Social Control of the Uses of Science*, London, 1969, p. 117.

to the USA from this shopping-for-brains operation equals and possibly exceeds American aid to under-developed countries.[8]

The Soviet Union is overstraining her resources over too many fields and cannot provide adequate material equipment for her scientists, with the result that highly qualified personnel squander thousands of man-hours on menial tasks. To estimate more precisely the time unproductively spent by specialists, several surveys have been carried out in the Ukraine (on members of the Ukrainian Academy of Sciences), in Leningrad, and in Novosibirsk. The time devoted to actual research was correlated to the scientists' age, qualifications (measured in terms of academic degrees), seniority, and fields of study. Productivity was measured in terms of publications and by calculating the number of new postgraduates trained under the supervision of the groups surveyed. As often happens with sociological surveys, the results confirmed what commonsense people had already suspected, namely that the most productive scientists were those who were enthusiastic researchers giving far more time to their work than the statutory 41 hours per week; those with higher qualifications and greater experience, but only up to a certain age when their position of seniority turned them from research to administration and the organising of the work of their team or their institute. Productivity was also higher in fields where greater 'mathematisation' cut down on time required for experimentation. Although in no way spectacular, the results of these surveys confirmed the importance of a scientific organisation of labour as well as the crying need for better equipment, ancillary staff, and methods of processing information.

On the credit side, the social structure of the Soviet Union may favour scientific advance. Education is free and opportunities for study are numerous, including part-time evening and correspondence courses for adults who may have missed the chance of studying for a degree earlier in life. Both sexes are given equal opportunities and this increases the pool of talent from which Soviet scientists are drawn. In the absence of competing private enterprises there is no danger of duplication of effort nor of useful information being concealed by one enterprise which is not interested in making use of it, yet withholds it from its rivals and may thus slow down the progress of society as a whole.

Since the purpose of science is to overcome natural handicaps, in the long run the progress of Soviet science may tilt the balance in Russia's favour. Yet it must be borne in mind that the fields of science are manifold and the social aims of the two countries may

[8] *Manpower Aspects of Recent Economic Developments,* p. 112; R. M. Titmuss, 'Trading in Human Capital', *Science Journal,* June 1967, p. 3.

lead them to pursue research in different spheres. Unfortunately, both concentrate on the costly and fundamentally sterile research in lethal thermo-nuclear weapons, of which the USA has already stockpiled enough to destroy all life in the Soviet Union a hundred times over and the Soviet Union all life in America thirty times over. They are also engaged in the space race, though both have more urgent problems to solve at home, let alone in the underdeveloped countries.

Admittedly, in both countries resources are allocated to other fields of science. In the USSR to the building of the material and technical basis which should be a first step towards new social relations and eventually the emergence of a new type of humanity. For the time being the Soviet Union is still bogged down in the first phase of development – the creation of the material and technical basis of communism – but she has a clearer vision of the future than the Americans, who, in the words of Nigel Calder, are like 'men who have stolen the fire of the Sun and do not know what to do with it'.[9]

The cover-to-cover translations of Russian scientific journals into English made in the USA, with and without subsidies from various Foundations, and commercially in Jerusalem, as well as the many translations of advanced Russian textbooks, testify to the recognition that Soviet science has gained in the English-speaking world.

So much for the natural sciences. In the humanities the position is different and for a long time has been distressing. A new, promising departure was the development of mathematical economics after the death of Stalin and the more recent resurgence of sociology, social psychology, ethnography, and allied fields of study. For too long research in these fields was discouraged, since inevitably it brought to light many unpleasant facts like rural poverty; the persistence of low educational levels among the majority of peasants and manual workers; tensions between the rulers and the ruled, reflected in the opposition of the pronouns 'they' and 'we'; tensions between generations, nationalities, occupational groups, between those who had been deported and those who had stepped into the jobs vacated by the deportees; it revealed, too, the coarseness of personal relations, exacerbated by housing shortages and mutual suspicion, fanned by campaigns for 'vigilance', as well as drunkenness, hooliganism, and the unaccountable survival, after years of indoctrination, of religious beliefs and customs.

The tendency to lay the blame on outside anti-communist propaganda and hostile psychological warfare is a facile explanation for social phenomena that have far deeper roots. To eradicate these

[9] N. Calder, op. cit., p. 295.

phenomena their existence must first be acknowledged and their causes identified. This is very slowly and cautiously being done by Soviet sociologists. However, bringing to light and admitting the existence of 'negative social phenomena', to the extent of compiling statistics about their frequency and distribution, is only a first step. To discover their *causes* will be a far more painful process, akin to psychoanalytic therapy which brings back to memory and to conscious understanding what was unbearably shameful and objectionable and has therefore been repressed and forgotten. Many are the shameful and objectionable deeds that the Party would like to forget and, above all, to be forgotten by others.

Some rather esoteric discussions have been broached apparently in connection with a book by Academician A. M. Rumyantsev (a former editor of the journal *Kommunist* and *Pravda*) entitled *Problems of the modern science of society (Problemy sovremennoi nauki ob obshchestve*, Moscow, 1969). The arguments revolve around the possible 'contradictions' within a socialist society which has not as yet achieved communism. One such contradiction might be between the growing needs of the population on the one hand and the level of production on the other; this is a contradiction that can be expressed as one between productive forces and productive relations. It would appear that this is a theoretical formulation relating to the gap between the needs and expectations of the people for a higher standard of living and their inadequate satisfaction. Popular pressure for higher living standards is manifested not in words but in behaviour, such as the rejection of substandard goods, flight from the land, and high labour turnover. Planners are beginning to accept the notion of customers' preferences, and the view that clothing is not merely a protection from cold but also a source of aesthetic satisfaction; that food may be a source of pleasure as well as sustenance; and that the buyer is entitled to choose. The right to choose is expanding into other fields, from that of a garment to that of a career. Educationalists accede to it in order to forestall the training of misfits; what started as a demand for vocational guidance may extend to a demand for the expression of personal tastes, and from personal aspirations to personal views. Vocal dissenters are few, but latent dissenters may be many. Something like public opinion might be shaping under the surface of Soviet conformism.

Public opinion and social attitudes can be manipulated and in the capitalist West public relations officers and sociologists are trained in the art of closing credibility gaps and de-fusing explosive situations. But this is a far cry from the imposition of a single, unchallengeable, infallible view by a Central Committee standing outside, above, and divorced from the life and thoughts of the silent majority. The Party maintains the opposite, namely that it always embodied and carried out the will of the people. Through Party primaries, the *Komsomol*, and the trade unions acting as 'driving belts', it has always been in touch with the masses. The point at stake is that these 'driving belts' transmitted motion solely in one direction, from the centre to the masses. There was no feed-back. Social sciences are beginning to introduce the notion of feed-back and mechanisms that could make a reality of it. In Lenin's words, it is the duty of the Party to teach the masses but also to learn from them. Has the present Party leadership the insight and tolerance needed to learn from the masses? Can it approach creatively and imaginatively the endless sequence of social problems that beset people who are still only beginning to adapt to a continuously changing modern industrial world, who are no longer content with jam tomorrow but yearn for jam *and* justice today? In other words, is Marxism an ossified relic of a nineteenth-century philosophy or a dynamic, perceptive, flexible, and creative science of society which can lead a vast country into the twenty-first century?

Chapter 10

Daily Life

To GENERALISE ABOUT the way of life of over 200 million people of different age, nationality, and level of education would indeed be overbearing, not to say ludicrous; yet some idea of people's daily life can be gleaned from a study of laws and customs governing traditional human institutions, such as marriage, family, and inheritance, as well as from that of modern welfare provisions for child care, for the sick, and for the aged.

Infant mortality, which was very high in pre-revolutionary days, has slowly decreased, particularly in the 1960s. By 1966–67 mortality was down to 6·9 per thousand among children up to four years old and 2·6 per thousand if the entire child population up to the age of fifteen is taken into account. The decrease in child mortality is due to the expansion of pre-natal and maternity care, the stamping-out of epidemic diseases such as smallpox, diphtheria, and cholera, and improved medical child-services. Indeed, of a total of over 600,000 fully qualified physicians working in the USSR, 12 per cent are child specialists and, of a total of nearly 2½ million hospital beds (excluding military hospitals), 225,000 or nearly 10 per cent were in maternity hospitals or wards, while there were another 140,000 hospital beds in gynaecological wards. In 1968 doctors specialising in gynaecology and midwifery numbered over 38,000 and there were, furthermore, 270,000 midwives and numerous outpatient departments and pre-natal clinics.

Medical care was better organised in towns than in rural districts, where the distance to the nearest hospital may be quite considerable in sparsely populated areas, because allocation of funds to the health service is based on the number of inhabitants and not on the size of the area. The average ratio of 25·9 doctors for every 10,000 inhabitants concealed also considerable local inequalities. Thus, in 1968, Georgia had 35·9 doctors for 10,000 inhabitants, Latvia 33·9, Estonia 32, and Armenia 30·1; whereas Belorussia (23·9), Kazakhstan (20·1), Uzbekistan (18·1), and in particular Tadzhikistan (15·4) had a much lower ratio.

Medicine in the Soviet Union, even more than teaching, is a female occupation; 72 per cent of all fully qualified doctors are women as against 70 per cent among teachers. The percentage of women in the health services in general is even higher, for among midwives, nurses, and other personnel with secondary medical education they account for no less than 90 per cent of the total.

The salaries of Soviet doctors employed in the health service approximate those in other occupations employing VUZ graduates, such as maintenance engineers and teachers. With truly male logic Western sovietologists take a dim view of a profession largely run by ill-paid female specialists. Yet over a vast territory, and despite the handicap of long distances, inadequate transport (rural doctors trudge on foot from village to village within their appointed areas), and the remoteness of some places accessible only to the tiny planes, distinguished by the red-cross sign on their tail which can be seen on Siberian aerodromes, these women have managed to increase life expectancy to seventy years; they are winning the battle against tuberculosis and have stopped the spread of venereal diseases, which had reached epidemic proportions during the Revolution with the break-up of family ties and the rejection of restraints that tradition puts on casual sexual relations. As in other advanced countries cancer and heart failure take a rising toll.

Much of Soviet medical care may be rough and ready because of the shortages of pharmaceutical preparations, overcrowding in urban hospitals, and low qualifications among personnel in certain fields regarded as of secondary importance, such as dentistry. The majority of Soviet dentists are still trained in secondary specialised schools, not in VUZ, and are better skilled in extracting decaying natural teeth than replacing them with artistically discreet bridges and dentures.

The present increasing prosperity allows for more attention to be devoted to the health of the population. Here, as in other spheres, the Supreme Soviet has adopted legislation – Basic Principles of the Health Service – with a definite emphasis on improved quality as well as a general expansion of the health services; among such improvements are greater variety and sophistication of pharmaceutical preparations, availability of visiting nurses to care for patients in their homes, and better ambulance transport.

Private practice is not forbidden, but earnings from treatment of private patients are heavily taxed like any other income from private employment. The maximum income-tax rate of 13 per cent levied on salaries of 100 roubles per month and over no longer applies. The rate rises to 29 per cent for private earnings of 100 roubles per month and may reach 69 per cent if earnings exceed 7,000 roubles per annum.

In line with a certain devolution of power inaugurated during the secretaryship of Khrushchev, institutions in health resorts (excepting sanatoria for patients suffering from tuberculosis) and rest and convalescent homes are the responsibility of the Central Committee of Trade Unions, of which the Medical Workers' Union is a member. All medical staff, from senior hospital superintendents to ward orderlies, belong to the same union, as is the case, also, in industrial enterprises where management and workers belong to a single union. Another form of enlisting public co-operation was the setting-up of local voluntary councils consisting of representatives of the medical personnel of a hospital, its trade union, Party and *Komsomol* primaries, as well as representatives of the urban (or district) Soviet. The activities of these voluntary councils depend on local conditions; they may canvass help to carry out repairs to the hospital building, or organise mobile dispensaries, or a roster of volunteers to carry prescriptions from an out-patient department to a central pharmaceutical depot, and bring back the drugs prescribed or deliver them to patients' homes. The Red Cross and the Red Crescent Societies are also voluntary associations with local primaries, provincial committees and a central committee which is a member of the International League of Red Cross Societies.

Medical consultations and hospital treatment are free, but medicines (apart from those supplied to hospital patients) are payable by the patient at fairly low prices because these prices are not inflated by the costs that have preceded actual manufacture, namely the cost of research and testing that goes on prior to the adoption of a new drug. The use of contraceptives is still a novelty, but abortions are quite common. They were legalised at the time of the Revolution, but forbidden in 1936, when other measures were taken to stabilise the family as an institution. They were again made legal but fairly expensive to the patient in 1954, and now form again part of the normal free medical service for all.

Child allowances are payable at the same rate to both married and unmarried mothers, starting with the third child, at the birth of which a lump sum of 20 roubles is paid to the mother; this sum is increased to 65 roubles for the fourth child and a monthly allowance of 4 roubles is payable to the mother for four years thereafter. Further increases in the family bring in larger benefits.

Although at first sight Soviet child allowances cannot be described as generous, they cost the state nearly half a billion roubles per annum and, in 1967, $3\frac{1}{2}$ million women benefited from this form of social welfare. Mothers with five and more children are awarded a medal and those with ten and over the title of 'mother heroine'.

The majority of Soviet women are gainfully employed; hence

the importance of nurseries, which have been increasingly subsidised from the state Budget. Nurseries are usually located either on the premises of an enterprise employing women or form part of a housing compound. Nursing mothers are entitled to half-hourly breaks every three hours to attend to their child, in addition to their normal lunch-hour. Gainful employment for women is regarded as an important factor of emancipation; personal earnings enhance the woman's standing in her family and contribute to her independence. It is said that collectivisation helped to emancipate the peasant woman because her labour days, however badly they may have been rewarded, were payable to her personally, whereas previously she had toiled in her husband's household without getting any individual pay. Be this as it may, women have been the mainstay of the country's work-force in the post-war years and with the potential shortages of labour in certain fields, their contribution to the national economy will remain indispensable in the immediate future. On the other hand, the desire to strengthen family ties and increase parental responsibility for the education of children is at last focusing attention on the difficulties experienced by women in their dual role. Various schemes under discussion are designed either to increase opportunities for part-time work or provisions for a temporary withdrawal of mothers of young children from gainful employment with a minimum financial loss to themselves as well as to the community at large.

Children start school at the age of seven and come of age at eighteen, when the full rights and duties of citizenship are bestowed on them. The rights include that of voting at elections, marrying, and entering into business transactions, while the duties are compulsory military service for boys, full responsibility for their actions in case of criminal proceedings being brought against them, and loss of privileges to a lighter work-load and shorter hours connected with the status of minor.

Laws on marriage and divorce have undergone several changes in the course of the last half-century. In the early years of the Revolution, marriage was more a question of fact than of law; a couple living together as husband and wife were regarded as married, whether they had registered their marriage with the Civil Status Registry or not. If they had registered and wished to divorce they went to the Registry together and had their marriage dissolved; if one spouse only wished to terminate the marriage, he (or she) informed the Registry of his (or her) wish and the latter notified the other spouse by postcard that the marriage had been dissolved and that he (or she) had the right to apply to a People's Court in case of dispute over property or custody of the children, if any. In 1936 a rather stiff fee was imposed to make divorce more difficult, stabilise the family, and make parents responsible for bringing up their offspring. One of the most distressing features of life in the Soviet Union in the years following the Revolution and again after collectivisation, both of which were followed by famines, was the numbers of abandoned children who were either the victims of unsettled family relations or children of parents who had been killed in the Civil War, or, later, those who had been arrested and deported as *kulaks* or counter-revolutionaries. Lunacharsky, the People's Commissar of Education, estimated their numbers at 2 million in 1921; they roamed along the railways and infested towns, living by theft, robbery, and prostitution, and growing into hardened criminals. The provision of orphanages was quite inadequate and the conditions in most were so bad that children escaped from them in search of food as well as freedom. The famous educationalist A. S. Makarenko made his name in rehabilitating those who were brought to the Gor'ky colony, where he worked in 1921–27, and the Dzerzhinski commune, which he ran in 1927–35.

World War II was not followed by a similar disaster because more was done to provide children's homes and also encourage adoption and *patronat*; the latter was the acceptance into a family of a child who was brought up by that family but not adopted; when the child reached the age of sixteen, all legal connections between him and his foster-family came to an end, though the human and emotional bond may have continued.

The Basic Principles of Marriage and Family, adopted in June 1968, make the registration of a marriage essential. In the larger towns Wedding Palaces are multiplying and there is much propaganda for greater solemnity to be attached to the event; the intention is to make young couples take marriage more seriously and also to counteract the attraction of a religious ceremony. A marriage can still be dissolved on application by both parties to the Civil Status Registry, provided there are no young children; otherwise divorce can be granted only by a People's Court. Usually, the court does not grant the divorce at once, but gives both parties a month to effect a reconciliation; if this is not achieved, the court will in most cases grant a divorce and may proceed to arrange for a division of property and the award of maintenance to one of the spouses (usually the one who gets custody of the children). The court may refuse to grant a divorce to a man whose wife is pregnant or has given birth to a child during that year, unless she agrees to the divorce.

Soviet citizens own little property as a rule, yet they do possess personal things and sometimes a house. Prior to the Revolution, the property of husband and wife was separate; this worked in favour of women who had dowries, because a husband was not entitled to interfere with the wife's financial affairs, but it put poorer women at a disadvantage because it was usually the man who earned wages and bought things, while the wife did the unpaid work of looking after the household and rearing the children. To preclude such injustice, Soviet law regards all property acquired during marriage as belonging jointly to husband and wife; in case of divorce it is divided equally, unless the court directs that it be shared out unequally in favour of the spouse who has custody of the children. Because of the dire housing shortage, a divorced couple may have to divide the house and go on living close to each other.

Old and incapacitated people are usually in receipt of a pension; yet adult children may be required to help maintain their old parents, grandparents, or even their in-laws.

Under a will, children both legitimate and born out of wedlock are entitled to inherit not less than two-thirds of their parents' property. If a man or woman dies without direct descendants, other next of kin may claim a definite share of the estate. The sharing-out of property between widower (or widow) and children may be complicated by part of the estate being common property and the surviving spouse being entitled to his (or her) share as well as to a share of the residue. Personal property in the USSR usually amounts to very little, but things such as clothing, furniture, tools, and farm implements, let alone sewing- and washing-machines, are still scarce and expensive and, therefore, even a small share in a legacy may be important to an heir. Moreover, there are successful writers, artists, and other well-paid citizens who are said to have collected pictures, books, and similar non-productive but valuable objects, so that laws of inheritance may be of greater importance to Soviet citizens than one would expect in a socialist society.

Workers who become temporarily or permanently disabled at their place of work are entitled to a temporary disablement benefit or a pension, if they become permanently disabled. Since trade unions administer the social insurance fund one of the duties of the factory union committee is to establish the fact of the accident (or the appearance of an occupational disease) and to allocate the temporary benefit. This is equal to the wage earned prior to the accident and is payable to the worker, even though the accident may have happened through his own fault. A reduction in the amount payable can be made only if it is established that a major contributory cause of the accident was the state of drunkenness of the victim at that time. There is no definite time-limit to the length of period during which a worker can draw a temporary benefit due to accident or occupational disease, but if it becomes evident that the disablement is of a permanent nature, the temporary benefit is replaced by a pension. This will depend on the degree to which the disability handicaps the life of the person and this is established by special 'medical-labour expert commissions', in accordance with the following classification : group I–disabled are people no longer capable of work and possibly in need of outside help; group II includes those who can look after themselves but can no longer work under normal conditions, though could be employed in special workshops for disabled; group III–disabled are those who can no longer perform the type of work for which they are qualified and have to accept lower-paid occupations.

Those disabled through industrial accident or occupational disease and classed in groups I and II are usually entitled to a pension equal to their former wage, but those in group III get a smaller pension. In certain cases compensation claims can be made against the enterprise if the cause of the accident is proved to have been connected with a breach of safety regulations or the provision of inadequate safety devices by the enterprise. Compensation is paid by the enterprise at fault to the social insurance fund, but a worker can bring a claim against the enterprise, and the courts may direct the latter to make compensation payments to the worker in addition to his pension. In awarding a disablement pension additional payments are made in respect of dependants.

Workers who fall ill are entitled to sickness benefits for periods not exceeding two consecutive months. Rates of pay depend on length of employment at the same place of work; if a worker has been employed at the same place for less than three years, sickness benefit amounts to 50 per cent of his wages; if his length of service was three to five years, the rate goes up to 60 per cent; for five to eight years, to 80 per cent; and for those who have worked at the same enterprise for eight years and more the sickness benefit paid is equal to their normal wage. Length of service at the same place of work is taken fairly broadly; periods of military service for men or childbirth and a year's absence connected with it do not affect 'length of employment'. In the case of Party and *Komsomol* members leaving employment to take up Party or *Komsomol* work, the interruption does not constitute a breach of continuous employment either.

Maternity benefits are paid to women for periods of fifty-six days before and fifty-six days after confinement at a rate equivalent to their wage, if they have been in employment in general for three years or for two years at the same place of work; otherwise the benefits are slightly less. Low-paid workers are entitled to a further 30 roubles for the child's layette.

Old-age pensions are normally paid to men at the age of sixty after twenty-five years' work and to women at fifty-five after twenty years' work. Men employed on underground, heavy, or dangerous work are entitled to retire earlier on somewhat larger pensions and the same applies to women who have borne and reared five children or more. The value of a pension is related to previous wages, length of service at one place, and responsibility for dependants, but within basic limits of not less than 30 roubles per month or more than 120 roubles. Families who lose their breadwinner are also entitled to pensions (orphaned children till the age of sixteen), particularly families of soldiers killed on active service. Generally speaking, war-disabled are entitled to various welfare priorities.

Distinguished Party and government officials may retire on a 'personal' pension, and their widows may also be awarded a special gratuity or 'personal' pension far in excess of the 120 roubles payable from the social insurance fund.

The complexity of this vast network of welfare provisions is naturally quite considerable, while the value of each benefit is of great concern to the individual. So there exists a sizeable literature on the subject. Indeed life is always raising problems unforeseen by the legislator and these are bound to increase with the extension of welfare provisions to the rural population. Already complications have arisen in respect of farmers who had worked most of their life on collective farms (which until 1966 were quite outside the social insurance scheme) when they were reclassified as agricultural workers because their collective was transformed into a state farm.

Since the late 1950s numerous handbooks have been published on various legal aspects of daily life: handbooks listing rights of workers to benefits, pensions, or holidays; handbooks designed for employees in specific occupations, e.g. teachers; handbooks relating to division of property between children at the death of their parents or between husband and wife in case of divorce; also handbooks setting out taxes payable by various categories of the population as well as on procedures to lodge complaints against wrongful assessments; and similar literature which is designed to strengthen legality, at least in the daily life of ordinary people, a kind of grassroot legality increasingly needed by a literate population whose standards of behaviour can no longer be regulated by an ill-defined traditional sense of equity.

For a long time the Soviet Union has been obsessed by the desire to 'catch up and overtake America', a desire which has not been fulfilled as yet and is unlikely to be fulfilled for a long time to come. There is, however, one field, namely welfare, where America might feel compelled to 'catch up and overtake' the USSR. The USA is a wealthy country which does little for its old, sick, disabled, and congenitally defective. Yet she could do so much more than the Soviet Union, where pensions and benefits are relatively modest, because the country is poor and cannot afford to be more generous. Nor is Russia yet in a position to allocate welfare in a more equalitarian way, for pensions are tied to wages and wages to the 'quantity and quality of work done'. However, the framework is there, as well as the conviction, that the young, the healthy, the gifted, and able-bodied must somehow share the wealth created by their work with the orphans, the sick, the old, and disabled, and the handicapped.

Chapter 11
Conclusion

THE SUBJECT OF THE present book has been the modernisation of the Soviet Union and her economic progress in the face of adverse geographical factors and despite the human failings of the people and their rulers. Among the adverse natural factors the most obvious are the severity of a cold climate affecting well over half of her territory; her limited outlets to international waterways, since she has access only to land-locked seas like the Baltic and the Black Sea, to the hardly navigable Arctic Ocean and the northernmost shores of the Pacific; the unfavourable location and wide dispersion of mineral resources, making heavy demand on long-distance haulage. The human factors that delayed rather than assisted economic development were the Revolution itself and the Civil War, which brought industry practically to a standstill and forced Lenin to adopt the New Economic Policy (NEP); according to Stalin the output of large-scale industry had been reduced by 1920 to one-seventh and that of the iron and steel industry to 3 per cent of what it had been in 1913.[1] During World War II the most productive and industrialised regions of the Soviet Union were overrun by the German armies and devastated by the scorched-earth policy enforced by both sides. Reconstruction started in 1945 and during the last twenty-five years the USSR has forged ahead so rapidly, that her present rank of a twentieth-century super-power is now fully accepted.

The Communist Party claims the credit for this achievement and attributes it to its doctrine of scientific economics and to the singlemindedness, unity, and dynamism of the Party itself. In the context of its spectacular achievements Stalin's senseless terrorism is glossed over as an unfortunate mistake put right by the Twentieth Party Congress. It is implied that during the war his unshakeable will-power was the mainstay of the people and an inspiration to victory, for 'it was he who in the years of trial never left his post of command'.[2] Without his autocratic drive the populace would not have put up with the hardships of post-war reconstruction,

[1] *Istoriya VKP (b), kratky kurs*, 1945 edition, chap. IX, p. 237.
[2] S. Smirnov in *Moskva*, October 1967.

when the rebuilding of mines, dams, and heavy engineering-works was given precedence over housing; while those who were doing the rebuilding huddled in dugouts and ramshackle hovels in near-famine conditions. Admittedly, the road to progress and prosperity had been hard, but the major obstacles were foreign invasions and inherited backwardness, not mistakes made by the CPSU.

Contrariwise, critics of the Soviet Union focus their attention on the wastefulness of convict labour, extensively used at a time when the workforce was already depleted by war losses running to over 20 million killed and an unspecified number of maimed and disabled; they emphasise the unjustifiable costs of maintaining a non-productive network of informers, interrogators, jailers, and executioners, as well as the stifling effect of terror on human initiative; even the promotion of science is seen as ambiguous, for although encouraged and lavishly financed, it was constricted by ideological controls; thus the ban on cybernetics resulted in the Soviet Union lagging in computer design and programming techniques.

Although on the rational level there seems to be no alternative to peaceful coexistence between capitalism and socialism, if the human race is to survive, too many people in too many countries are emotionally cave-men grinding their teeth and clenching their fists at real and imaginary enemies. Unfortunately, these half-rational bipeds, apart from grinding their teeth, can push buttons which will send multiple-head nuclear missiles flying over thousands of miles. Senior executives of powerful international corporations cast covetous and frustrated glances at maps showing oil-bearing lands they cannot buy up and mineral deposits to which their shareholders have no access. They are confronted by currencies that cannot be profitably manipulated, while unwelcome ships are plying oceans, probably to challenge and possibly to deny them the fabulous underwater riches still lying untapped under the sea-bed and which they regard as legitimate new sources of expansion and profits. In the division of world resources they have to contend with competitors who cannot become the object of takeover bids or be bribed into partaking of internationally disguised investment concerns. No less infuriating for the men in the Kremlin is the sight of a flourishing, prosperous, and expanding capitalism and the resourcefulness, viability, and obvious success of a mode of production that was proclaimed obsolete and doomed more than a century ago by the authors of the Communist Manifesto.

It is rather common among so-called kremlinologists to view the post-Stalin years as a kind of tug-of-war between liberals seeking to promote a freer society and conservatives clinging to the authoritarian methods of Stalinism. This is a very simplified view of extremely complex developments taking place over a vast territory and involving many people of different age, education, and national tradition. To give but a few examples. The merit of a bold policy of de-Stalinisation belongs to Khrushchev. To him goes the credit for handling the Twentieth Party Congress as he did and obtaining the rejection of terror as a method of government. Although the Hungarian uprising cut short further rapid de-Stalinisation, in 1961 Khrushchev renewed his denunciation of Stalin and had his body removed from Lenin's mausoleum. He intervened personally to allow the publication of A. Solzhenitsyn's story, *One day in the life of Ivan Denisovich*, about concentration-camp life. To reduce international tension he sought for personal contacts with President Kennedy and in 1960 went – uninvited – to a United Nations meeting in New York in a further attempt to promote peace. He agreed to lose face over the Cuba missile crisis in October 1962 and removed the objectionable weapons from Cuba without even demanding that the USA remove hers from Turkey and Pakistan, where they were deployed on the borders of the Soviet Union. Yet the same Khrushchev closed down seven of the ten Russian Orthodox seminaries that had been allowed to reopen during the war and transformed the famous Kiev Catacombs into an anti-religious 'museum of mummies', as yet another attack on what little religious freedom has been tolerated since World War II. He campaigned against peasant plots and privately owned cows and closed down collective-farm small-scale industries for fear that peasants acquire a little economic independence if given the opportunity to exercise their native wit and spirit of enterprise.

The policy of his successors has been, on the contrary, more liberal in economic matters and rigidly conservative in respect of ideology. For however limited the economic reforms inaugurated since 1965, they are a step towards giving more independence to individual enterprises and more powers of decision-making to the director (who still remains very much the boss), as well as to the factory trade union committees in matters of welfare and bonus payments. While grass-root democracy is promoted in local Soviets, writers are increasingly made to feel the iron grip of Party ideologists. Solzhenitsyn has not only been silenced and expelled from the Union of Writers, but even his name no longer appears in print.

International events have their repercussions on internal developments. Dangerously rapid liberalisation of the mass media and the campaign for market socialism in Czechoslovakia have made the Party very sensitive to all manifestations of dissent at home. That dissent exists is obvious from the very insistence on the need for the ideological struggle, a theme that pervades all authoritative pronouncements of Party leaders. There are, of course, various forms of dissent and not all of them are directed to better goals than those envisaged in the Party programme.

Western observers, particularly those with left-wing loyalties, hope that higher standards of education among Soviet people will preclude a return to Stalinism, which was, according to them, a product of the backwardness and therefore of the savage cruelty displayed by illiterate Russian masses at the time of the Revolution. This argument is contradicted by the acceptance of the no less cruel Nazi regime by the far more cultured German masses until it was overthrown by foreign armies. Nor can the scientists who work on devising diabolical means of warfare, such as nerve and other noxious gases, various strains of plague, and other agents of germ warfare, be regarded as uneducated or illiterate; yet they are aiding and abetting murder on a large scale, calmly preparing suffering and death for people and animals, either by direct poisoning or indirectly by the defoliation of forests or the spraying of toxic, crop-killing chemicals to induce famine. They probably condemn Stalin and his henchmen for mass murder, yet they themselves prepare horrors on a larger scale. Stalin thought that if he did not liquidate his enemies, they would liquidate him. He was probably right. Similarly, scientists working for their governments also think that if they do not liquidate the enemies of their country, the enemies will liquidate them. They, too, may be right. However, it does not occur to either that they are themselves *creating* their enemies.

To reverse the race to Armageddon is asking for a miracle. What would become of those in power, the marshals, the admirals, the generals, and other top brass in every country of the world if they were suddenly declared redundant? What would become of the hordes of instructors who teach soldiers to march, salute, polish buttons, shoot missiles, and drop bombs from supersonic planes? Or to the entire population of the Pentagon, if they were dismissed and sent to register at the nearest labour exchange as unemployed (and probably unemployable)? And, generally speaking, to all those who are engaged in the manufacture of a lot of dangerous waste and even more dangerous and explosive myth-making?

It would probably be easier for the Soviet leadership to beat their swords into ploughshares, because the Soviet Union is still badly in need of ploughshares and of other, more sophisticated, agricultural machinery; but would the fanatical and power-thirsty leaders of the CPSU agree merely to swell the ranks of tractor-drivers, of which the countryside is in dire need? More probably the leadership would wish to stay in power, though to lower tensions it may loosen its hold over the elected governmental bodies, such as local Soviets, or give more leeway to the expression of wishes cautiously conveyed on behalf of the electorate. By heeding the information of sociological surveys, the leadership may try to satisfy certain demands and reduce frictions, if that can be done without actually losing control. But reforms are more likely to be dictated by economic expediency than by other considerations. Agriculture will receive more investment because only further investment can make it more productive; rural infrastructures, such as all-weather roads and social amenities, are likely to get some attention in order to retain younger and more skilled labour in the countryside; otherwise the young will drift into towns where they can still easily find work. However, the denial of passports to peasants may continue in order to forestall a mass exodus. Certainly the demographic factor will be a compelling reason to provide better housing, if it is shown that larger flats can raise the birth-rate. More freedom of discussion of managerial techniques and organisational structure will be allowed if this leads to economic progress; and that in itself is quite a wide field; considering the ingenuity of the human mind and the voluminousness of Lenin's literary legacy, the sophistry of commentators is likely to produce a range of interpretations consonant with scientific discoveries made since his day. The raking-up of past blunders will not be tolerated, but the credibility gap between earlier ideological pronouncements and the direct experience of those who are taught advanced courses of Marxism-Leninism will have to be narrowed. People in the Soviet Union have increasingly wider contacts with foreign lands and foreign literatures. Not only diplomats and scientists attending international conferences go abroad, but also engineers and skilled mechanics connected with aid projects to underdeveloped countries, sailors manning Soviet merchant ships, and, more recently, sales promoters of Soviet goods. These contacts may have both the effect of sowing doubts and also that of confirming convictions, for instance the notion that poverty in underdeveloped countries is increased by imperialist exploitation.

Given these conditions, 'liberalisation' is bound to be a slow and very selective process, and outside dangers may shrivel manifestations of burgeoning tolerance. A struggle within the leadership may delay or hasten it; but it should be borne in mind that liberalisation is resisted most stubbornly at the lower echelons of power, because a bureaucrat securely entrenched behind his desk is not inclined willingly to vacate his comfortable seat. Resistance to younger men with scientifically progressive ideas by older men enjoying a possibly

CONCLUSION 235

well-deserved but obsolescent reputation and inclined to rest content with earlier achievements is a recurrent theme in Soviet fiction. The bitter struggle of less gifted authors whose major asset is Party backing against talented free-thinkers in the Writers' Union is a sad but well-established fact.

A return to Stalinism cannot be ruled out on the grounds that the population has achieved a higher educational level. On the contrary, scientific advance could make it more effective; bugging of flats, offices, and even public conveniences would be a better way of keeping the entire population under surveillance than the use of human spies; information retrieval techniques could provide those in power with the necessary data on every individual within a few minutes; the use of drugs could break down the resistance of the bravest prisoner. Although not impossible, a return to Stalinism is unlikely, because it would put back the clock of progress and, in Stalin's words, backward nations are beaten by the more advanced. Under neo-Stalinism the USSR could lose her front rank in science if her best scientists were made to work in special prisons, such as the one described by Solzhenitsyn in *The First Circle*. Economically, the country would also slip back, because the efficiency of convict labour is below that of modern machinery; the corollary would soon become apparent, namely that socialism leads to poverty while capitalism brings affluence. Nor could the international influence of the USSR be maintained if she could no longer risk sending abroad artists, athletes, technical advisers, and representatives on international bodies for fear of mass defections; she would have to seal off her frontiers again and take up a more rigid stance in foreign relations.

The way foreign relations would shape does not depend on the USSR alone, for it takes two to make a quarrel or an alliance. No one seriously believes in a sudden invasion of western Europe, except NATO's High Command, and then only when asking for further military credits and tactical nuclear weapons. East Germany is likely to be supported, though she is becoming much more of a liability than an asset. No Warsaw Pact ally will be allowed to join the other side.

The real danger lies in the Middle East, where Russia's involvement is particularly unfortunate because unnecessary. In the past Russia had no dealings with the Arab world one way or another. Distances precluded contacts. At present she does not need Arab oil. In the Central Asian republics sympathies probably go to the Arab side, but this is of minor importance. Connections with Israel are closer. The USSR was the first country to recognise the state of Israel. Her ideology is based on a doctrine fathered by Karl

Marx, who was a Jew. Among Lenin's close collaborators there were many Jews, Trotsky, Zinoviev, Kamenev, Sverdlov, Ioffe, for example, to name but a few. Even Stalin's first son-in-law was a Jew, and despite rumours of anti-semitism Jews are numerous and prominent in Soviet arts, sciences, literature, and the world of film-making and entertainment. The support of the Arab cause is part of the anti-imperialist struggle, and if the USSR does not support left-wing Arab states, China will not hesitate to supply arms to the Palestinian Liberation Army, who have a real cause to fight for since they have been driven from the land where they are believed to have dwelt for a longer period of time than their Jewish predecessors. The dispute between Egypt and Israel should be of no concern to the USSR, but having started as part of the anti-imperialist struggle, it is now further complicated by rivalry with China.

Frictions with China have developed from an ideological dispute over Stalinism into a confrontation between two nations along a very long and disputed frontier. A pre-emptive strike by the USSR against China, if ever contemplated, would now come too late. However limited China's nuclear power may be, it is already a deterrent. The will to fight it out is greater in Peking than in Moscow. After long years of toil to achieve industrialisation and prosperity, the Soviet Union has much to lose in case of war. She will also lose another asset to China, namely influence over the revolutionary movements of the world. That of China is in the ascendant, while that of the Soviet Union is waning. Since the Soviet Union still pretends to be a revolutionary force, the CPSU cannot make a clean break with its past and publicise its old mistakes. This adds to the ambivalence of the present leadership towards the personality of Stalin. We are back to the problem of Stalinism.

Although not inconceivable, a return to it would be the last stand of a desperate leader (or leadership) whose personal fate was at stake and who would put his own survival above the cause of socialism and the interests of the country. A slow, selective liberalisation is more likely, something reminiscent of a long-drawn-out rearguard action by a numerous and conservative bureaucracy using a variety of delaying tactics of greater or lesser effectiveness against the forces of change. These are the economic factors discussed in preceding chapters, the impact of new technologies, and the inarticulate pressures for more leisure and pay from the masses, whose demands are manifested by Monday-morning absenteeism, high labour turnover, and the disturbingly large consumption of vodka, due probably to the lack of something better to buy on pay-day.

CONCLUSION 237

In trying to describe the modernisation of the Soviet Union with its attendant hopes and difficulties, it has been assumed throughout that the establishment of an affluent society, where the distribution of material goods will be equitable and intellectual aspirations will find satisfactory outlets in scientific pursuit and artistic creativity, is in itself a desirable aim. Fundamentally, this aim does not conflict with the received ideas prevalent in any modern materialist society.

Human happiness organised by rational administrators has been satirised by Zamyatin in his novel *We* (1920), Aldous Huxley in *Brave New World*, and George Orwell in *1984*. But fiction-writers are notorious troublemakers and long ago Plato was at a loss to find a place for the poets of his *Republic*. However, poets are a statistically negligible percentage of the population, and what most critics reject is not a rationally and equitably organised society, but the methods used, that is, they reject the *means*, not the *ends*.

Those who reject the *means* are Western critics, particularly left-wingers, many Soviet citizens who have either suffered from their enforcement or are yearning for a humane socialism of the Dubček type and who would subscribe to the slogan of 'Soviets without Communists', put forward by the sailors of Kronstadt when they rebelled against the Soviet regime in 1921.

More thoughtful communists, and Lenin was one of them, posed as preconditions for the establishment of the good society not merely the nationalisation of the means of production but the evolution of Man himself. The somewhat naïve eighteenth-century optimism that good laws would make good citizens has been shattered by experience as well as modern psychology. Following Lenin, present-day Soviet educationalists, while believing that environmental factors will bring about the emergence of the New Man, envisage a spiral-type of progress; economic conditions improve because of public ownership of means of production and affect man for the better; a better man improves economic conditions and the latter improve the next generation; and so on. At first the spiral was thought to be quite short, made up of one or two generations; now it looks as if the spiral will be a lengthy one, measurable not in years but in generations.

However, there are people who, without rejecting the final aim of a secular millennium, doubt that external conditions can improve Man. They sense the innate wickedness, the irrational malice that will prompt him to break the most equitable and sensible laws or, like Dostoevsky's underground man, wantonly knock down the beautiful crystal palace built for his benefit, for no other reason than to exercise his self-will, knowing full well that what he is doing is to his own detriment. In other words, it is impossible to improve the world without first improving individual men. The path to the happiness of all is through self-improvement of each and every individual. The more optimistic Freudians hope that the intermittent flickering of reason may through self-knowledge become a steadier flame. Others believe self-improvement can be achieved through altruism, living to help others, a realisation of the futility of pointless ambitions and the vanity of material wealth. The next step is self-renunciation and the perennial question of the purpose of an individual human life. The search for truth may cease to be one for an earthly millennium and become one for the Kingdom of Heaven. Preoccupation with food and shelter and even good laws transcends into a search for the meaning of this short interval of eternity spent on a small planet in the infinity of space. The transient world is forsaken for something greater beyond space and time, for the absolute God. For such people the goals of communism become mere trifles and the purpose of life is no longer the building of an economic basis but a pilgrim's progress towards ultimate perfection, in other words, towards God.

This attitude is particularly obnoxious to communist leaders, since it distracts men from building communism and, furthermore, makes them indifferent to the goal, the importance of which dwindles if compared with life everlasting. Hence the unabating hostility to religious beliefs, the prohibition to preach any religion in general and to children in particular. Criminal proceedings may be taken against anyone preaching outside the precincts of a church, mosque, synagogue, or any other temple. Soviet leaders are too busy with material construction to waste time on insoluble questions that have engaged the attention of earlier philosophers 'who tried to explain the world instead of changing it'. Because of their lack of interest in and understanding of religious convictions, they measure them by external attributes, such as having or not having ikons in the house. Atheistic propaganda is directed mainly against ritual or dwells at length on discrepancies between geological data and biblical stories. Theoretically the practice of religion, in contradistinction to preaching it, is not proscribed, but priests are heavily taxed, like self-employed doctors, and they and godparents are liable to be prosecuted for assault if an infant catches cold after christening (which is by immersion in the Orthodox Church); seminaries have been closed on charges of homosexuality and churches with foreign connections, like the Baptists, accused of currency speculation if they received funds from abroad.

Apart from hostility to any organised religion, the CPSU fears all those who view things *sub specie eternitatis*. The major objection to Pasternak's *Dr Zhivago* was the poet's vision of the Revolution as just one event in the history of mankind, particularly in the poem where Christ watches the boats of centuries drifting towards Him.

It is also the deeper, the perennial questions of the meaning of death and the purpose of human existence raised in Solzhenitsyn's works that make them unacceptable to the Party leadership. His detractors were quick to perceive the link between *Cancer Ward* and Tolstoy's story *The death of Ivan Il'ich*, nor did they overlook the implications of his assertion that Man becomes spiritually free, when bodily he is in prison, stripped of all his material possessions, deprived of family affection, social position, and human dignity by humiliating searches, hunger, and beatings. Deprived of everything Man attains complete freedom. What is left is his real unalienable self or, in theological terminology, his immortal soul.

Solzhenitsyn knows suffering at first hand as well as degradation and the approach of death, which he saw near enough at the front, where he commanded a battery, during his trial which nearly ended in a death sentence, during his concentration-camp years, and in hospital where he was treated for cancer. Because he has so much to say, and what he says is important, he does not resort to involved symbolism like Western writers who fear to be accused of platitudes. All major themes, like the joy of life and the fear of death, love and lust, despair and anger, revenge and forgiveness, are eternal themes which have attracted all writers worthy of that name since the beginning of time. Anyone who returns to them is in danger of repeating what others have said, but because they are so fundamental, readers and listeners never tire of them, provided that he who conveys them has intensely felt those emotions, felt them so intensely as to infect his listeners with what he has experienced. This was Tolstoy's view of art; he maintained that all great art is simple and sincere and can be understood and enjoyed by all, a view that annoyed literary critics who sensed the danger of becoming superfluous. Simplicity is certainly a striking feature of Solzhenitsyn's style. He has an uncanny gift of outlining a character by using just a few sentences, every word of which is loaded with meaning and rich in implications. The lucidity and conciseness of his prose contrasts with the longwindedness of his Soviet colleagues. His parodies, in their tragic terseness, are permeated with 'laughter through tears'.

Like his great predecessors, Solzhenitsyn brings up the problems that have troubled mankind since the days when Job asked what was the meaning of suffering and the author of *Ecclesiastes* what was the purpose of man's toil and exertion if death effaced all. Who or what makes history? Who or what shapes the destiny of nations or simply a life worth living on earth? Solzhenitsyn sees wonder where others see none. Life in the countryside is made more tolerable because a warm-hearted old peasant woman is always ready to help her neighbours. A little yellow duckling miraculously emerges from the shell of his egg like others have always done without reference to any scientific theory. Nature so much wiser than men; the simple-hearted who are the backbone of a nation and retain their humanity even in prison camps; the mysterious bond between the land of the ancestors and the living of today; above all the reminder of death, the spectre that Soviet art and literature are meant to conjure away and keep out of sight; these are themes that disturb those who cannot see beyond the here and now.

He also questions many received ideas, even the importance of science to man. He objects to the right of doctors to decide for the patient, particularly if the treatment affects the personality; for who is entitled to decide what is normal? Cannot deviant behaviour be another form of normality?

From the Soviet point of view Solzhenitsyn is a deviant himself and his independence of mind is a challenge to conformity. This independence is particularly striking in a man born after the Revolution who, contrary to older writers (who might have preserved it from earlier days), has known nothing but Soviet reality.

This concentration on a nonconformist writer in lieu of a conclusion to a book designed to describe the modernisation of Russia is not entirely irrelevant. It is just a reminder that planners have to deal eventually not only with production targets and material incentives, but with living people as well; that there are among the latter a statistically negligible percentage who remain refractory to daily indoctrination, but whose voice might evoke echoes unexpectedly loud. The nonconformist mentioned happens to be a Russian. There may be others, people of different stock, in the mountains of the Caucasus and the oases of Central Asia.

Spontaneous mutations occur in nature very seldom, yet they are said to influence evolution even more than natural selection or environmental factors. When one comes to think of it, the eleven men who set out to preach the Gospel were a statistically negligible minority in the population of the Roman Empire. The human personality has not yet been reduced to a mathematical symbol in the USSR and the statistical data adduced in this book cannot reveal the richness and the variety of life in that country; they are far greater than could be expected from the uniformity of its daily press.

Appendix A

Chronology of Events

1870	22 April, birth of Lenin.
1881	1 March, assassination of Tsar Alexander II.
1891	Building of Trans-Siberian Railway begun.
1898	First Congress of the Russian Social Democratic Workers' Party (RSDRP) in Minsk.
1903	Second Congress of RSDRP held in Brussels and London. Split between Bolsheviks and Mensheviks.
1905	First Russian Revolution triggered off by Bloody Sunday, 9 January; first Council (Soviet) of Workers' Deputies set up in St Petersburg on 13 October; armed uprising in Moscow in December.
1906	First *Duma* convened.
1914	July, outbreak of World War I.
1917	25–26 February (8–9 March, according to Gregorian Calendar), February Revolution; 2(15) March, abdication of Tsar Nicholas II; Provisional Government set up by *Duma*.
	3 (16) April, Lenin returns to Russia from Switzerland.
	3–24 June (16 June–2 July), first All-Russian Congress of Councils (Soviets) of Workers' and Soldiers' Deputies.
	25–26 October (7–8 November), armed insurrection led by the Bolshevik Party, culminating in the October Revolution.
	8 November, Decrees on land nationalisation and peace with Germany adopted by the second All-Russian Congress of Soviets.
	2 December, formation of Supreme Economic Council.
	14 December Decree on the nationalisation of banks, followed by nationalisation of various industries in the course of the following months.
	20 December, setting-up of an Extraordinary Commission for Fighting Counter-Revolution and Sabotage (*Cheka*), and the beginning of Red Terror.
1918	12 March, Soviet government transfers capital to Moscow.
	15 March, Soviet-German peace treaty signed in Brest-

	Litovsk (abrogated on 13 November after Germany's defeat in the West).
1918	16 July, Tsar Nicholas II, his wife, and children murdered in Ekaterinburg (now Sverdlovsk) in the Urals.
1918–20	Civil War and foreign intervention.
1919	11 January, Decree on the requisitioning of all surplus grain from peasants and grain-traders.
	12 April, first communist *Subbotnik*, i.e. voluntary day's work at the Moscow Sortirovochnaya railway-yard.
1920	25 April–12 October, Soviet-Polish War.
	State Commission for the Electrification of Russia (GOELRO) set up.
1921	8–16 March, Tenth Party Congress. New Economic Policy (NEP) adopted; widespread famine.
1922	April, Stalin elected General Secretary of the Central Committee.
	December, the Union of Soviet Socialist Republics (USSR) comes into existence as a federation of republics.
1924	21 January, death of Lenin.
1925	December, Fourteenth Party Congress initiates measures to industrialise the country.
	6 December, Shatura peat-burning power-station goes into production, the first to be built under the GOELRO plan.
1927	Trotsky expelled from the Party.
	December, Fifteenth Party Congress adopts first Five-Year Plan for the development of the national economy.
1928–32	Implementation of first Five-Year Plan.
1928	First Machine-Tractor Station set up on the basis of the tractor column of the Shevchenko state farm (Odessa province).
1929	Mass collectivisation campaign decreed.
	Trotsky expelled from the USSR.
1930	1 May, opening of the Turkestan–Siberia (Turksib) railway.
	26 June–13 July, Sixteenth Party Congress.
1931	Japan occupies Manchuria.
1932	First generator of the Dniepr hydropower-station (Dnieproges) goes into production.
1933	19 January, Decree on compulsory grain deliveries to the state by collective farms and individual peasants.
1934	Seventeenth Party Congress adopts second Five-Year Plan.
1934	1 December, Kirov's assassination used as pretext for the intensification of terror and purges of the Party.

CHRONOLOGY OF EVENTS 243

1933-37	Second Five-Year Plan.
1935	Opening of the Moscow metro.
1936	5 December, the new Stalin Constitution adopted.
1938	December, introduction of Labour Books and general tightening of labour discipline.
1939	20-21 March, Eighteenth Party Congress adopts third Five-Year Plan for 1938-42, the implementation of which is interrupted by the German invasion of Russia. 23 August, German-Soviet (Molotov-Ribbentrop) Non-Aggression Pact. 1 September, Germany attacks Poland. 1-2 November, USSR occupies western Ukraine and western Belorussia, formerly parts of Poland.
1939-40	30 November 1939-12 March 1940, Soviet-Finnish War.
1940	26 August, USSR formally annexes Estonia, Latvia, and Lithuania.
1941	22 June, German armies invade the USSR.
1941-44	August 1941-January 1944, the 900-day siege of Leningrad by German and Finnish armies.
1941	December, German advance halted in the suburbs of Moscow.
1942-43	November 1942-February 1943, Battle of Stalingrad.
1943	28 November-1 December, Teheran Conference between Churchill, Roosevelt, and Stalin.
1944	6 June, Second Front opened, Allies land in France.
1945	4-11 February, Yalta Conference between Churchill, Roosevelt, and Stalin. 2 May, Soviet armies storm Berlin. 8 May, Germany's unconditional surrender. 6 August, Atomic bomb dropped on Hiroshima. 8 August, USSR declares war on Japan.
1946-50	Fourth Five-Year Plan for the reconstruction of the devastated areas and the rehabilitation of the national economy.
1947	14 December, monetary reform and abolition of wartime rationing.
1948	June, Stalin breaks with Tito.
1949	4 April, North Atlantic Treaty Organisation set up.
1949	23 September, USSR detonates her first atomic bomb. Formation of the Council for Economic Co-operation (*Comecon*). 1 October, Chinese People's government established by Mao Tse-Tung.
1950	14 February, Sino-Soviet Treaty of Friendship.

1952	Opening of the Volga–Don Canal. October, Nineteenth Party Congress adopts fifth Five-Year Plan, for 1951–55. The Party hitherto known as the All-Union Communist Party (bolshevik), or VKP (b), is renamed Communist Party of the Soviet Union (CPSU).
1953	5 March, death of Stalin. 14 March, N. K. Khrushchev becomes First Secretary of the Central Committee of the CPSU and Georgy Malenkov Prime Minister. 20 August, USSR detonates her first hydrogen bomb. September, Plenum of Central Committee adopts important measures to improve agricultural production.
1954	2 March, Decree on the ploughing-up of virgin and fallow lands. 14 May, Warsaw military Pact signed. 27 June, first Soviet atom-power station goes into production (5,000 Kw.). 1 October, USSR and Yugoslavia resume trade relations, broken off in 1949. 11 October, USSR and China issue text of friendship agreement. Port Arthur restored to China.
1956	Twentieth Party Congress adopts sixth Five-Year Plan. Khrushchev denounces Stalin's personality cult in a secret speech (published by the US State Department on 4 June). 20 October, Gomulka returned to power as First Secretary of Polish Communist Party. 20 October–4 November, Hungarian revolt against Soviet occupation; uprising crushed by Soviet armed intervention.
1957	7 May, legislation to decentralise the administration of industry initiated by Khrushchev. 3 July, Khrushchev defeats his rivals in an inner-party struggle for power. 4 October, launching of the first Earth satellite.
1958	31 March, abolition of Machine-Tractor Stations and sale of their equipment to collective farms.
1959	28 January–5 February, Twenty-first Party Congress adopts a Seven-Year national economic plan for 1959–65 to replace the unrealistically ambitious sixth Five-Year Plan approved at the Twentieth Party Congress. 12 September, launching of the first A-powered ice-breaker, *Lenin*. 4 October, first pictures of the dark side of the Moon.

CHRONOLOGY OF EVENTS 245

1960 April, Chinese leaders attack Soviet policy of peaceful coexistence.
12 April, Yury A. Gagarin first man in space.
1 May, US U-2 reconnaissance plane shot down over the Urals.
November, Moscow Conference of 81 communist parties endeavours to restore unity among communist parties.
14 November, new exchange value of rouble, one US dollar being made equal to 90 kopeks (0·9 roubles).

1961 17–30 October, Twenty-second Party Congress adopts new Party programme. Stalin's body removed from Red Square mausoleum.

1962 14 January, international pipeline taking Soviet oil to *Comecon* countries inaugurated.
22–29 October, Cuban Missile Crisis.

1963 14–19 June, V. F. Bykovsky and V. V. Tereshkova (first woman cosmonaut) in space flight.

1964 7 January, giant Bratsk hydropower-station in Siberia goes into production.
15 October, Khrushchev made to resign; succeeded by Leonid Brezhnev as First Secretary and Aleksei Kosygin as Prime Minister (Khrushchev held both posts, the former since 1953 and the latter since 27 March 1958).

1965 24–26 March, Plenum of Central Committee initiates legislation to increase agricultural production; Khrushchev's restrictive measures against peasant ancillary farming (individually owned livestock and vegetable plots) removed.
27–29 September, Plenum initiates economic reforms in industry.
2 October, measures to decentralise the administration of industry.

1966 March–April, Twenty-third Party Congress. Eighth national economic plan adopted for 1966–70.

1967 Fiftieth anniversary of the Revolution.

1968 20–21 August, Occupation of Czechoslovakia by the armed forces of the Warsaw Pact countries.

1969 5–17 June, Conference of 75 communist and workers' parties in Moscow boycotted by China.
2 and 15 March, 8 and 20 July, Sino-Soviet border clashes.

1970 Lenin's centenary.

Appendix B
Population Figures

BREAKDOWN ACCORDING TO UNION REPUBLICS
AND THEIR CAPITAL CITIES

	1959 thousands	1970	1970 as percentage of 1959
USSR (total)	208,827	241,748	116
1. RSFSR	117,534	130,090	111
Moscow	6,044	7,061	117
2. Ukraine	41,869	47,136	113
Kiev	1,110	1,632	147
3. Kazakhstan	9,153	12,850	140
Alma-Ata	456	730	160
4. Uzbekistan	8,261	11,963	145
Tashkent	927	1,385	149
5. Belorussia	8,056	9,003	112
Minsk	509	916	180
6. Azerbaidzhan	3,698	5,111	138
Baku	968	1,261	130
7. Georgia	4,044	4,688	116
Tbilisi	703	889	127
8. Moldavia	2,885	3,572	124
Kishinev	216	357	165
9. Lithuania	2,711	3,129	115
Vilnius	236	372	157
10. Kirghizia	2,006	2,933	142
Frunze	220	431	196
11. Tadzhikistan	1,981	2,900	146
Dushanbe	227	374	165
12. Armenia	1,763	2,493	141
Erevan	493	767	155
13. Latvia	2,095	2,365	113
Riga	580	733	126
14. Turkmenia	1,516	2,158	144
Ashkhabad	170	253	146
15. Estonia	1,197	1,357	113
Tallinn	282	363	129

POPULATION OF AUTONOMOUS REPUBLICS AND THEIR REPUBLICAN CENTRES

	1959	1970
	in thousands	
Within the RSFSR		
Bashkir ASSR	3,342	3,819
Ufa	*547*	*773*
Buriat ASSR	673	812
Ulan-Ude	*174*	*254*
Dagestan ASSR	1,063	1,429
Makhachkala	*119*	*186*
Kabardino–Balkar ASSR	420	589
Nal'chik	*88*	*146*
Kalmyk ASSR	260	268
Elista	*23*	*50*
Karelian ASSR	651	714
Petrozavodsk	*135*	*185*
Komi ASSR	806	965
Syktyvkar	*69*	*125*
Mari ASSR	648	685
Yoshkar-ola	*89*	*166*
Mordovian ASSR	1,000	1,030
Saransk	*91*	*190*
North Ossetian ASSR	451	553
Ordzhonikidze	*164*	*236*
Tartar ASSR	2,850	3,131
Kazan'	*667*	*869*
Tuva ASSR	172	231
Kyzyl	*34*	*52*
Udmurt ASSR	1,337	1,417
Izhevsk	*285*	*422*
Chechen–Ingush ASSR	710	1,065
Grozny	*250*	*341*
Chuvash ASSR	1,098	1,224
Cheboksary	*104*	*216*
Yakut ASSR	488	664
Yakutsk	*74*	*108*
Within Uzbekistan		
Karakalpak ASSR	510	702
Nukus	*39*	*74*

	1959	1970
	in thousands	
Within Georgia		
Abkhaz ASSR	405	487
Sukhumi	*65*	*102*
Adzhar ASSR	245	310
Batumi	*82*	*101*
Within Azerbaidzhan		
Nakhichevan' ASSR	141	202
Nakhichevan'	*24*	*33*

POPULATION OF AUTONOMOUS REGIONS (OBLAST')
AND NATIONAL DISTRICTS (OKRUG)

	1959	1970
Within the RSFSR	in thousands	
Adygei autonomous region	285	386
(within Krasnodar province)		
Gorno–Altai autonomous region	157	168
(within Altai province)		
Jewish autonomous region	163	173
(within Khabarosk province)		
Karachai–Cherkess autonomous region	278	345
(within Stavropol province)		
Khakass autonomous region	411	466
Taimyr (Dolgano–Nenets) national district	33	38
Evenki national district	10	13
(all within Krasnoyarsk province)		
Agin–Buriat national district	49	66
(within Chita province)		
Komi–Permyak national district	217	212
(within Perm' province)		
Koryak national district	28	31
(within Kamchatka province)		
Nenets national district	46	39
(within Archangel province)		
Ust–Ordyn Buriat national district	133	146
(within Irkutsk province)		
Khanty–Mansi national district	124	272
Yamalo–Nenets national district	62	80
(both within Tyumen' province)		
Chuktka national district	47	101
(within Magadan province)		

Within Georgia
South Ossetian autonomous region 97 100
Within Azerbaidzhan
Nagorno–Karabakh autonomous region 131 149
Within Tadzhikistan
Gorno–Badakhshan autonomous region 73 98

Appendix C

List of Personalities Mentioned in the Text

ENGLISH ABBREVIATIONS[1]

Acad.	Academy
Agr.	Agricultural
Assoc.	Association
Cand.	Candidate
CC	Central Committee
Coll.	Collected
CP	Communist Party
CPSU	Communist Party of the Soviet Union
Dept.	Department
Exec.	Executive
Grad.	Graduated
Inst.	Institute
Lit.	Literary
Maths	Mathematics
Prof.	Professor
Prov.	Province
Univ.	University

ABRAMOV, Fedor Alekseevich
 In 1954, published an article in the journal *Novy Mir* criticising idyllic descriptions of life on collective farms in fiction. Author of realistic stories set in the countryside, e.g. *Around and about*, 1962, translated into English as *The Dodgers*; *Two winters and three summers*, 1968; *Pelageya*, 1969.

AITMATOV, Chingiz, 1928–
 Novelist and scenario writer, born in the village of Sheker, Kirghizia; grad. from Kirghiz Agr. Institute, 1953; in 1956, senior zoo-technician on experimental farm of Kirghiz cattle-breeding Research Inst.; member of CP since 1960. Writes in both Kirghiz and Russian. His *Dzhamilya*, 1958, was translated into French by

[1] For Russian abbreviations see above, p. 15.

LIST OF PERSONALITIES MENTIONED IN TEXT 251

Louis Aragon; other novels include *My little poplar in the red kerchief*, 1961; *Mother's Heart*, 1963; *The Camel's Eye*, 1963, made into plays or films; *Farewell Gul'sary*, 1966, awarded Lenin Prize. Since 1967 on editorial board of *Novy Mir and Literaturnaya Gazeta*, member of board of USSR Union of Writers, deputy to XXIII Party Congress, member of USSR Supreme Soviet, etc.

AKHMADULINA, Bella Akhatovna, 1937–
Poetess, married first poet E. Evtushenko, then writer Yu. Nagibin. Collected poems: *Strings*, 1962; *My Genealogy*, 1965; *Rain*, 1968; also short stories and film scripts.

AKHMATOVA, Anna Andreevna Gorenko, 1888–1966
Poetess, associated with Acmeist school, married to poet N. Gumilev, later divorced. Author of collections of verse, e.g. *Evening*, 1912; *The White Flock*, 1917; *Anno Domini MCMXXI*, 1921; etc. In 1946, her poetry was attacked by Zhdanov for its lack of ideological content, preoccupation with personal feelings, and mysticism. An anthology of her *Poems of Various Years* was published in 1958.

AKSYONOV, Aleksandr Nikiforovich, 1924–
Member of CP since 1945, member of CC of USSR *Komsomol*, 1956–59. Minister of the Interior and member of CC of Belorussian CP; Chairman of Youth Commission of USSR Supreme Soviet.

AKSYONOV, Vasily Pavlovich, 1932–
Writer and physician; author of *A Ticket to the Stars*, 1961; *Half-way to the Moon*, 1962; *Oranges from Morocco*, 1963; *It's time, my friend, it's time*, 1965; *What a pity you were not with us*, 1969. Son of Evgenia Ginzburg, author of *Into the Whirlwind*, 1967.

ANDREYEV, Leonid Nikolaevich, 1871–1919
Decadent writer, author of *Red Laughter*, 1904; *King Hunger*, 1907; *Seven that were hanged*, 1908; *He who gets slapped*, 1914; and other stories and plays. Emigrated after October Revolution and died in Finland.

AVERBAKH (Auerbach), Leopol'd Leonidovich, 1903–
Theorist of the journal *On Guard* and the Proletarian Writers' literary movement; bitterly denounced non-communist writers and tried to secure a complete monopoly in literature for Proletarian Writers. After his brother-in-law, Yagoda, former head of the NKVD, was executed in 1938, A. was denounced as an enemy of the people and disappeared during the purges.

BABAYEVSKY, Semyon Petrovich, 1909–
Journalist and writer, member of CP since 1939, author of stories

Kuban' Kossaks, 1940; novels: *Knight of the Golden Star*, 1947; *Light over the Earth*, 1949; *The Wide World*, 1968; etc. Awarded several Stalin Prizes for literature, the Orders of Lenin and of the Red Banner of Labour.

BAIBAKOV, Nikolai Konstantinovich, 1911–
Chairman of State Planning Commission (*Gosplan*); member of CP since 1939; born and educated in Azerbaidzhan; Dr of Technical Sciences; specialist in petroleum engineering; Lenin Prize 1963; three Orders of Lenin, etc.

BELUKHA, Nikolai Andreevich, 1920–
Second Secretary of CC of Latvian CP. Member of Youth Commission of Supreme Soviet. Member of CP since 1948.

BELY, Andrei (Boris Nikolaevich Bugaev), 1880–1934
Symbolist poet, writer, and critic, author of *The Silver Dove*, 1910; *St Petersburg*, 1913; *Kotik Letaev*, 1917–18; etc; and of *Recollections of A. Blok*, 1922; *On the Borders of Two Centuries*, 1929; *The Beginning of a Century*, 1932; and *Between Two Revolutions*, 1933. Hailed the October Revolution in the poem *Christ is Risen*, 1918, then emigrated in 1921, but returned in 1923 and died in the Soviet Union.

BENES, Edvard, 1884–1948
Czechoslovak statesman; studied at the Univ. of Prague, Paris, and Dijon. During World War I formed with T. G. Masaryk in Switzerland a council for an independent Czechoslovakia; after break-up of Habsburg monarchy, became the first Czechoslovak Minister of Foreign Affairs, 1918–35; elected President of Czechoslovakia in 1935; forced to accept the 1938 Munich agreement ceding the Sudetenland to Germany. After Hitler's occupation of Prague, formed a government-in-exile in London. Returned to Prague to become again Head of State, 1945. In the 1946 elections the Communists emerged as largest single party and their leader Klement Gottwald was allowed to form a coalition government. In 1948, the Communists engineered a change of constitution, which Benes refused to sign and preferred to resign the presidency.

BERIA, Lavrenty Pavlovich, 1893–1953
Son of a Georgian peasant, joined Bolshevik Party in 1916, became head of Georgian security police, and in 1938 was appointed deputy chief of NKVD under Ezhov, whom he succeeded at the end of the same year; in 1945, elevated to the military rank of marshal; executed in December 1953, being held responsible for the excesses of police terror under Stalin.

BLOK, Aleksandr Aleksandrovich, 1880–1921
Symbolist poet, author of *Verses about the Beautiful Lady*, 1904; lyrical dramas, e.g. *The Puppet Show*, 1906; *The Rose and the*

LIST OF PERSONALITIES MENTIONED IN TEXT 253

Cross, 1913; poems about Russia: *Rus'*, 1906; *The Field of Kulikovo*, 1908; etc. Hailed the Revolution in his poem *The Twelve*, 1918, though realised later that his vision of it differed from reality. Died in Petrograd (Leningrad).

BOGDANOV (Malinovsky), Aleksandr Aleksandrovich, 1873–1928
Marxist economist, joined Bolshevik Party in 1904, broke with Lenin in 1909, and organised together with Lunacharsky and Maxim Gorky a Party school in Capri. In 1913, published the first volume of *Tectology* or 'universal organisational science'; final edition 1922. Served as military surgeon during World War I. Elaborated a theory of proletarian culture and was the major theorist of the 'Proletkult' literary movement.

BONDAREV, Yury Vasil'evich, 1924–
Writer, commanded an artillery battery during World War II, joined CP in 1944. Later studied at Gorky Lit. Inst. Author of *The Battalions are calling for supporting Fire*, 1957; *Peace* (Tishina), 1962, made into a film; second part *The Two*, 1964. Since 1967 member of Board of USSR Union of Writers.

BREZHNEV, Leonid Il'ich, 1906–
First Secretary of CC of CPSU. Born in Ukraine, educated Kursk Technicum for Land Utilisation and Reclamation, 1927; grad. Dneprodzherzhinsk Metallurgical Inst., 1935; during World War II head of Political Board Fourth Ukrainian Front, then deputy head, Main Political Board of Soviet Army and Navy. In 1950, First Secretary of CC of Moldavian CP; elected member of CC of CPSU at XIX Party Congress in 1952; replaced Voroshilov in 1960 as Chairman of the Praesidium of USSR Supreme Soviet, and in 1964 N. Khrushchev as First Secretary of CC of CPSU.

BRYUSOV, Valery Yakovlevich, 1873–1924
Symbolist poet, founder of the review *Scales* (Vesy), 1904–09; author of *The Fire Angel*, 1907, etc.; joined the CP in 1920, headed the Higher Literary and Art Inst. and contributed to the popularisation of culture among the masses.

BUDENNY, Semyon Mikhailovich, 1883–
Marshal of the Soviet Union since 1935, member of CP since 1919. Fought in the Russo-Japanese War, sergeant-major in Dragoon Regiment, 1908–17. In 1919–20, commanded First Cavalry Army against the Whites, then against Poland. During World War II did not take active part after south-western front was smashed by the Germans at Uman'.

BUKHARIN, Nikolai Ivanovich, 1888–1938
Joined Bolshevik Party in 1906 and was one of its leading theorists. In 1917, played a prominent part in preparations for the seizure of power by the Moscow Party organisation; with Lenin

drew up the 1919 Party programme; after Lenin's death supported Stalin against Trotsky; advocated the continuation of NEP; replaced Zinoviev as head of Comintern in 1925; led the 'Right opposition' against Stalin in 1928–29, yet remained a member of the CC until 1936 and took an active part in drafting the 1936 Stalin Constitution. Executed after a show trial in 1938. Author of *ABC of Communism*, 1919, in collaboration with E. Preobragensky, and other Marxist theoretical works.

BULGAKOV, Mikhail Afanas'evich, 1891–1940
Physician, journalist, and writer. His novel *The White Guards* was staged as a play in 1926 under the title *The Days of the Turbin family*; author of science fiction stories, a play about Molière, which was banned, and a symbolistic fantasy, *The Master and Margarita*, published posthumously in 1966–67.

BUNIN, Ivan Alekseevich, 1870–1954
Writer and poet, author of *The Life of Arsen'ev*, 1927 (in English translation *The Well of Days*, 1946). Emigrated in 1920. Awarded Nobel Prize for literature, 1933. Died in Paris.

CHAYANOV, Aleksandr Vasil'evich, 1888–19?
Specialist in agriculture; author of *The Theory of Peasant Economy*, a translation of which was published by the American Economic Association, 1966; opposed collectivisation and disappeared during the purges of the 1930s.

CHERNYSHEVSKY, Nikolai Gavrilovich, 1829–89
Literary critic and publicist; leader of the radical intelligentsia in the late 1850s and early 1860s; editor of the influential journal *Sovremennik*; his novel *What is to be done*, 1863, may be regarded as prototype of socialist realism. Arrested and exiled to Siberia for revolutionary activities. Usually viewed as founder of revolutionary Populism.

CHUKOVSKY, Kornei Ivanovich, 1882–1969
Journalist, lit. critic, writer of children's books, and translator of works by Oscar Wilde, Whitman, etc. Author of lit. studies, e.g. *Nekrasov's Artistry*, 1952; *People and Books*, 1958; children's books include *The Crocodile*, 1916; *Wash-to-Bits* (Moidodyr), 1923; *Doctor Oh-it-hurts* (Doctor Aibolit), 1927; and a book about children, *From two to five*, 1925, which went through many editions.

DANIEL, Yuly Markovich, 1925–
Translator and journalist on staff of *Komsomolskaya Pravda*, *Literaturnaya Gazeta*, etc. Under the pen-name of Nikolai Arzhak published abroad *Moscow calling*, *The Man from MISP*, and other stories; was arrested in Sept. 1965, arraigned with

LIST OF PERSONALITIES MENTIONED IN TEXT 255

Sinyavsky, and sentenced under article 70 of the Soviet Criminal Code to five years imprisonment for anti-Soviet activities.

DUDINTSEV, Vladimir Dmitrievich, 1918–
Writer, author of controversial novel *Not by bread alone*, 1956, and other stories as well as articles on biology and genetics, 1963–66.

EHRENBURG, Ilya Grigor'evich, 1891–1967
Versatile writer, journalist, author of memoirs entitled *Time, Years, Life*. Lived much abroad, especially in Paris; one-time foreign correspondent of *Izvestiya*. Author of *Julio Jurenito*, 1922, and other novels. The title of his short story *The Thaw*, 1954, has been used to describe the relaxation of lit. controls after Stalin's death.

EIKHENBAUM, Boris Mikhailovich, 1886–1959
Formalist lit. critic and member of the Society for the study of the theory of poetic language (OPOYAZ). Author of studies about L. Tolstoy, Lermontov, Anna Akhmatova, Mayakovsky, and others, as well as on stylistic devices and versification.

ESENIN, Sergei Aleksandrovich, 1895–1925
Poet of peasant origin, whose poetry is imbued with affection for the countryside; later member of the Imaginist lit. group. His 'populist' leanings led him to see in the Revolution a peasant millennium. Disappointed by its course, took to drink, married Isadora Duncan in 1921, a marriage that soon broke down, and committed suicide.

EVTUSHENKO, Evgeny Aleksandrovich, 1933–
Poet; came to prominence in 1956 by voicing the spiritual confusion of youth in post-Stalin Russia. Author of *Zima Railway Station*, 1956; *Baby Yar*, 1961; *The Bratsk Hydropower-station*, 1965; as well as an *Autobiography* published in Paris, 1964. Has travelled extensively at home and abroad. Repeatedly criticised by rigid Soviet ideologists.

FADEEV (Bulyga), Aleksandr Aleksandrovich, 1901–56
Writer; member of CP since 1918, author of *The Rout*, 1927, and *The Young Guard*, 1945, which he was made to rewrite to bring out more forcefully the role of the CP as the organiser of guerrilla resistance to the Germans. Member of the CC of CPSU and Secretary-General of USSR Union of Writers, 1946–55. Committed suicide after Khrushchev's denunciation of Stalin at the XX Party Congress.

FEDIN, Konstantin Aleksandrovich, 1892–
Novelist, First Secretary of the USSR Union of Writers since 1959; member of the USSR Acad. of Sciences since 1958. Formerly one of the Serapion Brothers lit. group; author of

Cities and Years, 1924; *The Brothers*, 1928; *First Joys*, 1945; *An Extraordinary Summer*, 1948; etc. Coll. works in 9 vols., 1962.

FURMANOV, Dmitry Andreevich, 1891–1926
Writer and journalist; joined CP in 1918 and served as political commissar of the Red Army detachment commanded by Chapaev. His novel *Chapaev*, 1923, is largely based on their personal experience. Other stories: *Red Sortie*, 1922, and *Riot*, 1923–25.

GARBUZOV, Vasily Fyodorovich, 1911–
USSR Minister of Finance since 1960, member of CC of CPSU since 1961, joined CP in 1939; two Orders of Lenin, etc.

GOMULKA, Wladyslaw, 1905–
Polish communist statesman, First Secretary of the CC of Polish CP. Member of Polish CP since 1926, arrested in 1932–34 and again 1936–39 for revolutionary activities. Took part in the defence of Warsaw against the Germans in Sept. 1939; emigrated to the USSR; returned to Poland in 1942 and was Secretary-General of Polish CP, 1943–48. In 1949, was removed from the CP and in 1951 arrested. Freed in 1954 after the death of Stalin, he was re-elected First Secretary of CC of Polish CP in Oct. 1956.

GORBACHEV, Georgy Efimovich, 1897–1942
Lit. critic, member of CP since 1919, belonged to the left wing of RAPP and was a militant advocate of proletarian hegemony in literature; disappeared during the purges of the late 1930s.

GOR'KY, Maxim (Peshkov, Aleksei Maksimovich), 1868–1936
Writer, born into a family of artisans, spent his childhood in the slums of Nizhny Novgorod (now Gor'ky), tramped across Russia taking on various menial jobs; first short stories in 1892; author of plays, e.g. *Lower Depth*, 1902; the novel *Mother*, 1907, highly praised by Lenin; and autobiographical tales: *Childhood*, 1913; *My Apprenticeships*, 1918; *My Universities*, 1923. Bought villa in Capri in 1906, where with Bogdanov and Lunacharsky established a school for workers. Supported financially the Bolshevik Party before and during the 1905 revolution. Although opposed to terror, remained friends with Lenin throughout 1917–21, and helped save many intellectuals and art treasures. Emigrated in 1921 after disagreements with Lenin; returned in 1928 and contributed to the formulation of the method of socialist realism. His last novels, including *Klim Samgin*, are set in pre-revolutionary Russia. A charge of poisoning him was brought against some defendants in the 1938 trial of Bukharin and accomplices.

LIST OF PERSONALITIES MENTIONED IN TEXT 257

GUMILEV, Nikolai Stepanovich, 1881–1921
Symbolist poet, later formed the Acmeist Group. First husband of Anna Akhmatova. Shot on a charge of participation in an anti-Soviet conspiracy.

GUSEINOVA, Zuleykha Ismail Kyzy,
Minister of Higher and Secondary Special Education of the Azerbaidzhan SSR; member of the Youth Commission of the USSR Supreme Soviet.

IOFFE, Adolf Abramovich, 1883–1927
Son of wealthy Jewish parents; joined Menshevik Party in 1903; in August 1917, together with Trotsky, went over to the Bolsheviks. Negotiated Brest-Litovsk peace treaty with Germany in 1918 and became first Soviet ambassador to Germany. After Lenin's death sided with Trotsky in the intra-party struggle and committed suicide when Trotsky was defeated.

IVANOV, Vsevolod Vyacheslavovich, 1895–
Playwright and novelist; after working in a variety of jobs joined the Serapion Brothers lit. group. Made his name with the publication of *Armoured Train 14–59*, 1922, later dramatised. Author of novels, plays, a semi-autobiographical story, *The Adventures of a Fakir*, 1934–35, and memoirs, *Meeting with Gor'ky*, 1947.

KAMENEV (Rozenfeld), Lev Borisovich, 1883–1936
Joined the RSDRP in 1901 and in 1903 its Bolshevik faction; arrested by Tsarist police, he later emigrated with Zinoviev and became a close associate of Lenin. Leader of Duma Bolshevik deputies in Nov. 1914, together with other deputies was banished to Siberia for anti-war propaganda. Returned after Feb. Revolution and with Stalin led Bolshevik Party until Lenin's return from Switzerland; opposed Lenin's policy of seizure of power, but rallied to him after October uprising and became first Chairman of the Central Executive Committee of the Soviets; in 1919–26, member of Politburo. After Lenin's death formed a triumvirate with Stalin and Zinoviev. In 1926–27 was ambassador to Italy. Expelled from the Party in 1927, readmitted upon recantation, but expelled again in 1932. Was one of the defendants at the 1936 trial of the 'Trotskyite-Zinovievite Terrorist Centre'. Sentenced to death and executed.

KAPITSA, Petr Leonidovich, 1894–
Physicist, member of the USSR Academy of Sciences since 1939 and of its Praesidium since 1960; 1921–30, worked at Cavendish Laboratory, Cambridge; 1930–34, director Mond Laboratory, Cambridge; 1935–46, director Inst. of Physical Problems of the USSR Academy of Sciences; reinstated as director in 1955. Member of the Commission for the Study of Cosmic Radiation; in-

ventor of equipment (turbodetonder) for the production of large quantities of liquid helium and oxygen. Stalin Prizes 1941 and 1943; four Orders of Lenin, Faraday Medal 1942, Franklin Medal 1945, Niels Bohr Medal 1964, etc.

KAVERIN (Silber), Veniamin Aleksandrovich, 1902–
Writer, member of Serapion Brothers lit. group. During World War II was correspondent of *Tass* and *Izvestiya*. Author of many novels, of which *Two Captains*, 1940–45, awarded Stalin Prize; lit. reminiscences, *At the desk* and *A few years*, published in *Novy Mir*, 1965 and 1966. Coll. works in 6 vols., 1966.

KELDYSH, Mstislav Vsevolodovich, 1911–
President of the USSR Acad. of Sciences since 1961; mathematician and mechanical engineer, grad. Moscow Univ.; 1932–46, prof. of Moscow Univ.; member of the USSR Acad. of Sciences since 1946; director of Steklov Maths Inst. (now Inst. of Applied Maths) since 1953. Research on vibration, aerodynamics, and wave propagation. Member of CP since 1959 and of CC of CPSU since 1961; six Orders of Lenin, three of the Red Banner, etc.

KHACHATURYAN, Aram Il'ich, 1903–
Composer, born in Tbilisi, Georgia. Grad. from Moscow Conservatoire, 1934. His 1937 piano concerto abounds in Armenian folklore themes. Wrote violin concerto for David Oistrakh, ballet *Spartakus*, 1953. Stalin Prizes 1941, 1943, 1946, 1950 and Lenin Prize 1959.

KHRUSHCHEV, Nikita Sergeevich, 1894–
Born in Kalinovka, village in Kursk prov., son of miner. Participated in October Revolution, was elected to Lugansk city Soviet, joined CP in 1918, and fought in the Civil War. Studied at the workers' (preparatory) faculty of Kharkov Univ. and did propaganda work in Ukraine, where he attracted the attention of L. Kaganovich, then First Secretary of CC of the Ukrainian CP. Went to Moscow for further study at the Industrial Academy in 1931; became Second, then First, Secretary of Moscow City Party Committee and member of CC of CPSU in 1934. As First Secretary of CC of Ukrainian CP carried out purges of Ukrainian CP. During World War II was a member of war councils of various fronts and took part in defence of Stalingrad. In 1949, returned to Moscow as member of CC of CPSU and First Secretary of Moscow Prov. Committee. In Sept. 1953, became First Secretary of CC of CPSU and in 1958 Chairman of the Council of Ministers of the USSR. In his secret speech to the XX Party Congress in 1956 denounced Stalin's crimes and promoted a policy of de-Stalinisation at home and peaceful co-existence abroad. Was made to resign by a plenary meeting of the CC in

LIST OF PERSONALITIES MENTIONED IN TEXT 259

Oct. 1964 on grounds of advancing age and deteriorating health.

KIROV (Kostrikov), Sergei Mironovich, 1886–1934
Born in Urzhum, Vyatka (now Kirov) prov.; joined Bolshevik Party in 1905 and carried on revolutionary activities in Tomsk (Siberia) and the Caucasus; arrested several times by Tsarist police. After October 1917 was active in establishing Soviet power in the Caucasus and forming Red Army detachments in Astrakhan. Elected member to CC; continued to be active in the Caucasus. In 1925, went to Leningrad and eventually replaced Zinoviev as First Secretary of the Leningrad Party organisation. Elected one of the secretaries of the CC at the XVII Party Congress, he was assassinated on 1 Dec. 1934 by a certain Nikolaev, allegedly on the instructions of the secret police.

KOCHETOV, Vsevolod Anisimovich, 1912–
Writer, editor of journal *Oktyabr'* since 1960, joined CP in 1944; grad. from an agr. technicum, worked as economist on a state farm and MTS; in 1941–45, war correspondent; 1955–59, chief editor of *Literaturnaya Gazeta*; 1956–66, member of Central Auditing Commission of CPSU, Author of *The Zhurbins*, 1952; *The Brothers Yershov*, regarded as an answer to Dudintsev's *Not by bread alone; Secretary of Provincial Committee*, 1961; *What do you Want?*, 1969. Two Orders of Lenin, 1962 and 1967.

KOLMOGOROV, Andrei Nikolaevich, 1903–
Mathematician, member of USSR Acad. of Sciences since 1939 and of Acad. of Pedagogical Sciences since 1965; dean of faculty of mechanics and maths, Moscow Univ., since 1931; specialist in the theory of probabilities, mathematical logic, etc. Three Orders of Lenin, Hero of Socialist Labour, 1963.

KOROLENKO, Vladimir Galaktionovich, 1853–1921
Writer, co-editor of 'Populist' journal *Russkoe Bogatstvo*; banished to Siberia for 6 years by Tsarist government. Author of stories, e.g. *The Dream of Makar, The Blind Musician*, 1886; and autobiographical tale *The History of my Contemporary*, part I, 1908, part II posthumously, 1922.

KOSYGIN, Aleksei Nikolaevich, 1904–
Chairman of USSR Council of Ministers since 1964; joined CP in 1927, grad. Leningrad Textile Inst. 1936; 1935–37, foreman, then shop superintendent Zhelyabov works, Leningrad; 1937–38, director, Oktyabr Spinning Mill, Leningrad; member of that city's Vyborg district Party Committee, 1939; then Chairman Leningrad City Exec. Committee; 1939–40, People's Commissar of Textile Industry; 1940–46, deputy Chairman USSR Council of People's Commissars; 1948–53, USSR Minister of Finance, then Minister of Light Industry, then Minister of Consumer

Goods Industry; 1956–57, first deputy Chairman of USSR *Gosplan*; 1959–60, Chairman of same; 1960–64, deputy Chairman of USSR Council of Ministers; since 1946 repeatedly member of CC of CPSU. Three Orders of Lenin, Hero of Socialist Labour, etc.

Kuprin, Aleksandr Ivanovich, 1870–1938
Writer, author of *The Duel*, 1905; *The Pit* (Yama), 1910; *The Garnet Bracelet*, 1913; and other stories. Emigrated in 1919, returned to the USSR in 1937, and died in Leningrad.

Kuznetsov, Anatoly Vasil'evich, 1929–
Writer, member of CP since 1955, worked as carpenter and bulldozer operator at Kakhovka hydropower-station; then on construction of Irkutsk hydropower-station; grad. Gor'ky Lit. Inst. 1960; published stories in *Pionerskaya Pravda* since 1946. His *Baby Yar* was translated into many languages. Defected during trip to London 1969, complaining of Soviet censorship and expressing intention to write henceforth under the name of Anatole.

Lavrent'ev, Mikhail Alekseevich, 1900–
Member of the USSR Acad. of Sciences since 1946, head of its Siberian branch; cand. member CC of CPSU since 1961; joined CP in 1952. Grad. Moscow Univ. 1922; 1931–42, prof. Moscow Univ.; since 1934 head of Dept. of Theory of Functions, Maths Inst., USSR Acad. of Sciences; 1939–41, director, Inst. of Maths and Mechanics, Ukrainian Acad. of Sciences; 1951–53 and 1954–57, Academic Secretary, Dept. of Physico-Mathematical Sciences, USSR Acad. of Sciences. Specialist in theory of functions of complex variables, hydrodynamics, and explosions; organised expedition to Dickson Island to study break-up of arctic ice and to Kamchatka to study subterranean heat. Three Orders of Lenin, Hero of Socialist Labour, etc.

Lelevich, G., 1901–45
Lit. critic, one of the militant advocates of the proletarian hegemony in literature.

Lenin (Ul'yanov), Vladimir Il'ich, 1870–1924
Founder of Soviet state and first Head of a communist government. Born in Simbirsk (now Ul'yanovsk), son of an inspector of schools, mother née Maria Blank, daughter of physician. Eldest brother Aleksandr executed for his part in an attempt on the life of Alexander III. Lenin joined revolutionary group while a student at Kazan, Univ., was expelled, 1887, but brilliantly completed his law degree externally at St Petersburg Univ. With Martov set up in St Petersburg the 'Union for the Struggle for the Liberation of the Working Class', 1895; arrested and exiled

LIST OF PERSONALITIES MENTIONED IN TEXT 261

to village of Shushenskoe in Siberia. Wrote there his *Development of Capitalism in Russia*, 1899. Lived abroad 1900–05, writing many articles on revolutionary Marxism, against revisionism, on the organisation of a militant Party, and the alliance of workers and peasantry. When the RSDRP split in 1903 into Menshevik and Bolshevik factions struggled to assume leadership of the latter. Returned to Russia in Oct. 1905 but had to emigrate again after defeat of the 1905 revolution. During World War I lived in Switzerland and led anti-war opposition. Returned to Russia in April 1917, organised armed uprising against Provisional Government in July (which failed), but in Oct. succeeded in overthrowing it and establishing the first Soviet state. Under his leadership the Brest-Litovsk peace treaty was signed and land, bank, and eventually most industrial enterprises nationalised. The suppression of other political parties and the ensuing Red Terror led to Civil War, backed by foreign intervention. Against tremendous odds the Soviet government overcame its enemies and reconquered most of the territories of the former Russian Empire. To help reconstruction small-scale private enterprise was allowed by the adoption of NEP. Promoted establishment of Third International. Suffered stroke in Dec. 1922, which partially paralysed him; died 22 Jan. 1924. His embalmed body preserved in Mausoleum, Red Square, Moscow.

LEONOV, Leonid Maksimovich, 1899–
Writer of peasant origin; studied at Moscow Univ.; served for three years in Red Army; author of *The Badgers*, 1924; *The Thief*, 1927; *Sot'* (in English translation *Soviet River*), 1930; *Skutarevsky*, 1932; *Road to the Ocean*, 1936; *Russian Forest*, 1953; and several plays. Two Orders of Lenin, Hero of Socialist Labour, 1965, etc.

LERMONTOV, Mikhail Yur'evich, 1814–41
One of Russia's greatest poets; studied at Moscow Univ. and Military School in St Petersburg; served in the army and participated in military operations against mountain tribes in Caucasus. Author of romantic poems *Mtsyri*, *The Demon*; the play *Masquerade Ball*; a psychological novel *A Hero of our Time*; and beautiful lyrical poems. Killed in a duel by N. Martynov, a fellow officer.

LIGACHEV, Egor Kuzmich,
Candidate member of CC of CPSU since 1966; First Secretary of Tomsk Prov. Party Committee since 1965; member of Youth Commission of USSR Supreme Soviet.

LUNACHARSKY, Anatoly Vasil'evich, 1875–1933
Active in revolutionary circles since 1892, joined the RSDRP in

1897, sided with Lenin's Bolshevik faction in 1903. Temporarily disagreed with Lenin but rejoined Bolshevik Party in 1917. First People's Commissar of Education, 1917–29; together with Gor'ky tried to preserve museums and monuments of the past. Wrote plays on historical subjects, articles on Marxist aesthetics, and lit. criticism.

Lunts (Lunz), Lev Natanovich, 1901–24
Writer and literary critic, member of Serapion Brothers lit. group, died during a visit to his parents in Germany.

Lysenko, Trofim Denisovich, 1898–
Biologist and agriculturist; grad. from Poltava School of Horticulture, 1917, and Kiev Inst. of Agr., 1925. President of the All-Union Acad. of Agr. Sciences, 1938; promoted seed vernalisation, said to endow spring wheat with qualities of winter wheat; supported theory of transmission of acquired characteristics and rejected Mendelian genetics. With Stalin's support had his opponents, including N. V. Vavilov, dismissed and arrested. Won favour with Khrushchev, although his theories had been disproved by better scientists. Remains head of experimental farm at Gorki Leninskie, near Moscow.

Mao Tse-Tung, 1893–
Chairman of the Communist Party of China and one of its founders. Son of well-to-do peasant, worked on father's farm, later studied at Hunan First Middle School and Hunan First Teachers' Training School, 1914–19. Library Assistant Peking Univ., 1918. Active in New People's Study Society; in 1920, organised Marxist group in Changsha whilst principal of an elementary school. Went to Shanghai to participate in inauguration of Chinese CP. Returned to Hunan to form a local CP organisation, 1921. At 3rd Congress of Chinese CP joined the Kuomintang. In 1924, organised peasant associations in Hunan; in 1926, took charge of Chinese CP peasant dept.; 1927, first president of All-China Peasants' Assoc.; organised Workers and Peasants Red Army first division and formed first Soviet region in Chialing on border of Hunan prov., established Kiangsi Prov. Soviet aimed at redistribution of land. In 1930, led attempts to capture cities; in 1931, Chairman of newly established Central Chinese Soviet Govt. Break with Nationalist govt. led to guerrilla warfare, 1927–36, and defeat by Kuomintang to Long March through Kweichow to Yunan in 1934. Maintained armed truce with Kuomintang during war against Japan, 1936–45; defeated Kuomintang throughout China, 1945–49; Chairman of Central People's Govt. of Republic of China, 1949–54; of People's Republic of China, 1954–58. Launched campaigns: 'Hundred

LIST OF PERSONALITIES MENTIONED IN TEXT 263

Flowers', allowing more freedom of thought, in 1956; 'Great Leap Forward', based on local crafts, which was criticised by Khrushchev, 1959; 'Great Proletarian Cultural Revolution', 1965, to break up bureaucratic apparatus. Chief delegate to the 40th anniversary of the Russian Revolution; signed peace manifesto of Communist and Workers' Parties of 64 countries, Moscow 1957; met Khrushchev in Peking, 1958, after which broke with CPSU. Author of numerous political essays and some poetry.

MAYAKOVSKY, Vladimir Vladimirovich, 1893–1930
Poet, born in Georgia, active in Futurist movement, intent on finding new means of expression and doing away with classical tradition. Author of biographical tragedy *Vladimir Mayakovsky*, 1914; poems *The Cloud in Trousers*, 1915; *Left March*, 1919; *150,000,000*, 1921; *Lenin*, 1924; etc.; plays *Mystery Bouffe*, 1918; *The Bedbug*, 1928; *The Bathhouse*, 1929; and a cycle of poems about America. One of the founders of the journal *LEF*, 1923, later renamed the *New LEF*. Committed suicide.

MEREZHKOVSKY, Dmitry Sergeevich, 1865–1941
Writer, critic, and religious thinker. With his wife Zinaida Gippius, one of the founders of the 'Religious and Philosophical Society', 1903. Emigrated in 1920 and lived in France. Author of the trilogy 'Christ and Antichrist', part I, *Julian the Apostate* (or the Death of the Gods), 1896; part II, *Leonardo da Vinci* (or the Resurrection of the Gods), 1901; part III, *Peter and Alexis*, 1905; and another trilogy: *Paul I*, 1908; *Alexander I*, 1911–12; and *14 December 1825*, 1918; critical essays include *Tolstoy and Dostoevsky*, 1901–02.

MEYERHOLD, Vsevolod Emil'evich, 1874–1942
Avant-garde producer, studied at Moscow Philharmonic Dramatic School, joined Moscow Arts Theatre, 1898–1902; worked in St Petersburg theatre of actress V. F. Komissarzhevskaya, then at Imperial theatres staging highly stylised productions. Joined CP in 1918 and promoted constructivism, then bio-mechanics and other novel theatrical trends. Arrested in 1939 and died allegedly in a concentration camp in 1942.

NAGY, Imre, 1896–1958
Hungarian Communist, emigrated to the USSR and returned in 1944. Succeeded Matyas Rakosi as premier in 1953 after Stalin's death, but was expelled from Hungarian CP in April 1955; readmitted in Oct., became Prime Minister again on 24 Oct. at the height of anti-Soviet rebellion; repudiated the Warsaw treaty and asked for immediate international recognition of Hungary's neutrality (31 Oct./1 Nov.). On 4 Nov. Soviet troops returned and put down uprising. Nagy sought asylum in

Yugoslav embassy, Budapest, was enticed out by a safe-conduct, but seized by Soviet agents; according to official statement executed in June 1958–after a trial held secretly in Romania.

NEIZVESTNY, Ernst, 1926–
Sculptor; son of physician; mother scientist. Volunteered in 1942 aged 16; seriously wounded. His abstract modernistic sculptures unacceptable to socialist realists. At exhibition organised by Moscow City Council, 1962, some of his works were shown and aroused the ire of N. Khrushchev, then First Secretary of CC of CPSU.

NEKRASOV, Viktor Platonovich, 1911–
Writer, grad. from Kiev. Inst. of Construction, 1936; worked as architect, theatrical set designer, and actor. Fought in World War II; author of *In the Trenches of Stalingrad*, 1946, an unembellished wartime novel; *In one's own home town*, 1954; and travel notes *On both sides of the Ocean*, 1962–63.

NICHOLAS II, 1868–1918
Last Emperor of Russia, 1894–1917, son of Alexander III and Maria Fedorovna (sister of Queen Alexandra of Great Britain). During his reign the following events took place: the construction of the Transsiberian Railway, the Russo-Japanese War, Russia's entry into the Franco-British Entente, the first Russian revolution, 1905, followed by the granting of a constitution and the election of a state Duma; the two first assemblies were dissolved because his government was not prepared to grant the Duma full parliamentary powers; the Third and Fourth Dumas promoted limited reforms. Participation in World War I precipitated the February Revolution and forced his abdication. First imprisoned in Tsarskoe Selo Palace, was moved to Tobolsk; on 16 July 1918 he, his family, and some retainers were shot in a cellar at Ekaterinburg, now Sverdlovsk, on the orders of Sverdlov, then Chairman of the Central Exec. Committee of the Congress of Soviets and Secretary of the Party CC.

NIKITIN, Nikolai Nikolaevich, 1895–
Writer, member of the Serapion Brothers lit. group; author of *Kirik Rudenko's Crime*, 1926, a story dealing with sexual problems amongst Soviet youth. In later works like *Aurora Borealis*, 1950, conformed more closely to socialist realism.

OKUDZHAVA, Bulat Shalvovich, 1924–
Poet and singer; son of an Ossetian father and Armenian mother who was exiled to Siberia for 19 years; grad. Tbilisi Univ.; 1942, in Soviet Army, later village teacher. Accompanies his own songs on guitar; a collection of his verse was published in 1964 and a historical novel *Poor Avrosimov* in 1969.

LIST OF PERSONALITIES MENTIONED IN TEXT 265

OSTROVSKY, Aleksandr Nikolaevich, 1821–86
Playwright, son of a government clerk; studied law at Moscow Univ., took clerical job in Moscow commercial court before completing course; author of 47 plays in prose or blank verse, including *The Bankrupt*, 1847; *Poverty is no vice*, 1854; *The Thunderstorm*, 1860; *The Forest*, 1871; *Wolves and Sheep*, 1875. His fairytale *The Snowmaiden* was made into an opera by Rimsky-Korsakov. Most of his plays describe the patriarchal, tradition-ridden, 19th-century merchant-class society, the power of money, and the disrupting impact of capitalism; few of his plays are available in translation.

PAPUTIN, V. S.,
Second Secretary of Moscow Prov. Party Committee; member of Youth Commission of USSR Supreme Soviet.

PASTERNAK, Boris Leonidovich, 1890–1960
Poet, son of painter and book-illustrator Leonid Osipovich P. Studied philosophy in Moscow and Marburg. Coll. early poems: *A Twin in Clouds*, 1914; *Over the Barriers*, 1917; *My Sister, my Life*, 1922; written under influence of Symbolism. Later in *Lieutenant Schmidt*, 1926, and *The Year 1905*, 1927, turned to revolutionary themes. The complexity and individualism of his poetry conflict with socialist realism; Pasternak's translations include Goethe's *Faust*, Shakespeare's *Hamlet*, *Othello*, *Macbeth*, *Antony and Cleopatra*, *Henry IV*, *King Lear*, and works by Georgian poets. The publication of his *Dr Zhivago* having been banned in the USSR, he sent the MS abroad, was awarded Nobel Prize in 1958, but renounced it under pressure from Soviet leadership and critics.

PAVLOV, Sergei Pavlovich, 1929–
Secretary-General of CC of All-Union *Komsomol* since 1959, member of CC of CPSU since 1961, member of CP since 1954. In 1944–45, worked in military hospital; 1950–52, studied at Moscow Inst. of Physical Training. From 1952 onward held various posts in Moscow city *Komsomol*, then in All-Union *Komsomol*. Headed delegations to many youth gatherings abroad.

PEN'KOVSKY, Oleg Vladimiovich, 1919–65
Colonel, senior Soviet intelligence officer; deputy Head of the Foreign Section of the Administration of Foreign Relations of the State Committee for the Co-ordination of Scientific and Research Work; between April 1961 and August 1962 passed on through Greville Wynne vital military information to the British and US secret services, in particular data on missile installations, including those set up in Cuba. Was tried for high treason and

sentenced to death in May 1963, but according to Greville Wynne was not executed but took his own life, in prison, in 1965.

PIL'NYAK (Vogau), Boris Andreevich, 1894–1942?
Writer and journalist; grad. from Moscow Inst. of Commerce, 1920. Early stories written in modernistic 'ornamental' prose, e.g. *The Naked Year*, 1920; *Machines and Wolves*, 1923–24; *The Story of the unextinguished Moon*, 1926, alluding to death of Red Army Commander Frunze from an operation to which Party pressure made him submit; *Mahogany*, 1929 (published in Berlin but not in the USSR). *The Volga flows to the Caspian*, 1930, was a more conformist production novel; *The Roots of Japan's Sun* and *Okay* based on his extensive travels to Japan and America. Arrested in 1938 and said to have died in a concentration camp in 1942.

POKROVSKY, Mikhail Nikolaevich, 1868–1932
Marxist historian. Joined Bolshevik Party in 1905, participated in revolutionary activities, 1905–07, emigrated, 1908, and lived abroad till 1917. After Oct. Revolution became first Chairman of the Moscow Soviet; from 1918 to his death was deputy People's Commissar of Education; also director of Inst. of Red Professors, Chairman of the Communist Acad., the Central Archives, etc. Author of textbooks, including *Concise History of Russia*, *Russian History from Ancient Times* (4 vols.), *Outline of the History of Russian Culture*, and editor of historical journals. In 1934 and in 1936 his views on economic materialism and the role of finance capital fell into disfavour and his textbooks were withdrawn from use in schools.

POWERS, Francis Gary,
Pilot of American U2 spy plane, shot down in May 1960 over the Urals. Exchanged for Soviet spy Rudolf Abel in 1962.

POZNER, Vladimir,
French novelist of Russian origin, member of Serapion Brothers lit. group, emigrated and settled in France. Author of *Le Mors au dents*, 1935; *Les Etats désunis*, 1938; *L'Espagne, premier amour*, 1965; and others.

PUSHKIN, Aleksandr Sergeevich, 1799–1837
Russia's greatest poet, educated at the Lyceum of Tsarskoe Selo; author of narrative poems *Ruslan and Ludmila*, 1817–20; *The Prisoner of the Caucasus*, *The Fountain of Bakhchisarai*, *The Gipsies*, 1820–24; *The Bronze Horseman*, 1833; the novel in verse *Eugene Onegin*, 1823–30; the historical drama *Boris Godunov*, 1824; and the little tragedies: *The Avaricious Knight*, *Mozart and Salieri*, *The Stone-Guest*, 1831; five short stories published together under the title *The Tales of Belkin*, 1831; *The Queen*

LIST OF PERSONALITIES MENTIONED IN TEXT 267

of *Spades*, 1831; the novel *The Captain's Daughter*, 1936; and numerous lyrical poems.

ROKOSSOVSKY, Konstantin Konstantinovich, 1896–1969
Marshal of the Soviet Union. Born in Warsaw, joined Bolshevik Party in 1919 and fought in Red Army. Arrested in 1937 during the Red Army purges, released after outbreak of World War II, during which became one of the outstanding Soviet commanders; 1949–56, was Commander-in-Chief of the Polish Army and Polish Minister of Defence; forced to resign from this post after the election of Gomulka as First Secretary of the Polish CP; returned to Russia in 1956.

Rozov, Viktor Sergeevich, 1913–
Playwright, author of *Her Friends*, 1949; *In Search of Joy*; *Before Supper*, 1962; *The Wedding Day*, 1964; and film scenarios.

SEMICHASTNYI, Vladimir Efimovich, 1924–
First deputy Chairman of Ukrainian Council of Ministers since 1967. Studied at Kemerovo Chemical Technological Inst., 1941–42; member of CP since 1944; 1946–50, Secretary, then First Secretary, of CC of Ukrainian *Komsomol*; 1950–58, Secretary, then First Secretary, CC All-Union *Komsomol*. 1961–67, Chairman of KGB; Order of Lenin, Red Banner of Labour, etc.

SHCHUSEV, Aleksei Viktorovich, 1873–1949
Architect, grad. from St Petersburg Acad. of Arts; restored tenth-century church in Ovruch, built by St Vladimir, and other ancient churches; builder of the Lenin Mausoleum in Moscow, the Marx-Engels-Lenin Inst., Tbilisi, combining classical and Georgian features (Stalin Prize 1941), the opera house in Tashkent, Komsomolskaya Kol'tsevaya metro-station in Moscow, etc.

SHELEPIN, Aleksandr Nikolaevich, 1918–
Chairman, All-Union Trade Union Council since 1967. Joined CP in 1940. Grad. 1941, Moscow Inst. of History, Philosophy, and Literature, where he was secretary of *Komsomol* organisation; 1940–43, head of dept. of Propaganda and Agitation, Moscow *Komsomol* Committee; 1952–58, First Secretary, CC All-Union *Komsomol*; in that capacity directed mobilisation of 350,000 *Komsomol* members for development of virgin lands, 1954; 650,000 to work in stock-raising, 1957; organised enlistment of all *Komsomol* members in DOSAAF and inaugurated voluntary contributions from *Komsomol* members to raise 5,000 million roubles for 13th All-Union *Komsomol* Congress. Two Orders of Lenin, of Red Star, etc.

SHKLOVSKY, Viktor Borisovich, 1893–
Writer and lit. critic; educated at St Petersburg Univ.; 1914–23, member of Society for the Study of Poetic Language (OPOYAZ);

formalist critic, later member of LEF. Author of *Art as a Device*, 1917; *The Theory of Prose*, 1925; *How to write Scenarios*, 1933; *Once upon a time: Recollections*, 1962–63; a biography of L. N Tolstoy, 1963; and scenarios for Pushkin's story *The Captain's Daughter* and own *Minin and Pozharsky*, 1940, and *Alisher Navoi*, 1948. Order of Red Banner of Labour, 1963.

SHOLOKHOV, Mikhail Aleksandrovich, 1905–
Writer, member of USSR Acad. of Sciences since 1939; Nobel Prizewinner 1965, Secretary USSR Union of Writers since 1967, member of CC of CPSU since 1961; joined CP in 1932. Author of *Stories of the Don*, 1927–28; *Quiet flows the Don* (4 vols.), 1928–40; *Virgin Soil Upturned*, vol. 1, 1931, vol. 2, 1959; *The Fate of Man*, 1957; Coll. Works, 8 vols. 1956–59. Two Orders of Lenin, 1955 and 1966, etc.

SIMONOV, Konstantin (Kirill) Mikhailovich, 1915–
Prolific poet, prose-writer, and playwright; member of CP since 1942; grad. from Gorky Lit. Inst., Moscow, author of *A Lad from our Town*, 1942; *Russian People*, 1942; *Days and Nights*, 1943–44; *The Quick and the Dead*, 1958; *People are not born Soldiers*, 1964; best-known poems *Wait for me*; *Remember, Alyosha*; *The Roads of Smolensk* and *Motherland*, 1941–42. 1941–45, war correspondent of newspaper *Krasnaya Zvezda*; 1954–57, chief editor of journal *Novy Mir*, removed apparently in connection with the publication in this journal of Dudintsev's *Not by bread alone*; 1952–56, candidate member of CC of CPSU; Stalin Prizes, Order of Lenin, 1965.

SINYAVSKY, Andrei Donatovich, 1925–
Lit. critic; grad. from Moscow Univ. 1953, senior associate, Gor'ky Inst. of World Literature, USSR Acad. of Sciences; contributor to a 3 vol. *History of Soviet Russian Literature*; author of articles on Soviet literature; under pen-name Abram Tertz published abroad stories deemed slanderous of the USSR and was sentenced to 7 years hard labour in 1966, for anti-Soviet activities.

SLONIMSKY, Mikhail Leonidovich, 1897–
One of the founders of the Serapion Brothers lit. group; author of *The Lavrovs*, 1926; *Frontier Guards*, 1937; *Chairman of the City Soviet*, 1941–45; *Engineers*, 1950; *Seven Years later*, 1963; *Together and Side by Side*, 1965.

SOLOUKHIN, Vladimir Alekseevich, 1924–
Writer, poet, and journalist; served in Red Army, 1942–46; grad. Gor'ky Lit. Inst. Moscow, 1951; member of CP since 1952; feature writer for journal *Ogonek*, 1951–57; author of *Along the Lanes of Vladimir Province*, 1958; *Dewdrop*, 1960; *Lyrical Tales*,

LIST OF PERSONALITIES MENTIONED IN TEXT 269

1961; *A Loaf of Scalded Dough Bread*, 1963; *Beloved Beauty*, 1969; etc.

SOLZHENITSYN, Aleksandr Isaevich, 1918–
Writer, grad. Physico-Maths Faculty, Rostov Univ.; commander of artillery battery in World War II; arrested 1945; spent 8 years in concentration camps and exile in Dzhambul province; rehabilitated in 1953; worked first as village teacher, then physics master in a Ryazan' school, 1957–63. Author of *One day in the life of Ivan Denisovich*, 1962, and 5 short stories, all published in the journal *Novy Mir*, 1963 and 1966. The publication of his novel *Cancer Ward* (expected in 1967) was banned but a typescript of it smuggled abroad allegedly by KGB agents for the purpose of then charging S. with anti-Soviet propaganda; novel published abroad in many languages; similarly the unfinished *In the First Circle* and other works. In 1969 Solzhenitsyn was expelled from USSR Union of Writers for not having taken adequate steps to prevent the publication of his works abroad.

STALIN (Dzhugashvili), Iosif Vissarionovich, 1879–1953
Of Georgian origin, son of a cobbler. Studied at theological seminary; expelled for revolutionary activities in 1899. Joined RSDRP in 1898. Though arrested several times, escaped and took part in party congresses in Finland, 1905, Stockholm, 1906, and London, 1907. With Caucasian terrorist Kamo organised 'expropriations' of banks including daring daytime robbery on 26 June 1907 in Tiflis to provide funds for Bolshevik Party. In 1912 went to Krakow to see Lenin and to Vienna, where he wrote (with Bukharin) *Marxism and the National Question*. Arrested on his return and banished to Siberia. Returned to St Petersburg in February 1917. Took active part in October Revolution and became People's Commissar for Nationalities, 1917–23; member of Politburo since its inception and of State Control, 1919–23. Senior political commissar during Civil War; from 1923 General Secretary of Party CC. After Lenin's death formed a triumvirate with Kamenev and Zinoviev; opposed slogan of 'building socialism in one country', to Trotsky's 'permanent revolution'. In intraparty struggle defeated Trotsky with the help of Kamenev and Zinoviev, then the two latter with that of Rykov and Bukharin; with the help of Molotov, Voroshilov, Kaganovich, Ordzhonokidze, and Kirov had these two expelled from the Party and executed during the bloody purges he organised in the 1930s. Ruling as undisputed leader carried out industrialisation and collectivisation of agriculture, intensified terror, and use of convict labour. In 1939, signed a non-aggression treaty with Germany which enabled the Soviet Union to occupy the Baltic provinces and

parts of Poland; nevertheless on 22 June 1941 Hitler's army invaded the USSR, penetrating as far as the Volga and the Caucasus. Stalin formally assumed the status of Head of State, Generalissimo, and Supreme Commander of all Soviet armed forces. His conduct of the war has aroused much controversy. The final victory over Germany enabled Stalin to bring to power communist parties in most countries of eastern Europe. Only Marshal Tito succeeded in selecting his own path to communism in Yugoslavia and broke with Stalin in 1948. At home rule by terror continued until Stalin's death on 5 March 1953. Stalin was married first to Catherine Svanidze; a son by her, taken prisoner by the Germans, disappeared during the war; by his second wife, Nadezhda Alliluyeva, he had a son Vasily, an airforce general who died an alcoholic in 1962, and a daughter Svetlana who defected to the USA in 1967, and subsequently married an American.

STOLYPIN, Petr Arkad'evich, 1862–1911
Statesman; studied natural sciences at St Petersburg Univ.; joined staff of Ministry of Agr.; governor of Grodno, 1902, and Saratov, 1903; in April 1906, Minister of the Interior and after the election of the First Duma, President of the Council of Ministers. Was instrumental in dissolving the First and Second Dumas and restricting franchise in election to Third Duma. Introduced court-martials and capital punishment against revolutionaries, but also agr. reforms designed to enable peasants to leave their communes and set up as landowning farmers, an opportunity which was taken by about 5 million peasants. Assassinated by a revolutionary in the presence of Nicholas II at Kiev Opera House during the Emperor's visit to that town.

SULTAN-GALIEV, Mirza, 1880–?
Volga Tartar; teacher of Russian in reformed Moslem school in the Caucasus; joined Bolshevik Party in 1917; member of the People's Commissariat for Nationalities; arrested in 1923 as bourgeois nationalist but released. Rearrested in 1929; said to have died in prison in the 1930s. Put forward a theory according to which the real forthcoming revolution would be that of colonial peoples seeking liberation from colonialism.

SVERDLOV, Yakov Mikhailovich, 1885–1919
Joined the RSDRP in 1901 and became a professional revolutionary organising Bolshevik groups in various localities, particularly the Urals and Moscow. Arrested several times by Tsarist police, banished to Siberia, but escaped. Elected to Party CC in April 1917 and to the Military Revolutionary Committee in Oct. First Chairman of Central Executive Committee of the Congress of

LIST OF PERSONALITIES MENTIONED IN TEXT

Soviets and Secretary of Party, making him with Lenin and Trotsky the most powerful man in Soviet Russia. The city of Ekaterinburg, where the Imperial Family was put to death on his orders in 1918, has been renamed Sverdlovsk in his memory.

TENDRYAKOV, Vladimir Fyodorovich, 1923–
Writer, author of *The Fall of Ivan Chuprov*, 1953; *Potholes* (Ukhaby), 1956; *The Miraculous Ikon*, 1958; *Ephemeride – a short lifetime*, 1965; *The End* (Konchina), 1968.

TITO, Josip Broz, 1892–
Yugoslav communist leader; born in Croatia, joined the Social Democratic Party of Croatia and Slovenia, 1910; mobilised in Austrian army, surrendered to the Russians in 1915. In 1920, returned and joined the Communist Party of Yugoslavia, arrested in 1928 by Yugoslav (royal) authorities. After completing his prison sentence renewed revolutionary activities; in 1937, elected to the CC and in 1940 General Secretary of CC of Communist Party of Yugoslavia. In 1941–45, commanded the People's Liberation Army and led guerrilla warfare against German occupation. In 1945, became President of the Council of Ministers and Commander-in-Chief of the Yugoslav Army. In 1948, broke with Stalin and inaugurated a different path to socialism, reflected in the renaming of the Communist Party the League of Communists of Yugoslavia; replaced the centralised, dictatorial state organisation by decentralised, self-governing associations of producers. In foreign policy strove to promote neutralism of non-committed nations.

TOLSTOY, Aleksei Nikolaevich, 1882–1945
Writer, probably son of his stepfather, A. Bostrom. Before the Revolution wrote novels, including *The Eccentrics*, 1911, and *The Lame Master*, 1912; emigrated in 1918, but returned in 1923 to become a major Soviet writer. Author of a trilogy translated into English under the title of *The Road to Calvary* (Khozhdenie po mukam): part I, *Sisters*, 1920–21; part II, *1918*, 1927–28; part III, *Gloomy Morning*, 1940–41; autobiographical tale, *Nikita's Childhood*, 1919–20; historical novel, *Peter I* (unfinished, 1929–45); science fiction, *Aelita*, 1922–23; and other stories, as well as a play in 2 parts, *Ivan the Terrible*, 1942–43, symbolically justifying Stalin's terror.

TOLSTOY, Count Lev Nikolaevich, 1828–1910
One of Russia's greatest novelists, author of *Childhood*, 1852; *Adolescence*, 1854; *Youth*, 1856. Took part in Crimean War and wrote *Sebastopol Stories*, 1856. In his estate 'Yasnaya Polyana' opened a school for peasant children, taught and later wrote stories and textbooks for them. In 1862, married Sofia Andreevna Behrs. *War and Peace* published in 1865–69; *Anna Karenina*,

1875–77. Religious, philosophical, and social problems which occupied Tolstoy found expression in *Confession*, 1880–82; *What I believe*, 1883; and stories and plays illustrating his convictions, including *Resurrection*, 1889–99, the royalties of which helped finance the emigration of the 'Dukhobory' (a sect of conscientious objectors) to Canada. Tolstoy's teachings were contrary to those of the Orthodox Church and led to his excommunication; a convinced pacifist, he rejected the military, judicial, and coercive powers of the state and preached the doctrine of non-resistance to evil by violence. Had a considerable following; expressed support for Gandhi during the latter's non-co-operation campaign in South Africa. Considered that land should belong to those who actually tilled it, denounced luxury and art without purpose. The contradiction between his views and those of his family led him to leave home; died from pneumonia at Astapovo railway-station.

TROTSKY (Bronstein), Lev Davidovich, 1879–1940
Revolutionary leader, born in the Ukraine of a middle-class Jewish family. Studied in Odessa, became a revolutionary in 1898, was arrested, exiled to Siberia, but escaped and joined Lenin in London in 1902. In the 1903 Party split, Trotsky opposed Lenin and with Parvus (Helfand) worked out his theory of permanent revolution. In 1905, became Chairman of the St Petersburg Soviet; arrested, exiled to Siberia, escaped again, and settled in Vienna. During World War I directed anti-war propaganda, first in France, then in New York. Detained by the British at Halifax, Nova Scotia, when returning to Russia in 1917, was allowed to proceed on the request of Milyukov, then Foreign Affairs Minister in Provisional Govt. Formally joined the Bolshevik Party in July 1917, became Chairman of St Petersburg Soviet and its Military Revolutionary Committee which organised the seizure of power, 26 Oct./7 Nov. 1917. First People's Commissar for Foreign Affairs, negotiated Brest-Litovsk peace treaty; 1918–25, People's Commissar for War and organiser of the Red Army; 1919–26, member of Politburo. After Lenin's death opposed formation of Stalin–Kamenev–Zinoviev triumvirate; then formed with Kamenev and Zinoviev a combined opposition against Stalin's policy of building communism in one country, was defeated, expelled from the Party, exiled to Alma-Ata, and in 1927 banished from the USSR. Went to Turkey, France, Norway, and eventually settled in Mexico City from where he waged an anti-Stalin campaign and formed the Fourth International. Murdered in his fortified villa in Mexico City, allegedly by a secret agent of Stalin.

LIST OF PERSONALITIES MENTIONED IN TEXT 273

TUKHACHEVSKY, Mikhail Nikolaevich, 1893–1937
Marshal of the Soviet Union; Tsarist officer during World War I. In 1918, joined Red Army, rapidly promoted to army commander; fought in the Caucasus, and against Poland in 1920; put down peasant rebellion led by the Social Revolutionary Antonov and that of the Kronstadt sailors in 1921. Chief of Staff of Red Army, 1925–28, deputy People's Commissar for Military and Naval Affairs, 1931, and deputy Chairman of the Revolutionary Military Council; in 1931, became one of the first five marshals of the Soviet Union. In 1937, accused of heading a military conspiracy and executed, together with other generals and senior officers of the Red Army.

TUPOLEV, Andrei Nikolaevich, 1888–
Aircraft designer; his TU-104 was the first passenger jet-plane to fly on European air-routes in 1957, followed by the giant 170-seater, 4-engine TU-114. Member of USSR Academy of Sciences and holder of many awards, including 8 Orders of Lenin.

VAVILOV, Nikolai Ivanovich, 1887–1943
Plant geneticist; grad. from Moscow Univ., 1911; prof. Saratov Univ., 1917–21; director All-Union Inst. of Plant-breeding, 1924–40, and of Genetics Inst., Acad. of Sciences, 1930–40. Participated in numerous plant-collecting expeditions throughout the world; worked on plant immunisation. Questioned soundness of Lysenko's theories and his assertion that stable new strains of grain plants could be satisfactorily selected in 4 years. With Stalin's backing Lysenko campaigned against Vavilov, which led to the arrest of the latter in 1940 and death in captivity; rehabilitated posthumously and acknowledged to have been a most distinguished scientist.

VIL'YAMS (Williams), Vasily Robertovich, 1863–1939
Soil specialist of American descent, prof. of Moscow Agr. Acad., member of USSR Acad. of Sciences. Joined CP in 1928. Advocated, as universally applicable, a system of crop rotation which included perennial grasses.

VOROSHILOV, Kliment Efremovich, 1881–1969
Marshal of the Soviet Union since 1935. A worker at the Lugansk locomotive plant, began his revolutionary activity in 1896. In 1903, joined RSDRP and took active part in 1905 revolution. Arrested and exiled to Siberia several times but escaped. In 1917, elected Chairman of the Lugansk Soviet; fought in Civil War against White Army on Polish front; put down the Grigoriev peasant uprising and that of the Kronstadt sailors in 1921. Rose rapidly to become People's Commissar for Military and Naval Affairs and, in 1925, Chairman of the Military Revolutionary

Council of the USSR; deputy Chairman of the Council of People's Commissars and Chairman of Defence Committee. Member of Party CC since 1921, of Politburo, 1926–52. Took part in 1943 Teheran Conference with Stalin, Churchill, and Roosevelt. Chairman of the Praesidium of the USSR Supreme Soviet, 1953–60.

VOZNESENSKY, Andrei Andreevich, 1933–
Poet; grad. Moscow Inst. of Architecture, 1957. Began writing poetry in 1953, frequently accused of formalism for his modernistic verses. Coll. poems : *Parabola*, 1960; *Mosaics*, 1960; *Triangular Pear*, 1961; *Longjumeau*, 1963; *Antiworlds*, 1964; *Oza*, 1964; *Requiem*, 1965; etc. Has travelled to France, England, and the USA.

VOZNESENSKY, Nikolai Alekseevich, 1903–1950
Economist, Chairman of *Gosplan* since 1938. Joined CP in 1919, became member of CC in 1939 and of Politburo, 1947. During World War II chief economic planner of State Council of Defence. Author of *The Economy of the USSR during the Great Patriotic War*. Shortly after Zhdanov's death disappeared and is said to have been executed in 1949 in connection with a purge of high-ranking Leningrad Party officials.

WYNNE, Greville M., 1919–
British businessman and spy; obtained Soviet military secret information from Pen'kovsky; was arrested in Hungary, brought to trial in Moscow in 1963, sentenced to 8 years imprisonment, but exchanged for Soviet spy Lonsdale. Author of *The Man from Moscow; the story of Wynne and Pen'kovsky*, London, 1967.

YAGODA (Yahuda), Genrikh Grigor'evich, 1891–1938
Chief of Secret Police; son of an artisan, joined Bolshevik Party in 1907, mobilised in 1915; during Civil War worked in the army inspection; in 1920, appointed member of the Praesidium of the *Cheka*; in 1924, deputy chairman of same (renamed GPU); in 1934, People's Commissar for Internal Affairs (then in charge of security police). Expanded use of forced labour; organised the first two major trials of Old Bolsheviks; in Sept. 1936, was transferred to the People's Commissariat of Communications, arrested 6 months later, tried in March 1938 with Bukharin, Rykov, and others, sentenced to death, and executed.

YAROSLAVSKY (Gubelman Minei Izrailevich), Emelyan Mikhailovich, 1878–1943
Joined the revolutionary movement in 1898, member of RDSRP since 1902, participated in 1905 revolution, arrested five times and served 5 years of hard labour and four terms of banishment during 1907–17. Took part in the Moscow insurrection of Oct.

LIST OF PERSONALITIES MENTIONED IN TEXT

1917; in 1921, Secretary of Party CC and its Control Commission. Promoted the League of Militant Atheists, was on the editorial boards of *Pravda* and the journals *Bolshevik* and *Istorik Marksist*, and head of the Dept. of the History of the CPSU at the Higher Party School of the CC of the CPSU.

ZAMYATIN, Evgeny Ivanovich, 1884–1937
Naval engineer and writer; member of the RSDRP since 1905, sent to England on official military mission during World War I. Founder member of the Serapion Brothers lit. group. Author of *The Islanders*, 1922, a satire on English life; *We*, 1924, forecasting a scientifically regimented future society; *A tale about what is most important*, 1923, etc. Was bitterly attacked by Averbakh and the Proletarian Writers; no longer able to publish, appealed personally to Stalin and was allowed to emigrate in 1932; settled in Paris, where he wrote *The Whip of God*.

ZHDANOV, Andrei Aleksandrovich, 1896–1948
Joined Bolshevik Party in 1915, headed party organisation of Nizhny Novgorod (now Gor'ky), 1924–34, and that of Leningrad, 1934–44. Member of Party CC and Politburo from 1939; took part in the defence of Leningrad during World War II; in charge of ideological affairs, in 1946, he attacked Anna Akhmatova and Zoshchenko who were expelled from the Union of Writers and prevented from further publishing. His son was the second husband of Stalin's daughter Svetlana.

ZINOVIEV (Radomysl'sky), Grigory Evseevich, 1883–1936
Joined the RSDRP in 1901 and its Bolshevik faction in 1903, emigrated after the 1905 revolution; 1909–17, closely associated with Lenin whom he accompanied in April 1917 back to Russia. Together with Kamenev opposed Lenin's policy of seizure of power but rallied to him and became Chairman of the Petrograd Soviet, member of Politburo 1921–26, and Chairman of the Exec. Committee of the Communist International, 1919–26. After Lenin's death joined Stalin and Kamenev to form a ruling triumvirate, then together with Kamenev and Trotsky opposed Stalin. Eventually expelled from the Party, sentenced to death in 1935, and executed.

ZOSHCHENKO, Mikhail Mikhailovich, 1895–1958
Satirical writer; member of the Serapion Brothers lit. group; gained popularity with short stories, depicting the little man, the philistine, surviving in and comically adapting to a new society. In 1946, his story *The Adventures of a Monkey* was attacked by Zhdanov; Zoshchenko was expelled from the USSR Union of Writers and no works of his were published until 1956.

Bibliography

The information used in compiling the present book was derived from the Soviet dailies *Pravda* and *Izvestiya*; the journals *Voprosy ekonomiki* and *Vestnik vysshei shkoly*. Major speeches and articles were usually available in English translation from the *Current Digest of the Soviet Press*, published formerly by the Joint Committee on Slavic Studies, appointed by the American Council of Learned Societies and the Social Science Research Council (since 1969 by the American Association for the Advancement of Slavic Studies).

The following books and articles were also used:

English

Armstrong, John A., *Ideology, Politics and Government in the Soviet Union*, Praeger, New York, 1962, revised edition, 1967.

Bor, Mikhail Z., *Aims and Methods of Soviet Planning*, translated from the Russian, with introductory note by Maurice Dobb; Lawrence & Wishart, London, 1967.

Brown, E. J., *The Proletarian Episode in Russian Literature, 1928–32*, Columbia University Press, New York, 1953.

Calder, Nigel, *Technopolis. Social Control of the Uses of Science*, Macgibbon & Kee, London, 1969.

Campbell, Robert W., *Soviet Economic Power: its Organisation, Growth and Challenge*, Macmillan, London, 1960, 2nd edition, 1967.

Clark, Alan, *Barbarossa, The Russian-German Conflict, 1941–1945*, Penguin, London, 1966.

Conolly, Violet, *Beyond the Urals: Economic Developments in Soviet Asia*, Oxford University Press, London, 1967.

Crowley, E. L., Lebed, A. I., and Schulz, H. E., *Prominent Personalities in the USSR*, The Scarecrow Press, Metuchen, N.J., 1968.

Drachkovitch, Milorad M., ed., *Marxism in the Modern World*, Stanford University Press, Stanford, Calif., 1965.

Eastman, Max, *Writers in Uniform: a study of literature and bureaucratism*, Knopf, New York, 1934.

Fainsod, Merle, *How Russia is Ruled*, Harvard University Press, Cambridge, Mass., 1954.

Florinsky, Michael T., *McGraw-Hill Encyclopedia of Russia and the Soviet Union*, McGraw-Hill, New York, 1961.

Franklin, S. H., *The European Peasantry–the Final Phase*, Methuen, London, 1969.

Grossman, Philip, 'A Note on Agricultural Employment in the USSR', *Soviet Studies*, January 1968, vol. XIX, No. 3.

Hanson, Philip, *The Consumer in the Soviet Economy*, Macmillan, London, 1968.

Hooson, D. J. M., *A New Soviet Heartland?* Van Nostrand, Princeton, 1964.

Hooson, D. J. M., *The Soviet Union*, University of London Press, London, 1966.

I.L.O., *Manpower Aspects of Recent Economic Developments in Europe*, I.L.O., Geneva, 1969.

Johnson, E. L., *An Introduction to the Soviet Legal System*, Methuen, London, 1969; Pergamon, New York.

Karcz, Jerzy K., ed., *Soviet and East European Agriculture*, University of California Press, Berkeley, Calif., 1967.

Korol, Alexander G., *Soviet research and development: its organisation, personnel and funds*, The M.I.T. Press, Cambridge, Mass., 1965.

McCauley, Mary, *Labour Disputes in Soviet Russia, 1957–1965*, Oxford University Press, London, 1969.

Mickiewicz, E. P., *Soviet Political Schools, The Communist Party Adult Instruction System*, Yale University Press, New Haven, 1967.

Muchnik, Helen, *From Gorky to Pasternak: six writers in Soviet Russia*, Vintage Books, New York, 1966.

Nove, Alec, *An Economic History of the USSR*, Penguin, London, 1969.

Nove, Alec, *The Soviet Economy*, Allen & Unwin, London; Praeger, New York, 1961, third impression, 1965.

Nove, Alec, *Was Stalin really necessary?*, Allen & Unwin, London, 1964.

Nove, Alec, and Newth, J. A., *The Soviet Middle East: a Communist Model for Development*, Allen & Unwin, London, 1967.

Nozhko, K., Monoszon, E., Zhamin, V., and Severtsev, V., *Educational planning in the USSR* (with observations of an I.I.E.P. mission to the USSR, headed by Raymond Poignant), UNESCO, Paris, 1968.

Observer, An, *Message from Moscow*, Jonathan Cape, London, 1969.

Parker, W. H., *An Historical Geography of Russia*, University of London Press, London, 1968.

Prociuk, S. G., 'The manpower problem in Siberia', *Soviet Studies*, October 1967, vol. XIX, No. 2.

Reavey, George, *The Poetry of Yevgeny Yevtushenko, 1953 to 1965*, translated with an Introduction by George Reavey, bilingual edition, Calder & Boyars, London, 1966.

Reavey, George, *The New Russian Poets, 1953–1968*, bilingual edition, Calder & Boyars, London, 1968.

Rigby, T. H., *Membership of the Soviet Communist Party 1917–67*, Princeton University Press, Princeton, 1968.

Riordan, J. W., 'The Olympic Games as a Mirror of Society', *Anglo-Soviet Journal*, January 1969, vol. XXIX, No. 2.

Sakharov, Andrei D., *Progress, Coexistence and Intellectual Freedom*, translated by *The New York Times*, with Introduction, Afterword, and Notes by Harrison E. Salisbury. André Deutsch, London, 1968.

Schapiro, Leonard, *The Government and Politics of the Soviet Union*, Hutchinson, London, 2nd edition, 1967; New York, 1965.

Schroder, Gertrude E. 'Soviet Economic "Reforms" : a Study in Contradictions', *Soviet Studies*, July 1968, vol. XX, No. 1.

Simmonds, G. W., ed., *Soviet Leaders*, Crowell Collier and Macmillan, New York, 1967.

Strauss, Erich, *Soviet Agriculture in Perspective, A Study of its successes and failures*, Allen & Unwin, London, 1969.

Titmuss, Richard M., 'Trading in Human Capital', *Science Journal*, June 1967.

Utechin, S. V., *Everyman's Concise Encyclopaedia of Russia*, Dent, London, 1961.

Voznesensky, Andrei, *Antiworlds and the Fifth Ace*, bilingual edition, edited by Patricia Blake and Max Hayward, Oxford University Press, London, 1968.

Vucinich, Alexander, *The Soviet Academy of Sciences*, Stanford University Press, Stanford, Calif., 1956.

Wädekin, K. E., 'Housing in the USSR–The Countryside', *Problems of Communism*, May–June 1969, vol. XVIII, No. 3.

Werth, Alexander, *Russia: Hopes and Fears*, Penguin, London, 1969.

Zaleski, E., Kozlowski, J. P., Wienert, E., Davies, R. W., Berry, M. J., and Amann, R., *Science Policy in the USSR*, OECD, Paris, 1969.

Russian

Arutyunyan, Yu. V., *Sovetskoe krest'yanstvo v gody velikoi otechestvennoi voiny*, Moscow, 1963.

Arutyunyan, Yu. V., *Opyt sotsiologicheskogo izucheniya sela*, Moscow, 1968.

Belyaev, E. A., Mikulinsky, S. R., and Sheinin, Yu. M., *Organizatsiya nauchnoi deyatel'nosti*, Moscow, 1968.
Burmistrov, D. V., *Nalogi i sbory s naseleniya v SSSR*, Moscow, 1968.
Buzlyakov, N. I., *Metody planirovaniya povysheniya urovnya zhizni*, Moscow, 1969.
Chuntulov, V. T., *Ekonomicheskaya istoriya SSSR*, Moscow, 1969.
Dobrov, G. M., ed., *Potentsial nauki*, Kiev, 1969.
Evtushenko, Evgeny, *Avtobiografiya*, Flegon, London, 1964.
Faddeev, N. V., *Soviet ekonomicheskoi vzaimopomoshchi*, 2nd edition, Moscow, 1969.
Ivanchenko, A. A., ed. *Ekonomicheskie problemy razmeshcheniya proizvoditel'nykh sil SSSR*, Moscow, 1969.
Knyazev, G. A., and Kol'tsov, A. V., *Kratky ocherk istorii Akademii Nauk SSSR*, Moscow, 1964.
Kamyshev, V. G., *Izdatel'sky dogovor na literaturnye proizvedeniya*, Moscow, 1969.
Kuznetsov, B. G., *Nauka v 2000 godu*, Moscow, 1969.
Lenin, V. I., *Sochineniya*, 4th edition, Moscow, 1941-50.
Morozov, V. A., *Trudoden', den'gi i torgovlya na sele*, Moscow, 1965.
Musatov, I. M., *Sotsial'nye problemy trudovykh resursov v SSSR*, Moscow, 1968.
Notkin, A. I., ed., *Struktura narodnogo khozyaistva SSSR*, Moscow, 1967.
Popov, V. E., *Problemy ekonomiki Sibiri*, Moscow, 1968.
Sergievsky, V. N., *Problemy optimal'nogo sootnosheniya proizvodstva i potrebleniya v SSSR*, Moscow, 1968.
Shutov, I. M., *Prirodnye bogatstva rodiny*, Moscow, 1969.
TS.S.U. (Central Statistical Administration of the Council of Ministers of the USSR),
 Narodnoye khozyaistvo SSSR v 1965 g., Moscow, 1966.
 Narodnoye khozyaistvo SSSR v 1968 g., Moscow, 1969.
Tul'chinsky, L. I., *Finansovye problemy professional'nogo obrazovaniya v SSSR*, Moscow, 1968.
Venzher, V., *Kolkhoznyi stroi na sovremennom etape*, Moscow, 1966.
Volkov, A. G., ed., *Izuchenie vosproizvodstva naseleniya* (Uchenye zapiski po statistike, vol. 14), Moscow 1968.
Volkov, B. A., Glozman, V. A., and Khvostov, A. M., *Yuridichesky spravochnik dlya naseleniya*, Minsk, 1969.
Zhamin, V. A., *Ekonomika obrazovaniya*, Moscow, 1969.
Zhamin, V. A., and Egiazaryan, G. A., *Effektivnost' kvalifitsirovannogo truda*, Moscow, 1968.

Index

Abel, Rudolf, 266
abortion, 130
Abramov, Fedor, 114n, 191, 250
absenteeism, 97, 98–9, 133
Academy of Arts, 214
Academy of Communal Economy, 214
Academy of Construction and Architecture, 214
Academy of Educational Sciences, 141, 149, 151, 154, 169
Academy of Medical Sciences, 133, 214
Academy of Sciences, 19, 32, 48, 50, 66, 78, 134, 149, 156, 159, 167, 168, 208, 209–14, 215
Academy of Social Sciences, 44
administrative areas: *see* autonomous regions; autonomous republics; national districts; Union republics
affluence, 48, 237
Afghanistan, 57
agricultural machinery, 69, 103–4, 108–10, 113, 116, 126, 137, 233–4; *see also* Machine-Tractor Stations
agriculture, 17–18, 20, 21, 37, 83, 89, 107–28, 137–8, 234; *see also* collectivisation
aircraft industry, 36, 106
Aitmatov, Chingiz, 203, 250–1
Akhmadulina, Bella, 194, 197, 199–201, 251
Akhmatova, Anna, 179, 189, 198, 202, 251, 255, 275
Aksyonov, Aleksandr, 65–6, 251
Aksyonov, Vasily, 192, 251
Alaska, 136
Albania, 82, 83
Alexander II, 241
Alexander III, 260, 264
Alexander the Great, 57, 174
Alexandra, Queen, 264
Alliluyeva, Svetlana, 270, 275
All-Union bodies: *see under* common title
All-Union Congresses: *see under* CPSU
Amann, R., 106n
Andreyev, Leonid, 179, 251
anti-communism, 26, 48, 49, 218–19

anti-religiousness, 60, 62, 232, 238
anti-semitism, 54, 60, 195, 236
apparatchiki, 34
applied economics, 47, 67; *see also* economic planning
arbitration, 95
architecture, 203–4
Arctic Ocean, 29
armed forces, 34, 53–4, 172, 233
Armenian SSR, 35n, 76, 209, 221, 246
Armenians, 55, 57, 58, 60
Armstrong, John A., 57n
art, 204
Arutyunyan, Yu. V., 109n, 122n
Associations of Proletarian Writers, 184, 187
ASSRs: *see* autonomous republics
astronauts: *see* cosmonauts
Austro-Hungarian Empire, 56
autonomous regions, 35–7
autonomous republics, 17, 35–7
Averbakh, Leopol'd, 185, 187, 251
Azerbaidzhanian SSR, 35n, 66, 130, 246, 248, 249
Azerbaidzhanians, 57, 58n
Azov Sea, 27

Babayevsky, Semyon, 189, 190, 251–2
Baibakov, Nikolai, 110n, 252
Baikal, Lake, 27, 139, 174
Baptists, 238
Bashkirs, 58n
Bebetov, 180
Belorussian SSR, 35n, 66, 211, 221, 246
Belorussians, 56
Belukha, Nikolai, 66, 252
Bely, Andrei, 179, 203, 252
Beneš, Edvard, 189, 252
Bergson, Abram, 89n
Beria, Lavrenty, 52, 194, 252
Berry, M. J., 106n
Bessarabia: *see* Moldavian SSR
Bezymensky, A., 184n
biological weapons, 29
Birobidzhan, 58
birth-rate, 129–40 *passim*
Blake, Patricia, 199n

INDEX

Blok, Aleksandr, 179, 182, 203, 252-3
boarding schools, 153
Bogdanov, Aleksandr, 179, 180-1, 253, 256
Bolshevik Party, 17, 18
Bondarev, Yury, 192, 253
Bratsk, 62, 71
Brezhnev, Leonid, 24, 28, 29-30, 35, 88n, 110n, 253
Britain, 17, 18n, 21, 67, 82, 129, 131
broadcasting, 49-50; see also mass communications
Brown, E. J., 184n
Bryusov, Valery, 179, 253
Buddhism, 43
Budenny, Semyon, 53, 253
Budget (USSR), 36, 72, 79, 133, 154-5, 206
Bukharin, Nikolai, 111, 182, 253-4, 256, 269, 274
Bulgakov, Mikhail, 187, 202, 254
Bulgaria, 29, 82, 83, 84, 86, 87
Bunin, Ivan, 179, 254
Burmistrov, D. V., 115n

Calder, Nigel, 216n, 218
Campbell, Robert W., 72, 108n
Camus, Albert, 202
Canada, 29
Castro, Fidel, 50
Catherine II, 54
CEMA, 82-7, 127
censorship, 52, 63, 178-9, 185-6, 187, 189-90, 195-6, 202, 203, 205
Central Committee (CPSU), 33-4, 35, 39, 44, 50, 59, 63-5, 142, 213
Central Institute for the Study of Languages and Writing of the Peoples of the USSR, 211
Central Statistical Administration, 50, 132
Chayanov, Aleksandr, 111, 254
Cheka, 37, 179, 185
chemical industry, 74, 75, 104, 106, 110
chemical weapons, 29
Cherepovets, 71
Chernyshevsky, Nikolai, 187, 254
child allowances, 132-3, 223-4
China, 19, 25, 50, 139, 172, 236
Christianity, 43, 56, 60
Chukotka, 131
Chukovsky, Kornei, 179, 183, 254
Chuntulov, V. T., 111n
CIA, 26
citizenship, 224
civil law, 38, 94, 224-6
Civil War, 17, 111, 118, 225, 230
clothing, 81, 102
coal, 69, 70, 71, 74, 75

Colbert, Jean-Baptiste, 67
collectivisation, 25, 32, 38, 50, 53, 107-28 *passim*
Comecon: see CEMA
Comintern, 82
Commission for Youth Affairs (USSR), 64, 65-6
Common Market, 87
communism, 28, 29, 41-2, 49, 51, 80, 170-1, 237-8; see also CPSU; Leninism; Marxism; socialism
Communist International: see Comintern
Communist Youth League, 19, 31, 32, 36, 60-6, 142, 166, 170, 171, 172, 175, 176-7, 220, 223
computers, 93, 103, 104, 106, 231
concentration camps, 52, 54, 130n, 133-4, 192, 239
concrete economics: see applied economics
Congress of Collective Farm Representatives, 123, 127
Congresses of CPSU: see under CPSU
Constantinople, 138
constituent republics: see Union republics
constitution (USSR), 17
consumer goods, 76, 78, 80-2, 89, 90, 93, 102, 106
copper refining, 84
cosmonauts, 25, 26-7
cottage industries, 119-20
Council for Economic Mutual Assistance: see CEMA
Council for the Study of Productive Forces, 68, 74
Council of Ministers, 34, 35, 36, 39, 213
Council of Nationalities, 35, 36
Council of the Union, 35, 36
Councils of Innovators, 104
CPSU, 17, 18, 19, 20, 21, 23-66, 167, 230-40 *passim*; All-Union Congresses, 19, 23-30, 53, 58n, 68
criminal law, 38, 238
Cuba, 26, 232
culture, 19-20, 37, 175-7; see also architecture; art; dancing; literature; singing
currency, 84, 86
cybernetics, 46, 48, 151, 231
Czechoslovakia, 29, 37, 40, 82, 83, 84, 172, 232, 252

Dagestanians, 57, 58n
daily life, 221-9
dancing, 203
Daniel, Yuly, 26, 27, 192, 254-5
Davies, R. W., 106n

decentralisation, 26
defence, 20–1, 42, 68, 106
delinquency, 49, 51, 63, 218
demographic factors, 51, 76–8, 129–40, 143, 234
dentists, 222
deportation: *see* concentration camps
deputies: *see* Supreme Soviet (USSR)
de-Stalinisation, 23–4, 25, 39, 53, 150, 194, 197, 232
Development of Capitalism in Russia, The, 174–5
de Witt, Nicholas, 208
dialectical materialism, 43, 47–8, 166
diamonds, 132
disablement benefits, 226–7
disease, 79
divorce, 224–6
Djilas, Milovan, 49
Dobrov, G. M., 208*n*
doctors, 221–2
Donbas: *see* Donetsky Basin
Donetsky Basin, 69, 71, 74
DOSAAF, 172
Dostoevsky, Feodor, 237
drama, 175–6
druzhiny, 49
Dubček, Alexander, 237
Dubna, 87
Dudintsev, Vladimir, 195, 255, 268

Eastman, Max, 183*n*
economic growth, 21, 24, 28, 29–30, 42, 230
economic planning, 17–18, 21, 26, 36, 51, 67–87, 88–106 *passim*, 120–1, 230; Five-Year Plans, 17–18, 21, 24, 30, 64, 67, 69, 90, 145
economic reforms, 102–6
education, 19, 20, 37, 65, 68, 78, 79, 80, 141–77, 217, 233, 235; *see also* further education; general education; political education; technical education; vocational training
educational expenditure, 154–60, 165
educational methods, 150–4, 169–71
educational planning, 143–7
educational research, 151–4
Egiazaryan, G. A., 159*n*
Ehrenburg, Ilya, 191, 255
Eikhenbaum, Boris, 183, 255
Einstein, Albert, 47–8
Eisenhower, Dwight D., 29
elections, 34, 35–6, 38, 39
electricity supply, 67, 80, 83, 123; *see also* hydro-electric power
emigration: *see* migration
employment, 98; *see also* labour force; workers
Engels, Friedrich, 19, 49, 58, 212

environmental factors, 138–40
Esenin, Sergei, 179, 182, 255
Establishments of Higher Education: *see* VUZ
Estonian SSR, 35*n*, 56, 76, 175, 221, 246
Estonians, 56
ethnic groups: *see* nationalities
Evtushenko, Evgeny, 52, 193–8, 201, 251, 255
Ezhov, 252

factories, 71–2, 90, 132
Fadeev, Aleksandr, 189, 255
Fainsod, Merle, 34
family allowances: *see* child allowances
family expenditure, 81–2, 135
family life, 38, 221–9
farming, 48, 79–80, 107–28, 137–8; *see also* agriculture
Fedin, Konstantin, 184, 255–6
Finland, 127, 251
First Secretary (CPSU), 33–4, 35
Five-Year Plans: *see under* economic planning
food processing, 120, 127
food production, 20, 81, 107, 110, 113, 117
football, 172
foreign trade, 36, 86, 103
France, 17, 67, 127, 128, 133, 143, 147
Freud, Sigmund, 141*n*
fruit, 120
Furmanov, Dmitry, 184, 256
further education, 44–6, 141–77 *passim*; *see also* VUZ

Gandhi, Mohandas, 188, 272
Garbuzov, Vasily, 72, 256
gas supply, 62, 80; *see also* natural gas
Gastei, A., 181
general education, 143–4, 147–9, 152–3, 154, 155, 160–1
General Scheme for 1971–1980, 73–4, 76
General Secretary: *see* First Secretary (CPSU)
genetics, 48, 141*n*, 150
Genghis Khan, 50
Gents, N., 45*n*
Geographical Society, 211
geography: *see* environmental factors
Georgian SSR, 35*n*, 209, 221, 246, 248, 249
Georgians, 55, 57, 60
Germans, 57–8
Germany, East, 29, 83, 84, 87, 131, 235
Germany, Nazi, 18, 25, 54
Germany, West, 21, 28, 84

INDEX

Ginzburg, Evgenia, 251
Gippius, Zinaida, 263
Gomulka, Wladyslaw, 23, 256
Gorbachev, Georgy, 185, 256
Gor'ky, Maxim, 179, 180–1, 182, 184, 187, 188, 192, 253, 256
Gor'ky Institute of World Literature, 211
Gosplan: see State Planning Commission
Gottwald, Klement, 252
government, 35–9
GPU, 37, 185
graduates, 208–9
gramophones, 81
'great terror': *see* oppression
Greenland, 29
Grossman, Philip, 109*n*
gross national product, 89, 136, 155, 157, 206
GTO, 172
Gumilev, Nikolai, 179, 251, 257
Guseinova, Zuleykha, 66, 257

Hayward, Max, 199*n*
health services: *see* medical services
Heisenberg, 47–8
higher education: *see* further education; VUZ
Hiroshima, 28
Hitler, Adolf, 18, 54, 141*n*, 189
Hoffman, E.T.A., 183
holidays, 137–8
Hooson, D. J. M., 139*n*
hospitals: *see* medical services
hours worked, 96–8
housing, 78–9, 80, 126–7, 135, 234
Hungary, 23, 29, 84, 86, 87, 232
Huxley, Aldous, 237
hydro-electric power, 62, 71, 72, 74, 123, 197
hydrogen bombs: *see* nuclear weapons

ideological instruction: *see* political education
immigration: *see* migration
income, 68, 76, 89
India, 57
industrial disputes, 94–5
industrialisation, 17–18, 25, 38, 42, 53, 55, 67, 68, 69, 84, 101, 111, 139, 185
industry, 67–76, 88–106; location, 71–2, 73–5, 76–7, 91, 92
innovation, 103–5, 128, 168, 215–16
Institutes of . . . : *see under subject*
International Bank, 86
International Conference of Communists and Workers' Parties, 39, 41

International Institute for Educational Planning, 143
international relations, 28, 234–6
Intourist, 173*n*
Ioffe, Adolf, 236, 257
Irkutsk, 214
'Iron Curtain', 54
iron ore, 69, 71, 139
Islam, 43, 57, 59, 60
Israel, 235–6
Italy, 127, 131
Itin, N., 214*n*
Ivanov, Vsevolod, 184, 257

Japan, 17, 28, 29, 53, 140
Jewish Doctors' Plot, 54, 194
Jews, 57, 58, 60; *see also* anti-semitism; Judaism
Johnson, Lyndon B., 67
Joyce, James, 187
Judaism, 43, 60
Jung, Carl, 141*n*

Kafka, Franz, 202
Kaganovich, Lazar, 258, 269
Kamenev, Lev, 236, 257, 269, 275
Kapital, Das, 148
Kapitsa, Petr, 212–13, 216, 257–8
Karaganda, 69*n*
Kaverin, Veniamin, 184, 258
Kazakh SSR, 35*n*, 134, 221, 246
Kazan University, 58
Keldysh, Mstislav, 66, 105, 258
Kennedy, John F., 232
KGB, 61, 193
Khachaturyan, Aram, 203, 258
Khrushchev, Nikita, 20–1, 23–4, 25, 29, 31, 40, 46–7, 49, 53, 73, 80, 93, 116, 117, 119, 126, 148, 149, 165, 194, 196, 197, 204, 223, 232, 253, 258–9, 263, 264
kibbutzim, 112
Kiev, 131, 195, 246; University, 151, 153, 163, 209
'Kieven Rus', 56
Kirghiz SSR, 35*n*, 58, 246
Kirillov, V., 181
Kirov, Sergei, 53, 259, 269
Klimenyuk, V. N., 208*n*
know-how, 86–7, 103; *see also* technology
Kochetov, Vsevolod, 189, 202, 259
Kola, 62, 211
Kolmogorov, Andrei, 150, 259
Kolyma, 54, 131
Komi, 87
Komissarzhevskaya, V. F., 263
Kommunist, 45, 219
Komsomol: see Communist Youth League

Komsomolskaya pravda, 62–3
Komsomolsk-on-the-Amur, 62
Konchalovskaya, N., 215n
Korol, Alexander, 208
Korolenko, Vladimir, 179, 259
Kosygin, Aleksei, 24, 30, 35, 89, 103, 259–60
Kremlin, 174
Krivoi rog, 71
Kronstadt rebellion, 237, 273
Kunitz, Stanley, 201n
Kuprin, Aleksandr, 179, 260
Kurakov, I. E., 159n
Kuzbas: see Kuznetsky Basin
Kuznetsky Basin, 69, 74
Kuznetsov, Anatoly, 195–6, 203, 260

labour camps: see concentration camps
labour force, 38, 42, 51, 68, 71, 75, 76–8, 84, 87, 94, 109, 129, 130–1, 132–4, 135–6, 137, 231; productivity, 77, 90, 157–9; see also technical education; vocational training; workers
labour-saving devices, 81–2
land use, 38, 107–28 *passim*
languages, 58–9
LAPP: see Associations of Proletarian Writers
Latvian SSR, 35n, 56, 66, 76, 105–6, 175, 221, 246
Latvians, 56
Lavrent'ev, M. A., 214, 260
League of Young Communists: see Communist Youth League
League of Yugoslav Communists, 18–19
Left Front in Art (LEF), 180
legal system, 37, 38–9
leisure activities, 62, 64, 78, 135, 171–7
Lelevich, G., 185, 260
Lenin, Vladimir, 17, 18, 19, 33, 39–43, 49, 52–5, 63, 66, 67, 111, 148, 174–5, 178, 179, 182–4, 188n, 210, 212, 220, 230, 232, 234, 236, 256, 257, 260–1, 272
Lenin Academy of Agricultural Sciences, 214
Leningrad, 53, 54, 71, 76, 105, 130, 131, 173, 204, 211; University, 153, 155–6, 163, 168, 209
Leninism, 39–43, 47, 50
Leonov, Leonid, 186, 188, 189, 261
Lermontov, Mikhail, 203, 255, 261
liberalisation, 230–40
Ligachev, Egor, 66, 261
liquidation: see oppression
literacy, 48–9, 58
literature, 52, 150, 178–205

Literaturnaya Gazeta, 50, 122, 195
Lithuanian SSR, 35n, 56, 175, 246
Lithuanians, 56, 60
living standards, 20, 51, 78–82, 90, 130, 135, 136–7, 219
location of industry, 71–2, 73–5, 76–7, 91, 92
lorry tyres, 73
Louis XIV, 67
Lukinov, I., 112n
Lunacharsky, Anatoly, 145, 180–1, 182, 210, 225, 253, 256, 261–2
Lunts, Lev, 184, 262
L'vov, 56
Lysenko, Trofim, 48, 150, 212, 262, 273

Macedonia, 101
Machine-Tractor Stations, 108–9, 113, 116, 126
Mackinder, 138
Magadan, 54, 131
Magnitogorsk, 69
management techniques, 105–6
manpower: see labour force
Mao Tse-Tung, 20, 24, 25, 216, 262–3
MAPP: see Associations of Proletarian Writers
Maria Fedorovna, 264
marriage, 224–6
Marshall Aid, 82
Marxism, 40, 43–7, 48–9, 50, 51, 58, 59, 148, 212, 220, 236
Masaryk, T. G., 252
mass communications, 19, 34, 44–5, 141, 232; see also broadcasting; press
maternity benefits, 227–8
Mayakovsky, Vladimir, 179, 180, 255, 263
medical services, 37, 38, 78, 79, 80, 135, 221–3
medicines, 223
Merezhkovsky, Dmitry, 179, 263
metal industry, 69
Meyerhold, Vsevolod, 180, 263
Mickiewicz, E. P., 45n, 47n
Middle East, 235–6
migration, 60, 131–2, 133–4, 136
Mikulinsky, S. P., 208n
minerals, 69–71, 230; see also under individual minerals
ministries, 36–7, 92–3; see also Council of Ministers
Ministry of Construction, 72; of Culture, 64; of Education, 141, 142; of Finance, 72; of Higher and Secondary Specialised Education, 142, 163, 166; of Light or Heavy Engineering, 72

INDEX

missiles: see nuclear weapons
Model Collective Farm Charter, 117–18, 123–6, 138
Moldavian SSR, 35n, 56, 131, 134, 209, 211, 246
Moldavians, 56–7, 60, 134
Molière, 187
Molotov, Vyacheslav, 269
Molotov–Ribbentrop Pact (1939), 189
Mongolia, 82
Mongols, 56, 57
Montenegro, 101
Morozov, V. A., 113n
Moscow, 29, 66, 76, 83, 105, 130, 131, 173, 175, 211, 246; University, 132, 153, 163, 168, 209
motor vehicles, 72–3, 102, 104
Mozhaev, B., 114n
Mstera, 120
Muromets, Ilya, 179
Murov, M., 215n
museums, 176n
music, 175, 203
'Muslim republic', 59

Nagasaki, 28
Nagy, Imre, 23, 263–4
Na Postu, 185
national districts, 17, 35–7
National Economic Plans: see economic planning
national income, 68, 76, 89
nationalities, 35, 54, 55–60, 218
NATO, 235
natural gas, 75, 139
natural resources, 27, 84, 131–2, 139–40; see also hydro-electric power; land use; minerals; natural gas; oil
Nazism, 43, 233; see also Germany, Nazi
Neizvestny, Ernst, 204, 264
Nekrasov, Viktor, 188, 264
neologism, 58–9
New Class, The, 49
Newton, Isaac, 207
New Zealand, 86
Nicholas II, 17, 241–2, 264, 270
nickel, 132
Nikitin, Nikolai, 184, 264
Nile, River, 67
NKVD, 37
nomenklatura, 32, 34
Norilsk, 132
North Atlantic Treaty Organisation: see NATO
Nove, Alec, 89n, 113n
Novgorod, 174
Novosibirsk University, 150, 153, 163, 167–8, 214

Novy Dvor, 83
Novy Mir, 203
nuclear power, 75, 86, 87
nuclear test-ban treaty, 21
nuclear weapons, 28–9, 140, 218, 231
nutrition, 81

obscurantism, 47–8
OECD, 143, 208
OGPU: see GPU
oil, 72, 73, 84, 85, 87, 136, 139
Oistrakh, David, 258
Okudzhava, Bulat, 201, 264
oppression, 52–5
Organisation for Economic Co-operation and Development: see OECD
Orwell, George, 181n, 237
Ostrovsky, Aleksandr, 190, 265
output: see production
Ovechkin, V., 114n
overtime, 96, 97, 98

Pakistan, 29, 232
Palekh, 120
Palestine Liberation Army, 236
Paputin, V. S., 66, 265
para-military training, 64
Paris Commune, 18
Parker, W. H., 139n
Parks of Culture and Rest, 176–7
Partiinaya Zhizn, 45
Pasternak, Boris, 187, 192, 202, 203, 238–9, 265
Pavlov, Sergei, 60, 61, 265
peasant crafts: see cottage industries
peasants, 107–28 *passim*
Pen'kovsky, Oleg, 26, 61, 265–6
pensions, 79, 129, 130, 133, 226, 228
People's Commissariat of Internal Affairs: see NKVD
People's Courts, 37, 224 225
Perevedentsev, V., 132, 133n, 134n
Pharaohs 67
Pil'nyak, Boris, 186, 266
Pioneer movement, 62, 142, 171, 172, 175, 176–7
Plato, 237
poetry, 179–81, 193–201
Pokrovsky, Mikhail, 180, 266
Poland, 23, 29, 56, 82, 83, 84, 87
Politburo (CPSU), 33
political education, 43–52
pollution, 27, 38
Polytechnical Museum, 151
population, 51, 76–7, 84, 129–40, 246–9; see also demographic factors
Potekhin, L., 214n
poverty, 49, 114n, 218

power industry, 72, 74
Powers, Gary, 29, 266
Pozner, Vladimir, 184, 266
Praesidium (CPSU), 36
Pravda, 44–5, 196, 219
President (USSR), 34, 36
press, 44–5; *see also* mass communications *and under individual papers*
prices, 88–9, 103, 105, 110, 112, 113, 116, 121
private enterprise, 55, 127–8
Prociuk, S. G., 135*n*
Procurator-General (USSR), 36, 37, 38
production, 20, 21, 42, 67–8, 73, 77, 78, 88–106, 107–28 *passim*
professional training: *see* vocational training
profitability, 93–4, 102, 105, 121
programmed learning, 151–2
proletarian literature, 179–85
Proletkult movement: *see* proletarian literature
property, 225–6
Proust, Marcel, 187
Pskov, 174
publishing houses, 182, 183
purges, 52–5
Pushkin, Aleksandr, 203, 266–7

Rabotnitsa, 45
racialism, 43, 48, 141*n*; *see also* antisemitism
Radio Liberty, 26
radios, 81
railways, 62, 83, 102
Rakosi, Matyas, 263
RAPP: *see* Associations of Proletarian Writers
'Ready for Toil and Defence': *see* GTO
Reavey, George, 197*n*, 199*n*
Red Army Choir, 175–6
Red Crescent Society, 223
Red Cross Society, 223
redundancy, 97
Rigby, T. H., 60*n*
Rimsky-Korsakov, Nikolai, 265
roads, 73, 127, 234
Rokossovsky, Konstantin, 54, 267
Roman Catholicism, 56
Romania, 29, 56–7, 82, 83, 86
Rostov, 174
Rozenfeld, L., 214*n*
Rozov, Viktor, 192, 267
RSFSR, 35*n*, 76, 131, 149, 209, 246, 247, 248
Rumyantsev, A. M., 219
rural depopulation, 115, 132; *see also* demographic factors

Russians, 56, 60
Rykov, 269, 274

Sakharov, Andrei, 52
Sal'nikov, I., 137*n*
Samarkand, 57, 174
Sarraute, Natalie, 202
Savel'ev, A. A., 208*n*
Scandinavia, 84
schools: *see* education
Schroder, G. E., 88*n*
Schwedt-on-Oder, 87
science, 19, 26–7, 42, 47–8, 63, 68, 103–4, 150–1, 206–20
Scientific Centre for Methods of Planning, 68
scientific research, 77–8, 86–7, 103–4, 155, 156, 167–8, 206–20 *passim*
Scientific Technical Societies, 104–5
scientists, 208–9, 216–17, 233
sea access, 138–9, 230
security forces, 37; *see also* Cheka; GPU; KGB; NKVD
Selskaya Zhizn, 45
Semichastnyi, Vladimir, 61, 267
Serapion brothers, 183–4
Sergievsky, V. N., 81*n*
SEV: *see* CEMA
sewerage, 80
Shakespeare, William, 187, 190, 203
Shchusev, Aleksei, 204, 267
Shelepin, Aleksandr, 61, 267
shipping, 83, 231
Shklovsky, Viktor, 183, 267–8
Sholokhov, Mikhail, 27, 186–7, 190, 268
Short Course of History of the VKP(b), 46–7
Shushenskoe, 174–5
Siberia, 29, 50, 54, 62, 71, 131, 134, 136, 137
sickness benefits, 227
Simonov, Konstantin, 190, 192, 268
Sinyavsky, Andrei, 26, 27, 192, 201, 268
Slonimsky, Mikhail, 184, 268
small-scale industries, 120, 125–6, 232
Smirnov, L. P., 208*n*
socialism, 40–3, 49, 51
Socialist State Productive Enterprise, 26, 38
social sciences, 50–1, 52, 63, 166–7, 169, 218–19, 220, 234
Society of Innovators and Rationalisers, 104
Soloukhin, Vladimir, 114*n*, 191, 268–9
Solzhenitsyn, Aleksandr, 192–3, 201, 203, 205, 232, 235, 239–40, 269
Sonin, M. Ya., 134*n*
South Africa, 141*n*

INDEX

Soviet Army Choir, 175-6
Soviets, local, 17, 19, 34, 37-8
space exploration, 26-7, 218; *see also* cosmonauts
spies, 26, 29, 53, 61
spiritual values, 237-40
sport, 62, 64, 171-3
SSRs: *see* Union republics *and under individual republics*
Stalin, Iosif, 17, 23, 24, 25, 35, 37, 40, 46-7, 49, 52, 54, 55, 59, 62, 98, 112, 121, 141*n*, 150, 186, 187, 190, 194, 195, 212, 231-2, 233, 235, 236, 269-70, 275
State Committee for Science and Technology, 104, 215
State Committee for Vocational and Technical Education, 142, 161-2
State Planning Commission, 54, 68, 74, 77, 82, 91, 106, 143-4, 214
State Political Administration: *see* GPU
State Prices Committee, 68, 106
State Security Committee: *see* KGB
Stolypin, Petr, 111, 270
strikes: *see* industrial disputes
Strumilin, S. G., 157-8
Sultan-Galiev, Mirza, 59, 270
Supreme Attestation Commission: *see* VAK
Supreme Court, 36, 37, 95
Supreme Soviet (USSR), 34, 35-7, 38, 65-6, 68, 127, 222
Surov, V., 45*n*
Suslov, I. F., 115*n*
Suzdal, 174
Sverdlov, Yakov, 185, 236, 264, 270-1
Sverdlovsk, 214

Tadzhik SSR, 35*n*, 76, 221, 246, 249
Tadzhiks, 58*n*, 59, 60
tape-recorders, 81
Tartars, 57, 58
Tashkent, 69, 246; Opera House, 204
teachers, 153-4, 166-7, 168-9
technical education, 144-7, 149, 152, 156-7, 162-3
technology, 103, 107, 110, 128, 210-11, 216, 236
telephones, 80
television, 81, 93
Tendryakov, Vladimir, 191-2, 271
Tereshkova-Nikolayeva, Valentina, 25
textiles, 69
thermo-nuclear weapons: *see* nuclear weapons
Theses (CPSU), 40-3
Titmuss, Richard M., 217*n*
Tito, Josip, 18-19, 50, 271
Tolstoy, Aleksei, 179, 188, 190, 239, 271
Tolstoy, Lev (Leo), 193, 255, 268, 271-2
Tomsk, 66
torture, 54
tourism, 173-5
trade unions, 38, 49, 64, 95-9, 220, 223
transport, 36, 37, 72-3, 74, 101, 114, 135
Trotsky, Lev, 55, 182, 183, 236, 257, 272
Tukhachevsky, Mikhail, 273
Tula, 119
Tul'chinsky, L. I., 157*n*
Tupolev, Andrei, 212, 273
Turkey, 29, 56, 57, 232
Turkmenian SSR, 35*n*, 76, 246
Turkmenians, 58*n*

Ukrainian SSR, 35*n*, 131, 134, 211, 246
Ukrainians, 56, 134
unemployment, 98
UNESCO, 39-40, 143
Union of Sport Societies and Organisations, 172
Union of Writers, 172, 178, 190, 192, 205, 232, 235
Union republics, 35-7; *see also under individual republics*
United Kingdom: *see* Britain
United Nations, 232; *see also* UNESCO
United States: *see* USA
universities: *see further education and under towns*
university graduates, 208-9
Urals, 74, 76, 139, 211
USA, 21, 25, 27, 28-9, 67, 82, 86, 89*n*, 106, 129, 140, 172, 216-18, 228-9, 232
Uzbek SSR, 35*n*, 131, 221, 246, 247
Uzbeks, 58*n*

VAK, 208
VAPP: *see* Associations of Proletarian Writers
Vavilov, Nikolai, 48, 212, 262, 273
Venzher, V., 120*n*
Vietnam, 28
Vil'yams, Vasily, 119, 273
VKP(b), 46-7
Vladimir, 119, 174
Vladivostok, 214
vocational training, 142, 149-50, 153, 154, 155, 161-2
Voice of America, 26
Volgograd, 74
Voluntary Society for Assisting the Army, Aviation, and the Fleet: *see* DOSAAF

Vorkuta, 71
Voroshilov, Kliment, 53, 253, 269, 273-4
Voznesensky, Andrei, 198-201, 274
Voznesensky, Nikolai, 54, 274
VUZ, 46, 146-70 *passim*, 210, 213

wages, 49, 51, 79, 80, 94, 96, 103, 121-2, 125, 135; overtime, 96, 97, 98
Warren, Robert Penn, 202
Warsaw Pact, 29, 235
water supply, 80
Wehrmacht, 21, 28
welfare services, 79-80, 98-9, 125, 129, 132-3, 135, 221-9
Western ideas, 50, 63, 94; *see also* liberalisation
women workers, 97, 132-3, 223-4
worker participation, 99-102
workers, 49, 51, 53, 79-80, 118, 135-6, 226-7; *see also* labour force; trade unions; wages
working conditions, 96-8
World War II, 24, 25, 28, 54, 64, 82-3, 88, 114, 188, 189

'World War III', 26
writers, 26, 27, 178-205 *passim*, 232, 235
Wroclaw, 87
Wynne, Greville, 26, 61, 265-6, 274

Yagoda, Genrikh, 185, 251, 274
Yakutiya, 132
Yaroslavl, 174
Yaroslavsky, Emelyan, 185, 274-5
Youth Commission: *see* Commission for Youth Affairs
youth movements: *see* Communist Youth League; Pioneer movement
Yugoslavia, 18-19, 86, 101-2, 127

Zaleski, E., 106n, 208n
Zamyatin, Evgeny, 181n, 183, 237, 275
Zetkin, Clara, 188n
Zhamin, V. A., 156-7, 158n, 159
Zhdanov, Andrei, 188-9, 251, 274, 275
Zinoviev, Grigory, 184, 236, 254, 269, 275
Zoshchenko, Mikhail, 184, 189, 275

---

*Printed in Great Britain by The Garden City Press Limited,
Letchworth, Hertfordshire*

FUNDERBURG LIBRARY

MANCHESTER COLLEGE

914.7
K849s